Create Full-Featured Web Sites

Configure and manage your Web server, page 583.

Create page banners automatically from titles assigned in Navigation view, page 382.

Guide visitors through your site with automatic navigation bars, page 202.

Give your pages a professional appearance with themes, page 189.

Add style to your pages with image bullets, page 265, and font control, page 271.

Create and maintain repeating page segments with the Include Page component, page 368.

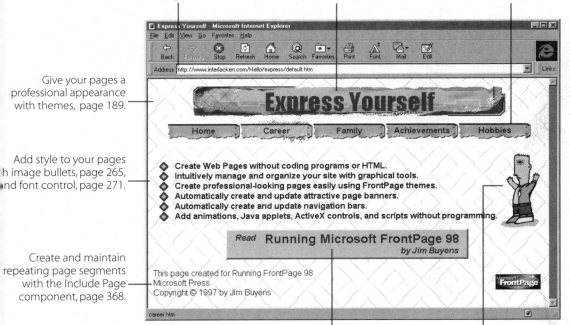

Display a constantly changing series of images with the banner ad manager, page 359.

Add spice with the built-in clipart gallery, page 278, and image editing tools, page 285.

About the Author

Jim Buyens is the senior PC-LAN administrator for AG Communication Systems, a leading provider of telephone switching equipment and software. An early proponent of TCP/IP connectivity, he administers a worldwide corporate network that includes several dozen Windows NT servers and more than 1,000 client personal computers. He was an early champion of World Wide Web applications for intranet use, and he administers a corporate Web site at *www.agcs.com*.

Jim received a Bachelor of Science degree in Computer Science from Purdue University in 1971 and a Master of Business Administration from Arizona State University in 1992. When not administering a network or writing books, he enjoys NHL hockey, NBA and WNBA basketball, and building theatrical scenery. He resides with his family in Phoenix.

RUNNING
Microsoft® FrontPage® 98

Jim Buyens

PUBLISHED BY
Microsoft Press
A Division of Microsoft Corporation
One Microsoft Way
Redmond, Washington 98052-6399

Library of Congress Cataloging-in-Publication Data
Buyens, Jim.
    Running Microsoft FrontPage 98 / Jim Buyens.
       p.   cm.
    Includes index.
    ISBN 1-57231-645-4
    1. Microsoft FrontPage.   2. Web sites.   3. Web publishing.
  TK5105.8885.F76B88   1997
  005.7'2--dc21   97-33680
                                         CIP

Printed and bound in the United States of America.

1 2 3 4 5 6 7 8 9   QMQM   2 1 0 9 8 7

Distributed to the book trade in Canada by Macmillan of Canada, a division of Canada Publishing Corporation.

A CIP catalogue record for this book is available from the British Library.

Microsoft Press books are available through booksellers and distributors worldwide. For further information about international editions, contact your local Microsoft Corporation office. Or contact Microsoft Press International directly at fax (425) 936-7329. Visit our Web site at mspress.microsoft.com.

Acquisitions Editor: Kim Fryer
Project Editor: Saul Candib

Chapters at a Glance

v

Table of Contents

Acknowledgments

Highest thanks go to my wife, Connie, and my children, Lorrill, Justin, and Lynessa, who provided me the time and understanding to write this book. To my parents, Harold and Marcella, go many thanks as well, not only for having me but for putting up with me all those years. To my new mother, Ruth, thanks immensely for your continued support and for putting up with my dad.

My brothers, Dave and Rick, put up with me almost as long as my parents, and perhaps even more so now when I get talking. Thanks, guys, and pass that along to Connie, Jenny, Michael, Steven, Matt, and Claire.

At Microsoft, thanks to Kim Fryer, who contracted me, to Lucinda Rowley, who managed the project, and to Saul Candib, the project editor.

Thanks to the people at Labrecque Publishing who repeatedly saved me from myself—at least that's what they tell me. Special thanks go to Lisa Labrecque, Curtis Philips, Mark Woodworth, Lisa Bravo, Erin Milnes, and Katherine Stimson.

Most of all, thanks to you, the readers, who make an effort such as this both possible and worthwhile. I hope we meet again.

Introduction

Welcome to *Running Microsoft FrontPage 98*. I'm glad you decided to create Web pages with Microsoft FrontPage, and doubly glad you chose this book to learn about it. I hope both the software and the book live up to your expectations.

For most of the brief history of the World Wide Web, text editors have been the tool of choice for creating Web pages. The inventors of hypertext markup language (HTML), the *lingua franca* of the Web, designed it so that anyone could produce Web pages with tools already at hand—that is, with text editors.

As Web page design approaches commercial art in its goals and audience, however, the original simplicity of HTML has become a hindrance. Not only has HTML grown continually more complex and difficult, but so have the techniques for living within its limitations. Meanwhile, as the Web penetrates the mainstream of society, more and more people seek ways to produce their own Web pages with less and less technical background. And organizations and businesses both large and small seek to avoid the high cost of hand-crafted Web pages, often priced at $1,000 each and more.

The solution to producing more complex output from simple input is a classic one: high-function software. This is the position that FrontPage occupies. FrontPage lets *you* concentrate on design while *it* writes the HTML.

The PostScript language, used for producing the pages of this book, consists of plain text—as does HTML. No one in their right mind uses a text editor to produce PostScript documents, though; instead, we use sophisticated word processing, drawing, and desktop publishing software that creates PostScript for us. PostScript, though, lacks hyperlinks and is built around the concept of a fixed page size. That, along with many historical factors, is why the Web uses HTML rather than Post-Script—and why you need a program like FrontPage, rather than a word processor or spreadsheet, to create your Web pages.

Still, for many of the pioneers of Web authoring, coding HTML by hand remains the time-honored method. Its adherents disdain other approaches as artless, but these purists might better criticize artists for not weaving their own canvas, not gathering their own pigments, and not plucking the animal hairs for their brushes. After all, art resides in the original concept and the finished product—*not* in the means of production.

Objectives of This Book

This book is primarily about using software and much less about style and graphic design. However, it does promote some principles of good style—usually in the context of the corresponding software features— as well as principles of good Web site management.

Running FrontPage won't teach you about specific elements of HTML, its syntax, or its techniques. This is what you bought FrontPage to avoid. Neither will it tell you how to design a specific Web page you have in mind; a book can no more design your Web page than arrange your living room, office, or computer niche.

Still, making the best use of software requires knowing the difference between good results and bad. To this end, the book discusses high-level principles for organizing your content, planning your page layouts, and choosing fonts and colors. The primary emphasis and the greatest amount of writing, though, is on using FrontPage to transform your designs into working Web pages.

How This Book Is Organized

Chapter 1 provides an overview of the FrontPage environment: a perspective on the major components and how they relate. All the material in this chapter is covered again later, in more detail, but Chapter 1 provides the initial basis for understanding the rest.

Chapter 2 provides some general thoughts about organizing the content, style, and production process for your Web site. You won't find specific recommendations about particular kinds of sites here; instead, you'll get general advice a level or two higher that may guide your thinking.

Chapter 3 provides background on the major components of the World Wide Web and how they work. It's not intended to make you a network or system administrator, but to describe the Web just enough so that you can understand its use as a publication medium.

Chapter 4 is a bit of an experiment; it covers principles of design, color, typography, and layout in a conceptual way. Artistic topics are generally considered difficult for technically inclined people, so I've approached these design issues as technically and factually as possible. While art is a human experience that will never be reduced to a set of algorithms, there's more order here than you might suspect. Give this chapter a try; I look forward to your feedback.

Before you build any Web pages you need a place to keep them. So with this in mind, Chapter 5 describes how to create a new, blank, FrontPage Web, a Web populated with sample pages, or a Web consisting of content previously managed elsewhere. It continues by describing how FrontPage manages the content, structure, and appearance of related Web pages. Planning, creating, and managing Web pages are highly related activities; thus, you should probably revisit this chapter as you gain proficiency with other parts of FrontPage.

Chapter 6 describes how to create, delete, and modify properties of blank Web pages. The next few chapters address adding and modifying content. Chapter 7 describes how to insert and format text, and Chapter 8 similarly describes the use of graphics, including clip art and the image editing now built into FrontPage. Chapter 9 explains how to set up hyperlinks, how to use HTML tables both for displaying data and for laying out pages, and how FrontPage creates and manages framesets. (*Great news:* Frame editing is now WYSIWYG!)

Chapter 10 describes using FrontPage Components, a series of nifty features that snazz up your Web pages, assist in managing content, or both. Formerly called WebBots, FrontPage Components produce complex HTML based on simple choices presented in dialog boxes.

Chapter 11 deals with HTML forms, a proven and popular way to collect data from visitors to your Web. The chapter details how FrontPage can add HTML forms to your Web pages, and how the FrontPage Server Extensions process form data when it arrives at the Web server.

Chapter 12 addresses another data-driven Web application: database access. FrontPage 98 begins a phase-out of the Internet Database Connector approach supported in FrontPage 97. Instead, it supports database queries with a facility called Database Regions, which uses the Active Server Pages feature of Microsoft's Web server for Windows NT—Internet Information Server.

Chapter 13 delves into a series of techniques that dynamically enhance your site: Web channels, animated page transitions, animated page effects, video, scripting, ActiveX controls, and Java applets. In degree of difficulty, these techniques range from clicking one button to complex configuration and programming. Pick those that suit your skills and meet your needs.

Chapter 14's topic is housekeeping: reorganizing pages and keeping them up-to-date; finding, replacing, and spell-checking text throughout your Web; auditing for inoperative hyperlinks; and performing other aspects of routine site management.

Chapters 15 and 16 conclude the book by discussing security and Web server management. Even on a stand-alone computer, FrontPage is a client-server system that accesses Web files not through the local file system, but through the network as a browser does. Most FrontPage users, therefore, run a personal Web server on their PC, and occasionally need to manage it. FrontPage Web administration and security are obviously topics of interest for system administrators as well. Thus, these two final chapters discuss the FrontPage security model, installation of the FrontPage Server Extensions, and administration of Microsoft's four Web servers.

What's New in FrontPage 98

FrontPage 98 provides a wealth of new and useful features. By category these are as follows:

Creating and Opening Webs

- **Improved Getting Started Dialog Box.** The Getting Started dialog box provides more options in a simpler way, providing a more direct and intuitive way to create new Webs and open existing ones.

- **Most Recently Used List.** The File menu in FrontPage Explorer lists the Webs you've most recently opened, providing a quick and direct way to open them again.

FrontPage Explorer

- **Views Bar.** FrontPage 98 Explorer displays a new Views bar, similar to the Outlook bar in Microsoft Outlook, that provides one-click access to all FrontPage views of your Web: Folders, All Files, Navigation, Hyperlinks, Hyperlink Status, Themes, and Tasks.

- **All Files View.** This view presents a flat view of every file in a Web, regardless of folder. This makes it easy to sort and find files that are duplicate, that are large or small, or that changed recently or long ago.

- **Manage Orphan Files.** All Files view also identifies orphan files—those with no links from other pages in your Web. This feature helps you identify and delete obsolete files.

- **Navigation View Site Maps.** A new Navigation view records and updates the hierarchical structure of your Web site. Visually, it resembles an organization chart. You can drag pages into and within this structure, expand and collapse your view, and shrink the view to fit the current window.

- **Navigation Bars.** FrontPage Editor can use the information in Navigation view to create menu bars for individual pages. These bars change automatically when you update the structure in Navigation view.

- **Print Navigation View Site Maps.** FrontPage can print your Web's Navigation view structure directly from FrontPage Explorer.

- **Hyperlink Status.** The Verify Hyperlinks command in earlier versions has been promoted from a dialog box to a view in the main Explorer window.

- **FrontPage Themes.** FrontPage 98 provides more than 50 professionally designed themes (graphical designs) you can apply to individual pages or entire Webs. Themes give a professional and uniform appearance to backgrounds, bullets, banners, hyperlinks, and navigation bars.

- **Task View.** The To Do list provided in prior versions is displayed now in Task view, where it has been promoted from a subordinate dialog box to a view in the main Explorer window.

- **Shared Borders.** This feature provides uniform content along any or all sides of the pages in your Web, as well as great flexibility in creating an attractive, consistently designed Web site.

- **Channel Definition Format (CDF) Wizard.** This feature allows users of Internet Explorer 4 to access your Web as a *channel*. A channel delivers your content to users automatically, using so-called *push* technology.

- **One-Button Web Publishing.** FrontPage 98 publishes your Web site to another server with the touch of a single button! FrontPage saves file transfer time by publishing only files changed since you last published, and it automatically detects changes made by others in a multiuser environment.

- **Web Publishing Wizard Version 1.5.** This wizard provides improved publishing to Web servers lacking the FrontPage Server Extensions. Working with the FrontPage one-button-publishing feature, the wizard helps you avoid common errors that frequently occur when publishing Webs using methods such as FTP or the America Online service.

FrontPage Editor

- **New Page Templates.** To provide starting points for your pages, FrontPage 98 Editor includes more than 17 new page templates, all professionally designed.

- **Improved Import Wizard.** FrontPage now imports files from Web locations as well as from the local file system. In addition, you can limit the number of link levels, kilobytes of data, or file types to import.

- **Editor Views Tabs.** FrontPage Editor has new tabs at the bottom of the screen that select alternate views of the current Web page. For most Web pages, these include the following:

  - **Normal**, which provides WYSIWYG (what you see is what you get) editing of Web pages, framesets, and frame targets.

  - **HTML**, which displays or edits the code for the current page or frame target.

  - **Preview**, a display-only mode, which most closely emulates a page's appearance in the browser.

  Two additional views appear when editing a frameset:

  - **Frames Page HTML** displays the code for the current frameset and lets you directly edit the HTML.

  - **No Frames** provides WYSIWYG editing of an alternate page that appears in browsers lacking frame support.

- **HTML Viewing and Editing.** Editing of native HTML has moved from a dialog box to a view that's selectable from the main FrontPage Editor window. In addition, basic operations such as search and replace are now supported.

- **Enhanced Support for Hand-Coded HTML.** FrontPage 98 better preserves the coding style of hand-coded HTML, and it generates easier-to-read HTML code.

- **WYSIWYG Frameset Editing.** FrontPage Editor can now create and modify framesets directly in true WYSYWIG fashion. At last you can edit framesets, edit frame contents, and see what you're doing—all at once.

- **Easier Hyperlinks.** Creating hyperlinks is now easier than ever. Redesigned dialog boxes make it easier to link to new pages, to existing pages in a Web, to pages on the Internet, to e-mail addresses, to bookmarks, and to targets within framesets.

- **Paste Plain Text.** The new Paste Special command works like those in other Microsoft Office applications, pasting text from various applications in a choice of formats.

- **Graphical Bullets.** FrontPage can create bullet lists using custom images rather than the plain bullets built into HTML. Once a graphical bullet list is configured, editing it involves the same procedures as editing a plain list.

- **Dynamic Outlining.** This feature uses Dynamic HTML to display expanding and collapsing outlines in your Web pages on supporting browsers.

- **Cascading Style Sheet Support.** FrontPage now supports cascading style sheets (CSS), a powerful set of more than 60 formatting options you can specify at the page or object level. FrontPage can apply these options explicitly or through named styles. CSS is endorsed by the World Wide Web Consortium and implemented by Microsoft Internet Explorer versions 3 and 4 and by Netscape Navigator 4.

- **Improved Table Editing.** FrontPage 98 provides improved visual control over the structure and layout of tables. New facilities include dragging to move or copy table rows and columns, dragging borders to resize rows and columns, and using Distribute Evenly commands for rows and columns.

- **Table Drawing Tools.** New tools in FrontPage Editor create tables of any size or shape, using the equivalents of a pencil and an eraser to draw the tables and their cells.

- **Image Preview.** The dialog box for selecting and opening images now displays a preview of each image you select, making it easier to pick the right image.

- **TWAIN Support for Image Acquisition.** FrontPage's built-in TWAIN support accepts images directly from your scanner or digital camera.

- **Clip Art Gallery.** FrontPage now ships with more than 1,000 clip art images and uses the same Clip Art Gallery interface as other Microsoft Office applications.

- **Clip Art Gallery Live.** From within the Clip Art Gallery dialog box you can download thousands of clip art images directly from the Microsoft Web site.

- **Text Overlays on Images.** FrontPage now permits entering text on top of images, making it easy to create page elements such as titles and graphical buttons.

- **Improved Image Editing Tools.** New image editing tools can bevel, crop, flip, rotate, wash out, resize, or resample images in FrontPage Editor.

- **Auto Thumbnail.** This feature automatically creates a small thumbnail image of a graphic and links it to the larger original image from which it was created. This is great for quickly building "picture gallery"–type Web sites.

- **Page Transitions.** Remote users with Internet Explorer 4 can experience stunning visual effects when navigating between pages. FrontPage can configure your pages to take advantage of this striking feature.

- **Text Animations.** FrontPage can create animations of text flying onto the screen or words revealed letter by letter.

- **Hit Counter.** This FrontPage component graphically displays a count that increases by one each time a user accesses your Web page.

- **Banner Ad Manager.** This component displays a timed series of images with transitions. It creates easy-to-use, eye-catching banner advertisements.

- **Hover Buttons.** These buttons provide an animated alternative to hyperlinks. A hover button can change its colors or shape, display an image, or play a sound when users pass the mouse over it or click it. Hover buttons are Java applets supplied with FrontPage and configured through dialog boxes in FrontPage Editor.

- **Enhanced Form Creation.** Whenever you add the first form field to a Web page, FrontPage automatically creates Submit and Reset buttons as well.

- **Form Field Extensions.** FrontPage can control the tab order and Alt+ key shortcuts for elements in HTML forms. This makes HTML forms easier to use without the mouse—benefiting laptop users and providing improved accessibility for other users.

- **Improved Saving of Form Results.** FrontPage 98 includes simplified dialog boxes that configure how the FrontPage Server Extensions process submitted HTML forms. Not only are these dialog boxes more intuitive, they're more powerful too.

- **Save Form Results to E-mail.** FrontPage now creates HTML forms that collect data from the remote user, send it to the Web server, and deliver it to you by electronic mail. In addition, the FrontPage Server Extensions now support outbound e-mail.

- **Database Region Wizard.** FrontPage can automatically program Active Server Pages to dynamically retrieve and display database information from a Microsoft Web server.

- **Improved Active Server Page Interoperability.** FrontPage 98 manages hyperlinks found within ASP script code. In addition, FrontPage Editor provides enhanced editing of ASP source code.

- **Dynamic HTML Support.** Browsers supporting Dynamic HTML can change portions of a Web page already on display, providing a degree of interactivity impossible with static, unchanging pages. FrontPage provides a variety of predefined Dynamic HTML functions, and it supports custom Dynamic HTML programming with browser-side scripts and special HTML tags.

- **Design-Time ActiveX Control Support.** Third parties can extend the authoring capabilities of FrontPage by writing these special ActiveX controls. The controls run in FrontPage, not in the browser. Settings are made when the page is created, and the control writes the necessary HTML when the page is saved.

Integration with Other Programs

- **FrontPage Editor Integrated with Internet Explorer.** When browsing a page with Internet Explorer, you can press the Edit button to edit the page in FrontPage Editor and then save changes back to the server.

- **FrontPage Editor Integrated with Netscape Communicator.** FrontPage can become the default editor invoked by Netscape Communicator.

- **Microsoft Commercial Internet Services Membership Integration.** User authentication in FrontPage integrates with the Membership feature of the Microsoft Commercial Internet System (MCIS), providing single login to all authorized services from an Internet service provider.

- **Microsoft Office Integration.** FrontPage emulates the intuitive visual interface and command structure of other Microsoft Office applications. It also provides the best cut and paste, the best drag and drop, and the best file compatibility with other Office applications of *any* Web authoring tool.

Other Enhancements

- **Performance Improvements.** The time needed to start Front-Page, the time to save a page, and the time to open a Web are all reduced. The ability to work with very large Webs is also enhanced.

- **Server Extensions Improvements.** Refinements to the Front-Page Server Extensions make it easier for server administrators to host multiple FrontPage Web sites.

Using the Companion CD

The compact disc that accompanies this book contains most of the sample Web pages that appear in the book's figures. This provides a way to view the pages in color on your own monitor, to examine how they're constructed, and to experiment. These pages can also form the basis for your own work.

⊗ CAUTION

FrontPage cannot open the Hello Web directly from the CD. Whenever it opens a Web, FrontPage writes information to certain internal files. On CD, of course, these files are unwritable.

The files are located in a CD folder called \hello. For casual browsing, you can open files in this folder with your browser by pointing it to your CD-ROM drive. To savor the full FrontPage experience, however, including modifying the pages and seeing certain components in action, you should import this folder to your hard drive as a FrontPage Web. Proceed as follows.

1 Open an MS-DOS window and copy the \hello folder from the accompanying CD to a folder on your local hard disk. Assuming your hard disk is drive C: and your CD-ROM is drive D:, the necessary MS-DOS command would be

```
xcopy d:\hello\*.* c:\hello\ /s
```

2 Issue the following DOS command to ensure that none of the copied files are flagged as Read-Only.

```
atttrib -r c:\hello\*.* /s
```

3 Close the MS-DOS window.

4 Start FrontPage. When the Getting Started dialog box appears, click the More Webs button.

5 In the box titled Select A Web Server Or Disk Location, enter c:\hello and then click the List Webs button.

6 In the list titled FrontPage Webs Found At Location, click <RootWeb>. Then, click the OK button at the bottom of the window. This will open the Hello Web.

7 To use the Hello Web as a disk-based Web only, stop here. To install the Hello Web on your Personal Web Server (or any other Web server), continue as directed.

8 Click the Publish button on the FrontPage Explorer toolbar.

9 If the Publish dialog box appears, make sure the following check boxes are turned off, and then click the More Webs button.

- Publish Changed Pages Only

- Include Child Webs.

10 When the Publish FrontPage Web dialog box appears, enter the following location in the text box provided:

`http://<server>/hello`

where `<server>` is the network address of the destination Web server. Click OK when this entry is complete.

11 If prompted, enter the destination server's Root Web administrator password.

12 Once publishing is complete, you should be able to open the Hello Web on the destination server.

   a Choose Open FrontPage Web from the File menu.

   b Click the More Webs button.

   c Enter the destination server's network name in the box titled Select A Web Server Or Disk Location.

   d Click the List Webs button.

   e Choose Hello from the list titled Frontpage Webs Found At Location, and then click OK.

Please view the Hello Web as a collection of exercises and sample pages constructed primarily for figures in this book.

- Various hyperlinks and form handlers may be incorrect or missing if they aren't relevant to the point at hand.

- Some functions may use facilities that were present in the author's lab but located outside the Hello Web.

- The Hello Web has been tested on a Windows NT 4 server runing IIS 3, with FrontPage 98 running on Windows 95, and with Internet Explorer 3 running on Windows 95. Results may vary with other configurations.

While not a fully functioning, integrated Web site, the Hello Web illustrates many FrontPage features and gives you a starting point for your own explorations.

Contacting the Author

Hearing from happy readers is always a welcome and pleasant experience, and hearing from the less-than-satisfied is important as well. My e-mail address is

buyensj@primenet.com

I'm most interested in your impressions of this book: what you liked or disliked about it, what questions it did or didn't answer, what you found superfluous and what you'd like to see added in the next edition. (I'm not privy to any inside information, but FrontPage 98 hardly seems the last of its kind.) I'll post errors, omissions, and corrections on my Web site at

http://www.primenet.com/~buyensj

I can accept enhancement requests only for this book, and *not* for the FrontPage software itself. The Microsoft phone number for suggesting product enhancements is

(425) 936-WISH [that is, (425) 936-9474]

Please understand that I'm just one person and I can't provide technical support for FrontPage—not even for readers. Please try other channels, including the following newsgroups:

microsoft.public.frontpage.client
microsoft.public.frontpage.extensions.windowsnt

Also try the following Microsoft Web locations:

http://www.microsoft.com/frontpage/
http://www.microsoft.com/frontpagesupport/

If all else fails, please write. While I can't promise to answer each message, I'll try to provide at least a useful suggestion. Even when I can't answer your e-mail messages directly, I find it instructive to learn what problems users like you are experiencing—and therefore how I can make this book more useful to everyone in its next edition.

Setting the Stage

For the last several years I've spent most of my spring weekends helping produce a rather large dance recital. There are four performances of about 32 dances each, with different scenery for each number. About 500 dancers participate, including my daughter.

Despite my having worked on these recitals for several years, I still get choked up at the start of a show. We set the opening scenery 15 or 20 minutes before the performance starts and line up the second act scenery in the wings. At about the same time the opening dancers come out, sit around the stage floor in groups, chat, and stretch. The opening number is always performed by the top dancers. Over the years these girls have repeatedly made the cut; now they're principal dancers, and taking over the stage with an easy confidence is one or their perks.

The stage hands stand around in small groups, chatting casually and waiting for the action to start. Hopefully there are no last-minute repairs to make. The dancers for the second number line up in the hallway behind the stage. The director thanks the teachers, rewards the year's top achievers, and accepts a few flowers.

Finally the talking stops, the introduction plays, and the working lights go out. The girls on stage rise in the dark, take their positions, straighten their costumes, flex out any kinks, and strike their opening poses. The curtain draws, the girls put on their smiles, the lights come up, and the music and dancing begin. The event that hundreds of people worked many long months to produce is happening.

It takes five hundred people to put on each performance, and each performance is a unique, once-in-a-lifetime work of art. And then, three hours later, we do it all again.

With this sense of anticipation, let's make Web pages.

PART I

Web Publishing with FrontPage 98

The FrontPage Approach to Web Authoring

In the space of a few short years, the World Wide Web has become the predominant electronic publishing medium on the planet. Once considered obscure technical details, Internet addresses now receive prominent mention at sporting events, in presidential debates, in television commercials, and in print advertising and marketing materials everywhere. More and more, organizations of all types are using Web technology to disseminate internal information and develop new kinds of client-server applications.

As the Web itself has moved from obscurity into the mainstream, so has its authoring community. Many new Web authors have neither interest nor aptitude for coding hypertext markup language—the stuff of which Web pages are actually made—but nevertheless they expect to create Web pages with high-level tools as sophisticated and easy to use as their favorite word processing, spreadsheet, or desktop publishing applications. This facility is exactly what Microsoft FrontPage provides.

At some fundamental level, word-processed documents, spreadsheets, slide-show presentations, and database reports are all documents. Nevertheless, each of these types represents a different mind-set and requires a different program to handle its unique requirements. So it is with Web pages. Concept divisions, and not the physical dimensions of paper, govern breaks from one Web page to another. Because Web pages have no fixed width or length, they reformat automatically with changes to the display window. Web pages do so depending on the current date, the capabilities of the end-user's computer, user input, or other factors. For all these reasons and more, producing Web pages is a task with unique requirements and challenges. As you will discover from this book, FrontPage provides a corresponding set of features uniquely suited to the task at hand.

The remainder of this chapter introduces the major components of FrontPage, explains their purpose, and provides an overview of how they work. Once you understand FrontPage conceptually, you'll be ready for the details presented in later chapters that will give you mastery on the Web.

Why FrontPage Was Created

The operation of the World Wide Web is quite simple. It involves the exchange of information between a computer that requests information, often called a *client,* and one that delivers the information, often called a *server.* The client's software, called a *browser,* requests Web pages from a server located somewhere on a network, whether it's a corporate intranet or the global World Wide Web. The browser identifies the requested file by its name in the server's file system and requests that the server send it. After receiving the requested file, the browser displays it to the end user. If the Web page calls for additional files, the browser requests them, using the same mechanism.

The creator of a Web page can designate areas of text, images, and other objects as *hyperlinks.* Each hyperlink specifies the network address and filename of another Web page. Clicking a hyperlink in the current Web page instructs the browser to retrieve and display the associated page.

Browsers expect Web pages to be in a format called hypertext markup language—HTML. This is a format anyone can produce using a simple ASCII editor, such as Windows Notepad. Text in an HTML page is entered as ordinary ASCII text, and so are formatting commands. Formatting commands are enclosed in <angle brackets> while ordinary text is not.

People around the world have produced millions of Web pages using simple ASCII editors, often with excellent results. The ability to produce Web pages just this way—using only simple, universally available tools—has been a key factor in the growth of the Web itself and remains a common practice. For many people, though, coding Web pages by hand presents serious obstacles.

- Coding Web pages manually requires intimate knowledge of a variety of markup commands such as `<H1>` to denote a heading typeface, `<B>` and `</B>` to start and stop boldface, and `<IMG SRC="/images/logo.gif">` to insert a specific graphic file.

- Lack of a graphical interface provides no visual feedback of what the Web page will look like to the end user and offers no visual cues regarding commands and options.

- The relationships among text, images, and other kinds of files in a typical collection of Web pages are highly detailed and complex. Errors result if a single file is misnamed or misplaced. Initially creating such a structure is difficult, but maintaining it over time can be daunting.

FrontPage provides a rich variety of features to relieve Web page creators of problems like these, and many more. The rest of this chapter will introduce them briefly. As you review each feature, consider how much more difficult it would be to achieve the same results with only a simple text editor.

FrontPage Webs

Most electronic documents reside in a single file regardless of the number of pages they contain. Web documents, by contrast, store each page in a separate file. There are several reasons for this practice.

- Storing each page in a separate file provides small, easily downloaded units of content.

- Using a separate file for each page provides a convenient means of hypertext addressing. Links to a given Web page simply point to the corresponding filename.

- Web pages scroll and have no fixed length, so there's no need to set page breaks every 11 inches.

Web pages, then, are like ducks, buffalo, and barracuda; they usually occur in groups. For all but the smallest or most unusual publishing projects, you should produce a set of interrelated Web pages rather than a single, large document file. Creating a one-page Web site is like producing a one-slide presentation or a one-chapter book—not only boring, but also a poor use of the medium.

To facilitate content management and administration, FrontPage organizes Web pages into units called FrontPage Webs. A FrontPage Web server has one Root Web plus any number of User Webs (sometimes called SubWebs). The system administrator, nicknamed the Webmaster, typically delegates administration of User Webs to individual owners but retains control over the Root Web.

There are no concrete rules or technical requirements that dictate how many Webs a server should have, or what they should contain. Certain principles apply, however:

- Pages with many hyperlinks among themselves usually belong in the same FrontPage Web. That is, distinct bodies of content should generally reside in a single Web.

- Groups of pages administered by different people should generally be in different Webs.

- The larger the Web, the longer it will take to load and update. For purposes of both performance and content management, FrontPage Webs generally shouldn't exceed a few hundred pages.

Graphical Site Organizer

Keeping all but the smallest Web page collections organized would be difficult without a graphical organizer like FrontPage Explorer. To suit various needs, FrontPage Explorer provides seven distinct views of a FrontPage Web site. To select a particular view, click its icon at the left of the FrontPage Explorer window or choose it from the View menu.

- Folders view

- All Files view

- Navigation view

- Hyperlinks view

- Hyperlink Status view

- Themes view

- Tasks view

Headings later in this section discuss each view in detail. Regardless of the view in effect, FrontPage Explorer's menu bar and toolbar provide rich options to

- Create, modify globally, or delete Web sites

- Import pages from existing sites not controlled by FrontPage

- Run spelling checks and text searches throughout a site

- Copy sites from one server to another

- Control security

NOTE

The Explorer also serves as the launch point for all other FrontPage functions.

Folders View

This view provides a representation, strongly resembling Windows Explorer, that displays the files and folders in a Web site. Figure 1-1 shows an example of Folders view.

FIGURE 1-1.
FrontPage Explorer's Folders view gives a graphical view of the files and folders that make up a FrontPage Web site.

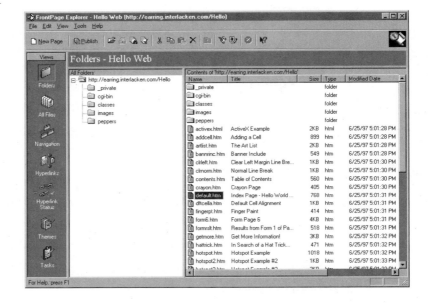

Folders view works very much like Explorer in both Windows 95 and Windows NT 4.0. Note the extra column for Title, however. As in Windows Explorer, double-clicking folders navigates through them. Double-clicking Web pages invokes FrontPage Editor, and double-clicking an image file invokes either Microsoft Image Composer or another bitmap editor of your choice. As you'll learn in detail in this book, the FrontPage Editor is a program that works in unison with FrontPage Explorer and enables you to create and edit individual Web pages much as you would use a word processor. Microsoft Image Composer, which ships along with Frontpage, helps you prepare graphics for your Web pages.

Right-clicking an item in Folders view results in this menu.

- **Open** opens the file with FrontPage Editor, Image Composer, or another program appropriate to the type of file.

- **Open With** opens the file with another editor of your choice.

 TIP

> You can maintain the list of available editors by choosing FrontPage Explorer's Tools menu, selecting Options, and clicking the Configure Editors tab.

- **Cut** puts the clicked file in the Clipboard and adds a **Paste** option for storing the file elsewhere. After pasting, the original file is deleted.

- **Copy**, like Cut, puts the clicked file in the Clipboard and adds a **Paste** option. However, the original file is retained after pasting.

 TIP

> When you move or rename a file by any means in FrontPage Explorer, FrontPage will automatically update references from other files in the same Web.

- **Rename** opens the filename to editing.

- **Delete** permanently removes the file. (There is no Undelete.)

- **Add Task** adds a reminder to Tasks view regarding this page.

- **Properties** displays a dialog box showing the object's characteristics and settings.

FrontPage Explorer's Folders view supports all the drag and drop operations you've grown accustomed to in Windows 95 or Windows NT 4.0. The difference is that if you move or rename files in Windows Explorer, you have to (1) manually locate each hypertext link from other pages in your site to the moved or renamed one and (2) update each of these pages manually. When you move or rename a file in FrontPage Explorer, FrontPage updates the other pages in your Web automatically.

All Files View

This view provides a list of all files in a FrontPage Web, regardless of the folder in which they reside. Figure 1-2 provides an example.

FIGURE 1-2.
Front Page Explorer's All Files view lists all files in the current Web, showing folder location as an attribute.

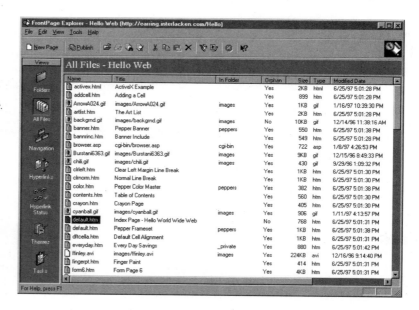

The All Files view provides all the capabilities of Folders view except for moving files among folders. Having a single list of all files in your Web can be convenient for locating files with a particular attribute.

As with many columnar lists in Windows, you can sort the All Files list on any field by clicking its column heading. Clicking Modified Date, for example, makes it easy to identify all files—in any folder—changed within a certain time span. (Click a second time to reverse the sort direction of any column.)

The Orphan column in All Files view might be particularly interesting to sort and review. If the Orphan column for a given file is Yes, Front-Page has detected no hyperlinks within the current Web that refer to it. Orphans bear investigation to determine if hyperlinks are missing or if pages have become obsolete.

Navigation View

Most Web authors organize their content hierarchically—that is, much like an organization chart. The Web begins at the top level with a home page and continues downward with a child page for each primary choice on the home page menu. Children at the second level might be parents to other groups of children at a third level, and so forth.

FrontPage Explorer's Navigation view provides a way to enter, view, and print just such an organization chart for any Web. Figure 1-3 provides a typical example.

FIGURE 1-3.
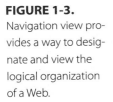
Navigation view provides a way to designate and view the logical organization of a Web.

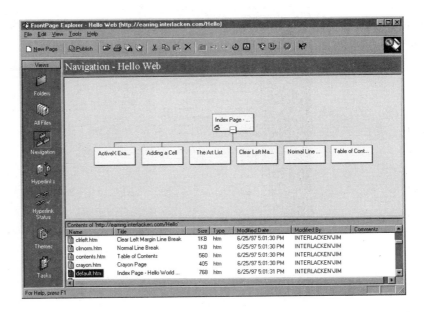

For new Webs, FrontPage will create a home page named default.htm and place it in the center of the upper Navigation view window. For existing Webs, FrontPage will identify the home page if possible. If FrontPage can't identify a Web's home page, clicking the New Page toolbar icon will create one.

Once Navigation view knows the Home page, you can identify its children by dragging their filenames out of the bottom pane and dropping them just below the home page. The pages will remain ordered left to right, depending on where you drop or subsequently drag them. If a page's parent is other than the home page, drop it under its parent. As you drag a page around the Navigation view window, FrontPage draws shaded lines to indicate its parentage if dropped at the current location.

As the diagram becomes larger and more complex, you might want to zoom in, zoom out, collapse branches, and then expand them. Navigation view provides all these commands.

Storyboard Your Site with Navigation View

Once you have a basic structure drawn—even if it consists of nothing but a home page—you might find it convenient to *always* create new pages in Front-Page Explorer. Without leaving Explorer, you can title the new pages, add them to Navigation view, and update the Tasks view with a reminder to supply the actual content. This process is similar to storyboarding your Web site with index cards and pushpins, though much more flexible.

Documenting the structure of your Web can seem like redundant work; you might argue that analyzing hyperlinks or folder structures should produce the same information. On reflection, however, you'll find that neither of these methods will produce the same results as good human judgment.

- Hyperlink analysis fails because most Web pages contain hyperlinks that are convenient for the reader but extraneous to the Web's primary content structure. Also, if a page is the target of hyperlinks on several other pages, there's no way to determine via hyperlinks which is the *true* parent in terms of the Web's content.

- Folder analysis fails because most sites become disorganized over time and because utility pages are often added beyond the Web's main structure.

For these reasons, FrontPage takes an opposite approach to eliminating double work: Rather than inducing the Web's structure from its HTML, FrontPage generates HTML from information you provide about your Web's structure.

Figure 1-4 shows the FrontPage Editor dialog box for automatically building a navigation bar—what most people call a menu bar—from the information in FrontPage Explorer's Navigation view.

FIGURE 1-4.
This dialog box in FrontPage Editor adds a navigation bar to the current Web page. Items on the bar will show the structure and page names as they were entered in Explorer's Navigation view.

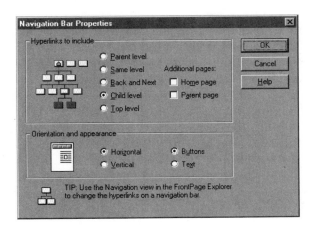

A navigation bar inserted in FrontPage Editor automatically reflects the current structure in FrontPage Explorer's Navigation view—you can change the bar's options and appearance in FrontPage Editor, but not its content. To change the bar's content, update Explorer's Navigation view and FrontPage will propagate the changes to each affected page.

Hyperlinks View

This view provides the hyperlink-based structure analysis you may have expected in Navigation view. It provides a display, centered on any page in the FrontPage Web, that illustrates graphically which other pages are related by hyperlink. Figure 1-5, on the following page, illustrates this view.

In Hyperlinks view, selecting a page in the left pane moves it to the center position in the right pane. Lines connecting one page to another indicate hyperlinked pages; the arrowhead points *from* the page containing the hyperlink *to* the page being linked.

Pages marked with plus-sign icons contain hyperlinks to still more pages; you can display these hyperlinks by clicking the plus sign on the icon (which then changes to a minus sign). Clicking the minus sign

FIGURE 1-5.
FrontPage Explorer's
Hyperlink view
provides a graphical
view of the hyperlink
relationships within
a Web site.

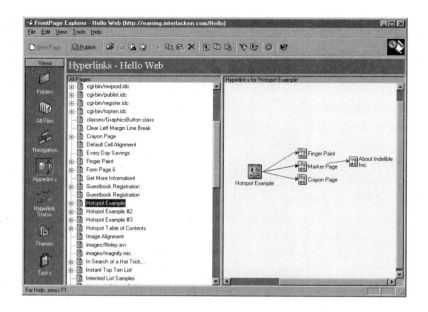

restores the original view. Resting the mouse over the central page icon in the right pane displays that page's filename, while pausing the mouse over its links displays their filenames and information about the type of link.

Double-clicking the body of a Web page icon brings up FrontPage Editor for viewing or editing the page. To move a linked page to the center of the view, right-click it and then choose Move To Center.

Hyperlink Status View

The Hyperlink Status view shown in Figure 1-6 displays each hyperlink in a FrontPage Web, tells where it occurs, and indicates whether the link's status is OK, Broken, or Unknown.

FrontPage uses its own internal indexes to verify the status of hyperlinks involving only pages in the same FrontPage Web. As long as these indexes are correct, FrontPage will provide instant, always-up-to-date information on these links.

Checking links outside the current Web requires attempting actual connections. This can be a time-consuming operation, especially when connections time out, so FrontPage doesn't verify these links

Web Publishing
with FrontPage 98

FIGURE 1-6.
Hyperlink Status view
displays the status of
all internal hyperlinks.
To update hyperlinks
pointing outside the
current Web, choose
Verify Hyperlinks from
the Tools menu.

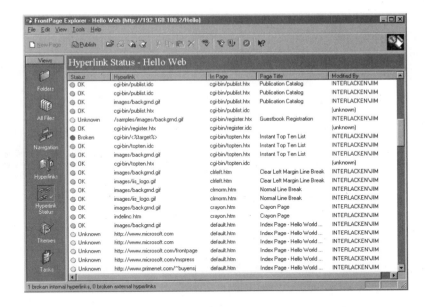

automatically. To initiate external hyperlink checking, choose the Verify Hyperlinks command from the Tools menu.

To fix a broken link, open the Edit Hyperlink dialog box:

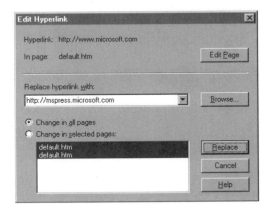

If you know the correct hyperlink address, you can type it directly into the Replace Hyperlink With text box. If not, clicking Browse will start your Web browser so that you can locate the desired page. When you return to the Edit Hyperlink dialog box, FrontPage will get the current page location from the browser and insert it for you.

Themes View

Themes are a new feature of FrontPage 98 that provides an assortment of professionally designed Web page styles. You can apply themes a page at a time or throughout an entire Web. Choosing a theme in FrontPage Explorer applies it to the entire Web. Figure 1-7 shows the Blue Print theme being previewed in Themes view.

FIGURE 1-7.
Choosing a theme in FrontPage Explorer applies it to every page in the current Web.

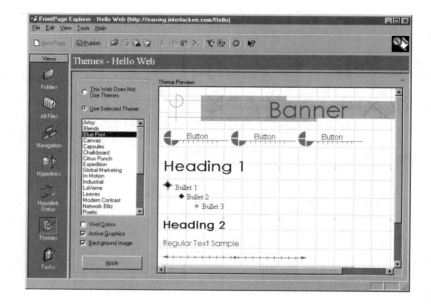

A theme is essentially a predetermined set of style choices. The theme overrides—and in fact makes unavailable—many of the formatting options you would otherwise have available in FrontPage Editor. If you want guaranteed consistency from page to page and you prefer professionally designed and packaged styles to your own, this can be an excellent facility. If you want more flexibility than a theme provides, you can achieve all the same effects and appearances manually, or can use themes on individual pages only.

To apply a theme to an individual page, open the page in FrontPage Editor and choose Theme from the Format menu.

? SEE ALSO

For more information
on themes, see "Work-
ing with Themes," 189.

FrontPage has no integrated facility for building or modifying themes.
However, you can find the necessary tools in the FrontPage SDK (Soft-
ware Development Kit). The SDK is available on the FrontPage 98 CD-
ROM or from Microsoft's Web site at *www.microsoft.com.*

Tasks View

This view displays a list of pending tasks for the current FrontPage
Web. You can create tasks either manually as you think of them or
automatically as a result of other processes.

? SEE ALSO

For more information
about FrontPage
Explorer, see Chapter 5,
"Structuring Your Web."

There are several ways to create a new task. From the Tasks view,
shown in Figure 1-8, you can simply click the New Task button on
the toolbar. From any view, you can choose New from FrontPage
Explorer's File menu and select Task. However, you can also create
tasks pertinent to a given page by right-clicking that page in Explorer
and choosing Add Task. In FrontPage Editor you can choose Task from
the Edit menu, and in some cases you can create a New Page task
rather than the new page itself.

FIGURE 1-8.
The Tasks view displays
a listing of all known
pending issues with
your Web. As you
resolve each issue, you
can mark the task
complete.

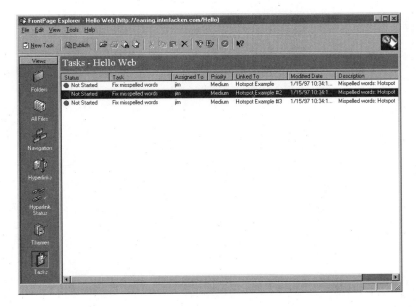

Certain global FrontPage operations also create tasks. For example, you can check the spelling on your entire Web and, rather than stopping at each error, simply create tasks pointing to any pages that contain errors.

Right-clicking an entry in Tasks view produces this contextual menu.

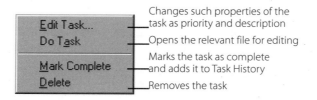

Changes such properties of the task as priority and description

Opens the relevant file for editing

Marks the task as complete and adds it to Task History

Removes the task

HTML Editors and WYSIWYG

A key decision in the invention of the World Wide Web was to throw away ten years of progress in word processing. Instead, Web pages consist of plain ASCII text "marked up" with tags such as <P> for new paragraph, <UL> for unnumbered list, and <LI> for list item. There was no way to know what size screen the end user had or what screen fonts were available, however, so these details were left to the discretion of each user's browser and system configurations, and not to the author. Text would flow within whatever document window the user chose. The author assigned style codes such as <H1> through <H6> for progressively smaller headings, for example, but every computer in the world could theoretically display a different font and size for each of those styles.

The file format that resulted from this early work is hypertext markup language (HTML). Objectively, it's one of the worst page description languages around. Its greatest strength and its greatest weakness are one and the same: simplicity. Its simplicity allows anyone with a plain text editor (such as Notepad) to create Web pages and lets anyone with a browser on any computer system read those pages—but at the same time it constrains page designers so harshly that they spend huge amounts of time trying to overcome its limitations. Page designers should be designers, stylists, and artists, not technicians required to create intricate program code.

To be charitable, early versions of HTML were designed for publishing scholarly and technical papers—and simple ones at that. There was no provision for publishing equations, charts, or tables, for example. Nevertheless, the HTML specification developed in those days still provides the basis for the most complicated Web pages we see today. In fact, plain text editors remain among the most common tools for creating Web pages, no matter how complex the page or how cryptic the HTML codes might be.

Web page authors working with a text editor typically keep a browser running in the background and displaying the page they're working on. To preview the appearance of a page, the author saves it to disk, and then clicks the browser's Refresh button to load it from disk. "But this is crazy," you say. "Why doesn't someone invent a Web page editor that displays what the end user will see—in true WYSIWYG (what you see is what you get) fashion—and not a bunch of HTML gibberish?"

To a large extent, the FrontPage Editor provides an answer to this question: Someone has done just that. Figures 1-9 and 1-10, on the next page, show how Internet Explorer and the FrontPage Editor display the same page with remarkable similarity.

There are, of course, limits to the extent that any HTML editor can provide a WYSIWYG view. The remote viewer's system still controls the screen resolution, color depth, page width, typeface, font size, and other visual aspects, according to its operating system, browser software, installed fonts, and so forth. No HTML editor can predict what these settings will be at display time, so no HTML editor can accurately preview them. FrontPage Editor, however, does provide a reasonable preview of what a user with similar browser settings would see.

If you compare Figures 1-9 and 1-10, it's apparent that FrontPage Editor displays certain structural elements that the browser doesn't. FrontPage Editor by design displays invisible table borders, invisible line breaks, and in some cases even invisible colors, all as aids to editing. Even though the end user won't see these elements, *you* need to, in order to edit them.

FIGURE 1-9.
Internet Explorer displaying a reasonably complex Web page belonging to the author.

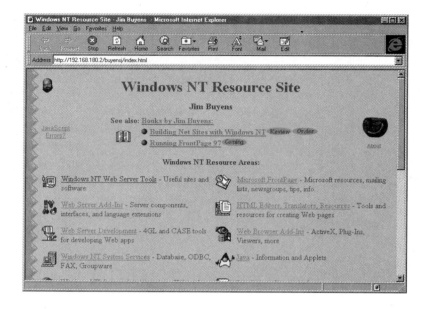

FIGURE 1-10.
FrontPage Editor closely matches Internet Explorer's display of a Web page (Figure 1-9) and also provides a great assortment of editing commands and tools. Note that the Normal view tab is selected at the bottom of the screen.

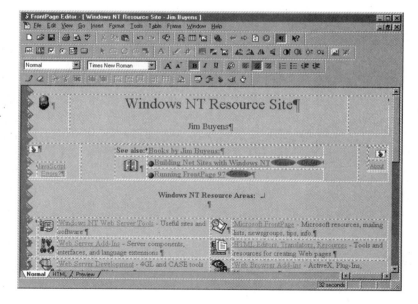

Figure 1-11 shows FrontPage Editor displaying the HTML code that actually creates the Web page shown above. As you can see, for the vast majority of Web page creators, editing with FrontPage Editor will offer tremendous advantages over editing raw HTML code.

FIGURE 1-11.
Select the HTML tab at the bottom of the Editor screen to view the HTML behind the current page. You can edit the code directly and then return to Normal view to see the results.

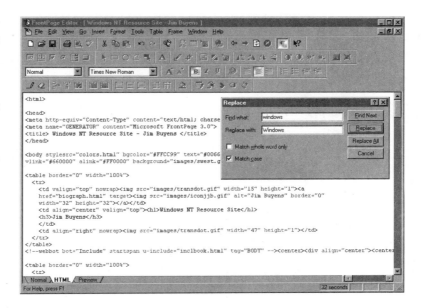

Special FrontPage Features

In addition to expected similarities like overall appearance, menu organization, icon assignment, dialog box similarity, keyboard shortcuts, and drag and drop, FrontPage supports

- **File format conversion to and from Microsoft Office Formats and HTML.** This includes inserting entire Microsoft Office files into Web pages as well as copying content from an Office application and pasting it into FrontPage. For example, if you copy a Microsoft Word table, a range of Excel cells, or a block of Access records, FrontPage will paste it as an HTML table.

- **Uniform table commands.** The FrontPage procedures for creating and editing tables are, to the maximum extent possible, the same as in other Office applications. This single feature alone provides an order of magnitude improvement over editing HTML with a text editor.

- **Uniform layout commands.** Wherever possible, FrontPage uses familiar Office commands and dialog boxes for aligning objects, setting fonts, and controlling bullets and other paragraph properties.

- **Creation of HTML forms.** HTML supports a variety of user interface objects such as text boxes, drop-down lists, option buttons, and push buttons. A grouping of such elements is called an *HTML form*. FrontPage Editor provides a WYSIWYG, drag and drop environment for designing HTML forms and menu-driven configuration of all form elements.

? SEE ALSO
For more information about FrontPage Editor, see Part III, "Building Your Site."

FrontPage Editor also provides extensive support for dragging and dropping objects from one location on a page to another, from one Web page to another, and from Windows Explorer onto Web pages.

Style Tools

Rock bands notwithstanding, members of a group should generally be united by a common appearance. This is just as true for Web pages as it is for marching bands, store clerks, armies, executives, and Girl Scouts. FrontPage offers a number of tools with which you can create a unified and attractive style for all your pages.

Themes

Its collection of themes is the most pervasive, all-encompassing style facility FrontPage has to offer. If you want to guarantee that your site has consistent style and colors, nothing else has the force of FrontPage themes. Applying a theme to a page or Web locks in a professionally designed appearance and disables any command that could override it.

By design, themes aren't open to modification by ordinary users. If you're into control and uniformity, this is good. The same is true if you don't fully trust your own artistic judgment or perhaps believe you have none. If artistic freedom is your passion, though, themes are likely to be frustrating (unless you're the one who gets to use the Software Development Kit and design themes for others).

Themes were discussed earlier in this chapter and will be covered in greater detail in "Working with Themes," page 189.

Color Masters

Somewhat less drastic than Themes, color masters provide a way for one page in a Web to inherit the text colors and background of another. Any page can be the source (or master) of colors and background for another, though the best approach is usually to create a special page for each shared color combination in your Web.

To create a color master, simply create a new page, assign the colors and background you want, and save it. This page may or may not actually appear in your Web, but its properties can be used for pages that do appear.

To assign colors to a Web page from a color master

1 Open the Web page in FrontPage Editor.

2 Choose Page Properties from the File menu.

3 Click the Background tab. The following dialog box will result.

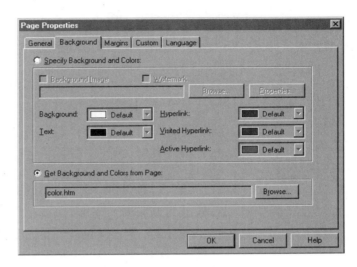

4 Click the button titled Get Background And Colors From Page.

5 Click the active Browse button and locate the page whose colors you want to assign to the current page.

6 Click OK to select the color master page, and then click OK again to close the Page Properties dialog box.

Changing the colors or background on a color master will automatically change the same attributes of any page set up this way to inherit its colors.

Shared Borders

This new FrontPage 98 feature applies any combination of top, bottom, left, and right borders—including the content within them—to selected pages or to an entire Web. Shared borders are very handy for applying standard heading styles, standard footers, and standard margin content to an entire Web.

The following dialog box in FrontPage Explorer activates shared borders for an entire web. The Borders To Include graphic shows the approximate position for each border.

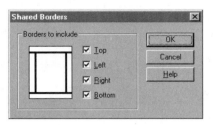

FrontPage Editor also has a Shared Borders option, located on its Tools menu, which enables you to apply or remove borders from individual pages rather than the entire Web.

The borders themselves are actually table cells. FrontPage surrounds the normal page content with an all-encompassing table; if all four borders are used, this would be a 3×3 table, with all three columns in rows 1 and 3 merged. Figure 1-12 shows a page with four shared borders open in FrontPage Editor.

FIGURE1-12.
The rectangular areas at the top, bottom, left, and right of this page are shared borders and will be applied to all pages in the Web.

Shared borders

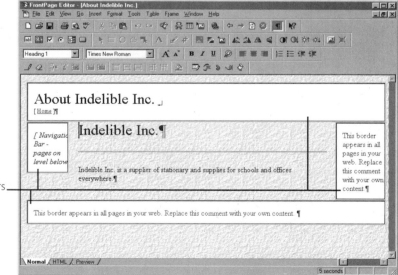

You can edit the shared border areas within any page that uses them, but remember that changes may affect every page in your Web. The contents of each shared border are contained in four files, named

_borders/bottom.htm

_borders/left.htm

_borders/right.htm

_borders/top.htm

By default, top.htm contains a page banner component, left.htm contains a vertical navigation bar component, and the other two files contain only comments.

Page banners will be discussed later in this chapter, but for now it's enough to know that they display the current page's Title (as configured in a Page Properties dialog box) as text. The page banner component allows top.htm to show the correct Title for every page in the Web, even with a single copy of top.htm that doesn't change.

Templates

FrontPage helps you create a consistent Web appearance with a feature called *templates*. Using a template is simple.

1 Use FrontPage Editor to create a Web page with the color scheme, background, and other standard features you want in the template.

2 Use FrontPage Editor's Save As feature to save the page as a template. Figure 1-13, on the following page, illustrates this function in progress.

? SEE ALSO

For more information about templates, see "Planning and Managing Reusable Components," page 195.

3 When creating a new Web page that should have the given template features, select that template in the File New dialog box shown in Figure 1-14, on the next page.

As you can see in Figure 1-14, FrontPage also provides its own assortment of standard templates.

FIGURE 1-13.
FrontPage Editor can save draft Web pages as templates, which then serve as models for other pages.

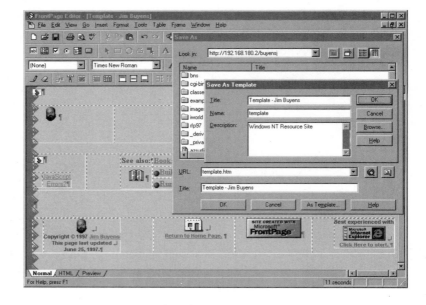

FIGURE 1-14.
You can choose any stored template as the starting point for a new Web page.

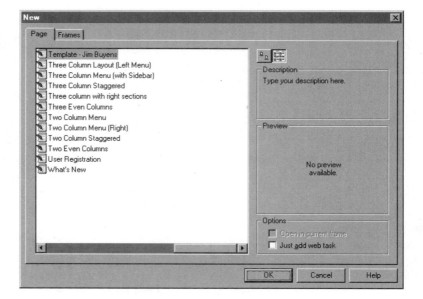

Framesets

A frameset is a special Web page whose sole purpose is dividing the user's browser window into several rectangular areas called *frames*. Each frame has a name and can display a different Web page within itself.

Hyperlinks clicked in one frame can load pages into another frame. A common application is therefore to define a menu in one frame and content in another. Clicking a menu item can then replace the content area but not the menu itself. This avoids the need to keep menus up to date on multiple pages. Of course, many other applications are possible as well; anytime you wish to replace only portions of the browser window, framesets are an option worth considering.

Figure 1-15 shows a frameset open in FrontPage Editor. Users of Front-Page 97's frames feature will rejoice; the fully editable, WYSIWYG view is new in FrontPage 98. Note the title frame at the top of the page, the menu bar at the lower left, and the large content frame at the lower right. This is a fairly typical arrangement.

FIGURE 1-15.
FrontPage 98 provides full WYSIWYG editing of framesets. Four HTML files are open in this example: the frameset itself, plus one ordinary HTML page for each of its three frames.

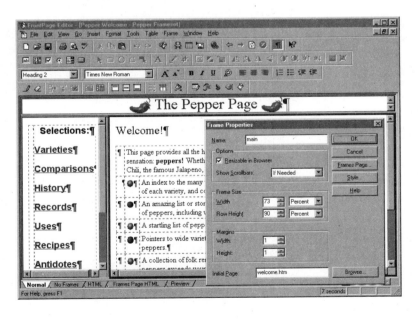

Standard Active Components

The fact that computers deliver Web pages on demand and display them interactively means that computer programming instructions can be inserted at any step of the process: storing pages to the server, processing user requests, delivering requested pages, and displaying the pages. This is a significant difference between the Web and other mass media. Newspapers, magazines, books, radio, and television all provide very little interactivity or customization.

Developers have invented a wide range of technologies for adding programmed intelligence to the Web experience. These include

- **CGI, WinCGI, and ISAPI programs.** These are programs that run on the Web server and produce Web pages as output. Users on the Web invoke these programs by submitting a special Web page request, and the server returns the generated page to the user who submitted the request. Creating such programs is beyond the objectives of FrontPage, but FrontPage does provide a useful, prewritten set of them—the FrontPage Server Extensions.

- **Script languages.** Scripts are short sections of program code inserted directly into Web pages and set off by special tags so that the source code doesn't appear on the displayed page. Scripts can run on either the browser or the Web server, subject to the design of the script and the capabilities of the environment.

    Two common uses for scripts are inserting variable information, such as the current date or the date a page was saved, and responding to user events, such as resizing the browser window or clicking a button. Script languages can also interact with ActiveX controls and Java applets on the same page, and with the browser or server itself.

    FrontPage Editor supports script languages by (1) providing a way to insert user-written scripts into FrontPage Web pages and (2) automatically generating script code for common functions such as field validation. FrontPage supports both VBScript (Microsoft Visual Basic Scripting) and JavaScript, the two most popular browser script languages. Figure 1-16 show three lines of JavaScript inserted into a Web page.

FIGURE 1-16.

FrontPage can insert JavaScript or VBScript code at any position on a Web page.

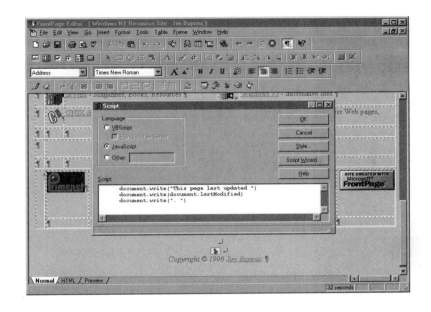

- **Java applets.** Java is a programming language capable of running on almost any computer. Java programs compile to a format called bytecode, and then run on any computer that has another piece of software called a Java bytecode interpreter. The interpreter creates an environment called the Java Virtual Machine that, in theory at least, can run any Java program written. This frees programmers from having to write different versions of their software for each type of computer. The interpreter must be matched to the type of computer, but the Java program need not.

  A Java applet is a Java program designed to run as part of a Web page. The applet usually occupies a portion of the browser window, controls its contents, and responds to any user events that occur there. For security reasons, applets can't access files and other resources on the local computer, and they can initiate network connections only to the machine the applet was downloaded from. (These restrictions are frequently compared to a sandbox, inside of which Java applets must play.) FrontPage isn't a development environment for Java applets, though it does support placing existing applets onto a page and displaying them in their initial state.

- **ActiveX controls.** Like Java applets, ActiveX controls are programmed objects capable of providing a given function in a variety of contexts. Unlike Java applets, however, ActiveX controls are based on the OLE (object linking and embedding) approach developed for Microsoft Windows. ActiveX is a very flexible specification that defines not only Web page objects, but objects that run on the Web server, operating system, and non-Web applications as well.

  Controls designed to run within a browser window occupy a portion of the Web page and accept input from the HTML, the user, or other controls. In response, they change their appearance and make results available for transmission back to the Web server. ActiveX controls running on a Web server don't create visual output directly, but they perform server-side functions such as writing and retrieving data in files and databases. They typically get their input from requests originating from a browser client or from a script that invokes them. To express output, they return values to the script that invoked them or write HTML for transmission to the remote user.

  ActiveX controls are compiled for a specific computer type and operating system, and a separate version is therefore required for each environment. There's no "sandbox" limiting what an ActiveX control can do, but each control is digitally signed so that the end user can verify that it arrived both intact and from a trusted source. While FrontPage isn't a development environment for ActiveX controls, it supports placing such controls on a page and displaying them in their initial state.

- **Plug-ins.** This is another category of software module, first developed by Netscape Communications, that integrates into the display of a Web browser. Plug-ins typically provide interactive and multimedia capability.

TIP

Unlike Java applets and ActiveX controls, plug-in programs don't install automatically when a Web page needs them. When using plug-ins, be considerate and provide links to the plug-in vendor's download site.

- **Design-time controls.** The purpose of design-time controls is to preview Web functions and create the required HTML. As such, design-time controls run in the authoring environment only. The HTML or other created objects can run either on the server when a request is received, or at the browser when it receives a response. However, servers and browsers use the output of a design-time control and not the control itself.

  Eventually, design-time controls might permit users to seamlessly add new functions at will to Web editors like FrontPage. For now, FrontPage will accommodate them—but not seamlessly.

FrontPage Components

In addition to the active components already mentioned, FrontPage provides its own intelligent features called FrontPage Components. FrontPage Editor inserts these wherever you specify, prompts you for any variable information, and then generates the corresponding HTML codes when it saves the page. Along with the HTML, FrontPage saves the dialog box fields you specified so it can redisplay them in future editing sessions or re-create the HTML if some other factor has changed.

In almost every case, FrontPage components provide active output; that is, their content or appearance will change automatically based on events beyond the Web page that contains them. This may occur because

- The generated HTML includes a browser-side or server-side script that produces variable output.

- The generated HTML invokes a program on the server, such as a database query or full text search.

- The generated HTML reflects information located elsewhere within the FrontPage Web. If you change the information located elsewhere, FrontPage will automatically correct all the Web pages that reference it.

FrontPage provides 16 FrontPage components. Of these, the 13 described next operate totally within the FrontPage environment or the user's browser. Because they involve no components on the server, they don't require the FrontPage Server Extensions to work.

■ **Banner Ad Manager.** This component displays a series of images, each for a specified number of seconds. Whenever remote users load the page, their browsers load a FrontPage Java applet that continuously retrieves and displays the specified images.

■ **Comment.** This component displays text in FrontPage Editor, but has no visible effect on the Web page as viewed with a browser.

■ **Hover Button.** HTML provides a built-in button object commonly used to submit forms or trigger other actions, but such buttons have become boring and mundane. FrontPage hover buttons provide much more flexibility in appearance, and they allow buttons to change appearance in various ways when the user passes the mouse pointer over them.

■ **Include Page.** FrontPage replaces this component with the contents of another page in the same site. Whenever you have the same features appearing in many Web pages and might need to change them in the future, you should consider using the Include Page component.

■ **Insert HTML.** If you know how to code HTML and wish to insert some special code directly into a Web page, this component provides the method. FrontPage will insert any HTML you provide directly into the Web page without interpretation, validation, or correction.

 TIP

To fully integrate your HTML into the HTML generated by FrontPage, insert the new HTML lines after switching FrontPage Editor into HTML view. This will permit subsequent WYSIWYG viewing and editing. Use the Insert HTML component only for HTML you don't want FrontPage to process in any way.

- **Marquee.** This component creates an area of text that moves across the Web page. FrontPage provides a rich assortment of colors, effects, and timing options that control the marquee's appearance at browse time.

  Some browsers, such as Netscape Navigator, don't display marquees actively. In these cases, the marquee text will appear but remain stationary.

- **Navigation Bar.** Using FrontPage Explorer's Navigation view records the structure of the pages in your Web but, for various reasons, it can't automatically add the corresponding hyperlinks to each page. Principal among these reasons is that FrontPage can't guess how you want the links formatted or positioned on each Web page.

  The navigation bar component builds a set of text or graphic hyperlinks—usually consisting of the current page's children—and inserts the set wherever you want on the current Web page. Changing the structure in FrontPage Explorer's Navigation view will then automatically update the navigation bars in any relevant pages.

  Navigation bars can provide links not only to child pages, but also to the current page's parent, to all pages at the parent level, to all other pages at the same level, to the previous and next pages, to the Web's home page, and to all pages at the top level. A single Web page may contain any number of navigation bars.

- **Page Banner.** This component inserts a text or graphic object containing the current page's title, as specified in various Page Properties dialog boxes. This is particularly useful when constructing page templates or standard page headings. Each time the template or heading is used, the page banner component will display the title of the current page.

- **Scheduled Image.** FrontPage replaces this component with a specified image every time the page is saved during a specified time period. After the time expires, FrontPage no longer displays the image. Figure 1-17, on the following page, shows the dialog box that controls the Scheduled Image FrontPage component. In this example it labels an element on the Web page as *New!* for a period of one month.

- **Scheduled Include Page.** This component works like a Scheduled Image except that the FrontPage component replaces itself with a Web page (or page segment) rather than an image.

SEE ALSO

For an explanation of Web configuration variables, see "Global Site Parameters," page 37.

- **Substitution.** This component replaces itself with a page or Web configuration variable.

- **Table of Contents.** This FrontPage component creates an outline with hyperlinks to each page in your FrontPage Web. It also updates the outline when the Web changes.

- **Timestamp.** FrontPage replaces this component with the date and time of your last update to the page.

FIGURE 1-17.
The Scheduled Image component starts and stops displaying an image based on date.

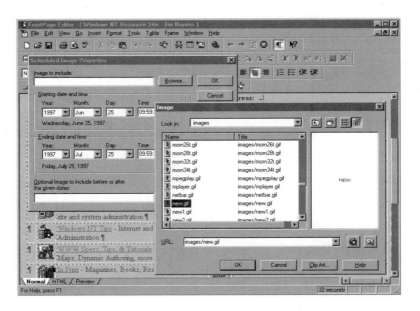

The three FrontPage components listed below operate at least partially on the Web server. Be sure your Web server has the FrontPage Server Extensions installed before using them.

- **Confirmation Field.** FrontPage replaces this component at run time with the submitted contents of a form field. This is useful for displaying the contents of a form to the user for verification. For example, if a user fills out a name-and-address form, this component can redisplay the information for the user to verify before it is filed away on the server.

- **Hit Counter.** This FrontPage component increments and displays a counter every time a user accesses the page that contains it.

- **Search Form.** The Search Form component creates a form for full-text searching of a FrontPage Web. The user submits a form containing words to locate, and the Search Form component returns a list of hyperlinks to relevant pages.

(?) SEE ALSO

For more information about FrontPage components, see Chapter 10, "Using FrontPage Components."

All FrontPage components depend on the FrontPage Editor's invoking them whenever a page is saved. If you make changes to your Web with *another* editor, the FrontPage component won't be invoked at save time and might not function correctly. Scheduled FrontPage components will take effect only when you save the affected pages on or after the specified start and stop dates.

FrontPage Server Extensions

FrontPage achieves its maximum potential when the FrontPage Server Extensions are installed both on the Web author's machine and on the server that eventually delivers those pages to the end users. The extensions are a set of programs that

- Communicate with FrontPage Explorer (and therefore FrontPage Editor) at authoring time, and

- Provide various centralized services—such as data collection, mailing, and search—for remote users who visit an Extensions-enabled Web site.

Server extensions are available for a variety of popular Web servers and computing platforms including both Windows NT and Unix. If you're a server administrator planning to support users running FrontPage, you should definitely install the extensions and keep them up to date. If you're a FrontPage Web author, you should definitely encourage your server administrator to do so. If you have a Web site hosted by an Internet service provider (ISP), check to see if they have installed (or will install) the FrontPage Extensions.

Wizards

Like other Microsoft Office applications, FrontPage provides wizards to perform complex operations. Wizards prompt you for options in a structured way, first prompting for options with a series of dialog boxes like the one shown below and then completing their work uninterrupted. This avoids prompts for unnecessary options and minimizes the chance of a partially completed update.

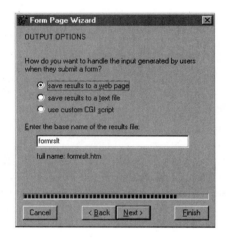

These are some of the Wizards FrontPage provides:

- **Corporate Presence Wizard.** Creates a typical set of Web pages for representing a company on the Internet. The wizard contains generic pages you can use as a starting point, and leaves notes in purple text indicating what you should update and what kinds of information to include.

- **Customer Support Web.** Creates a set of Web pages for a company offering customer support on the Internet. It's particularly designed for computer software companies.

- **Discussion Web Wizard.** Creates a special FrontPage Web designed for interactive discussions. Users can submit topics by entering text in a form, review existing articles listed in a table of contents, or locate articles by word searching.

- **Import Web Wizard.** Adds an existing set of Web pages to a new or existing FrontPage Web.

- **Personal Web Wizard.** Creates a Web that represents an individual, with pages for interests, favorite sites, and photos.

The following wizards help you to create a Web page.

- **Database Region Wizard.** Prompts for the name of an ODBC Data Source (a database), an SQL statement, and the database columns to display. It then creates the necessary VBScript code to run the query on a Web server, format the results, and provide a display to the remote user.

- **Form Page Wizard.** Creates an HTML form based on the type of information you need to collect.

- **JavaScript and VBScript Authoring Wizard.** Creates both browser-side and server-side scripts based on prompted user input.

- **Web Publishing Wizard.** Copies a FrontPage Web to a server on which the FrontPage Server Extensions aren't installed.

Global Site Parameters

FrontPage provides a facility whereby you can save frequently used data once, in a central location, and then reference it by name in any Web pages you create.

? SEE ALSO

For more information about site parameters, see "Reviewing Web Settings," page 166.

Suppose, for example, that the names of key people at your site change from time to time. You could set up a site parameter for each position in your organization chart and assign each incumbent's name as a value. At this point, you could have each page in the site reference the parameter name (say, *vprad* for your Vice President of Research and Development) rather than the explicit name (say, "Frank P. Jones"). When someone new takes over a position, you can then change the one site parameter rather than having to find and update each affected page by hand, possibly missing some in the process.

Figure 1-18, on the next page, shows the FrontPage Web Settings dialog box for adding and maintaining site parameters. You change the

FIGURE1-18.
FrontPage can accommodate any number of global parameters for a site.

Two parameters with their current values

Adding a new parameter and its starting value

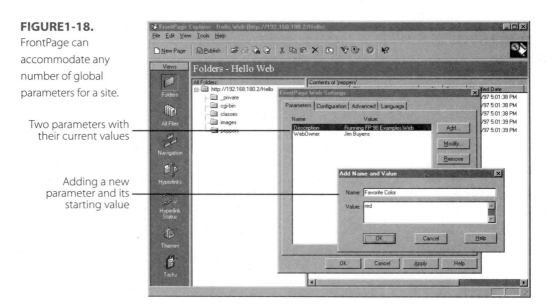

settings in FrontPage Explorer by choosing Web Settings from the Tools menu and then clicking the Parameters tab.

Built-In Upload/Download

SEE ALSO
For more information about HTTP, see "Hypertext Transfer Protocol," page 61.

Because FrontPage uses HTTP (hypertext transfer protocol), rather than the local file system to retrieve and store Web pages, there's no need to transfer Web files manually. FrontPage keeps the Web server automatically updated for you.

FrontPage can also copy Webs from one server to another. This is an excellent feature if you want to maintain separate sites for authoring and production. More information about the role multiple servers can play in a FrontPage environment is provided in "Organizing Your Web Server Environment," page 145.

Image Editing

Graphics (also called images) are among the most important components of any Web page—so important that it's rare to see a page without them. In addition to providing tools to edit and manage

HTML files, FrontPage therefore provides a rich assortment of tools for editing images.

Image Editing in FrontPage Editor

FrontPage provides a number of tools for directly modifying images when a page containing them is open in FrontPage Editor. You can find these on the Image toolbar.

- **Select.** Tells FrontPage that clicking an image selects it. This is the default; all remaining tools require that an image first be selected.

- **Rectangle.** Marks a rectangular area within an image as a *hotspot*. At browse time, clicking any pixel within a hotspot activates an associated hyperlink.

- **Circle.** Marks a circular area within an image as a hotspot.

- **Polygon.** Marks an irregular, straight-sided area as a hotspot.

- **Highlight Hotspots.** Displays all current hotspots within an image.

- **Text On GIF.** Allows entry of text superimposed over an image.

- **Make Transparent.** Converts any single color in an image to transparency by clicking on a pixel of that color.

- **Crop.** Provides a way to display only a rectangular subset of an image. You can adjust the rectangular area using the mouse.

Imposing Text on GIF

This is a very cool feature. When you overtype a graphic with text, FrontPage remembers the filename of the original image, the text string you enter, and the font characteristics you specify. It then formats the text onto the image, saves the results using an internally generated filename, and displays the combined text-and-graphics image rather than the original.

This feature is useful not only for labeling images, but also for creating headings and titles that use special fonts or colors. To create headings and titles, you would typically choose a textured surface, solid color, or completely transparent image as the background.

- **Washout.** Adds whiteness to all the colors in an image, making it look washed out. This is frequently desirable for images used as backgrounds.

- **Black And White.** Converts an image to monochrome.

- **Restore.** Returns an image to its original appearance. However, this may not be possible after the image is saved.

- **Rotate Left / Rotate Right.** Rotates the selected image 90 degrees counterclockwise or clockwise.

- **Reverse.** Converts the selected graphic to a mirror image of itself.

- **Flip.** Turns the selected image upside down.

- **More Contrast / Less Contrast.** Increases or decreases the contrast in an image. Increasing contrast means light colors get lighter and dark colors get darker; decreasing contrast means the reverse.

- **More Brightness / Less Brightness.** Increases or decreases the brightness of an image. Increasing brightness means that dark colors get brighter; decreasing brightness means that light colors get darker.

- **Bevel.** Adds a three-dimensional border around the image. Front-Page will lighten the top and left edges while darkening the bottom and right edges.

- **Resample.** Converts a visual image to one with the actual desired size. Suppose, for example, you resized a 200×100 pixel image to 100×50. This would download the original, 200×100 image to the browser and tell the browser to resize it. The Resample command would create a new image whose actual size is 100×50, and it would download in $\frac{1}{4}$ the time of the original.

In addition, FrontPage lets you copy, cut, and paste graphics (using the traditional Windows commands or shortcut keys), move them around the page by dragging and dropping, and resize selected graphics with the mouse.

Microsoft Image Composer

FrontPage 98 ships with Microsoft Image Composer, a feature-laden bitmap editor. Image Composer, shown in Figure 1-19, accepts images in a wide variety of formats or directly from your scanner, and it offers more than 500 transformation functions. Among the things Image Composer can do:

- Adjust color, tint, and brightness

- Apply hundreds of different and configurable transformations such as drop shadow, bas relief, spattering, texturing, and smudging

- Convert image file formats

- Create text images using any font on the system

- Fill, paint, and replace colors using a variety of brush shapes

- Optimize the palette and palette depth

- Rotate, flip, crop, shrink, and enlarge images

FIGURE 1-19.
Microsoft Image Com-
poser has numerous
editing and transforma-
tion features.

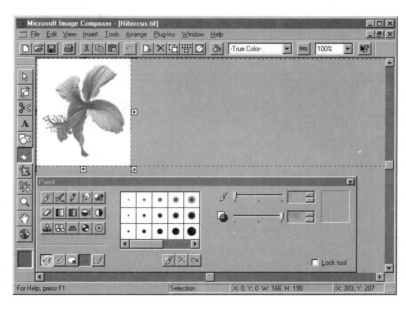

Microsoft GIF Animator

Animated GIF files have become a popular feature on the Web. Unlike ordinary GIF files, the animated type contains (1) a series of images and (2) instructions on how long to display each one. Displaying an ordered set of images fast enough produces the illusion of continuous motion.

FrontPage 98 comes with a simple program called Microsoft GIF Animator that, as you might expect, creates animated GIFs. GIF Animator, shown in Figure 1-20, is neither an image editor nor an animation studio; you must create each image in the series using some other program, paste them one-by-one into GIF Animator, and then set all the timing parameters. This is animation at its most elemental level, but at least in simple cases it gets the job done.

FIGURE 1-20.
This is Microsoft GIF Animator displaying a 13-frame animation, three frames at a time. The animation mimics the moving lights of a theater's marquee.

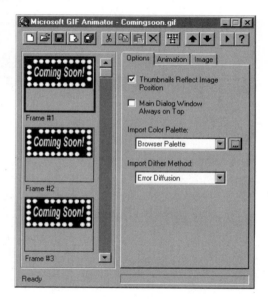

Clip Art

FrontPage provides an extensive library of buttons, horizontal rules, backgrounds, images, and other figures you can use to enhance your Web pages. This collection is shared with the rest of the Microsoft Office 97 suite, making clip art you install for any other Office applications (such as Publisher) automatically available to FrontPage as well.

For ease of use, FrontPage lists clip art by category in the Clip Gallery and provides the graphical clip art selection dialog box shown in Figure 1-21.

FIGURE 1-21.
To insert clip art, choose Image from FrontPage Editor's Insert menu and then click the Clip Art tab.

Advanced User Interface

The FrontPage 98 user interface follows all the style and organizational conventions of other Office 97 applications. If you're familiar with other Office applications, most of FrontPage 98's commands and toolbar icons will be just as you expect them to be.

Finally, if nothing yet has convinced you that organizing a Web site with FrontPage is easier than doing it with a scratch pad, consider this: look back to Figure 1-1, on page 8, which clearly shows the top of the Web site as a URL, or uniform resource locator—a Web address—and *not* as a local file location. Unless you specify otherwise, FrontPage opens, modifies, and saves all information about your site via HTTP, the communications language of the Web itself. As a result, you and your team, regardless of physical location, can use FrontPage to maintain Web sites not only on your local machine or on your LAN (local area network), but also on any Web server in the world! The server's Webmaster simply needs to install the FrontPage Server Extensions and grant you the necessary permissions.

PART II

Plumbing, Art, and Media—A Web Primer

CHAPTER 2

Planning and Organizing a FrontPage Web

Whatever your site's size and purpose, proper advance planning will produce a better appearance, more organized content, faster construction, and easier ongoing maintenance. More importantly, a well-planned site will attract more visitors, better meet its original goals, and be cheaper to run.

Every site should have a consistency suited to its purpose. Pages should be unified by a common theme, a common organization, and a common style. The words, images, colors, and layout should lead the visitor to the messages—both overt and subtle—that justify the site's existence.

This chapter and the next two address the core aspects of planning and producing a Web site. The chapters are highly interrelated; you can't plan without understanding the work to be done, and without a sound plan you can't properly do the work. Their approach to organizing and producing Web sites is therefore somewhat iterative, with increasing levels of detail.

Identifying Your Message

Step one in building or maintaining a Web site is understanding the message its sponsors want to send. Whether your site describes yourself, an area of interest, your organization, your client, or a large multinational corporation, the message you want to send probably isn't, "I'm just learning HTML," "I'm scatterbrained," or "I'm trying to increase ugliness and confusion in the world."

"Establishing a presence" is probably the most common reason for starting a Web site, but this is terribly vague. It usually means following a perceived trend, keeping up with competitors, or responding to requests from others. More focused (and more useful) reasons for starting a Web site include

- Increasing knowledge and awareness of a person, a topic, or an organization

- Releasing information in accordance with law or an organization's charter

- Promoting a desired public image

- Advertising products and services

- Selling products or services directly to Web visitors

- Providing post-sale product support information

You'll almost certainly need to drill through several levels of detail to fully understand your site's mission. Investigating each level generally leads to questions for the next. The end result should be a mission statement, even if informal, that describes the site's purpose and objective.

Understanding the Audience

As important as knowing your site's message is knowing its audience. "Everyone on the Web" is too vague an audience to be useful; you should have some particular *kinds* of people in mind—perhaps even specific people to use as models. Some typical audiences are

- Everyone in a certain industry

- Practitioners of a certain skill

- Purchasers of a certain type of product or service

- Users of a specific product

Once you know who's in your audience, you should learn whatever you can about them. Are they technical, artistic, or people-oriented? What are their skills and interests? What's their level of vocabulary and education? Do they respond more to detailed text or to color, style, and visual metaphors?

You hope, of course, that your audience will find your site's message inherently interesting and attractive. Often, however, some other enticement is needed. Perhaps you can entice visitors with a free clip art library and then, while they browse, sell them your graphics program. Perhaps you can sell art supplies as people browse a library of works or techniques. If they come for information about a product they already own, perhaps you can sell them another.

The ultimate enticement, according to recent thinking, is to make your site the meeting place for a community of some kind—presumably a community with an interest in your product or message. The goal is then to make your site such a valuable resource—such a compelling place for people in your target audience to find each other and interact—that the site becomes a "must visit." This generally requires some sort of added content that's updated frequently and not available anywhere else. It also requires a means for visitors to enhance the site themselves and to find other visitors without invading anyone's privacy. Achieving this sort of community is more often talked about than achieved in practice, though it remains a lofty goal. It also illustrates the importance of providing a magnet to attract targeted visitors.

Addressing the Politics of Organizations

Anything involving two or more persons involves politics. Unless you're building a personal Web site or a site for your own entrepreneurial business, you'll probably need to discuss your ideas with someone else, get their approval, or reach consensus. This might seem like an extra task up front, but it generally results in improved content and fewer problems when it's time to go online. In a large organization

II

Plumbing, Art, and
Media—A Web Primer

that's putting up a new external Web site, for example, it's generally best to get input and approval from higher-ups in outer-directed departments such as Public Affairs and Marketing.

A greater problem arises when key authorities are asked to render decisions on something they don't understand. Education into the intricacies of Web publishing is obviously critical in such situations, especially when it includes review of established and successful sites with a similar mission. Unfortunately, it's often difficult to get enough time with the right people.

A related problem occurs when key decision makers lack empathy with the intended audience. Some principals from Manufacturing or Engineering, for example, might insist on content with internal rather than external relevance—even for an external Web site. Perhaps you can get customer profiles from Marketing or Public Affairs and discuss them with the inner-directed departments.

These general tips might help you deal with organizational conflict or obstructionism:

- If two key people disagree, try shuttle diplomacy. Speak to them both privately, try to formulate a compromise, and then speak to them privately again.

- If two key groups disagree, identify the opinion leaders and revert to the bullet point immediately above. Remember, the key opinion leaders aren't necessarily the highest-ranking individuals.

- Play the expert. Using long technical explanations of why poor decisions won't work, bore them until they break.

- Don't assume that a person's view won't change. Asking the same question a different way on a different day frequently produces a different answer—quite possibly a more workable one and even a more effective solution.

- The best way to get action from bureaucrats is to let them know you've found a way around them.

- The second best way to get action from bureaucrats is to make a deal.

- The hardest way to get action from bureaucrats is to figure out their agenda and attack it. A folksy old saying warns, "Don't ever fight with pigs; you both get dirty and the pig likes it."

- Use your boss, project sponsor, or contract authority to the hilt when necessary. They probably occupy their positions because they're better at organizational dealings than you are.

Identifying Content Categories

If your site is typical, the home page will be the most time-consuming of all to construct. There are several reasons for this:

- The home page presents the site's first impression, and therefore is usually the most elaborate page in the site. Remember another old saw: "You get only one chance to make a first impression."

- Despite being the site's most elaborate page, the home page must download quickly. Otherwise, users will give up after a minute or two and go elsewhere.

- The home page often serves as the prototype for the entire site's visual appearance. It sets the tone and image for every page that follows.

- If you're new to creating Web pages, a home page will probably be your initial learning experience.

- The options on the home page intrinsically represent the site's primary structure.

The first four points usually work themselves out, but the last is critical. If you can identify the top few options in your site, you probably have a good understanding of its message and audience. If you can't get your home page organized, your content plan probably isn't organized either.

FrontPage provides built-in templates and wizards that create typical pages for many kinds of sites, but at best they produce only starting points. No two sites are exactly alike; your site's content and organization are ultimately your unique creation.

Here are some terrible ways to organize a site:

- An option for each member of the design committee

- An option for each person who reports to the top executive

- An option for each category someone thought of, in chronological order

- The same options you used at a previous site

All the above share the same problem: They ignore the target visitor's likely interests and mind-set. They indicate a lack of defined message, defined audience, or both.

Choosing a Visual Concept

Visual appearance plays a critical role in the way visitors perceive your site and receive its message. No matter how interesting and well-organized your site's content may be, a drab presentation will provide a poor viewing experience for your Web visitors and indicate a lack of interest on your part. Because most Web sites devote the best visual presentation to the most important content, many Web visitors now associate drab presentation with boring, outdated information.

Visual presentation is no substitute for well-organized and useful content; both are necessary to produce an effective site. Except for a few highly specialized sites, content doesn't *consist* of presentation; instead, presentation is a means to *convey* content. HTML is such a weak page description language that the challenge of achieving visual appeal frequently overshadows that of developing content; don't let this happen to you.

Your site's graphic design should complement its message and appeal to its audience. An abstract, garish design patterned after an album cover might be appropriate for a rock group, but certainly not for a bank or a brokerage house. A site's overall graphic design conveys messages just as surely as its text and images, and you should strive to have those messages reinforce each other rather than clash.

If it happens you're not an experienced graphic design professional, don't despair. In many cases the site's organization will already have logos, colors, and style guidelines designed by professionals for use in other media. If so, these can be adapted for Web use as well. This might even be a requirement of the Legal department.

In the absence of other guidelines, choose a theme related to some aspect of the site's content. For a school, consider the school colors, emblem, and mascot. For an athletic league, consider the colors and textures of the playing field or equipment. For a restaurant, consider the scenes and colors related to the cuisine, locale, fixtures and objects from the restaurant's decor, the style of the restaurant's menu, or ingredients and cooking utensils.

Beyond these relatively obvious approaches, consider a theme based not on products themselves, but rather on settings where the product is used, cities or sites where it's manufactured or sold, or aspects of the organization's history or technology. Your site's theme should suggest colors, images, and icons you can use throughout the site or its principal sections. If a particular theme doesn't suggest a set of workable colors and images, move on to another. You'll probably get an "aha!" feeling when you've found it.

? SEE ALSO
For help in choosing colors that display correctly on Web pages, see "Achieving Accurate Rendition—Safe Colors," page 124.

The default colors on most browsers are black on gray or black on white. This is every bit as interesting as black-and-white slides projected on a basement wall. Black, white, and gray aren't necessarily colors to avoid, but they *do* deserve augmentation with adjacent frames, images, and borders. When choosing text and background colors, choose dark text on a light background. Bright text on a dark background is harder to read, especially for small type sizes. It's usually a good idea to maintain color contrast as well as brightness contrast between text and background.

Planning Your Pages

Given a mission, an audience, a content plan, management go-ahead, a visual concept, and knowledge of what HTML can and cannot do, you're finally ready to design pages in detail. To at least some extent, this will probably involve storyboards and sketches.

The classic storyboard consists of index cards pinned to a wall. You write up an index card for each Web page, annotate it to indicate planned content, and then arrange all the cards in some kind of hierarchy or

II

Plumbing, Art, and
Media—A Web Primer

sequence. Web visitors will traverse the site along these sequences and hierarchies. Team members and your project sponsor will review the chart, suggest revisions, and someday pronounce it worthy of prime time.

Storyboards so archetypical are rare—but the concept is sound. Your storyboard might be notes on a yellow pad, an outline in a word processor, a draft set of menu pages, or even a Navigator view in Front-Page Explorer. No matter: The key result is a well-organized set of pages and not the method used to achieve it.

It's easy to go wild with menus. Visitors are unlikely to find pages more than two or three clicks away from the main page, however, so don't nest menus too deeply. Avoid long pages of hypertext links by using drop-down lists, option buttons, check boxes, and other HTML form elements. A drop-down list of 10 product names and another with 4 kinds of information efficiently supports 40 menu choices.

You should also start sketching or drafting pages at this point. Identify each type of page you plan to use, and then make up a draft or template for each type. Identify changeable components that will exist on multiple pages—menu bars, signature blocks, contact names, and the like—then plan site parameters and include blocks to support them. Accumulate stock images, too. These are logos, icons, buttons, bars, and theme images that, if standardized, will help the site achieve a unified appearance.

Lengthy text, either as content or HTML commands, is seldom the cause of excessive download times. Images, Java applets, and ActiveX controls are far more often the culprits. As you plan your pages and accumulate your images, keep a rough total of download bytes for each type of page. There are no hard and fast rules on the size of Web pages, and this is less a consideration on high-bandwidth intranets than on public Internet sites accessed by dial-in users. Pages having more than 25,000 to 30,000 download bytes are generally considered too large for dial-in users. This is equivalent to 15 to 20 pages of double-spaced plain text or one uncompressed image 170 pixels on a side.

A final bit of planning advice: You *can* have too much of a good thing. All Web sites are always under construction, so trying in advance to nail down every nit for every page is probably a futile exercise. If you try to plan too much detail, the site's rate of change will exceed the rate of planning. Don't let "Paralysis by Analysis" happen to you.

Achieving Effective Page Layout

The normal progression of topics on a page, whether on the Web or in your morning paper, is top to bottom and left to right. Every Web page should have both a meaningful title and a meaningful heading. As Figure 2-1 illustrates, the title appears in the browser's title bar and the heading appears somewhere near the top of the page. The title serves to identify the page externally to processes like FrontPage Explorer and search engines (such as Yahoo, Lycos, AltaVista, and InfoSeek). The heading immediately informs the viewer what content appears on the page. If the user has chosen a wrong link, they can immediately jump back to the previous page. Otherwise, the user should find confirmation that they've arrived at the correct page. If the page is long, bookmark links should provide pathways to each major subsection, to avoid extensive scrolling (at least on the home page).

FIGURE 2-1.
The title of this page is "Microsoft FrontPage Home Page" and its heading is "Microsoft FrontPage 98, Professional Web Sites Without Programming."

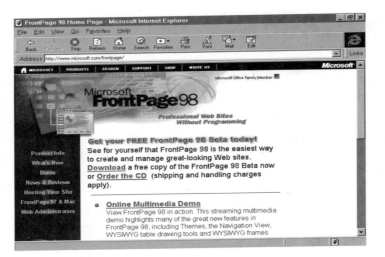

Experienced page designers often find HTML's weak page-layout features extremely frustrating. This reflects a fundamental conflict between the HTML goal of device independence and the artistic desire for precise control. This conflict isn't likely to subside any time soon, though FrontPage does support a number of recent HTML page layout facilities.

- **Alignment tags.** The normal flow of HTML text is down the left margin, wrapping lines automatically when they reach the right margin, with a hard-coded line break and an explicit or implied paragraph ending. Images, Java applets, and ActiveX controls retain their relative positions within the HTML text.

Implied paragraph endings occur in several situations:

- Before and after tables

- At transitions in paragraph style

- Before and after numbered and bulleted lists

? SEE ALSO

For more information about using alignment tags to control page placement, see "Aligning Text," page 275.

Recent versions of HTML support tags to left-align or right-align images and other objects, flowing text around them. A centering tag centers the same kinds of objects, but no text flows to the right or left of the centered image. Additional tags align non-text objects vertically with the surrounding text flow. FrontPage supports all these tags.

? SEE ALSO

For information about using FrontPage to create HTML tables, see "Creating and Editing Tables," page 313.

■ **HTML tables.** Originally designed to display tabular data, HTML tables have become one of the premier means to place items spatially on a page. Anytime you'd like to draw an imaginary grid on a page and align items within it, an HTML table should be your choice.

? SEE ALSO

For more information about frames, see "Creating and Editing Frames," page 338.

■ **Frames.** This feature provides a way to divide a Web page into tiled rectangles and to independently control the content of each rectangle. One Web page defines a *frameset*—an object that controls the number, sizes, and placement of the frames—while additional Web pages provide the content for each frame. Standard frames have visible borders between them and scroll bars for moving up, down, left, and right within each frame. Borderless frames have no visible borders and are simply page layout areas that corral your text where you want it.

In the next chapter we'll broaden this discussion of HTML to include the new active components that increasingly are becoming vital parts of Web pages. We'll also look at how the World Wide Web moves this information around the globe.

Looking at the Web—Inside Out

I n all probability, your interest in FrontPage reflects a distinct lack of interest in HTML. Nevertheless, publishing in any medium—whether print, broadcast, or online— requires a certain knowledge of its technology, strengths, limitations, and mind-set. Therefore, in this chapter we broadly review the structure of both HTML and the World Wide Web itself.

If you're an old hand at creating Web pages and communicating via the Web, you may wish to skip ahead to Chapter 4, or treat this chapter as a review, or place it at the bottom of your bird cage. If you're a beginner, proceed in confidence that no arcane syntax or hexadecimal codes lie in waiting. (Well, maybe a little....)

Relationships Between Browsers and Servers

Like most Internet applications, the Web is a client server system. The clients are machines where users submit interactive commands and view responses using software called a *browser*. Microsoft Internet Explorer (IE) and Netscape Navigator are the most popular browsers. Servers typically are located some distance from the users, service simultaneous requests from multiple users, and have no need for a keyboard, mouse, or monitor other than for system administration. Most servers support several applications at the same time, but the software that supports the World Wide Web is called an *HTTP server*. HTTP is the hypertext transfer protocol.

> **NOTE**
>
> The term *server* is a bit ambiguous. Sometimes it refers only to the hardware, sometimes to a specific piece of background software, and sometimes to the combination of all hardware and software on a machine. Because this is a book about the Web, the term *server* will mean all the hardware and software required to service HTTP requests—that is, requests to deliver Web pages.

Another distinction between clients and servers is that clients generate requests and servers provide responses. Obviously, the client must formulate its requests and submit them in a way the server understands. Likewise, the server must formulate its responses in a way the client can deal with. The rules governing these interchanges are called *protocols*.

> **NOTE**
>
> A protocol is nothing more than a way of acting. Life is full of little protocols, such as the conventions we use to avoid bumping into people on sidewalks, in hallways, and when entering and leaving elevators. If an individual (or computer) acts outside established protocols, interaction with others will generally fail.

There are millions of computers on the Internet, and they interact in quite a variety of ways. As a result, many different Internet protocols are used. People can hardly talk about anything on the Internet without talking about protocols. Protocols govern how telephone numbers must be dialed, how modems link to each other, how dial-up networking software negotiates settings and logs onto the network of an ISP (Internet service provider), and how machines on a local network (or intranet) communicate via Ethernet. There are hundreds more protocols, but fortunately most of them can be ignored in a discussion of browsers and HTTP servers.

Browsers and HTTP servers always communicate by TCP/IP (see the sidebar below). This means each computer needs an IP address. IP addresses are four bytes long, with the value of each byte typically stated as a decimal number; for example, 192.168.180.2 is a typical four-byte IP address. If your PC is permanently wired into a local area network, or LAN—perhaps in an office or university environment—an administrator or an automated service on the network will assign its IP address. If you dial into an Internet service provider, the process of connecting and logging in assigns a temporary IP address for your computer to use.

Servers are usually situated on local area networks and generally have administrator-assigned IP addresses. Administrators also publicize the server's IP address by assigning an easy-to-guess, easy-to-remember name and providing lookup through a globe-spanning network service called the Domain Name System.

Plumbing, Art, and Media—A Web Primer

World Wide Web Protocols

The two most important protocols involved in Web browsing are TCP/IP and HTTP. In fact, TCP/IP is two protocols: TCP and IP.

- TCP—the transmission control protocol—opens and closes connections, breaks data into manageable chunks for transmission, reassembles incoming chunks, and checks incoming data for completeness and accuracy.

- IP—the Internet protocol—gives each computer a unique address and specifies how data finds its way through the network from one computer to another.

- HTTP—the hypertext transfer protocol—specifies the types of requests Web browsers can submit and the types of responses a Web server should make.

Reserved IP Addresses

Certain blocks of IP addresses are reserved for special purposes, and two of these are frequently employed by FrontPage users.

First, the *loopback address*, 127.0.0.1, always refers to the local machine; in essence, it's a shortcut that means *myself*. If you're running a Web server and a client (that is, FrontPage or a browser) on the same machine, the client can access the local Web server by connecting to 127.0.0.1. This can be extremely convenient if you don't know your IP address or if your only network is dial-in. In most cases, the name *localhost* is synonymous with 127.0.0.1.

Second, IP addresses of the form 192.168.*xxx.yyy* are reserved for private networks. To set up an IP network connecting two or more computers not on the Internet:

1   Install a network card in each machine and connect them with suitable wiring.

2   Install the TCP/IP software that comes with your operating system.

3   Give each machine an IP Address of the form 192.168.*xxx.yyy* where

- All the machines have the same *xxx* number between 1 and 254.

- Each machine has a different *yyy* value between 1 and 254.

4   Assign a Subnet Mask of 255.255.255.0.

5   Leave the Default Gateway field blank.

IP addresses beginning with 192.168 aren't valid on the Internet, though you can use them to connect private networks for a home or small business. No conflict results if machines on the private network occasionally dial into an Internet service provider, or if you later connect the private network to the Internet using software called a proxy server.

Internet Computer Names

Computers on the Web actually connect by means of numeric IP addresses and not by name. Site names like *www.microsoft.com*, *ftp.microsoft.com*, and *www.msn.com* are only for the convenience of users. Names like *www.microsoft.com* are simply easier to remember than numeric addresses like 207.68.137.36. With users preferring names and computers using numbers, some means is clearly needed to translate from one to the other. The Domain Name System (DNS) provides that service.

DNS names are built in levels. Periods separate the levels, with the highest level at the right end of the name. Names get looked up a level at a time, possibly on different servers for each level. Table 3-1 lists a few of the most common high-level DNS names.

TABLE 3-1. Common Domain Name Suffixes (Root Domains)

Suffix	Meaning	Example	Site
com	Commercial	www.microsoft.com	Microsoft Corporation
edu	Educational	www.nd.edu	University of Notre Dame
gov	Government	www.odci.gov	Central Intelligence Agency
mil	Military	www.army.mil	United States Army
org	Nonprofit Organization	www.pbs.org	Public Broadcasting Service
ca	Canada	www.canoe.ca	Canadian Online Explorer
uk	United Kingdom	www.ox.ac.uk	Oxford University, England
us	United States	www.state.az.us	State of Arizona

Your Internet service provider or network administrator will either give you the IP address of a local DNS server or arrange to have it configured into your PC automatically. This is an important setting because without it you can only connect to other machines by numeric IP address.

Hypertext Transfer Protocol

Like so many other technologies, HTTP started out simple and later grew to be complicated. As originally conceived:

1 The browser opened a connection to the computer and port specified in the desired Web page address.

2 The browser transmitted the word GET followed by a space, a folder path, an optional filename, and a carriage return (equivalent to pressing Enter). The command to request a server's home page, for example, was

   GET /

II

Plumbing, Art, and Media—A Web Primer

3 The server sent back a status code, a file type indicator, a blank line, and the contents of the requested file.

4 The server then closed the connection.

Nowadays, in addition to the basic GET request, browsers transmit *headers* that convey additional information about the connection. In the recording below, for example, the browser indicates what kinds of files it can accept, what human language it prefers (English), the size and color depth of the user's screen, the user's operating system and CPU type, the name and version of the user's browser and any compatibilities, the computername the browser is trying to contact, and an indication that the browser is willing to use the same connection for several transfers rather than opening new connections for each file.

```
GET / HTTP/1.0
Accept: image/gif, image/x-xbitmap, image/jpeg, ↵1
   image/pjpeg, */*
Accept-Language: en
UA-pixels: 1024x768
UA-color: color8
UA-OS: Windows 95
UA-CPU: x86
User-Agent: Mozilla/2.0 (compatible; MSIE.3.0; ↵
   Windows.95)
Host: www.interlacken.com
Connection: Keep-Alive
```

In response to the GET request printed above, the server responded with the following headers. They indicate the status code "200 OK", the name and version of the Web server software, the willingness to reuse connections, the date and time, the file type "text/html", the ability to supply a byte-numbered portion of a page, the date the returned page was last modified, and the length in bytes of the returned page.

```
HTTP/1.0 200 OK
Server: Microsoft-IIS/2.0
Connection: keep-alive
Date: Sun, 03 Nov 1996 22:41:10 GMT
Content-Type: text/html
```

---

[1] The ↵ symbol indicates a single line of code that had to be broken onto two or more lines to fit on the book page. Always treat such lines as if they were one continuous line.

```
Accept-Ranges: bytes
Last-Modified: Sun, 03 Nov 1996 03:50:15 GMT
Content-Length: 5574
```

A second type of request, POST, is often used by Web pages containing HTML forms. The POST method uses additional HTTP headers to transmit all the names and values from an HTML form. This provides more flexibility and data handling capacity than using the GET method with a query string.

A complete explanation of HTTP headers is beyond the scope of this book, but Web designers should be aware that browsers and Web servers exchange a variety of information about themselves during each

---

Understanding HTTP and Stateless Connections

The greatest limitation of HTTP connections is that they are *stateless*. This means that the connection is closed immediately after a page is transmitted and the server retains no useful memory of it. This becomes a real nuisance when a single transaction requires several Web pages to complete. Suppose, for example, that a user brings up the first Web page, submits some information, and gets a second screen prompting for more data. When the user submits the second page, the server has no memory of what transpired on the first.

Three common solutions to this dilemma are the following:

- Have the server write all the data about a transaction out to each Web page, and have the browser transmit it back with every transaction. This usually involves an invisible form field for each item of data.

- Have the server and browser exchange transaction data as *cookies*. Cookies are data fields that the browser and server exchange by means of special HTTP headers. Cookies may apply to a specific Web page, folder, or site, but cookies from one site can never be sent to another.

- Have the server keep transaction data in a file or database record designed for that purpose. Transmit a transaction identifier to and from the server using hidden form fields, path data, query strings, or a cookie.

By default, cookies reside in the browser's memory and disappear when the user closes the browser. However, a Web page can specify that its cookies should be saved persistently in a special file on the user's disk. Once cookies exist for a given Web page, folder, or site, the browser transmits them with every request to that location until the cookies expire. The server specifies an expiration date every time its sends the cookies.

request. Information supplied by the browser, for example, can be used on the server to customize the server's response.

Web Site Folders and Files

Any folders and files you create as part of your Web site will become folders and files on the computer where your Web server runs. Factors such as allowable characters, allowable length, and case sensitivity of names depend on the operating system running the Web server. If you develop and test Web sites under an operating system with a different file system than the production Web server, you'll need to understand and account for any file system differences.

Unix file systems are case sensitive, so asking for a file named Index.html will fail if the actual filename is index.html. Windows file systems aren't case sensitive, however, so the same request would work on a Windows-based Web server.

 TIP

> Case-sensitive names are relatively confusing even to hard-core Unix users, and the normal solution is to use lowercase filenames only. This is an excellent habit to acquire.

The FAT file system used for years under MS-DOS and Windows 3.x supported an eight-character filename base plus an optional three-character extension. You should conform to these restrictions if there's any chance of moving your site or any of its files to such a platform, even temporarily. This will involve shortening HTML and JPEG filename extensions to HTM and JPG, respectively. (Note that for clarity extensions standing alone in this book are printed in capital letters.)

The maximum length of a filename or folder name under Unix is 32 characters—certainly a reasonable bound for Web pages as well. Extremely long filenames and folder names constitute cruel and unusual punishment when the need to hand-type a Web page address arises; further, they invite error, frustration, and ultimately perhaps the user's moving on to a simpler site.

Finally, it's good practice to use only letters, numbers, hyphens, and underscores in pathnames and filenames used on the Web. Even if allowed by the Web server's file system, characters such as commas, slashes, apostrophes, backslashes, dollar signs, ampersands, and spaces aren't allowable in Web addresses; a percent sign followed by a two-digit hexadecimal code is required in lieu of most special characters. A "simple" folder name like What's New? thus becomes What%27s%20New%3F—decidedly less friendly than whatsnew or whats-new.

Uniform Resource Locators

A uniform resource locator (URL, pronounced "u-r-l") provides, in a single string, all the information required to access a file on the Web. It consists of the following structure:

```
<protocol>://<computername>:<port>/<directory>/<filename>
```

For example:

```
http://www.microsoft.com:80/frontpage/learn.htm
```

The protocol HTTP (often supplied automatically when you hand-type *www* into your browser) tells the browser to use hypertext transfer protocol for formatting and transmitting a request to the named computer. It also sets the default port number to 80. The browser will ask the remote computer to send a file named learn.htm from the /frontpage directory on that site.

In URLs that appear within Web pages, protocol, computername, port, pathname, and filename are all optional.

- Protocol defaults to that of the page currently on display.

- Computername also defaults to that of the current page.

- If the URL specifies a computername, port defaults to the default for the protocol. (For HTTP, the default is 80.) If the URL takes the computername from the current page, the default port is also taken from the current page.

> **NOTE**

In URLs, filenames and folder names are always separated by a slash (/)—even if the Web server is running an operating system (such as MS-DOS or Windows) that normally uses a backslash (\) separator.

Additional URL Features

Three optional subfields can follow the filename in a URL.

Bookmarks. Web designers can give names to certain spots within a page. Hypertext links from within the same page or other pages can then jump directly to those spots. The syntax for a link to a bookmark is a pound sign (#) and the name of the bookmark, appearing immediately after the filename. If the URL consists of the pound sign and bookmark name only, the full path to the current page will be the default. The following are examples of URLs that jump to bookmarks.

```
http://www.foo.com/far/out/place.html#space
#earth
```

Query strings. In some cases, rather than the name of a file to transmit, a URL specifies the name of a program the server should run. Such programs may require command-line arguments, and the query string provides a way to transmit them. As shown in the following example, a question mark indicates the beginning of a query string.

```
http://www.foo.com/scripts/lookup.exe?cust=123&order=456
```

The query string contains one or more name=value pairs, separated by ampersands (&).

Path information. Anything that appears between the name of an executable file and the beginning of a query string is passed to the executing program as path information. The URL below contains the string "zonkers" as path information.

```
http://www.foo.com/scripts/lookup.exe/zonkers?cust=123&order=456
```

Query strings, path information, and the POST method are three different ways of sending data from a browser to a program on a Web server. The method required by any given program depends on how that program was written.

- If no pathname appears, the path from the current page applies.

- If no filename appears, the browser simply doesn't transmit one. The Web server responds by searching the directory path for one or more preconfigured, default filenames. If the path contains no default file, the server transmits either a list of files or a Not Found message, depending on its security configuration.

- Although pathname and filename are both optional, at least one is required.

Note that except for the filename, these defaults work from within Web pages and not from the Address or Location field of your browser window. Suppose, for example, the browser window displays the following URL:

```
http://www.microsoft.com/frontpage/learn.htm
```

To jump to the What's New page, you'd have to change the browser's Address or Location box to:

```
http://www.microsoft.com/frontpage/brochure/whatsnew.htm
```

This entire string isn't required within the definition of the learn.htm file, however. Within learn.htm, you could specify simply:

```
brochure/whatsnew.htm
```

and allow the rest of the URL to default. The browser will add `http://www.microsoft.com/frontpage/` in front of `brochure/whatsnew.htm` for you.

In general, it's best to allow URLs to default whenever possible. This minimizes changes when you move pages from one site or folder to another.

Hypertext Links

(?) SEE ALSO

For more information about links, see "Creating and Managing Hypertext Links," page 308.

The essence of the Web is hypertext links. Without them, users would have to hand-type the URL of each page they wanted to visit. Given the length and cryptic nature of many URLs, users probably wouldn't visit many pages, or would get lost in a thicket of typos along the way.

Hyperlinking Text

The most common form of Hypertext link is the *anchor*. With this type of link clicking underlined text or an outlined picture takes you to another page. A simple anchor has the following HTML syntax:

```
<A HREF=/contact.html>Click here for Contact ↵
   information.</A>
```

Plumbing, Art, and
Media—A Web Primer

The browser would display this code as:

`Click here for Contact information.`

and clicking it would jump to the contact.html page in the current server's home folder. The A in `<A HREF=` stands for anchor, and `HREF` means Hypertext Reference. Content that appears between the `<A...>` and `</A>` appears as a link, and clicking on it jumps to the HREF location.

Of course, a major reason FrontPage exists is to isolate you from HTML tags such as `<A HREF=>`. The procedure for creating a Hypertext link in FrontPage Editor is as follows:

1 Highlight the text, images, or both that will trigger the jump.

2 Choose Hyperlink from the Edit menu.

3 Specify the hyperlink using one of the options shown in Figure 3-1.

4 Click OK.

FIGURE 3-1.

FrontPage provides handy dialog boxes for building hypertext links. Here, the user is building a hyperlink to another page in the current Web.

Link to another page in the current Web.

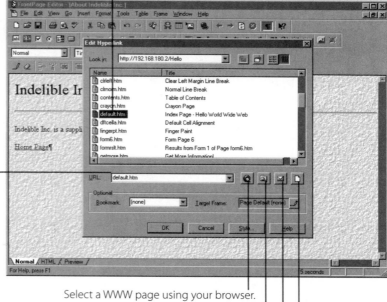

Type a URL address into the text box.

Select a WWW page using your browser.
Select a file on your computer.
Create a hyperlink to an e-mail address.
Create a new file and link to it in one step.

Image Maps and Hotspots

Image maps provide another form of hyperlinking—one that permits assigning different URLs to different parts of an image. FrontPage calls this feature *hotspots*.

Web pages use two basic kinds of image mapping (hotspots): server-side and client-side. When the user clicks on an image with server-side hotspots defined, the browser transmits the *x-y* coordinates of the spot clicked, along with the name of the image map file. Using the hotspot definitions already set up in the image map file, the server can then translate the clicked coordinates into a URL and finally takes one of two actions:

- If the URL points to a file on the same server, the server transmits that file.

- If the URL points to a different server, the local server sends a command to the browser instructing it to retrieve the mapped URL.

? SEE ALSO

For more information about image maps, see "Establishing Hotspots," page 292.

There are three formats for server-side image map files: CERN, NCSA, and Netscape. The CERN and NCSA servers were the first and second HTTP servers ever written, and most subsequent servers have used one of these two formats. The Netscape format is derived from NCSA. Microsoft Internet Information Server uses CERN image map files.

Client-side hotspots sidestep the server entirely by including all hotspot coordinates and associated URLs as part of the original HTML. The browser locally translates the clicked coordinates to an associated URL, and then jumps to it.

Figure 3-2, on the following page, shows how FrontPage Editor can manage image mapping in WYSIWYG fashion.

MIME Types and Other Curiosities

The GET response in the previous section included the following line in the HTTP headers:

```
Content-Type: text/html
```

The string `text/html` is a MIME file-type code that indicates the type of data that will follow. MIME stands for Multipurpose Internet Mail

FIGURE 3-2.

FrontPage hotspots jump to different pages, depending on which part of an image is clicked.

Use the rectangle, circle, and polygon buttons to outline portions of the image.

Specify the associated hyperlink location in the dialog box.

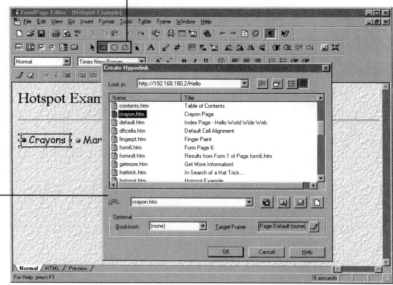

Extensions and, as you might expect, was first defined as a way to handle e-mail attachments. The MIME type simply provides a system-independent way to indicate the format of a file; mail programs use it to launch an appropriate viewing program when file attachments arrive with electronic mail. It makes sense to use the same MIME-type associations for viewing Web files as well.

Figure 3-3 shows the Internet Explorer version 3 dialog box for configuring MIME types. To display it, choose Options from the View menu, click the Programs tab, and then click the File Types button. Each file type in the resulting table has associations with one or more file extensions, a MIME type, and a program capable of opening the file.

The Web doesn't use filename extensions to identify file types, because not all operating systems support them. The Macintosh is a case in point. Instead, Windows-based Web servers usually have a table that translates filename extensions to MIME types, and browsers use local MIME tables to select appropriate viewer programs. If you run into problems with Web content displaying incorrectly or prompting the user for a download location, investigate the MIME tables on both the server and the client.

FIGURE 3-3.
Web Servers identify file types with MIME Content Type codes. The browser uses this information to invoke the proper viewing program.

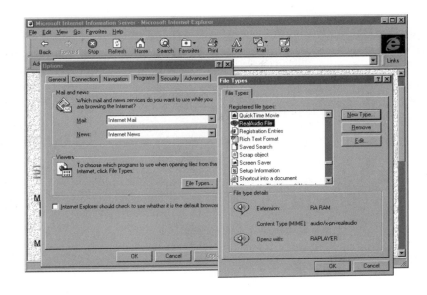

Hypertext Markup Language

? SEE ALSO
For more information about HTML and text formatting, see Chapter 6, "Getting Started with Web Pages."

HTML, or hypertext markup language, arose from an earlier format called Standard Generalized Markup Language (SGML). SGML had been a fixture in the technical publishing industry for years because of its ability to assemble uniform documents from the writings of many contributors. This was possible because the contributors submitted only plain text intermixed with style codes that indicated headings, captions, bulleted and numbered lists, and other structural elements. Publishing specialists then chose fonts, margins, and other aspects of page layout independently from the original authors.

The first use of HTML was to publish technical papers at the European Laboratory for Particle Physics in Geneva, Switzerland. The technical contributors there were familiar with SGML, so HTML was designed along the same principles—plain ASCII text marked up with ASCII style codes. This produced documents like the one in Figure 3-4, on the next page.

As use of the Web grew beyond the scientific community and entered the mainstream community, Web page creators wanted to match the appearance of other high-visibility mass media. Browser manufacturers sought market share by adding markup tags that would appeal to these creators, and the result has been pages such as that shown in Figure 3-5, on the following page.

II

Plumbing, Art, and Media—A Web Primer

FIGURE 3-4.
This is HTML doing what its inventors intended—displaying simple text documents.

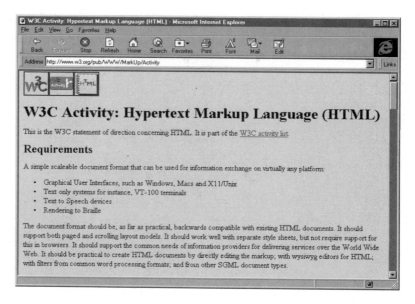

FIGURE 3-5.
Complex Web pages test the limits of HTML's capabilities.

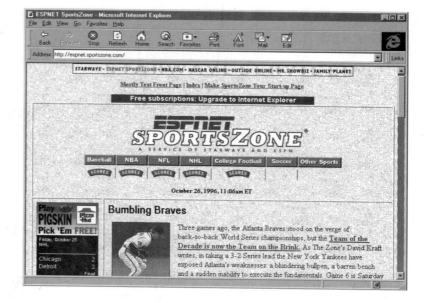

The creator of a page like the one in Figure 3-4 has very little control over paragraph formatting, font selection, page width, or line endings. The creator *can* specify paragraph styles such as <H1> for Heading Level One and font styles like <B> for Bold, but the end user's browser and computer system control the typeface, point size, and color used for each style. There are no controls for paragraph indentation, line spacing, or margins. Everything is flush left (left-aligned).

? SEE ALSO

For more information about frames, see "Creating and Editing Frames," page 338.

By contrast, the page shown in Figure 3-5 is divided into *frames* and makes considerable use of graphic images, even as the text within each frame follows the same rules as the text in Figure 3-4. The limitations of HTML tempt many Web creators to make each page a single large graphic, but this usually results in unacceptably long download times for users who access the Web by modem.

The original HTML specification provided no means for placing text, images, or other objects spatially on the page; contents flowed left-to-right, top-to-bottom, left-aligned only. Frames provide a way to divide a page into areas and control each area, but *tables* provide an additional technique for *x-y* positioning.

? SEE ALSO

For more information about tables, see "Creating and Editing Tables," page 313.

Figure 3-6 shows a Web page that uses tables to organize six topics into a three-column by two-row grid. A second table ("Island Excursions"), near the bottom of the figure, has four columns. The first two columns contain bulleted items, the third provides white space, and the last provides some unbulleted hyperlinks. Note that the heading for the first two columns spans both of them.

FIGURE 3-6.
This page uses HTML tables to arrange information horizontally and vertically.

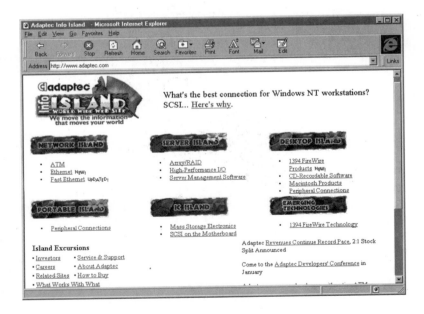

Plumbing, Art, and Media—A Web Primer

HTML Forms

? SEE ALSO

For more information on HTML forms, consult Chapter 11, "Using HTML Forms and FrontPage Form Handlers."

Forms created in HTML provide a limited *graphical user interface (GUI)* that's useful for constructing data entry screens. Figure 3-7 shows Front-Page Editor creating such a form. Note the use of an HTML table to arrange the field titles and form.

Each element within the form has a name assigned by the Web designer plus a value assigned by the user. When the user clicks the Submit button in the form, the browser sends the name and value of each field to a program on the Web server. The server program uses the form data to send mail, update a database, or perform some other action.

⊗ CAUTION

Radio (option) buttons are the only form elements where duplicate names are valid. Normally, each element in the form must have a unique name.

Figure 3-7 shows the configuration of a radio button (or option button). The Group Name (for example, location) identifies all radio buttons in the same group; selecting one button automatically deselects all other buttons with the same Group Name. Value is the string transmitted to the server if the form is submitted with this button selected. Initial State controls whether this button is selected when the form is first displayed. Tab Order optionally indicates the sequence this button occupies as the user tabs from one form element to another.

FIGURE 3-7.
FrontPage Editor provides a graphical way to easily construct HTML forms.

Use these six tools to insert form elements.

To quickly configure a form element, open its associated dialog box by right-clicking the element and choosing Form Field Properties from the pop-up menu.

Radio Button Properties dialog box

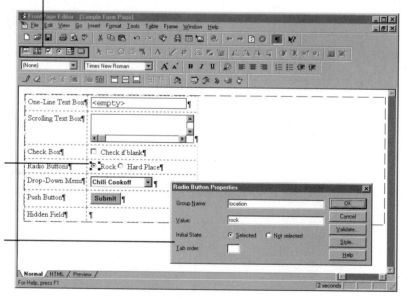

A single Web page may contain any number of HTML forms. If there are several forms on a single page, the only elements transmitted are those in the form whose Submit button was clicked.

What "Activating the Internet" Is All About

During the first few years of the Web's existence, most activity consisted of publishing information in fixed HTML pages and building hyperlinks. What was termed progress consisted of getting HTML to render more and more attractive pages—a challenging task both technically and artistically. This kind of progress hasn't reached its zenith and probably never will, but a second challenge has arisen: that of making pages respond more interactively than simple hyperlinks ever can. Microsoft calls providing this kind of interactivity "Activating the Internet."

The software foundation for Activating the Internet has four layers.

- HTML provides basic page layout and presentation.

- Scripts provide simple application logic and coordinate interaction among other components. Script languages typically require no compilation, no declaration of variables, and no installation. They are comparable to macro languages in applications. On the Web, scripts typically reside within the HTML files of pages they affect. The script may execute either on the server, just before the HTML gets transmitted, or on the browser. Browser scripts can execute as the page loads, later as timers go off, or as users operate controls on the Web page.

- Components usually provide more complex or intricate services than scripts. Programmers write them in rigorous, compiled languages such as C++, Java, and Visual Basic. Because of the development time required, it usually isn't practical to write component objects for a single Web page. Well-written components are versatile, fast, and designed to be used by scripts or other components.

- The operating system and services provide basic functions such as file input and output, database management, and network communication.

These layers are arbitrary and, in practice, the lines between them sometimes blur. Nevertheless, they provide a useful model. Components and services provide a way to implement functions of any complexity in a reusable way. Scripts and basic HTML provide ways to complete jobs in hours rather than days or months. The rest of this chapter examines scripts and components in greater detail.

Script Languages

? SEE ALSO

To learn how Front-Page can generate JavaScript or VBScript code without programming, refer to "Generating Browser Scripts," page 514.

A full explanation of script language programming is beyond the scope of this book. Still, the increasing use of such languages makes Front-Page's support of them a critical feature.

FrontPage can process JavaScript and VBScript code from three sources.

- User-written code

- Code written by a FrontPage Script Wizard

- Code written by FrontPage to validate form fields

JavaScript

Netscape Communications invented JavaScript to provide browser-side scripting for its popular Navigator browser. The language was originally named LiveScript, but Netscape renamed it when the company adopted Sun Microsystem's Java language for use in components. JavaScript and Java both resemble C++ but otherwise have little in common.

JavaScript has access to a variety of built-in objects belonging to the browser, the current window, the current URL, and HTML objects such as form elements, hyperlinks, and images. Each of these objects has an assortment of properties, some of which the script can modify.

Developers place JavaScript statements within `<SCRIPT>` and `</SCRIPT>` tags in the HTML. JavaScript statements are executed as the browser loads the page, and may write data into the browser's input stream. The following statement, for example, writes the page's Last-Modified value into the browser window as if the data had come directly from the HTTP server:

```
document.write(document.lastModified)
```

If the browser finds a subroutine defined within <SCRIPT> and </SCRIPT> tags, the browser stores it for future use. Code found later in the page can then execute the routine.

Events on the page can also trigger JavaScript code. There's an *onClick* event, for example, that occurs when the user clicks a button. If the Web page designer supplied code for that event, the code executes when the event occurs.

Figure 3-8 shows FrontPage Editor inserting some JavaScript into a Web page. FrontPage does nothing with such code after inserting it; it merely displays a J icon where the code resides. FrontPage doesn't verify the code for correctness or try to execute it; to see the code run, you'll have to open the page with a browser.

FIGURE 3-8.
FrontPage can insert JavaScript or VBScript into Web pages. This script displays the date the page was last updated.

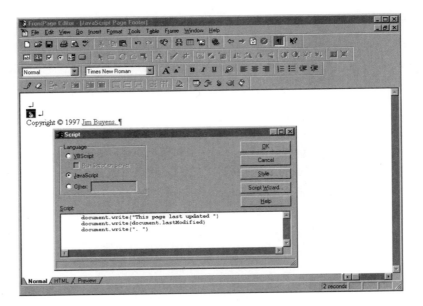

The JavaScript language tends to be a work in progress; various bugs and limitations appear and disappear with every browser version. Be sure to test your scripts under all recent versions of each browser you care about. As long as JavaScript remains the only script language available on both Netscape Navigator and Internet Explorer, it will probably remain the preferred language for populations of mixed browsers.

VBScript

The VBScript language serves all the same purposes and objects as JavaScript, but is based on Visual Basic Scripting Edition. VBScript lacks many familiar Visual Basic features such as a GUI development environment, GUI run-time displays, file input and output, and the ability to call system services. However, its syntax is very familiar to thousands of Visual Basic developers, and it interfaces very well with ActiveX controls.

As of version 3, Internet Explorer is the only browser to support VBScript. This severely limits the usefulness of browser-side VBScript in environments where Netscape Navigator is common. Internet Information Server 3, however, provides server-side support for VBScript. Although scripts running on the server can't interact directly with the user, they produce "plain vanilla" HTML as output and thus operate the same with any browser. They can also interact with server-side components and with such services as database systems.

On the browser, VBScript provides roughly the same capabilities as JavaScript. In addition, it can interact with ActiveX components residing on the same page.

Programmed Components

Script languages are wonderful for providing simple Web functions, but they don't work well (or at all) for more complex functions. This is where the need for full-fledged Web programming arises.

Server-Side Programming with CGI and ISAPI

The first server-side components for the Web were CGI programs. CGI stands for common gateway interface. The term *gateway* in this case refers not to a network device, but rather to the fact that CGI programs provide a software gateway between Web pages and other services on the same server.

CGI programs are relatively inefficient. For each execution the operating system must create an address space, start a process, load the program, run it, and then shut everything down. CGI programs get input data from environment variables, from the command line, and from data piped into standard input. They write HTML to standard output piped into the Web server, and the server transmits this HTML to the originating computer for display. In short, CGI programs greatly resemble MS-DOS command-line programs with console input and output.

Because it was the first server-side programming technology, CGI is supported by virtually every Web server. The most common programming languages used to create CGI scripts are Perl and C. In general, CGI programs don't interact with script languages.

To solve performance and flexibility problems of CGI, Microsoft and other developers invented ISAPI—the Internet Server Application Programming Interface. ISAPI programs run as DLLs (dynamic-link libraries), so only one copy needs to be in memory regardless of the number of users. ISAPI programs also run in the Web server's address space and therefore avoid the constant startup/shutdown memory overhead of CGI.

For these performance reasons, most server-side utilities for Internet Information Server, Microsoft's flagship Web server, are supplied as ISAPI programs.

Java Applets

SEE ALSO
For more information about using Java applets, see "Incorporating Java Applets," page 542.

Like images and form elements, Java applets are objects you can add to your Web page. Also like images and form elements, Java applets normally appear as visible objects on the page; unlike those other objects, however, Java applets are programs that produce real-time animation or other programmed behavior.

Programmers write applets using the Java programming language, a process that's beyond the scope of this book. Once compiled, however, Java applets can run within any browser on any operating system as long as a suitable Java interpreter is present; there are no separate Windows, Macintosh, or Unix versions of Java applets. You can locate many freeware or shareware applets on the Web, download them to your own site, and use them in your pages.

Figure 3-9, on the following page, shows how FrontPage Editor can insert Java applets into a Web page. Prior to this editing session, the developer downloaded an applet called GraphicsButton and imported

Plumbing, Art, and Media—A Web Primer

FIGURE 3-9.
FrontPage Editor can add Java applets to Web pages and configure them too.

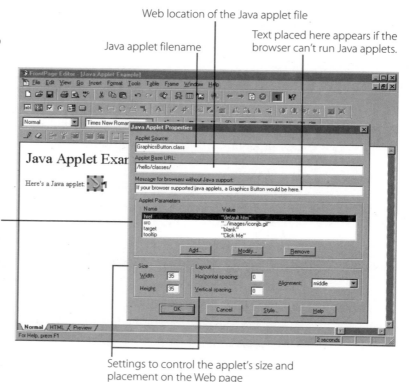

Web location of the Java applet file

Java applet filename

Text placed here appears if the browser can't run Java applets.

Values that control how the applet runs (usually documented in a file downloaded with the applet or on a Web page maintained by the applet's author)

Settings to control the applet's size and placement on the Web page

it into a FrontPage Web folder called classes. GraphicsButton displays a button with a specified picture on its face and jumps to a specified Web location when a user clicks it.

To add a Java applet with FrontPage Editor, choose Advanced from the Insert menu, and then select Java Applet. This places a Java placeholder on the browser page and opens the Java Applet Properties dialog box shown in Figure 3-9.

Figure 3-10 shows the page from Figure 3-9 in action. Note that an image and button face now appear on the page rather than the placeholder that FrontPage Editor displayed. FrontPage Editor only inserts applets—it doesn't execute them—so it can't display their output. Clicking the button opens a new browser window for the page specified in the applet's HREF property.

FIGURE 3-10.
Internet Explorer displays the page created in Figure 3-9.

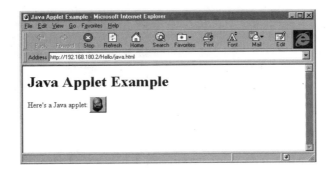

ActiveX Controls

? SEE ALSO

For more information about ActiveX controls, see "Incorporating ActiveX Controls," page 532.

The Java programming language and the concept of Java applets are both inventions of Sun Microsystems. The Microsoft alternative, based on existing Windows technology, is the ActiveX framework. As you might suspect, FrontPage supports ActiveX controls at least as well as it does Java applets. To add an ActiveX control to a Web page, choose Advanced from FrontPage Editor's Insert menu and select ActiveX Control. The dialog box shown in Figure 3-11 results.

At the top of the dialog box, the Pick A Control drop-down list box contains the names of all the ActiveX controls on your system. You'll probably discover many more controls than you expect; the list includes all controls installed on your system by any software, plus any controls you've downloaded from Web pages.

FIGURE 3-11.
FrontPage Editor can add any ActiveX control available on your system to a Web page.

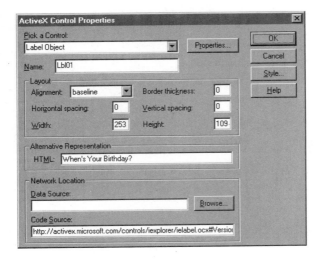

II

Plumbing, Art, and
Media—A Web Primer

Some ActiveX controls support *local property editing*, a feature that allows FrontPage to display and edit ActiveX controls in WYSIWYG mode. FrontPage also supports controls that lack local property editing, though display and editing of these are at the moment quite rudimentary.

Calendar Control 8.0 is an ActiveX control that supports local property editing. When this control is selected, clicking the Properties button brings up two more windows, as shown in Figure 3-12. The left window provides an active preview and direct manipulation of some properties. The Properties window at the right provides access to all settings applicable to the control. The FrontPage Editor window displays the control in full WYSIWYG mode.

FIGURE 3-12.
FrontPage Editor provides full-function editing and WYSIWYG preview of ActiveX controls that support local property editing.

Configure HTML attributes here.

Full WYSIWYG preview

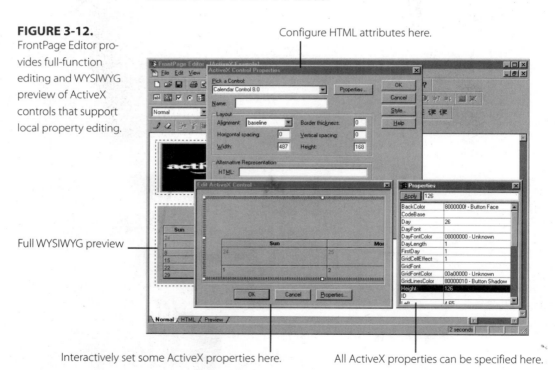

Interactively set some ActiveX properties here.

All ActiveX properties can be specified here.

The Label Object is an ActiveX control that doesn't support local property editing. As Figure 3-13 illustrates, FrontPage can't display this control in WYSIWYG mode; instead it displays a generic ActiveX Resources icon. There's no preview window when editing the control's properties, and the Object Parameters window requires that each parameter name and its corresponding value be entered manually.

FIGURE 3-13.
FrontPage Editor offers manual editing and size preview of ActiveX controls that lack local property editing.

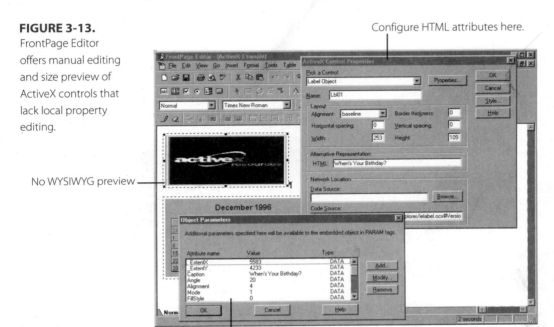

Configure HTML attributes here.

No WYSIWYG preview

Specify the control's properties and values here.

Plumbing, Art, and Media—A Web Primer

As you can imagine, local property editing is a much-appreciated feature among Web page developers who use ActiveX controls, and most new controls include it. Local property editing does increase the size of the control, however, making it bulkier and thus slower for the end user.

Figure 3-14, on the following page, shows a finished Web page that makes use of both the Label Object and the Calendar Control.

FIGURE 3-14.
The end user perceives no difference whether a control supports local property editing or not. Both types appear in fully WYSIWYG fashion at browse time.

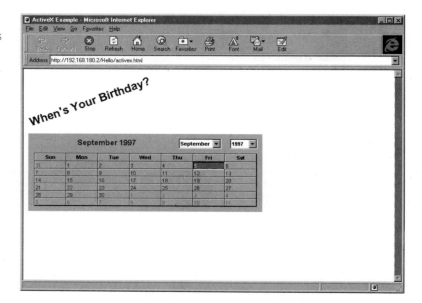

CHAPTER 4

Achieving Visual Impact—Graphic Communication

C reating attractive and effective Web pages is a surprisingly difficult proposition. First, Web pages require a different organization and layout than letters, memos, presentations, books, reports, or other documents that beginning Web authors may be more familiar with. The aesthetics and metaphors of Web pages are more like graphic arts compositions: brochures, magazine pages, posters, handbills, and the like. Second, limitations inherent in HTML severely constrain use of the most common graphic composition techniques: images, typography, color, and page placement and orientation.

Reading this chapter won't magically transform you into a graphic artist, but it does provide a brief introduction to the graphic and artistic design of Web pages. If you find the material intriguing, try browsing the graphic arts section of your local bookstore or library, or visit a large art-supplies store. As long as you keep your handheld computer out of sight, no one will point or laugh.

Elements of Design

Artistic design isn't an exact science, so many technically inclined people conclude it's beyond them—or at least something that gives them a headache. Even if you lack the talent to become a professional artist, though, you can use certain principles of good design to enhance your work and communicate your message more effectively. Contrast and symmetry are two such principles that appear in a variety of contexts.

Contrast Versus Clash

The polar bear at the north pole and the black cat in the coal bin figure in two old jokes involving contrast. In both cases, lack of contrast makes the key element indistinguishable from its surroundings.

Graphic contrast serves two important purposes in Web pages or, for that matter, any other document.

- Contrast enhances legibility. For example, the black type and white background in this book make it easier to read than if one color were gray.

- Contrast visually communicates distinctions among various page elements. In this book, for example, contrasting typography makes it easy to distinguish headings from body type.

The contrast knob on your monitor or TV set controls the difference in brightness between the lightest and darkest parts of an image. Contrast, however, occurs in many other dimensions as well: contrast between adjacent colors, contrast between differently sized or shaped fonts, contrasting position on a page, and many more. The total contrast between two page elements thus involves the number of contrasting attributes as well as their individual extents.

The need for contrast is generally intuitive; document creators ordinarily realize that items like titles, headings, body text, and captions are intrinsically different and that a unique appearance should identify each such element. They run into greater problems deciding what kind of contrast to provide and how much. Too much or too little contrast can be illegible, confusing, or just irritating to the eye. Consider the four type samples below.

Contrast enhances appearance.

Contrast enhances appearance.

Contrast enhances appearance.

Contrast enhances appearance.

If the first sample, the word Contrast is presented in the Bookman font and the rest of the sentence in Garamond. These are both *old style* fonts: they both have slanted serifs and nonuniform line widths, while the thinnest top and bottom portions of each circular or elliptical shape align at an angle. In short, there's very little contrast between text set in Bookman and Garamond. This sentence looks like a typesetting error and bothers the eye. The reader's concentration is diverted to figuring out "What's wrong with this picture?" and thus misses the information being conveyed.

The second sample has more contrast. The word Contrast appears in Myriad Bold, which lacks serifs, has uniform line widths, and is much thicker than Garamond. The font size is larger as well. In brief, there's considerable contrast in appearance between the first word and the rest of the sentence. This example works.

The third example uses a decorative font called Syntax Ultra Black. Like Myriad, Syntax Ultra Black lacks serifs and is much thicker than Garamond, but this font is very gimmicky and just doesn't look right with the relatively formal Garamond. This example clashes, like a clown on a concert stage.

The last example simply italicizes the emphasized word. There's only one kind of contrast between italicized Garamond and normal (roman), namely the overall slant. Nevertheless, this technique catches the eye and provides nearly as much emphasis as examples two and three.

Real life offers—as does Web design—a countless variety of potential contrasts. Contrasts of color, of size, of alignment, and of motion immediately come to mind. If something doesn't look right, consider increasing or reducing the number of contrasts as well as varying their intensities. And remember: The visual equivalent of screaming in someone's face isn't necessarily the best way to communicate your message. When contrast is required:

- Don't be a wimp.

- Don't be a screamer.

- Don't mix signals.

Symmetry Versus Monotony

In any page layout, like elements should have a like appearance, and elements that differ should have a different appearance. Neither contrast nor uniformity should be random. This is the principle of symmetry.

All the chapter headings in this book are set in the same font, color, size, and position on the page. When you encounter some text that visually resembles all the other chapter headings, you assume that text is a chapter heading as well. You also assume that any text with a different appearance is *not* a chapter heading.

Note that chapter headings are similar to each other, but not to body text. Because chapter headings and body text are quite different elements, there's much contrast between them. There's essentially no contrast (other than distance) between one chapter head and another, because all chapter headings are alike.

The same reasoning applies to this book's figures, tables, and side notes such as See Also, Caution, and Tip. These elements each have their own unique style that aids the reader in identifying them and generally makes the book appear cohesive. It would be confusing if See Also notes in this chapter and the next appeared differently.

The principle of symmetry (or parallelism) is equally applicable to Web pages. Make all your level 1 headings look the same, for example, not just within each page but within an entire Web site or major section. Use the same color scheme, the same typography, the same alignment (left aligned, centered, right aligned, or justified), the same menu appearance, the same title conventions, and so forth. Avoid monotony by adopting (and testing on your eyes and the eyes of others) an attractive set of designs up front and not by making each page look completely different.

An overall site design should be a guide, never a straitjacket. Certainly you'll have several different types of pages, and each type of page should have unique elements that visually alert the Web visitor. The number of page types and their corresponding appearances are strictly your decision, but each page type should have

- Symmetry that unifies it with all other pages in the same site.

- Distinctive contrasts that visually identify each unique type of page or content.

- Symmetry among like types of page or content.

In short, similar types of content call for fewer contrasting elements having a narrower range of contrast. Dissimilar types call for a greater variety and degree of contrast.

Color

You'll find color and the study of color to be remarkably multifaceted. Perception of color is a biological and emotional process, not a technical one, and it defies precise scientific analysis. Computer graphics deals with color literally by the numbers, while the artist's view of color—arguably the far better developed—is totally subjective. No graphics card or monitor deals with colors as cool, warm, happy, sad, playful, or serious. Nevertheless, these are the moods we as Web designers seek to convey through our use of technology.

This section briefly introduces the physical nature of color and describes how the human eye perceives it. It then explains how computers (and thus Web browsers) create color images, and then integrates into these discussions several artistic views of color. Finally, it returns to the technical details of implementing the aesthetic colors you choose.

Grasping this material will give you at least a jump-start at under-standing how Web visitors will respond to the colors in your site and how to choose colors that invoke the emotional responses you wish to convey, to get the maximum impact you want.

Technical Models of Color

In the physical world colors correspond to different wavelengths of light. Focusing a beam of white light through a prism—as shown in Figure 4-1—divides it into many beams, each with a single unique hue. The prism works by deflecting each wavelength by a different amount.

FIGURE 4-1.

A glass prism divides white light into its constituent wavelengths.

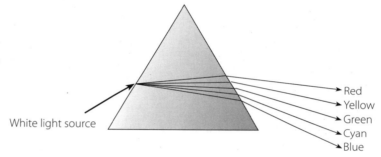

Objects in nature emit or reflect various amounts of light at various wavelengths, and the human eye interprets these combinations as colors. Astonishingly, experts estimate the eye can discriminate about two million different colors.

Fortunately, producing lifelike color images doesn't require monitors and video cards capable of generating all the wavelengths found in nature. The eye interprets the infinite range of natural colors in terms of just three: red, green, and blue. Rather than emitting true yellow light, for example, a video system can emit equal amounts of red and green light instead.

If you shone a beam of true yellow light through a prism, a single yel-low beam would emerge. The same prism would separate a mixture of red and green light into red and green beams. Nevertheless, both beams, the true yellow and the red-green mix, would look the same to us humans.

RGB—The Red, Green, and Blue Primary Colors

Computer monitors emit only three colors of light: red, green, and blue. Mixing and blending these three colors in various intensities allows the monitor to mimic any color our eyes can perceive. The face of the monitor is divided into a series of dots called *pixels* (picture elements), while a graphics card inside the PC controls the red, green, and blue intensities of each pixel.

> **NOTE**

An image 200 dots wide and 75 dots tall contains 15,000 pixels.

All current graphics cards trace their ancestry to the original Video Graphics Adapter (VGA) developed by IBM. This device produced a display 640 pixels wide, 480 pixels high, and 16 fixed colors in depth. Since then, capabilities have grown to typical resolutions of 800×600, 1024×768, 1152×864, 1280×1024, 1600×1200, and other variations, and color depth has increased from 16 fixed colors to 256, 65,536, and 16,777,216 programmable colors.

Video cards supporting 256, 65,536, and 16,777,216 colors devote 8, 16, or 24 bits of video memory per pixel. The 24-bit color system is the easiest to understand and program. For each pixel on the display, the graphics cards provides 8 bits of memory that specify 256 intensities of red. An additional 8 bits specify 256 intensities of green, and 8 more control 256 intensities of blue. A value of zero indicates no color; 255 indicates maximum color. Each color value of 0–255 occupies 8 binary digits, so the entire scheme is called 24-Bit RGB (Red, Green, Blue) Color. Multiplying 256 reds times 256 greens times 256 blues equals 16,777,216 combinations. Therefore, 24-Bit RGB Color is synonymous with 16 Million Color Mode.

FrontPage and many other Windows applications prompt for colors using the Windows dialog box shown in Figure 4-2, on page 93. You can choose from the basic or custom colors at the upper left by clicking on them. The large rectangle at the right shows a pixel-by-pixel array of colors you can choose by clicking, and the vertical bar at the far right controls darkness or lightness.

II

Plumbing, Art, and
Media—A Web Primer

Color Notation by the Numbers

With 16,777,216 colors available, referring to them all with vague names like Blanched Almond, Honey Dew, and Moccasin quickly becomes tiresome. Instead, most Web applications denote colors in terms of their red, green, and blue (RGB) intensities. Here are some typical colors specified as RGB combinations.

| | Decimal | | | Hexadecimal | | |
Color	Red	Green	Blue	Red	Green	Blue
Black	0	0	0	00	00	00
White	255	255	255	FF	FF	FF
Gray	128	128	128	80	80	80
Bright Red	255	0	0	FF	00	00
Bright Green	0	255	0	00	FF	00
Bright Blue	0	0	255	00	00	FF
Dark Red	128	0	0	80	00	00
Dark Cyan	0	128	128	00	80	80

A 256-color graphics adapter also uses a 24-bit color notation. Despite dedicating only 8 bits per pixel, these adapters can display any 24-bit color a programmer desires; the trick is that 8-bit video cards can only display 256 different 24-bit colors at any given time. The video driver supplies the card with a table of 256 colors, and then tells the video card which of these 256 colors to display in each pixel. The phrase that describes this is "256 colors from a palette of 16,777,216."

Some 16-bit graphics adapters display 65,536 colors from a palette of 16,777,216; some display 65,536 fixed colors. An adapter that provides 65,536 fixed colors in "64K mode" usually produces better results if configured to use 256 programmable colors instead. Note that a graphics adapter operating in 64K mode can display 65,536 colors because 64KB = 64×1,024, or 65,536.

? SEE ALSO

For information on choosing colors that Web browsers will display smoothly with 256-color display adapters, see "Achieving Accurate Rendition—SafeColors," page 124.

The Red, Green, and Blue values at the lower right of Figure 4-2 specify color intensities in the range 0–255, the range discussed earlier in this section. For the most part, this book will refer to colors by RGB value. The currently selected color in Figure 4-2, for example, would be 255–153–153.

FIGURE 4-2.
This standard color choice dialog box is provided by Windows and used by FrontPage and many other applications.

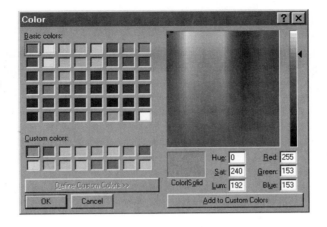

 SEE ALSO

For an explanation of the color array and the Hue, Sat, and Lum settings shown in Figure 4-2, see "HSL— The Hue, Saturation, Luminance Color Model," page 112.

Some applications require hexadecimal, rather than decimal, RGB values. In hexadecimal (sometimes called simply "hex") the first digit is the 16s place, so hex 23 is (2×16) + 3, or decimal 35. Hex 80 is (8×16) + 0, or decimal 128. The letters A through F are the hex digits that represent decimal 10 through 15. In Web pages you'll often see color codes like #9900CC. This represents hex RGB colors 99, 00, and CC, which are 153, 0, and 204 in decimal. A few really detestable programs require entering the true decimal equivalent of hex 9900CC, which is 10,027,212.

TIP

You can use the Microsoft Windows Calculator (in Scientific View) to convert decimal values to hexadecimal and vice versa. To convert hexadecimal to decimal, click Calculator's Hex button, enter the number, and then click Calculator's Dec button. To convert decimal to hex, reverse these steps.

CMY—The Cyan, Magenta, and Yellow Subtractive Colors

The RGB (Red, Green, Blue) color system described above is an *additive* system; it describes how to form colors by combining beams of light from luminous sources. The colors red, green, and blue are called primary colors because the eye responds to them directly.

Paints and pigments absorb light rather than generate it, and thus require a completely different model of color. If you mix red and green light, the result is yellow. If you mix perfectly red and perfectly green paint, the result is black. This is the subtractive color system.

Subtractive colors are passive. The ink or paint isn't luminous of itself; it only reflects light shone upon it. Red paint reflects red light but absorbs green and blue. Green paint reflects green light but absorbs red and blue. Combining two such paints produces a surface that absorbs all three colors—that is, a surface that appears black.

> **NOTE**
>
> In practice, pigments don't reflect or absorb all colors of light perfectly. This is why mixing red and green paint usually produces a brown or gray color.

The simplest and most elementary subtractive colors are those that absorb only one primary color. As shown in Table 4-1, these colors are Cyan, Magenta, and Yellow. Most color reproduction processes, such as color printing and color photography, work by blending these three colors. The CMY color scheme is as common in the printing industry as RGB is for computers. Because of its use in printing, the subtractive color scheme is sometimes called *process color*.

TABLE 4-1. Additive and Subtractive Colors

Subtractive Color	Absorbs Primary	Reflects Primaries
Cyan	Red	Green, Blue
Magenta	Green	Red, Blue
Yellow	Blue	Red, Green

To produce red, the subtractive process uses a combination of magenta and yellow pigments. The magenta pigment absorbs green and the yellow pigment absorbs blue, so the combination reflects only red to the viewer.

In practice, producing black through a mixture of cyan, magenta, and yellow pigments is quite difficult; natural pigments are seldom so perfect that light of all wavelengths is absorbed completely. Most printing equipment therefore provides black ink as well as cyan, magenta, and yellow. You might think that a cyan, magenta, yellow, and black system would be called CMYB but it's not; the actual term is CMYK.

Both the CMY and CMYK systems use percentages between 0 and 100 for measuring intensity. Zero means no absorption and 100 means complete absorption. A typical CMYK color specification appears below.

C	40
M	100
Y	0
K	45

It's extremely unusual to specify computer display colors in terms of the CMY or CMYK systems; the RGB system is much more appropriate. Occasionally, though, the need may arise to convert CMY color values to RGB. In such cases, the following approximate formulas will help.

Converting CMYK to CMY

Cyan $= Min(1, Cyan*(1–Black)+Black)$

Magenta $= Min(1, Magenta*(1–Black)+Black)$

Yellow $= Min(1, Yellow*(1–Black)+Black)$

To convert the CMYK color 40-100-0-45 to CMY, the equations work out to

Cyan $= Min(1, 0.40*(1–0.45)+0.45)$ $= Min(1, 0.22+0.45)$ $= 0.67$

Magenta $= Min(1, 1.00*(1–0.45)+0.45)$ $= Min(1, 0.55+0.45)$ $= 1.00$

Yellow $= Min(1, 0.00*(1–0.45)+0.45)$ $= Min(1, 0.00+0.45)$ $= 0.45$

Converting CMY to RGB

Red $= 255*(1–Cyan)$

Green $= 255*(1–Magenta)$

Blue $= 255*(1–Yellow)$

To convert the CMY color 67-100-45 to RGB, the computation would be

Red $= 255*(1–0.67)$ $= 255*(0.33)$ $= 84$

Green $= 255*(1–1.00)$ $= 255*(0.00)$ $= 0$

Blue $= 255*(1–0.45)$ $= 255*(0.55)$ $= 140$

II

Plumbing, Art, and Media—A Web Primer

Converting RGB to CMY

Cyan	= 1–(Red/255)
Magenta	= 1–(Green/255)
Yellow	= 1–(Blue/255)

Converting the RGB color 84-0-140 to CMY produces the expected result:

Cyan	= 1–(84/255)	= 1–0.33	= 0.67
Magenta	= 1–(0/255)	= 1–0.00	= 1.00
Yellow	= 1–(140/255)	= 1–0.55	= 0.45

Converting CMY to CMYK

Black	= Min(Cyan, Magenta, Yellow)
Cyan	= (Cyan–Black)/(1–Black)
Magenta	= (Magenta–Black)/(1–Black)
Yellow	= (Yellow–Black)/(1–Black)

Converting the CMY color 67-100-45 to CMYK works as below (find the black value *first* so that you can use it in the C, M, and Y formulas).

Black	= Min(0.67, 1.00, 0.45)	= 0.45	
Cyan	= (0.67–0.45)/(1–0.45)	= 0.22/0.55	= 0.40
Magenta	= (1.00–0.45)/(1–0.45)	= 0.55/0.55	= 1.00
Yellow	= (0.45–0.45)/(1–0.45)	= 0/0.55	= 0.00

Artistic Color Models

The RGB and CMY color models provide a way to numerically classify and then mechanically reproduce colors. This is valuable information for Web page creators, who almost universally need a way to specify colors and be relatively confident that Web browsers can reproduce them on the end user's computer. However, neither the RGB nor CMY color models provide any guidance on choosing colors that look good together, display well, and convey a desired image or mood. Providing this kind of advice is the province of art, artists, and artistic expression.

Artists seldom deal with colors numerically; to them, colors are tubes of pigment having traditional names and obtained from art supply stores. The artist is far more concerned with human perception of color than the technology of color reproduction; mixing pigments to produce desired colors is a means to an end and not an end in itself.

Think about the front outside wall of your house or building. Most scientific or technically oriented folks would say that the wall is always the same color; very few would say its color constantly changes. In an artistic sense, however, the wall is many colors at once, and those colors change all the time! It's completely obvious, in an artistic sense, that the wall appears to be a different color in the morning and in the afternoon, a third color in the evening, and another at night. A painting would have to use different colors to show the wall in sunlight or in shade, on sunny days or overcast, in winter or summer. (Think of Monet's series of paintings of water lilies.) The paint on the building wall doesn't change, but the human perception of it does. The artist is concerned with reproducing the human perception of the wall rather than the original color of the house paint.

Fortunately, Web authors seeking to produce attractive pages needn't become proficient oil painters or artists. There are no absolutes in the field of art, but there *are* relatively simple guidelines you can use to choose colors intelligently—colors that work well together and transmit the message you desire.

Color Wheels

A common artistic approach to color involves arranging hues around the edges of a wheel, as shown in Figure 4-3, on the following page. Colors appear around the wheel's edge in spectral order: the order produced by splitting white light with a prism.

The arrangement of colors in Figure 4-3 seems technically correct—the primary colors red, green, and blue are spaced evenly, in spectral order, and diametrically opposed to their subtractive opposites. Note that 180° across from red is cyan, which absorbs red and reflects only green and blue.

FIGURE 4-3.

This color wheel arranges the standard RGB and CMY colors uniformly. This is correct in a technical sense—but seldom produces artistic results.

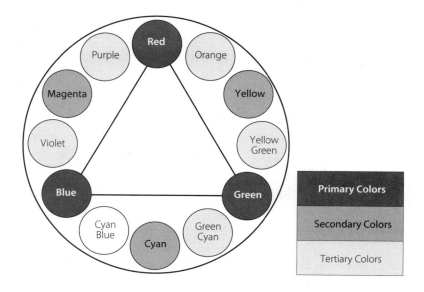

There's nothing hard and fast about a color wheel; you can arrange any number of colors in any order you want. The Corel Draw dialog box shown in Figure 4-4, for example, includes a color wheel with six labeled color positions, red at 3 o'clock rather than 12, and the colors red, green, and blue arranged counterclockwise.

FIGURE 4-4.

This color dialog box from Corel Draw features a technically oriented color wheel. Moving the highlight around the triangular area controls saturation and brightness.

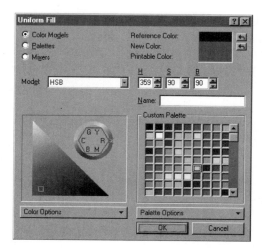

Purple, the Unnatural Color

The visible spectrum of color extends continuously from red to blue, with stops along the way as shown below.

Red—Yellow—Green—Cyan—Blue

The eye sees yellow in either of two ways:

- When it sees true yellow light

- When it sees a mixture of red and green light

A similar effect occurs with cyan. We see this color either because we see real cyan light or because we see a mixture of green and blue light.

Something interesting happens when the eye sees a mixture of red and blue light—it sees purple, a color that doesn't exist as a single wavelength of light. Purple, in this sense, is an artificial color.

Purple pigment has rather exacting requirements: It must absorb the broad middle of the visible spectrum and reflect only the high and low extremes. This explains somewhat why purple is a color seldom found in nature.

Color Harmony

Properly constructed color wheels serve a very important purpose for beginning designers and artists: They provide guidance in selecting colors that work well together. This technique is called *color harmony*.

The theory of color harmony maintains that drawing a regular polygon inside a color wheel automatically selects colors that are harmonious—that is, pleasing together, like the musical notes that constitute a chord.

Colors opposite each other on the wheel are complementary—that is, opposites in a pleasing way. Adjacent colors are similar—that is, they transition smoothly. Stating this another way, opposite colors have maximum contrast of hue, whereas adjacent colors have minimal contrast of hue.

Color harmony provides an appealingly simple approach to choosing attractive color schemes for Web pages or any other purpose. Here's how to achieve color harmony:

1   Select a key color—a color that must appear in the color scheme because of requirement or preference.

II

Plumbing, Art, and Media—A Web Primer

2 Locate that color on the color wheel.

3 Select two, three, or four harmonious colors by imagining a line, triangle, or square inside the wheel and noting the colors at the ends or corners. (See the first three examples in Figure 4-5.)

4 Alternatively, choose the complementary (opposite) color plus one or two similar colors—similar either to the key color or to the complement. (See the last example in Figure 4-5.)

FIGURE 4-5.
Colors spaced evenly around the wheel are harmonious—that is, they're usually pleasing when used together. Opposite colors are complementary and adjacent colors are similar.

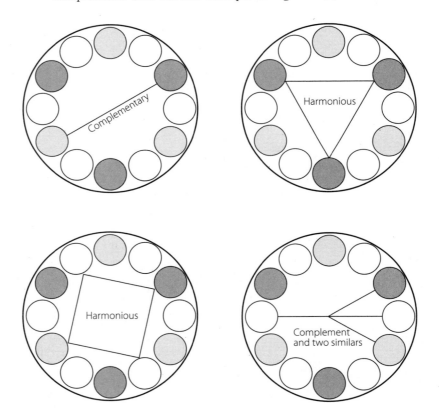

If this seems too simple, you're right; there are several details we haven't discussed yet. Nevertheless, the simple techniques of color wheels and color harmony prove you needn't be van Gogh or Andy Warhol to design an attractive color scheme.

The Artistic Color Wheel

The first step to achieving true color harmony is adjusting the colors in the wheel. A color wheel with red, green, and blue evenly spaced— and with cyan, magenta, and yellow in direct opposition—doesn't take the flesh and blood characteristics of the eye and mind into account.

Artists, with hundreds of years of art history to guide them, consider the primary colors to be red, yellow, and blue. You can show artists all the prisms, computer monitors, and printer's inks you want, but they'll swear that red, yellow, and blue are the colors with the most visual contrast and the highest recognition. Conversely, blue and green have too little visual contrast for both to be artistic primaries.

A color wheel with red, yellow, and blue as the primaries appears in Figure 4-6, on the next page. Green, cyan, and magenta appear interspersed among the primaries in their usual order; in fact, the overall order of the wheel is unchanged. The colors from red to green have simply been stretched to occupy the entire right side of the wheel, and the colors from green through blue and back to red have been compressed into the left semicircle. This arrangement fulfills two objectives.

- It takes into account the color perception of the human eye and mind.

- It produces better—more harmonious—results.

Figure 4-7, on the next page, shows the same color wheel as Figure 4-6, except that color names are replaced by RGB values. Note that the additive and subtractive primaries have color values of 0 or 255 only; these are extremely vivid—some would say fully saturated—colors. The remaining colors are quite vivid as well; the extreme intensities of 0 and 255 predominate except where it's necessary to generate hues between two adjacent colors.

The terms hue, shade, tint, and color deserve some explanation. Many people use these terms somewhat randomly or interchangeably, but in color theory they have very specific meanings.

- A color's hue is its true, pure color. A hue relates to a single wavelength of light.

FIGURE 4-6.
Here is the sort of color wheel most artists use. The primary colors are red, yellow, and blue.

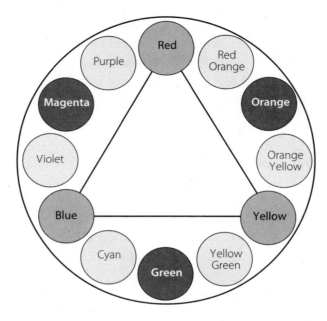

FIGURE 4-7.
This artistic color wheel shows RGB color values that correspond to the color names in Figure 4-6.

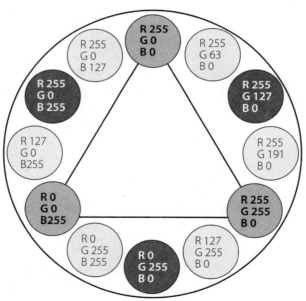

- Tints are a mixture of the pure hue with white.

- Shades are a mixture of the pure hue with black.

- The same hue can have thousands of tints and shades.

Elementary Color Schemes

Because human judgment and interpretation are involved, choosing effective color combinations can never be a completely scientific process. Nevertheless, some approaches are more consistently successful than others. The 10 schemes listed below have been used repeatedly and have stood the test of time.

- **Achromatic.** Use no color at all; the composition consists entirely of grays. A black-and-white photograph is achromatic.

- **Monochromatic.** Use various tints and shades, but only one hue. This lends a soft appearance and sense of unity.

- **Neutral.** Use a single hue, but neutralize it by adding its complement or black. The result is more muted than a monochromatic scheme might be.

- **Analogous.** Use tints or shades of three consecutive color wheel colors.

- **Complementary.** Use two colors 180° apart on the wheel. Beware of excessive contrast, especially when choosing vivid colors.

- **Clash.** Choose a starting color for this extremely harsh yet eye-catching scheme, and then choose the hue to the left or right of its complement. That is, choose two colors 150° or 210° apart.

- **Split Complementary.** Use a starting color and the two colors adjacent to its complement—that is, 150° or 210° degrees around the wheel. Two similar colors clashing with another often produces a certain balance, especially if you avoid vivid colors.

- **Primary.** Use red, yellow, and blue.

- **Secondary.** Use green, violet, and orange.

- **Tertiary.** Use any colors other than red, yellow, blue, green, violet, and orange, but that are equally spaced around a color wheel.

Perhaps by now you've realized there are many ways to choose contrasting colors that are pleasing and compatible. In fact, there are seven. These are the topic of the next section.

II

Plumbing, Art, and
Media—A Web Primer

Seven Kinds of Color Contrast

Johannes Itten, a pioneer in the study of color, identified seven kinds of contrast that occur between colors:

- **Contrast of Hue.** Choosing colors from different positions on the color wheel (or spectrum) is the simplest and most obvious way to achieve color contrast. Contrast of hue is greatest among primary colors, less among their complements, and least among tertiary and other mixed hues. Stained glass windows have very high contrast of hue.

- **Contrast of Light-Dark (Brightness).** Two colors of the same hue can differ greatly; a dark, near-black shade and a light, near-white tint of the same color exhibit this kind of contrast. A black-and-white photo consists entirely of light-dark contrasts, though this kind of contrast can occur with any hue. The human eye responds more precisely and reliably to contrast of light-dark than to contrast of hue. Extreme light-dark contrast is usually more legible and less jarring than extreme contrast of hue. In the absence of light-dark contrast, fine text is usually illegible.

- **Contrast of Cold-Warm.** Colors on the green-blue side of the color wheel are classified as cool, while those on the red-yellow side are warm. Compositions involving all warm or all cool colors are usually more pleasing than those in which colors of both types appear. Cool colors are usually deemed sedate and warm colors stimulating (wall and fixture colors in psychiatric wards and fast-food restaurants are designed accordingly).

- **Contrast of Complements.** This is the contrast that occurs between any two colors that are directly opposite on a continuous color wheel. Combined, they will always produce black, white, or gray; adding their respective RGB components will produce three equal numbers. Using complementary colors, especially in combination with intermediate colors, can produce a strong yet pleasing sort of contrast. Vivid complements, however, can clash violently.

- **Simultaneous Contrast.** When two colors are adjacent, the eye sees the duller color as tinged by the complement of the brighter color. When the eye shifts away from a bright color, such as yellow, to a dull color, such as gray, it experiences a sort of boomerang or overshoot effect and mistakenly senses the opposite of the "missing" color. This explains why a gray spot in a yellow background appears blue, or a black thread in a red fabric looks green. Color experts can use this effect constructively, but for beginners it's more often an explanation of why their work doesn't look as expected.

■ **Contrast of Saturation.** The purity of a color is expressed as its degree of saturation. Painters and artists control saturation by starting with an extremely vivid pigment and then diluting it with white, black, gray, or the original color's complement.

In computer graphics, saturated colors have RGB components as extreme as possible; the three primaries red, green, and blue, for example, are fully saturated at RGB values of 255-0-0, 0-255-0, and 0-0-255. Cyan, magenta, and yellow are fully saturated at 0-255-255, 255-0-255, and 255-255-0. Intermediate hues are fully saturated when one RGB component is 0 and another is 255.

Here's how you can control the saturation of a color:

- To add white to a color, increase its low RGB values uniformly. Adding some white to vivid blue (0-0-255), for example, could produce 102-102-255. Adding even more white would produce colors like 151-151-255 and 204-204-255.

- To add black to a color, uniformly decrease its high RGB values. Adding some black to vivid blue (0-0-255) might produce a color like 0-0-153. Adding more black would produce 0-0-102 or 0-0-51.

- To add gray, increase the color's low RGB values and decrease its high RGB values simultaneously. Adding gray to vivid blue (0-0-255) produces colors like 102-102-153.

- To create the complement of a color, invert its RGB values. The complement of vivid blue (0-0-255) would be 255-255-0 (yellow).

II

Plumbing, Art, and
Media—A Web Primer

■ **Contrast of Extension.** The extent to which a color predominates a composition depends on both its intensity and its extent—that is, on both its brightness and its percentage of total surface area. If all the major colors in a composition have equal impact on the viewer, based on their intensities and extents, the result is harmonious. If not, the result is expressive. Expressive results have greater visual contrast.

A complicating factor in judging contrast of extension is that the eye reacts more strongly to some colors than to others. Comparing yellow and violet colors of equal intensity, for example, the eye will perceive yellow as about three times as bright. The following relative intensities are generally accepted.

Yellow	Orange	Red	Violet	Blue	Green
9	8	6	3	4	6

Because orange appears twice as bright as blue, blue must have twice the area of the orange for the two colors to have equal impact. Intermediate combinations are also possible. Here are three possible brightness effects controlled by the extent of the two colors:

Extent of Color	Perceived Brightness
Blue area is twice orange area	Blue appears as bright as orange
Blue area equals orange area	Orange appears twice as bright as blue
Orange area is twice blue area	Orange appears four times as bright as blue

Contrast of extension is a tool, not a rule. To reduce the impact of a color, use less of it in terms of area, brightness, or both. To increase a color's impact, increase its brightness or surface area.

Of these seven contrasts, three are physical properties of light and four are properties of human perception. Cold-warm, complements, simultaneous, and extension contrasts are perceptual and serve primarily to explain human perception of color in compositions—Web pages or any other. These contrasts are important, but the page creator achieves them indirectly by manipulating the physical color properties.

Color Contrast on Web Pages

A rule of thumb states that attractive color schemes consist of three (or at most four) predominant colors. On Web pages, these are usually the background color, the normal text color, and a highlight color.

- For easy reading, the most contrast is between normal text and the background. The background is usually light and the text dark.

- The highlight color is used for elements like edge trim, icons, and headings. Consider using a complement of the background hue, but with similar saturation and brightness. Contrast between the highlight and background should generally be less than the contrast between normal text and the background. More contrast against the background may be required for heading text, though, if heading text and normal text will be different colors.

- Use icons and graphics related to the background color. Against a light blue background, for example, use icons featuring either dark, cool colors or complementary earth tones. Avoid icons with poor edge contrast against the selected background color; these confuse the eye.

- Choose similar colors for hyperlink text and visited hyperlink text. These should probably be similar hues with equal saturation and brightness rather than equal hues of different saturation. Make sure that both hyperlink colors have enough contrast against the background to be legible, but near enough to each other to suggest a like function. Hyperlink text and visited hyperlink text are usually brighter than normal text.

- Avoid not only more than three major colors per page, but also more than two or three contrast types. Using too many kinds of contrast on the same page is visually disorienting.

The physical properties of perceived color are hue, saturation, and brightness. Choosing and blending computer graphics colors using these dimensions is clearly more natural than specifying direct RGB value, and this is the objective of the HSB color model described in the next section.

II

Plumbing, Art, and
Media—A Web Primer

HSB—The Hue, Saturation, Brightness Color Model

Figure 4-8 shows a typical color dialog box that selects colors based on hue, saturation, and brightness.

- Hue is specified as degrees of counterclockwise rotation around the color wheel, starting from red at 3 o'clock.

- Saturation varies along the vertical axis of the triangle from 100 at the bottom to 0 at the top; 0% saturation (at the top corner) results in white.

- Brightness varies along the horizontal axis of the triangle from 100 at the left to 0 at the right; 0% brightness (at the right corner) is black.

- The selected hue is most vivid at the lower left corner of the triangle, where saturation and brightness are both 100%.

- For any given hue, the triangle displays every possible tint and shade.

FIGURE 4-8.
This color dialog box from Corel Photo-Paint selects hue as degrees of rotation around the color wheel, saturation along the vertical edge of the triangle, and brightness along the horizontal edge.

Figure 4-9 shows how Microsoft Image Composer supports the HSB model, but Image Composer uses the alternate term HSV, which stands for hue saturation value. The top edge of the banded rectangle is essentially a color wheel rolled out flat.

- The slider marked with a triangle along the top edge (or the Hue slider to the right) selects hue.

- The slider next to the tall narrow rectangle (or the Sat slider to the right) controls saturation.

- The slider marked with a triangle along the left edge of the banded rectangle (or the Value slider to the right) controls brightness.

HSB color dialog boxes provide a natural way to make and refine color choices. Finding a pleasing hue with an RGB dialog box requires varying three independent color components in search of a satisfactory combination; the same operation in HSB requires varying only one dimension.

FIGURE 4-9.
Microsoft Image Composer supports HSV selection (essentially the same as HSB) through this color dialog box.

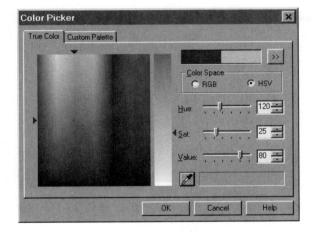

Choosing tints and shades is also quite intuitive under the HSB system. Artists lighten vivid colors by adding white pigment; to accomplish the same result with computer graphics, you can either calculate proportional increases in all three RGB components (using the RGB system) or simply vary the saturation setting (using HSB).

Similarly, artists darken vivid colors by adding black. In computer graphics, you can either calculate proportional decreases in all three RGB components or simply decrease the brightness setting.

Table 4-2 and Table 4-3 compare the RGB and HSB settings for various shades and tints of blue and orange. Blue, being a primary color, has a relatively simple progression of RGB values; to decrease brightness, decrease the blue value. To decrease saturation, increase red and green. Increasing brightness and saturation work the same, in reverse.

 NOTE

Ignore the HSL column for now. The next section will discuss this additional color model.

TABLE 4-2. Saturation and Brightness Settings for the Color Blue

Color	RGB Model				HSB Model			HSL Model		
	Red	Green	Blue	Hue	Satura-tion	Bright-ness	Hue	Satura-tion	Lumi-nance	
Black	0	0	0	240	100	0	160	240	0	
Shade of blue	0	0	51	240	100	20	160	240	24	
Shade of blue	0	0	102	240	100	40	160	240	48	
Shade of blue	0	0	153	240	100	60	160	240	72	
Shade of blue	0	0	204	240	100	80	160	240	96	
Vivid blue	0	0	255	240	100	100	160	240	120	
Tint of blue	51	51	255	240	80	100	160	240	144	
Tint of blue	102	102	255	240	60	100	160	240	168	
Tint of blue	153	153	255	240	40	100	160	240	192	
Tint of blue	204	204	255	240	20	100	160	240	216	
White	255	255	255	240	0	100	160	240	240	

Varying orange—a more complex, tertiary color—is more difficult. Decreasing brightness requires proportional decreases in both the original red and green values, and decreasing saturation requires proportionally increasing green and blue. Varying the appearance of a color while maintaining the same hue is considerably easier using the HSB model than the RGB model.

TABLE 4-3. Saturation and Brightness Settings for the Color Orange

Color	RGB Model				HSB Model			HSL Model		
	Red	Green	Blue	Hue	Saturation	Brightness	Hue	Saturation	Luminance
Black	0	0	0	48	100	0	32	240	0
Shade of orange	51	41	0	48	100	20	32	240	24
Shade of orange	102	82	0	48	100	40	32	240	48
Shade of orange	153	122	0	48	100	60	32	240	72
Shade of orange	204	163	0	48	100	80	32	240	96
Vivid orange	255	204	0	48	100	100	32	240	120
Tint of orange	255	214	51	48	80	100	32	240	144
Tint of orange	255	224	102	48	60	100	32	240	168
Tint of orange	255	235	153	48	40	100	32	240	192
Tint of orange	255	245	204	48	20	100	32	240	216
White	255	255	255	48	0	100	32	240	240

In summary:

- To obtain progressively lighter tints using the RGB model, proportionally increase any components not already at maximum. To obtain lighter tints using the HSB model, decrease saturation.

- To obtain progressively darker shades using the RGB model, proportionally decrease any nonzero components. To obtain darker shades using the HSB model, decrease brightness.

Any Color Black You Want

According to legend, someone once asked Henry Ford to start manufacturing cars in more than one color. Ford reportedly answered, "Fine. We'll build cars in any color black you want."

Sharp-eyed readers may notice that while the RGB columns in Tables 4-2 and 4-3 (on the previous two pages) both show black as 0-0-0 and white as 255-255-255, the HSB values for black and white differ:

Color	Table	Hue	Saturation	Brightness
Black	4-2	240	100	0
	4-3	48	100	0
White	4-2	240	0	100
	4-3	48	0	100

In the HSB model, a brightness of zero indicates zero light—the color black. Hue and saturation are irrelevant under these conditions. Think of it this way: If you were sitting in a dark room, leaving a red light turned off would produce the same effect as leaving a green light turned off.

Similarly, there are no hues of white. Zero percent saturation of any hue is still zero. When saturation is zero:

- Hue is irrelevant.

- Varying brightness from 0% to 100% produces a gray scale extending from black to white.

Although irrelevant, the hue values for both black and white in Table 4-2 and Table 4-3 were repeated, for the sake of uniformity, as they appeared elsewhere in the same table. The black saturation values were treated similarly.

HSL—The Hue, Saturation, Luminance Color Model

For reasons no doubt lost in antiquity, the standard color selection dialog box provided with Windows and used by most applications doesn't support the HSB color model. Instead, it supports RGB and another model called HSL—hue, saturation, luminance.

- Hue is the same measurement used in the HSB system, except that the color wheel is divided into 240 (rather than 360) increments.

- Saturation ranges in value from 0 to 240, and has a different meaning than saturation in the HSB model. In HSL, a saturation of 0 means the color is gray and 240 means the color contains no gray.

■ Luminance denotes the brightness of gray referred to by saturation. A luminance of 240 means white, 120 means 50% gray, and 0 means black.

HSL's fascination with gray stems from its origins in the television industry. Luminance is the black-and-white portion of a television signal. The inventors of color television modified the black-and-white television signal, adding hue and saturation data in such a way that monochrome sets would ignore them.

Figure 4-10 shows a typical Windows color dialog box with HSL support.

■ The top edge of the banded rectangle corresponds to the hues in a standard, continuous color wheel. You can select hues by dragging the crosshairs within the banded rectangle left and right, or by typing a number between 0 and 239 into the Hue text box.

■ The banded rectangle's vertical dimension represents saturation. Note that the lower edge is 50% gray, not black or white. To vary the saturation setting, either move the crosshairs up or down, or type a number between 0 and 240 into the Sat text box.

■ The tall narrow rectangle at the right of the dialog box controls luminance. To vary luminance, drag the slider up and down, or type a number between 0 and 240 into the Lum text box. Remember, 240 means white, 0 means black, and the value 120 produces the most vivid hue.

II

Plumbing, Art, and
Media—A Web Primer

FIGURE 4-10.
This standard Windows color dialog box simultaneously supports the HSL and RGB color models.

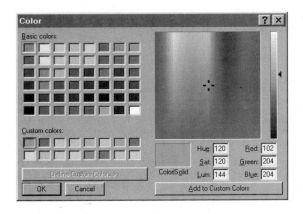

As illustrated in Table 4-4, varying HSL saturation is equivalent to varying *both* HSB saturation *and* HSB brightness. This makes sense when you consider that varying gray (which HSL defines as saturation) is equivalent to simultaneously varying a mixture of white (HSB saturation) and black (HSB brightness).

TABLE 4-4. Corresponding Effects of HSL Saturation

Color	HSL Model			HSB Model			RGB Model		
	Hue	Saturation	Luminance	Hue	Saturation	Brightness	Red	Green	Blue
Gray	160	0	120	240	0	50	127	127	127
Dull blue	160	48	120	240	33	60	102	102	153
Dull blue	160	144	120	240	74	80	51	51	204
Vivid blue	160	240	120	240	100	100	0	0	255

Most Web page creators find the HSL model more difficult to understand than either RGB or HSB. However, it does provide a way to vary colors without affecting hue, and its frequent appearance in Windows color dialog boxes makes learning it worthwhile.

Other Dimensions of Color

Most of us have developed rich associations between colors, other sensory perceptions, and the moods they invoke. Some of these associations are physical, such as red, the color of fire, denoting warmth. Some are societal, such as purple being associated with royalty, and others seem quite arbitrary. Whatever the origins, these associations identify color as a communications channel—a channel by which your Web pages will, by design or by default, communicate with your visitors. Some of these associations are as follows:

- **Hot.** A combination of highly saturated red hues produces red at its strongest and conveys an image of heat. Hot colors are strong and bold, and attract attention strongly. They stimulate the nervous system, sometimes to the point of raising blood pressure.

■ **Cold.** Consisting of highly saturated blues, cold colors are directly opposite hot. They invoke sensations of snow and ice; they slow bodily functions and induce a sense of calm. Saturated greens and blue-greens are cold colors.

■ **Warm.** Any hue containing red is warm, but mixtures of red and yellow are particularly so. Warm colors are spontaneous, soothing, and enticing.

■ **Cool.** These colors differ from cold by containing yellow; this produces yellow-green, green, and blue-green hues such as turquoise. Cool colors are lush, deep, spring-like, soothing.

■ **Light.** Light colors are mostly white, with just a tint of hue; hues appear in such small proportion that contrast among them is minimal. They convey airiness, free flow, rest, and relaxation. Light colors have all three RGB components at or near maximum, or an HSB brightness near maximum.

■ **Dark.** Vivid hues mixed with black produce dark colors. Electronically, none of the RGB components is likely to exceed 127. In HSB terms, brightness will be less than 50. Dark colors are dense, somber, and masculine in effect, and they suggest autumn or winter. Compositions composed entirely of dark colors are seldom effective, but dark colors provide excellent contrast against light.

■ **Pale.** These are soft pastel colors formed with diminished hues and at least two-thirds white—that is, with all three RGB components at 170 or more. Pink, light blue, and ivory are typical results. Soft and calming, pale colors are frequently used for interiors of homes and offices.

■ **Bright.** Colors lacking black or white dilution are vivid, saturated, and therefore bright. Bright colors attract attention from a distance, but if overused at close quarters they can be overpowering and harsh.

Transparency and Alpha Channels

At times it's quite desirable for parts of a computer graphics image to be transparent:

- When the edges of an object are irregular—that is, anything but rectangular

- When parts of an image must appear translucent

- When parts of an image should blend gradually into the background

Irregular Edges

Figure 4-11 shows a Web page containing two versions of the same image. The version at the left has a solid white background that clashes with the textured background of the Web page. The image at the right has a transparent background that allows the texture to show through clearly.

FIGURE 4-11.
Compare the white background in the image at the left with the transparent background of the image at the right.

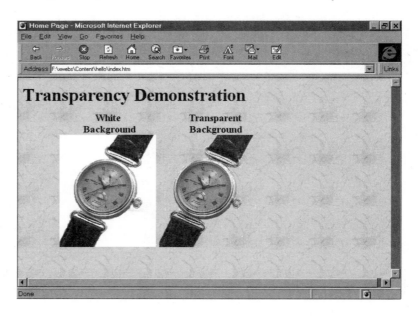

No amount of editing on the left image will make it look as good as the image on the right. No solid color can possibly blend evenly with the surrounding texture, and even adding a textured background to the image will produce slight mismatches as the user resizes the browser window.

Using a solid, rather than textured, Web page background makes it easier to use images with nontransparent backgrounds—though each different background color then requires its own set of images with matching backgrounds. A transparent background allows using the same image file on any Web page.

Anti-Aliasing

Another application that greatly benefits from transparency is anti-aliasing. This is a technique that reduces the jagged appearance of curved lines when displayed on a computer monitor. Pixels along a curved edge, rather than being either the object's color or the background color, take on a mixture of the two. Figure 4-12 shows the string "abc" aliased at the left and anti-aliased at the right.

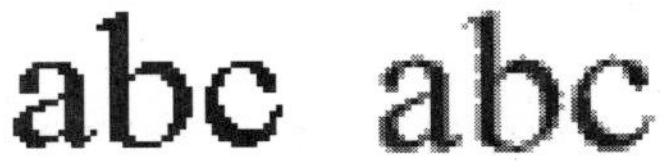

FIGURE 4-12.
Anti-aliasing, shown here at the far right, softens edges to make them look less jagged.

abc abc

Figure 4-13, on the following page, provides an enlarged view of anti-aliasing. Pixels entirely in the white area are entirely white, and those entirely in the black area correspondingly black. Pixels along the border, however, are colored gray in proportion to the amount of black or white space that would be occupied at much higher resolution.

The use of anti-aliasing isn't confined to black-and-white drawings; the concept of proportionately shading edge pixels can apply to any intersection of two colors.

Many graphics programs anti-alias everything by default, but this isn't always desirable. Anti-aliased edges sometimes appear blurry, like a slightly out-of-focus photograph, and sometimes the sharpness of aliased images is more important than the elimination of jagged edges. For this reason, it's important to have both aliasing and anti-aliasing tools at hand.

FIGURE 4-13.
Pixels along the aliased curve are either light or dark. Pixels along the anti-aliased curve use various shades of gray for a smoother effect.

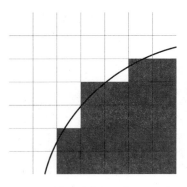
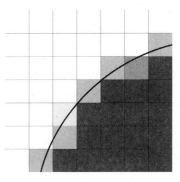

Aliased (jagged) curve

Anti-aliased (smoothed) curve

Translucence

Figure 4-14 shows Microsoft Image Composer editing an image that contains a transparent *sprite*—the magnifying glass. An Image Composer sprite is a sort of image within an image; when you combine several images to form a single composition, Image Composer remembers each subimage as a separate component you can later rearrange or modify. The magnifying glass, the gray background, and the darker gray stripe are each sprites.

FIGURE 4-14.
Note the transparency present in the magnifying glass. The gray background and dark gray stripe show through the glass only partially.

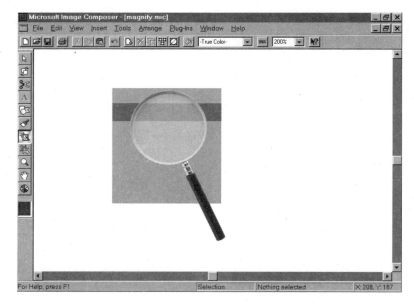

The background and stripe were actually drawn with solid colors; they appear lighter through the magnifying glass because the glass is partially transparent. This is possible because Image Composer uses a 32-bit color model with an 8-bit *alpha channel*.

Implementing Transparency

A problem arises when preparing anti-aliased graphics (or, for that matter, nonrectangular graphics of any kind) for use on various colored or textured backgrounds. One color is known—that of the image—but the second color varies depending on where the graphic is used. The edge pixels need to be shaded not from one color to another, but from a solid color to various degrees of transparency—degrees that allow background colors to partially show through. Complicating the problem, each pixel in the image may require a different amount of transparency.

An *alpha channel* stores a fourth value along with the normal red, green, and blue intensities for each pixel. Each pixel's alpha value indicates the degree of transparency for that pixel, normally with the same precision used for red, green, and blue values. The addition of an alpha channel expands 24-bit color (8 bits each for red, green, and blue) to 32-bit color.

Unfortunately, neither of the two graphics formats commonly used on the Web supports a true alpha channel. Advanced image editors such as Microsoft Image Composer *do* support alpha channels, but saving an image in Web format converts the transparency information to fixed colors based on the editor's current background color. Having alpha channel support in the image editor and its native file format is less useful than if Web graphics fully supported the feature, but having alpha support in an editor at least provides an easy way to create multiple versions of an image with different background colors.

A common problem involves images anti-aliased for one background but used on another. This results in a sort of halo around the opaque portions of the image. Unfortunately, even editing the image with a program that supports alpha channels won't restore the original transparency information; the alpha channel was lost when the image was saved with a fixed color background. Pixel-by-pixel editing along the edges is often the only remedy to this halo effect.

SEE ALSO
For more information on graphics file formats, see "Graphic File Formats," page 122.

The graphic interchange format—GIF—does support an all-or-nothing sort of transparency. The creator of a GIF file can designate one color in the image as denoting transparency, and a browser will then render pixels that color as transparent. This is better than nothing—but nowhere near as powerful as a full alpha channel.

Gamma Correction

In a perfect world—or at least a simple one—the brightness of each pixel displayed on a monitor would vary precisely in accordance with the brightness values set by software. For example, a pixel with RGB values of 200-200-200 would appear twice as bright as one with values of 100-100-100. The relationship between software intensity, display card voltage, and hardware intensity would all be linear. Optimally, the brightness of a monitor pixel would vary directly with the signal from the display adapter, as shown in the first graph of the following figure.

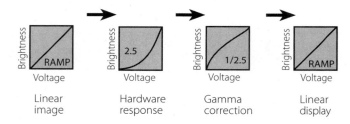

| Linear image | Hardware response | Gamma correction | Linear display |

Of course, real life is nowhere near so simple. Monitors work by blasting electrons at glowing phosphors; the more electrons the brighter the phosphors, but the relationship is hardly linear. For most monitors, brightness equals voltage raised to the 2.5th power:

$$\text{Brightness} = \text{Voltage}^{2.5}$$

 NOTE

In the above formula, voltage is a relative value between 0 and 100 percent, expressed in the range from 0 to 1.

The second graph in the figure shows a typical, real-world graph of monitor brightness versus display adapter output.

The exponent 2.5 is called a *gamma coefficient*. The exact value varies somewhat, depending on the particular device, but 2.5 is a typical value. The resulting curve relating brightness to voltage is shown in the second graph of the figure.

Gamma correction is an adjustment that restores linearity between software color values and monitor brightness. It supplies an inverse function, shown in the third graph, and corrects the nonlinearity of the hardware, as shown in the final graph.

Without gamma correction, changes in RGB values close to zero have far less effect than changes closer to 255. Also, a true 50% gray would occur at an RGB value of 193-193-193, not (as you would expect) at 127-127-127:

$$\left(\frac{193}{255}\right)^{2.5} = .49836$$

? **SEE ALSO**
For more information about gamma and gamma correction, browse the Web site *http://www.cgsd.com/papers/gamma_intro.html*.

Uncorrected gamma can also have a serious effect on color blending. Doubling each of the intensities in RGB color 50-75-100, for example, would create a nonlinear color shift because doubling 50 would have less effect on the red component than doubling 100 would have on the blue component.

Gamma correction can occur in application software, in the operating system, in the video driver, in the display adapter, or in the monitor. In the PC and Unix environment, however, gamma correction normally appears

Plumbing, Art, and Media—A Web Primer

PC vs. Macintosh Gamma Correction

Macintosh computers have a gamma correction of 1.4 built into the hardware. Since 2.5 divided by 1.4 is 1.8, 1.8 is the normal gamma correction setting for Macintosh software. This accounts for the muddy appearance of Macintosh-created graphics on a PC, and the bright, washed-out appearance of PC-created images on a Mac. The Mac hardware brightens dark colors in hardware, while PC hardware does not.

Measuring the gamma of a particular monitor, graphics card, printer, or other device is called *color calibration*. Color calibration requires special color measurement hardware and specially adjustable software, and is generally beyond the scope of this book. However, this may be an area to explore if you plan on doing the most exacting, professional-quality graphics work.

only in application software. Figure 4-15 shows the Gamma tab of the Microsoft Image Composer options dialog box.

FIGURE 4-15.
Microsoft Image Composer contains this tab to provide control over gamma correction.

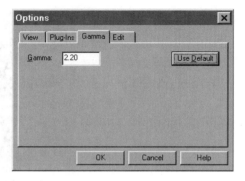

Graphic File Formats

Graphics on Web pages must be in one of two formats for you to view them in current Web browsers without using additional software: GIF (graphic interchange format) or JPEG (Joint Photographic Expert Group). Table 4-5 compares these two formats.

TABLE 4-5. Characteristics of GIF and JPEG Formats

	GIF	JPEG
Colors available	16,777,216	16,777,216
Colors per image	256	16,777,216
Compression	Lossless	Lossy
Transparency	Yes	No
Animation	Yes	No

 NOTE

FrontPage lets you import graphics in any of several other formats—BMP, TIFF, MAC, MSP, PCD, RAS, WPG, EPS, PCX, and WMF—and insert them as GIF or JPEG images.

Table 4-5 identifies some important differences between GIF and JPEG images.

- **Lossy versus lossless compression.** Storing a bitmapped image may require several bytes of information for each pixel and, if the image is large, may result in very large files. Most bitmapped file formats therefore include provisions for *compression*. Compression uses complex mathematical formulas to identify and abbreviate repeating patterns in the data.

GIF compression uses a formula that results in zero loss of data from the compression/decompression process—that is, it provides *lossless* compression. The JPEG format supports varying degrees of compression, but most of them fail to guarantee an exact reproduction of the original. Depending on the creator's choice of settings, the resulting image typically loses a measure of color fidelity, sharpness, or contrast. This is called *lossy* compression. The more loss tolerated, the smaller the image file.

? SEE ALSO

For information about setting transparency in FrontPage Editor, see "Setting Transparency," page 297.

■ **Transparency.** Images saved as GIF or JPEG files are always rectangular. The number of horizontal and vertical pixels can be whatever you want, but there's no way to save an image in these formats with circular, ovate, or irregular borders.

One way to avoid rectangular image shapes is to fill the edge with the same color as the background of your Web page. However, this won't work if the page uses a complex image as a background, or if the end user has configured the browser to override incoming background colors and images.

A better solution involves specifying a *transparent* color in the image. Instead of displaying pixels from the image having that color, the browser displays whatever pixels lie behind them— usually the background color or image.

■ **Animation.** The GIF format includes a provision to accommodate multiple images in the same file, and to specify timing sequences among them. This provides a way to present simple animations within the browser without requiring the end user to install additional animation software.

Most Web designers prefer the GIF format for text, line art, and icons because of its lossless compression and transparency. JPEG finds use in backgrounds, photographs, and other areas where maximum compression and color fidelity are more important than sharpness.

II

Plumbing, Art, and
Media—A Web Primer

Portable Network Graphics—PNG

A new graphic format called PNG—portable network graphics—supports full 32-bit color with an alpha channel, multiple compression methods, gamma information, and additional features that ease cross-platform difficulties. Unfortunately, PNG support in browsers remains far from universal and PNG images tend to be larger than GIF or JPEG images.

For detailed information about PNG, browse *http://www.w3.org/TR/REC-png-multi.html*.

Images on Web pages remain in separate files and don't become part of the HTML. Instead, the HTML merely includes a reference to the image file's name. As the browser receives the HTML for a page, it identifies any image files needed and downloads them for display.

Avoid using more than 20 to 30KB of image files on a Web page. Doing so leads to slow download times for users who connect to the Internet by modem.

Achieving Accurate Rendition—Safe Colors

A large percentage of Web users have 256-color displays. Such systems can display 16,777,216 different colors, but only 256 at once. This isn't a problem when displaying a single GIF image, because most graphics programs adjust the video hardware to display the same 256 colors that appear in the image. However, three problems arise when displaying GIF images on a Web page:

- On most computers with 256-color displays, not all 256 colors are programmable. On Windows-based computers, for example, 20 colors are reserved for use by Windows so that window borders, menu bars, button faces, and other elements of the user interface maintain a consistent appearance. This leaves only 236 colors that can be adjusted to match those in an image.

- Web pages can contain any number of GIF images. Each GIF image can contain only 256 colors, but two images on the same page—if they have no colors in common—can require a total of 512. Three images can require 768 colors, and so forth. This presents a problem if the display hardware can only accommodate 256 colors in total.

■ A single JPEG picture can contain far more than 256 colors: up to 16,777,216 (assuming the image has that many pixels). A 256-color system has no hope of rendering such an image accurately.

Most browsers solve this dilemma by programming 256-color displays with a fixed 216-color palette. The 216 colors are all combinations of six evenly spaced levels of red, the same six levels of green, and the same six levels of blue. Table 4-6 shows the six levels.

To display colors with RGB intensities other than 0, 51, 102, 153, 204, or 255, the browser either *dithers* or *substitutes*. When dithering, the browser displays nonstandard colors as a mixed pattern of standard-color pixels. In theory, the viewer's eye perceives the mixed pattern as a smooth area, but in practice the perception is often grainy. Dithering usually works better on continuous-scale images, such as photographs. It's most objectionable on images with large solid areas, such as text, flood fills, and line art.

TABLE 4-6. Safe Palette Color Intensities for 256-Color Video Systems

Intensity	Decimal	Hex
Minimum	0	00
	51	33
	102	66
	153	99
	204	CC
Maximum	255	FF

When substituting, the browser simply replaces nonstandard colors with its idea of the closest standard color. Browsers normally apply substitution rather than dithering for background colors, because dithering a background can seriously affect the readability of text.

Both dithering and substitution result in Web visitors seeing something other than you intended. To avoid this take one of these steps:

- Specify only the following RGB values for text, backgrounds, and solid images: 0, 51, 102, 153, 204, or 255.

- If you must supply RGB color values in hexadecimal, specify only values 00, 33, 66, 99, CC, or FF.

If you have an image that displays properly in an editor or stand-alone viewer but appears grainy in the browser, you should try converting its *palette*. A palette is simply a collection of colors, and most image editors can store, edit, and save palettes—both with individual images and as stand-alone palette files. If you open an image having one palette and then open a palette file with another palette, most editors provide several options to reconcile the differences. One such option is usually to convert each pixel in the image to the nearest color in the new palette. If the palette consists solely of 216 safe colors, each pixel in the original image will take on a safe color value and no dithering or substitution will subsequently occur.

The fixed 216-color palette explains two other problems Web designers often encounter.

1. Black-and-white photograph rendition is usually terrible. This is because the browser has only six levels of gray, and four if you exclude black and white. The six available gray levels are

Color Name	Decimal	Hexadecimal
Black	0-0-0	00-00-00
	51-51-51	33-33-33
	102-102-102	66-66-66
	153-153-153	99-99-99
	204-204-204	CC-CC-CC
White	255-255-255	FF-FF-FF

These six aren't enough shades of gray to display continuous tone grayscale images such as black-and-white photographs.

2   Screen shots look terrible because only 8 of the 20 colors reserved by Windows are in the safe palette. Early, 16-color VGA adapters had the following colors indelibly fixed in hardware, and these colors are, by default, now fixed in the Windows user interface as well. They are

Color Name	Bright	Dark
Black	0-0-0	192-192-192 (light gray)
Red	255-0-0	128-0-0
Green	0-255-0	0-128-0
Blue	0-0-255	0-0-128
Cyan	0-255-255	0-128-128
Magenta	255-0-255	128-0-128
Yellow	255-255-0	128-128-0
White	255-255-255	128-128-128 (dark gray)

All the colors in the Bright column appear in the safe browser palette, but none of those in the Dark column are in the safe palette. This explains why screen shots converted directly into GIF files don't appear as clearly on Web pages as they did when originally displayed. To obtain a clear display, you'll need to use an image editor to convert the dark VGA colors to their nearest safe palette equivalents.

Using the safe color palette significantly reduces the choice of colors in a harmonious scheme. This presents a dilemma that won't be solved until all Web visitors have 24-bit color displays. For now, you must decide whether to optimize colors for 8-bit displays or 24-bit displays, and at this time 8-bit displays predominate.

Typography

Although the bulk of this chapter covers color principles, two other important topics merit discussion as well: typography, and layout and design. Typography is the umbrella term for the use of typefaces, a fundamental tool of graphic design, whether on paper or on screen. The shape, color, and style of the letters and symbols that make up text convey meaning as surely as the words and sentences themselves. Effective use of type will enhance and amplify your message, just as ineffective use will weaken it and even confuse viewers or readers.

Originally, fonts used on the Web were totally outside the page creator's control. The page creator specified text styles such as "Heading1," or "Normal," and each remote user configured their browser with desired fonts for each style. In practice, most fonts ended up being a form of Times Roman or Courier.

Choosing fonts for normal text presents a problem because computer monitors typically display only 72 pixels per inch. At such resolutions there are simply not enough pixels to differentiate similar typefaces. Often, there aren't even enough pixels to make fonts legible. For these reasons, overriding the default font for normal text is generally a bad idea.

Headings and titles generally use larger type sizes and thus provide more opportunity for artistic type selection. The problem is that there's no good way to ensure that end users have the specified fonts on their systems; nor is there any widely accepted technology for providing temporary, downloadable fonts as Web page components. As a result, and as a workaround, most Web page typography involves text rendered as graphic images.

As always, similar page elements should look alike and dissimilar elements should look different. This means, for example,

- All first-level headings should look alike.

- All normal text should look alike.

- First level headings and normal text should look different.

Similarly, all hypertext links should look alike, but something other than a link should never look like one. Many other examples are possible.

The extent of contrast between different page elements is a matter of judgment, but the result should be a mixture of contrast and unity. If something deserves typographical treatment to make it look different, then make it look *really* different. Insufficient contrast makes the reader stop reading and start analyzing the tiny differences you've created. Insufficient contrast confuses and distracts the reader.

Excessive contrast is similarly distracting. Each Web page should have a unity among all its elements, and all Web pages on the same topic or site warrant a certain unity as well. Choosing different styles and conventions for every page forces your readers to constantly reorient themselves, diverting their attention away from your message.

There are two main uses for bolding and italics on Web pages. In normal text, **bolding** indicates words bearing special emphasis and *italics* denotes special terms—especially the first instance of a special term.

Bolding and italics can also be useful in designing heading fonts. In this context, the entire heading phrase is bolded or italicized to distinguish it from normal text, other headings, or other page elements.

Underlining, by the way, is a crude substitute for italics carried over from the days of typewriters. Now that italics are readily available, there's no longer any need to emphasize text by underlining. Such text can also be confused with a link, because browsers are often configured to display hyperlinks with an underline.

The primary dimensions that provide contrast between different kinds of text are

- **Size.** Font size is normally measured in points, where one point equals 1/72 of an inch. It refers to the vertical range of the entire typeface as measured from the top of the tallest character to the bottom of the lowest "descender," such as the tail of the letter *j*.

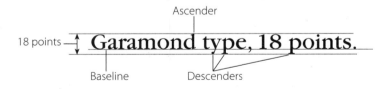

- **Color.** Text, like any other page element, can appear in any selected color. Text color should naturally be integrated with the overall color scheme for the page.

- **Typeface.** There are thousands of typefaces, and more are being created every day. It's remarkable there can be so many variations on an alphabet of only 26 letters, and even more remarkable that so many variations of the same letters can be recognizable. Some of the characteristics that differentiate one typeface from another include

- **Presence or absence of serifs.** Serifs are small, angular extensions added to the ends of character strokes. Fonts such as Times Roman and Garamond have them; Arial and Helvetica don't.

- **Slant of serifs.** Serifs may be angled relative to the baseline or parallel to it, particularly for lowercase letters.

- **Thickness of serifs.** Serifs may be hairline thin or as thick as main character strokes.

- **Stroke transition.** Strokes are the lines and curves that form the body of a character. Stroke transition refers to the difference between the thickest portions of a character and the thinnest.

- **Stress.** This term refers to the angle of an imaginary line drawn through the thinnest portions of a rounded, symmetrical character such as *O*.

- **Weight.** The difference between bold and normal text is one of weight, but other degrees of thickness are possible as well. Some typefaces are always thicker than others by design; very thick fonts often have the word *black* or *ultra* in their names. In general, the heavier the font, the more attention it attracts. (Recall contrast of extension.) However, a predominance of heavy fonts greatly reduces their effectiveness.

- **Direction.** This property sometimes refers to curvature or rotation of the baseline (effects that, by the way, are more often abused than used properly). Beyond baseline alignment, though, direction can refer to the dimensions of text flow. Sentences or paragraphs fitted into tall, narrow columns have a more vertical direction than text fitted into the full width of a page. The rows and columns of cells in a table have horizontal and vertical dimensions. Items in a list can appear horizontally, in sentence format, or vertically, as bullets in a list (like this one).

- **Proportional versus monospaced.** Most typefaces are proportional, meaning some characters are wider than others. This is and should be the normal situation; there's no reason for small *l* and capital *W* to occupy the same amount of space on a line.

  Monospaced typefaces allocate the same amount of space for every character, much like a typewriter. They are significantly less attractive and less readable than proportional fonts, but may be preferable for program code listings and other applications that need equally spaced characters to align text without using tabs.

- **Form.** This property refers to the overall shape of the letters, numbers, and symbols in the typeface. Uppercase and lowercase letters in the same font obviously have different forms, as do the characters in distinctly different typefaces. In a sense, form is the sum of all the technical properties above.

- **Style.** This is a catchall property that covers everything not covered above. Typefaces are collections of artistic images, after all, and combining a set of technical and artistic properties into a useful and legible font is an artistic endeavor.

Every typeface has a name, but font names may reveal little about their properties. Some, such as Garamond and Baskerville, have a rich history and are named for their designers of a century or more ago, but many are recent creations, driven by market forces, or derivations of the classics. To analyze the contrast or similarity of typefaces, general categories such as the following are more useful.

- **Oldstyle.** These are some of the oldest, most readable typefaces in common use. They feature slanted, lowercase serifs; moderate transition in strokes; and left-leaning diagonal stress. These characteristics are highlighted in Figure 4-16, on the following page. Typical oldstyle typefaces include Times Roman and Garamond.

II

Plumbing, Art, and
Media—A Web Primer

FIGURE 4-16.
Oldstyle fonts have a classic appearance and are among the easiest to read.

Slanted lowercase serifs   Moderate transition in strokes   Diagonal stress

Times Roman

 NOTE

Many oldstyle fonts are difficult to display on the limited resolution of computer monitors. The limit of 72 pixels per inch simply doesn't provide enough detail to display moderate stroke variations and slanted pixels, especially at small point sizes. Modern fonts are therefore more common in online environments than in print. One aid to viewing fonts is software that automatically smoothes (anti-aliases) the typefaces, such as Win95 Plus or Adobe Type Manager. Another is higher resolution video cards used on larger monitors that can combine to display type up to about 120 pixels per inch, making each character more fully formed.

■ **Modern.** These fonts were invented to have a more mechanical, colder look than oldstyle fonts. Stroke transitions are extreme, stress is vertical, and serifs are horizontal. Bodoni and Elephant are typical modern fonts. See Figure 4-17.

FIGURE 4-17.
Modern fonts eliminate many angular features found in oldstyle type.

Horizontal serifs   Vertical stress   Extreme transition in strokes

Bodoni

■ **Slab serif.** Fonts in this category are designed for extra visibility by eliminating fine strokes. They have less stroke transition and thicker serifs than modern fonts, but retain the vertical stress. Century Schoolbook, New Century Schoolbook, and Clarendon are slab serif fonts. See Figure 4-18.

FIGURE 4-18.
Slab serif fonts eliminate the fine details of other serif fonts to enhance casual readability.

■ **Sans serif.** These fonts have no serifs and display uniform stroke thickness throughout. With no stroke transition there is, of course, no stress. Sans serif fonts have a clean, technical appearance but in general aren't quite as legible as serif fonts. The contrast between serif and sans serif is quite extreme yet attractive, accounting for the common practice of using serifs for body text and sans serifs for headings. Common sans serif fonts include Arial and Helvetica. Figure 4-19 provides an example.

FIGURE 4-19.
A complete lack of serifs gives the sans serif category its name. Sans serif fonts provide an attractive contrast to oldstyle and modern fonts.

■ **Script.** Fonts that resemble handwriting or calligraphy fall into the script category. These are highly stylistic fonts typically used for wedding invitations and advertising. Most are inherently hard to read and even worse at computer monitor resolutions. Exercise great caution when considering a script font for use on a Web page. Figure 4-20 uses Zapf Chancery, a typical example.

FIGURE 4-20.
Script fonts look like excruciatingly correct handwriting or lettering.

■ **Decorative.** This category includes a wide variety of highly stylized fonts—you could almost call them fonts with a gimmick. They're eye-catching but hard to read, and overusing them can drive people screaming from the room. Small point sizes look terrible on computer monitors. Used properly, decorative fonts can produce eye-catching logos, headlines, and banners, but overuse is much more common than proper use. Tread carefully. Figure 4-21 illustrates Giddyup, a decorative font with a rough 'n' ready western flair.

FIGURE 4-21.
Decorative fonts are fonts with a gimmick. Use them carefully, if at all.

■ **Symbol.** These fonts range from useful symbols to visual clutter, and don't even pretend to contain letters, numbers, and punctuation; they're actually icon collections. Formatting normal characters with a symbol font produces seemingly random sequences of mathematical symbols, foreign language characters, bullets, road signs, or images of almost anything. Figure 4-22 shows the Zapf Dingbats font. (A dingbat is a typographer's term for a symbol or decorative "thingie.")

Symbol fonts are more useful in printed documents than in Web pages. There are far better (and more colorful) icon collections in clip art libraries and on the Web than any symbol font can provide.

FIGURE 4-22.

Symbol fonts display small icons, bullets, or other non-English characters.

Special characters and icons —

Zapf Dingbats

The primary value in considering these font categories lies in understanding the most common conventions and variations among fonts. The eye is so accustomed to reading different fonts that it takes quite a difference to be obvious.

Figure 4-23 shows an attractive but unusual font—Optima. This is a sans serif font with stroke transition, normally an oldstyle or modern characteristic. Despite its attractiveness, Optima's partial similarity to both the sans serif category and to oldstyle and modern makes it difficult to use with either. This highlights the importance of providing sufficient contrast among typefaces used on the same page.

FIGURE 4-23.

Optima is a sans serif font with stroke transition. The blend of oldstyle and sans serif characteristics makes Optima difficult to use with either.

No serifs   Vertical stress   Moderate transitions in strokes

Sans Serif

Optima

There are dozens of lookalike typefaces that are modeled on (or ripoffs of) the classic designs of Optima, Garamond, Times Roman, Helvetica, and the like.

Contrast in color and size are far more obvious than contrast in the shape of letters. If you decide to use multiple fonts on a page, topic, or site, make sure they're markedly different yet legible and that they work together. When in doubt, use the default font (typically an oldstyle) for body text and a larger sans serif for headings.

Layout and Design

Robin Williams, in *The Non-Designers Design Book*, identifies four key elements of effective graphic arts page design. The first two concepts should be quite familiar from earlier discussions regarding color and typography. The third and fourth concepts, however, are new to this chapter.

- **Contrast.** This is the idea that different kinds of page objects should each be identified by a different look. Titles, headings, body text, hyperlinks, and legal disclaimers, for example, should each be differentiated by a unique appearance.

- **Repetition.** This concept directs that similar page objects should look alike. All body text should look the same, as should all level-1 headings, all level-2 headings, and so forth. Giving like objects different appearances can be extremely confusing to the reader.

- **Alignment.** This concept addresses the positioning of each element in a composition. Elements should appear to be organized according to some plan, not haphazardly.

  Proper alignment generally involves drawing imaginary horizontal and vertical lines through the composition, and then aligning related objects along those lines. Similar objects should generally be aligned similarly to each other. Unlike objects may likewise have unlike alignment, but they can also be differentiated in some other way.

- **Proximity.** This principle holds that related objects should be closer together than unrelated objects. This leads to techniques such as ordering similar items together, decreasing blank space between related items, and increasing blank space between unrelated items.

? SEE ALSO

For the technical details of HTML page layout, consult Chapter 7, "Adding and Formatting Text"; "Creating and Editing Tables," page 313; "Creating and Editing Frames," page 338; and "Managing Page-Level Cascading Style Sheets," page 232.

HTML is a relatively poor page layout environment. HTML, after all, was designed for simple documents and simple authoring—no one at the time thought of assembling graphic compositions rivaling brochures and magazine ads. Basic HTML had almost no typographical or page layout controls, thus stripping page designers of their most important tools. HTML page layout is further complicated by its variable page dimensions (according to the viewer's browser dimensions), which in turn complicate spatial positioning.

HTML provides only a basic assortment of paragraph styles. Normal text, headings, code listings, and so forth are all *flush left*—that is, aligned to the left margin, with no provision for indentation. Only a few styles such as bulleted lists, numbered lists, and definition lists provide built-in horizontal alignment.

More advanced objects, such as images, tables, Java applets, and ActiveX controls, are flush left by default but can also be centered or *flush right* (aligned to the right margin). When aligned to the left margin, text can optionally flow around nontext objects. Text always flows around right-aligned objects.

Tables and frames are the most common tools used for HTML page layout. Of the two, tables offer the most flexibility. The cells in an HTML table can have visible or invisible borders. Tables are required for most page layout applications, and invisible borders are usually preferable. Creating a page layout with tables first involves deciding how many horizontal and vertical cells the composition requires, and then merging cells for objects that need to span more than one row or columns. Chapter 9, "Hyperlinks and Page Layout," provides several examples of these techniques.

Using HTML frames begins with defining a *frameset* that divides the browser window into zones called *frames*. Each frame displays a different Web page, and clicking hypertext in one frame can change the page displayed in another. A typical use of frames involves a menu list in one frame and an information display in another. As the user clicks different menu items, the information frame displays corresponding Web pages.

Tables and frames both divide the browser window into horizontal and vertical areas, but they solve two quite different problems. Tables are relatively static *x-y* grids, but you can define as many rows and columns as you need. Frames provide a means to replace parts of the browser display while preserving others, but their size and positioning is much less precise. A 5-row by 5-column table is relatively easy to work with, but a 25-frame frameset would be a nightmare.

For a simple example of alignment and proximity, consider the following block of text.

Planes

The Wright brothers are generally regarded as the originators of mechanical flight. The concept, of course, was centuries old, and the efforts and failures of countless inventors undoubtedly formed the basis for the Wright brothers' accomplishment.

Trains

Of all the factors that won the American West, the locomotive was among the most important. Railroads provided the transportation necessary for the western economy to flourish.

Automobiles

Henry Ford's greatest invention was not mass production, but the concept of making automobiles cheap and serviceable enough to permit mass consumption.

The preceding segment is legible and the headings are clearly identified by bolding, but additional indentation clearly increases the contrast and recognition of headings versus body text.

Planes

The Wright brothers are generally regarded as the originators of mechanical flight. The concept, of course, was centuries old, and the efforts and failures of countless inventors undoubtedly formed the basis for the Wright brothers' accomplishment.

Trains

Of all the factors that won the American West, the locomotive was among the most important. Railroads provided the transportation necessary for the western economy to flourish.

Automobiles

Henry Ford's greatest invention was not mass production, but the concept of making automobiles cheap and serviceable enough to permit mass consumption.

To apply the principle of proximity, add space between each element of body text and the next heading by shifting each head closer to the text that follows it.

Planes

The Wright brothers are generally regarded as the originators of mechanical flight. The concept, of course, was centuries old, and the efforts and failures of countless inventors undoubtedly formed the basis for the Wright brothers' accomplishment.

Trains

Of all the factors that won the American West, the locomotive was among the most important. Railroads provided the transportation necessary for the western economy to flourish.

Automobiles

Henry Ford's greatest invention was not mass production, but the concept of making automobiles cheap and serviceable enough to permit mass consumption.

Further variations might involve increasing the size of the heading text, changing its color, or switching its font to sans serif. The possibilities are endless; go for it!

II

Plumbing, Art, and
Media—A Web Primer

PART III

Building Your Site

CHAPTER 5

Structuring Your Web

No piece of software can automatically organize your content effectively or achieve artistic excellence. These are tasks for talented human beings. Software can, however, expedite the flow of ideas from concept to expression, from dream to reality. It should certainly never get in the way. FrontPage provides strong tools to help you plan, construct, and manage your site.

- **Navigation view.** This new feature provides a way to graphically design and record the logical structure of your Web. FrontPage can then generate the corresponding hyperlinks among your pages automatically.

- **Themes.** These are professionally designed color and style combinations that FrontPage can apply to selected pages or an entire Web. You can't override themes except by removing them, but you can design your own themes using the FrontPage Software Development Kit.

- **Templates.** In essence, these are the most useful blank pages you'll ever find. FrontPage lets you create any number of Web page starting points, save them as templates, and then create new pages based on any desired template. FrontPage also provides a library of predesigned templates plus a selection of wizards for initializing entire sites.

- **Color masters.** In FrontPage, you can configure any page to get its color scheme and background from another. By having all the pages in a site or topic get their appearance from a single master page, you can fine-tune or totally redesign the site's color scheme at will.

- **Shared borders.** FrontPage can apply a standard heading, footer, right edge, or left edge to every page in a Web or to selected pages. Each such border displays exactly the same content on every page, so that changing a shared border on one page changes it everywhere. Note, however, that certain FrontPage components, with no change to their configuration, appear differently depending on the page in which they appear. The Navigation bar and page banner are two of these.

- **Site parameters.** FrontPage can store frequently occurring strings as named *variables*, and then insert the value of the variable everywhere it occurs in your site. Later, if the information changes, you can modify it everywhere by changing the value of the variable in a single location.

- **Include page components.** For longer and more complex page segments, FrontPage provides the ability to include one Web page in another. This means you can store any sort of repeating content in a small Web page, and then include that page wherever you want the content to appear. When it becomes necessary to change the content of the page segment, changing it once updates its occurrence in the entire Web. This is perfect for navigation bars, signature lines, and other elements that appear on many pages and need to be kept in sync.

- **Folder organization.** FrontPage Explorer provides an intuitive file and folder manager for Web sites, even those not accessible on the local hard disk or through conventional file sharing. What's more, using FrontPage Explorer to rearrange files and folders maintains the integrity of all hyperlinks in the site.

- **Task List.** Most sites, especially new ones, have a long list of unfinished business—pages to be created, completed, corrected, or removed. FrontPage can maintain this list for you, with automatic links to the pages needing the work.

Once your initial planning is complete, you're ready to start building. We'll assume FrontPage is installed on your computer; if not, follow the installation instructions that came with FrontPage and install it now.

Organizing Your Web Server Environment

Even more than you might expect, the workings of FrontPage are rooted deeply in the Web.

- When FrontPage loads a file, it does so using a Web request—as a browser would do—and not by reading a file off your disk as other applications do.

- When FrontPage updates a file or any other information, it issues an HTTP POST and asks the Web server to update the data. This is the same mechanism used to process HTML forms.

- The FrontPage Server Extensions, on which FrontPage relies for some of its most advanced functions, are designed to run not as ordinary Windows programs, but rather as processes within a Web server.

For these reasons and more, making best use of FrontPage requires access to at least one FrontPage Web server and preferably two. One server will be your development environment, for storing work in progress and for testing Web pages you create. The second server will be your production server, where you publish finished work and make it available for high-volume public browsing.

III

Building Your Site

Having two Web servers isn't a hard-and-fast requirement; if your needs are simple and control over content changes isn't critical, a single server will suffice. If your needs are complex, a battery of servers might be needed. These are decisions only you, your organization, or your client can make.

Here are two common scenarios.

- You create Web pages in your home or small office, and connect only periodically to the network where your production Web server resides. An Internet service provider, a Web presence provider, or your corporate MIS department operates the production server. The development server would run on your own PC—the same machine where you run FrontPage Explorer and FrontPage Editor.

- You create Web pages in an office or campus having a permanent network connection. In this case, your development server and your production server might be one and the same, running on your PC. Alternatively, either or both could be located on systems operated by your MIS department or network support staff.

By default, Setup will install Microsoft Personal Web Server on Windows 95 or its successors at the same time it installs FrontPage. If you're running Windows NT Workstation, Microsoft Peer Web Services are required. These personal Web servers are quite suitable for doing FrontPage development, though both have limitations that interfere with high-volume production use. Microsoft's Internet Information Server, which runs on the Windows NT Server operating system, is a better choice for production environments.

You should definitely have the FrontPage Server Extensions installed on your development server, and preferably on your production server as well. FrontPage Setup installs the server extensions automatically when it installs a personal Web server or finds one already installed. If your proposed development server is administered by someone else and they don't want to install the extensions, consider running a personal Web server.

If your production server doesn't have the server extensions, publishing your Web won't be quite as smooth, and FrontPage services that run at browse time—like Search, Save Results, and Database Access—won't be available. This may present a crisis or not, depending on your requirements.

If both your development and production Web servers are provided by someone else—such as an Internet service provider, network administrator, or support staff—there's no need to install a personal Web server on your PC. Instead, contact your provider for instructions and network settings.

If you're working remotely or, like the author, are cursed to *be* the network administrator, skip ahead to Chapter 16, "Choosing and Configuring Your Web Server." This explains in more detail how to choose the proper Web server for your platform and how to coordinate installation of the Web server, the FrontPage Server Extensions, and the FrontPage client.

Initializing a FrontPage Web

From one perspective, a FrontPage Web is any collection of HTML pages and support files that FrontPage administers as a unit. From another, each FrontPage Web occupies a first-level folder in a Web server's HTTP root location. A FrontPage Web named "sample" and created on the Web server *www.interlacken.com* would have URLs that begin *http://www.interlacken.com/sample/*.

Here's the procedure to create a new FrontPage Web.

1 Start FrontPage.

2 When the Getting Started dialog box appears, choose the option Create A New FrontPage Web and click OK. Figure 5-1, on the next page, illustrates this dialog box.

 TIP

If FrontPage is already running, skip steps 1 and 2. Instead, choose New from FrontPage Explorer's File menu and select FrontPage Web.

III

Building Your Site

FIGURE 5-1.
Start creating a Front-Page Web by choosing Create a New Front-Page Web in the Getting Started dialog box.

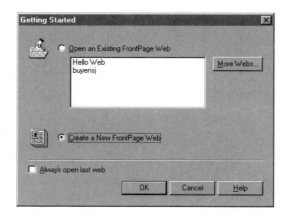

CAUTION

Import An Existing Web won't convert a folder in the Root Web into a normal Front-Page Web. For that procedure, see "Initializing a New Web from a Folder in the Root Web," page 160.

3 The dialog box in Figure 5-2 will next appear.

a To create a nearly blank Web containing only a simple home page, choose One Page Web.

b To create a new Web initialized with existing content, choose Import An Existing Web.

c To create a new Web with pages from a FrontPage wizard or template, choose From Wizard Or Template and select a type of Web from the list.

d Give your Web a friendly, descriptive name—a name in words.

FIGURE 5-2.
Here you specify the initial content and location of a new FrontPage Web.

e Verify the Web location suggested just above the Change button. FrontPage will propose a location such as *http://<computer>/<folder>* that will form the basis for URLs within the new Web.

To locate the Web on a different computer or folder, click the Change button to display this dialog box:

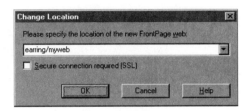

You can overtype the computer name, the folder name, or both, but the two must remain separated by a slash. You can name the Web anything that's valid as a folder name on the target Web server, but the following restrictions will minimize later problems.

- Use only lowercase letters or numbers.

- Don't use any spaces or special characters.

- Create a name that's meaningful, but no longer than 8 or 10 characters.

TIP

You should choose a Web name, folder names, and filenames for your Web that are valid on any server that will host it. This is one reason to avoid special characters, spaces, and uppercase when choosing these names.

f Click OK.

4 At this point FrontPage will begin building your Web, and might prompt you for the Root Web administrator name and password. Figure 5-3, on the following page, illustrates this dialog box.

Root Web (shown on screen with brackets, as in "<Root Web>" is the first Web on any FrontPage server; it gets created when you install the FrontPage Server Extensions. All other Webs on that server reside within the Root Web, so the Root Web's administrator account is required to create them. If you installed your own copy of FrontPage Personal Web Server or Microsoft Personal Web Server, you would have chosen your Root Web administrator name and password during the installation.

If FrontPage doesn't prompt for Root Web account information, it means your credentials are already established. Microsoft Internet Information Server and Microsoft Peer Web Server, for example, won't prompt for a Root Web password if you're already logged onto the Windows NT system as an administrator.

FIGURE 5-3.
To create a FrontPage Web on a given server, you'll need the server's Root Web administrator name and password.

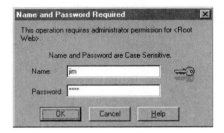

5 If you chose to import an existing Web or use a wizard, Front-Page will now prompt you for additional input. Figure 5-4, for example, shows one screen from the Corporate Presence Web Wizard. Answer the questions to the best of your ability but don't agonize; you can always delete the new Web and start over. In fact, you *should* expect to delete the new Web and start over several times until you get the results you want.

FIGURE 5-4.
This is a prompt from the Corporate Presence Web Wizard. Your answers will determine the initial content of the new Web.

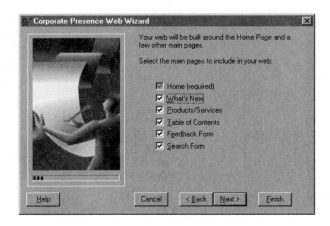

6 When FrontPage finishes building the new Web, it displays it in FrontPage Explorer, as shown in Figure 5-5.

 NOTE

When creating a new Web on a given server, FrontPage uses that server's default page name as the filename of the new Web's home page.

FIGURE 5-5.
FrontPage Explorer will display a new Front-Page Web like this.

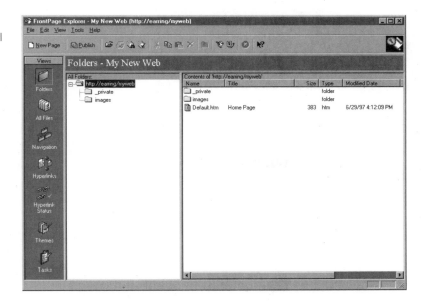

Choosing One Page Web in step 3 created a site with one blank Web page. Choosing other options will produce the results listed in Table 5-1.

TABLE 5-1. New FrontPage Web Templates and Wizards

Template or Wizard	Description
Corporate Presence Wizard	A comprehensive Internet presence for your organization
Customer Support Web	A Web for providing customer support services
Discussion Web Wizard	A discussion group with threads, a table of contents, and full-text searching

(continued)

III

Building Your Site

TABLE 5-1. *continued*

Template or Wizard	Description
Empty Web	A Web with nothing in it
Personal Web	A personal Web, with pages for your interests, photos, and favorite web sites.
Project Web	A Web for a project team; it includes a list of members, status, schedule, archive, and discussions

Creating a Project Web, for example, produces the 25 generic Web pages listed in Figure 5-6. The Web's name is baseball. Figure 5-7 shows two unmodified pages from the baseball project Web: the Home page and the Discussions page.

FIGURE 5-6.
All these pages result from choosing the Project Web template.

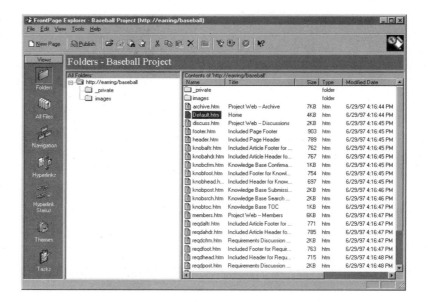

The difference between wizards and templates lies in their degree of automation. While a template is relatively static and preformatted, a wizard prompts you for local information and then custom-builds your site accordingly. The Corporate Presence Wizard, for example, displays 15 pages of prompts that affect the resulting site. While detailed discussion of these wizard prompts is beyond the scope of this book, the

FIGURE 5-7.
These are the Home and Discussions pages in a new FrontPage Project Web.

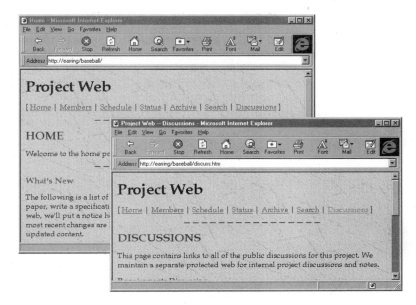

prompts are fairly obvious and there's on-screen Help for each. The Corporate Presence Wizard prompts you for information such as company name, company address, color scheme, and background. It also presents lists of pages you can choose to generate or not.

- Note in Figure 5-8, on the following page, that the Corporate Presence Wizard has created Site Parameters for changeable information and Task list items reminding you to finish the generated pages.

- Figure 5-9, on the next page, shows the FrontPage Editor displaying the Corporate Presence home page that Explorer generated; note the boilerplate text suggesting information you should enter under each heading. This Web's appearance resulted from specifying the Value Added theme while running the wizard, but themes can be changed at will from Themes view in FrontPage Explorer.

- Figure 5-10, on page 155, shows the Navigation view of the Corporate Presence Web. The wizard prompted the user for the number of press releases, products, and services. The Feedback, Contents, and Search page aren't actually part of the hierarchy; they're peers at the Web's top level and, by virtue of a navigation bar included in a shared border, have links available from every page in the Web.

? SEE ALSO
For information on the following topics, refer to the applicable sections. "Templates," page 196; "Themes," page 197; "Navigation Bars," page 202; "Site Parameters," page 205; and "Include Page Components," page 208.

III

Building Your Site

FIGURE 5-8.

The FrontPage Corporate Presence Wizard built this Web.

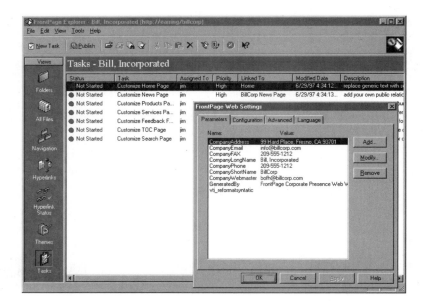

FIGURE 5-9.

FrontPage Editor is ready to modify the default Corporate Presence home page. Boilerplate text suggests typical content.

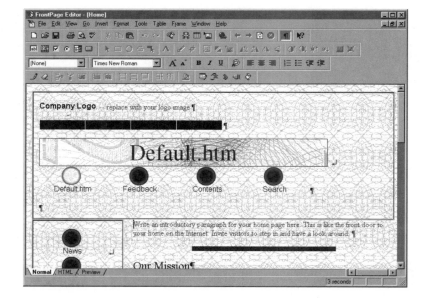

FrontPage's wizards for creating a new Web can produce so many unique variations that describing them all is impossible. The best advice is simply to try them and judge the results for yourself. Create, decide, delete, and re-create until you have the starting point you want, and then begin your own modifications.

FIGURE 5-10.
This is the Navigation view of a Corporate Presence Web.

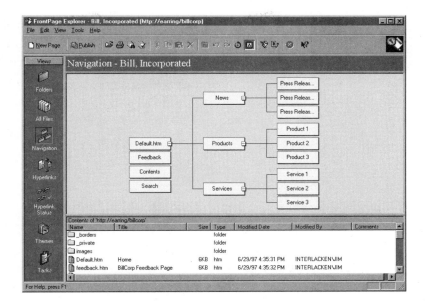

Importing an Existing Web

⊗ CAUTION
The Import command on FrontPage Explorer's File menu doesn't create a new Web; its purpose is adding files to an existing Web. To create a new Front-Page Web from an existing Web, follow the instructions on the next several pages.

Creating new FrontPage Webs is relatively straightforward, but converting an existing Web site to FrontPage is perhaps a more common task. This is especially true for new FrontPage users, who frequently have an existing body of work. FrontPage 98 provides an Import Wizard that builds a new FrontPage Web from existing content; its ease of use, however, depends greatly on how the existing pages are organized.

The following sections will describe three scenarios for initializing a new Web with existing content.

1 Initializing a new Web with files from a file system folder

2 Initializing a new Web from another Web server

3 Initializing a New Web from a folder in the Root Web

Initializing a New Web from a File System Folder

Having FrontPage create a blank or standardized Web provides a good start for new projects, but converting existing Web sites to FrontPage is

? SEE ALSO

To learn about adding individual files to a FrontPage Web, see "Importing Web Pages," page 214.

equally important, especially for new users and clients. FrontPage therefore provides an option, called Import An Existing Web, that creates new Webs from existing file system folders and existing sites.

The Import An Existing Web option appears on the New FrontPage Web dialog box shown in Figure 5-2, on page 148. To initialize a new Web with existing content from disk:

1 Choose Create A New FrontPage Web on the FrontPage startup page, or choose New from the File menu and then choose FrontPage Web.

2 Choose Import An Existing Web from the New FrontPage Web dialog box, specify a title, and then adjust the default server and folder location, if necessary.

3 Click OK.

4 FrontPage will prompt you for Web server and FrontPage Web names, and then might ask for the user name and password of that server's FrontPage Root Web. This follows the pattern described earlier for creating a new Web.

5 FrontPage displays the Import Web Wizard dialog box shown in Figure 5-11, asking you for the location of your existing Web files. Because this procedure assumes that you're importing files from a local computer or network, choose the first option (From A Source Directory...).

   a Specify the file location by typing it in the Location text box or by using the Browse button.

   b To import files in the specified source folder only, leave the Include Subfolders box blank. To import all folders contained within the source folder, turn on the box.

6 The wizard next displays the Edit File List dialog box shown in Figure 5-12. Here you can exclude any files from the existing Web that aren't necessary for the new FrontPage Web. After making your selections, click the Next button.

7 Click the Finish button on the final dialog box.

FIGURE 5-11.
FrontPage can popu-
late a new Web with
files from a local disk
location or from a
remote Web site.

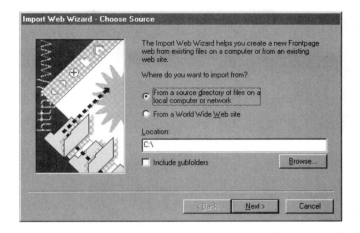

FIGURE 5-12.
You can choose which
files are imported into
your new FrontPage
Web.

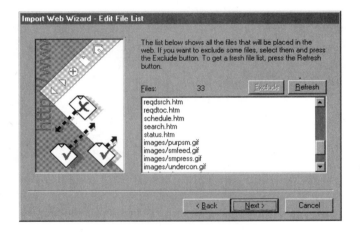

When the import process completes, you'll have a new FrontPage Web
that contains all your former pages. You might also have a mess.
Unless you've been extraordinarily meticulous in the past, you'll probably discover many cases of inconsistent filenames, missing page titles,
and files not residing in the most logical location. Repairing these problems is the subject of the next main section in this chapter, "Planning
and Managing Folders," page 171.

III

Building Your Site

Initializing a New Web from Another Web Server

The best way to copy a Web from one server to another is by using the Publish FrontPage Web command. This requires that both servers have the FrontPage Server Extensions installed. If they do:

1 Open the existing FrontPage Web in FrontPage Explorer.

2 Choose Publish FrontPage Web from the File menu.

3 Specify the Destination Web Server and the FrontPage Web.

4 Click OK.

If the server hosting the source Web doesn't have the FrontPage Server Extensions, proceed as follows:

1 Create a New FrontPage Web from the FrontPage startup page, or choose New from FrontPage Explorer's File menu and select FrontPage Web.

2 Choose Import An Existing Web, specify a title, and adjust the default server and folder location if necessary.

3 Click OK.

4 FrontPage will prompt you for the target Web server and Front-Page Web names, and then might ask you for the user name and password of the target server's FrontPage Root Web.

5 When FrontPage displays the Choose Source dialog box shown in Figure 5-11, on the previous page, choose From A World Wide Web Site.

6 The dialog box changes to that shown in Figure 5-13.

   a In the Location text box, specify the URL of the site's home page.

   b Turn on the check box titled Secure Connection Required (SSL) if the source Web server requires a secure connection.

7 Click the Next button.

FIGURE 5-13.
FrontPage presents this dialog box for populating a new Web with files from a remote Web site.

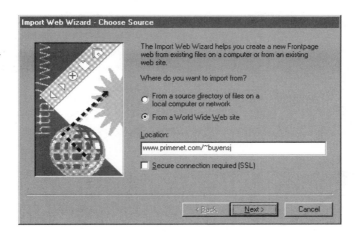

8 The Choose Download Amount dialog box shown in Figure 5-14 optionally limits the amount of material added to the new Web.

a To limit the depth of retrieval, turn on the check box titled Limit To This Page Plus and specify the maximum number of levels between an imported page and the home page. Specifying 1, for example, means FrontPage will import the home page and any files referenced on it. Specifying 2 means FrontPage will import the home page, any files referenced on it, plus any files referenced on those pages.

FIGURE 5-14.
FrontPage provides three ways to avoid excessive downloading when importing an existing Web site.

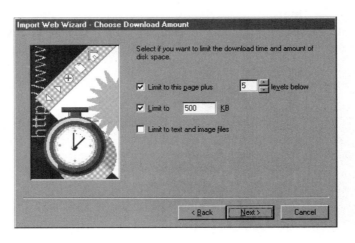

III

Building Your Site

When determining which Web files to download, FrontPage ignores hyperlinks and other references external to the requested site. That is, FrontPage imports files only from the requested site, and not from other sites it may refer to.

b To limit the number of bytes downloaded, turn on the Limit To check box and specify the maximum number of kilobytes.

c To download text and image files only, turn on the box titled Limit To Text And Image Files. This imports Web pages and graphics, but skips content such as ZIP files and executables.

9 Click the Next button and then click the Finish button on the final dialog box.

Initializing a New Web from a Folder in the Root Web

Installing the FrontPage Server Extensions on an existing Web server creates only one Web: the Root Web. If the server supports multiple groups or customers, it's usually best to create a separate FrontPage Web for each one.

In many cases, the existing files owned by each authoring group will be located in a first-level Root Web folder. Creating such a folder for each user is a common way to organize Web servers. If the files targeted for a particular new Web aren't in a first-level Root Web folder, you'll need to move them. Suppose, for example, you have the following folders on your Web server.

    finance/acctpay

    finance/acctrecv

    finance/costacct

    finance/payroll

Converting the finance folder to a FrontPage Web called finance would be easy, but perhaps each of the four departments wants its own Web.

FrontPage doesn't support hierarchies of Webs, so you can't set up four departmental Webs inside an overall Finance Web. Instead, you'll need to move acctpay, acctrecv, costacct, and payroll—making them first-level folders—and then convert each folder using the procedure described below.

If possible, you should move all required content folders to the first level of the Root Web before converting any of them into FrontPage Webs. As long as all such folders remain in the Root Web, FrontPage will automatically adjust hyperlinks among their Web pages. On the downside, processing FrontPage Webs containing thousands of Web pages can be quite time-consuming. The more folders you convert to Webs, the faster Root Web operations will be.

Once you've positioned the existing content, proceed as follows.

1   Start FrontPage and select Create A New FrontPage Web, or choose New from the File menu, and then choose FrontPage Web.

2   Choose From Wizard Or Template, and then select Empty Web from the list.

3   Choose and enter a title for the new Web.

4   Verify that the server name and folder displayed just below the Web title are the server where the Root Web resides and the folder where the existing content resides. If not, click the Change button and correct them.

5   Click OK. FrontPage will transform the Root Web folder into a new FrontPage Web, retaining all prior contents.

SEE ALSO
Before deleting a Web, see "Deleting a Front-Page Web," page 163.

6   If you're not satisfied with the results, *don't* delete the FrontPage Web without backing it up first! FrontPage preserves existing content when it creates a new FrontPage Web, but deleting a Web deletes the contents as well.

Like all updates in place, the above procedure is quick, convenient, and unforgiving. Always ensure that you have a good backup before proceeding.

III

Building Your Site

The following procedure will also define a FrontPage Web in place.

1 Copy the existing folder to another location.

2 Delete the existing folder using FrontPage Explorer.

3 Import the copied content by choosing the New command on the File menu and selecting FrontPage Web.

Unfortunately, FrontPage Explorer erases hyperlinks to pages it deletes; so deleting and reimporting a folder will remove links from outside that folder.

Examining the structures in Figure 5-15 may clarify the import process and the options you have. This figure shows two views of the same file area: one in FrontPage Explorer and one in Windows 95 Explorer.

FIGURE 5-15.
The FrontPage Root Web contains only those files and folders that aren't part of any other FrontPage Web and aren't part of FrontPage itself.

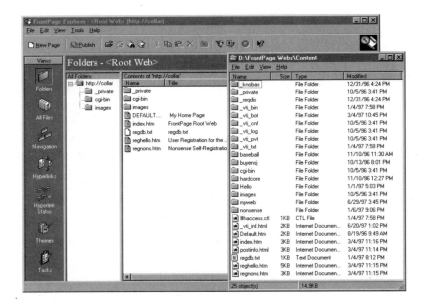

The FrontPage view excludes _knobas, _reqdis, and six _vti folders because these belong to the FrontPage Server Extensions. It also excludes the folders baseball, hardcore, hello, myweb, and nonsense; these folders contain other FrontPage Webs and thus aren't part of the Root Web. The files #hacess.ctl, _vti_inf.html, and postinfo.html don't appear as part of the Root Web because they are FrontPage system files.

> **FrontPage and the File System**
>
> Within the Root Web, FrontPage maintains information not only about the Root Web itself, but also about each normal FrontPage Web. In addition, each normal Web maintains indexes and other information about itself. You should be extremely cautious about moving, renaming, or otherwise updating file areas under control of FrontPage.
>
> Once you make a folder a FrontPage Web, you should use FrontPage for making changes whenever possible. If you add, change, or delete any content files without going through FrontPage, be sure to later open the Web with FrontPage and choose Recalculate Hyperlinks from FrontPage Explorer's Tools menu.
>
> Never use Windows Explorer or any other programs to update FrontPage systems files or folders. This might create situations that are very difficult to recover from.

Deleting a FrontPage Web

To delete a FrontPage Web

1 Open the Web in FrontPage Explorer.

2 Choose Delete FrontPage Web from the File menu.

3 Click Yes on the resulting Confirm Delete dialog box.

⚠ WARNING

> Deleting a FrontPage Web deletes absolutely everything it contains—Web pages, images, text files, FrontPage system files, and all folders. If you want to save the Web pages, images, and other content, back them up before deleting the FrontPage Web.

Configuring Your FrontPage Web

Before starting to work on your Web, you may wish to review the FrontPage options that control your work environment.

Reviewing FrontPage Settings

The Options command on Explorer's Tools menu controls how FrontPage works on your computer. The three tabs on the Options dialog box are General, Proxies, and Configure Editor. Figure 5-16, Figure 5-17, and Figure 5-18 (page 166) display each of these.

FIGURE 5-16.
The General tab of the Options dialog box.

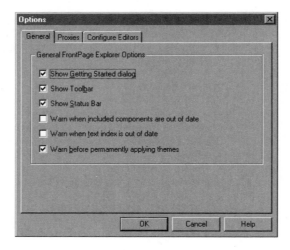

The General tab contains the following options, which you can set by turning each box on or off:

- **Show Getting Started Dialog.** If this option is turned on, starting FrontPage will display the Getting Started dialog box shown in Figure 5-1, on page 148. If the option is turned off, starting Front-Page will open the most recently used Web and display it in FrontPage Explorer.

- **Show Toolbar.** FrontPage will display the Explorer toolbar if this option is turned on.

- **Show Status Bar.** FrontPage will display a status bar only if this option is turned on. The status bar displays informational messages at the bottom of the window.

- **Warn When Included FrontPage Components Are Out Of Date.** If this option is turned on, FrontPage Explorer will inform you if any included components are out-of-date. If an out-of-date condition occurs, use the Recalculate Hyperlinks command from the Tools menu of FrontPage Explorer.

- **Warn When Text Index Is Out Of Date.** If this option is turned on and you open a Web whose text index is out-of-date, FrontPage will notify you and ask whether to recalculate the index.

- **Warn Before Permanently Applying Themes.** With this option turned on, FrontPage will display an *Are You Sure?* dialog box before permanently applying a theme to a site. Note that applying a theme overwrites existing formatting in your Web pages, with no possibility of Undo.

FIGURE 5-17.

The Proxies tab of the Options dialog box.

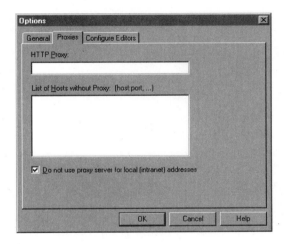

The Proxies tab contains three settings:

- **HTTP Proxy.** If your network is connected to the Internet (or some other network) through a proxy firewall, enter the firewall's DNS name in this text box.

- **List Of Hosts Without Proxy.** To avoid using the HTTP proxy specified above for accessing certain hosts, enter their names here.

- **Do Not Use Proxy Server For Local (Intranet) Addresses.** Check this box if you don't want FrontPage to use the proxy server for requests that are obviously local in origin.

NOTE

A proxy firewall receives HTTP requests from client computers on a local network, satisfies the requests using an outside network, and then sends the responses back to the client computer. This allows *inside* computers to access *outside* resources, but prevents *outside* computers from accessing *inside* resources. Consult your network administrator to determine what settings are required at your site.

TIP

If your copy of Internet Explorer needs proxy information to access outside sites, you should enter the same information here.

The Configure Editors tab lists file types and the editors associated with them. Double-clicking a file or using the Open command from the Edit menu in FrontPage Explorer will invoke the editor specified in this list, according to the extension of the filename you click. Use the Add, Modify, and Remove buttons to configure your favorite editors.

FIGURE 5-18.
The Configure Editors tab of the Options dialog box.

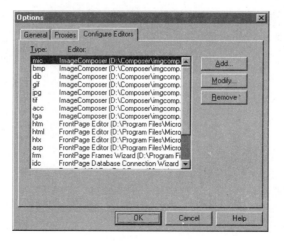

Reviewing Web Settings

The Web Settings command on the Tools menu of FrontPage Explorer governs settings for the current FrontPage Web. There are four tabs on the Web Settings dialog box: Parameters (Figure 5-19), Configuration

(Figure 5-20, page 168), Advanced (Figure 5-21, page 168), and Language (Figure 5-22, page 169).

The Parameters tab displays a list of Web parameters or variables and their current values. After defining these variables once here, you can use them in any number of Web pages by choosing Substitution from the FrontPage Component command of FrontPage Editor's Insert menu.

- **Add.** To define an additional variable, click the Add button, enter the desired name and value, and then click OK.

- **Modify.** To change the value of a variable, first select it in the list, and then click the Modify button. When the prompt appears, make your edits and then press OK.

- **Remove.** To remove a variable, select it and then click the Remove button.

FIGURE 5-19.
You can define any number of variables from the Parameters tab in FrontPage Explorer's Web Settings dialog box.

The Configuration tab contains two text boxes:

- **Web Name.** This entry specifies the name of the current Web. To rename the Web, you must be an administrator of the server's Root Web.

- **Web Title.** Here you can enter a more descriptive, textual name for the Web.

III

Building Your Site

FIGURE 5-20.
The Configuration tab of the Web Settings dialog box specifies the Web's name and title and provides additional server information.

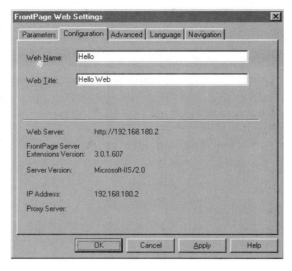

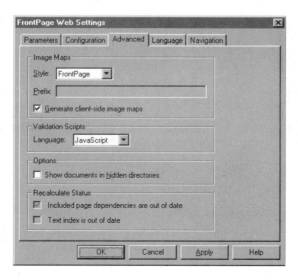

> **NOTE**
>
> The Configuration tab also displays the Web server's URL, the version number of the FrontPage extensions on that server, the name and version of the Web server itself, and the name (if any) of the proxy server in use.

FIGURE 5-21.
The Advanced tab of the Web Settings dialog box contains settings for such advanced items as image maps and validation scripts.

The Advanced tab contains areas for setting four advanced Web features:

SEE ALSO

For more information on how image maps work, refer to "Hypertext Links," page 67.

- **Image Maps.** If you want to use server-side image maps, you must find out what type your server supports and enter it in the Style box. Choose <None> if you don't want FrontPage to generate server-side image maps.

  - If you specify a server-side image map style of CERN, NCSA, or Netscape, specify the relative URL of the server-side handler in the Prefix text box. The handler is the program on the server that processes image map requests.

  - Select **Generate Client-Side Image Maps** if you want FrontPage to generate client-side image maps in the HTML. Client-side image maps operate on the browser, avoiding server-side complications, but some older browsers don't support them. If you specify both client-side and server-side image maps, client-side mapping will be used whenever the user's browser supports it.

- **Validation Scripts.** When FrontPage generates code to validate form input at the browser, it will use the programming language specified in the Language box. As of version 3, both Microsoft Internet Explorer and Netscape Navigator supported JavaScript, but only Internet Explorer supported VBScript. If you choose <None>, FrontPage won't generate any browser-side validation code.

- **Options.** If you turn on **Show Documents In Hidden Directories,** FrontPage Explorer will display files in hidden folders. Such folders contain system information and have names beginning with an underscore. To view accumulated discussion group files while in FrontPage, you must select this option.

- **Recalculate Status.** These two check boxes inform you if any pages in your Web have an outdated Include component **(Included Page Dependencies Are Out Of Date)** or if the Web's index is out-of-date **(Text Index Is Out Of Date)**.

The Language tab contains two boxes for setting language defaults for your Web:

- **Default Web Language.** This setting controls the language used for sending error messages from the FrontPage Server Extensions to the Web browser. Match this setting to your audience.

- **Default HTML Encoding.** FrontPage will use the character set specified here for all new Web pages it creates.

 TIP

> To override the default HTML Encoding setting for individual pages and use a different character set, open each page in FrontPage Editor and choose Page Properties from the File menu , and then edit the HTML Encoding settings on the Language tab.

Understanding Web Pages and Language Encoding

Because the Web is world-wide, it must accommodate the character set of every written language on Earth. Yet, because the Web is bandwidth-constrained, it uses single-byte character sets.

A single-byte character set provides only 256 different codes, which isn't nearly enough to represent all the characters in all the languages on Earth. As a result, each language uses the 256 codes in its own way. To display a Web page properly, a browser must know what character set its author intended. The following HTML, for example, indicates the US/Western European character set.

```
<meta http-equiv="Content-Type" content="text/html; ↵
    charset=iso-8859-1">
```

The Default HTML Encoding setting in FrontPage Explorer specifies the character set FrontPage will assign to new pages created in the current Web. You can also modify HTML Encoding for individual pages by using the Language tab of the Page Properties dialog in FrontPage Editor. The setting for most Western languages is US/Western European.

Specifying an HTML Encoding causes some browsers to display the resulting Web pages twice, as if they notice the charset= parameter on the first pass and then apply it on a second. To avoid this behavior, specify HTML Encoding = <none>. Specifying <none>, however, implies complete trust that the default character set on the remote user's browser will display your page correctly.

FIGURE 5-22.
The Language tab of the Web Settings dialog box controls whether server error messages will appear in English or another available language, as well as the default character set for saving pages.

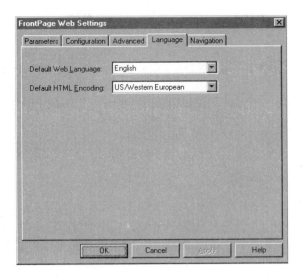

The final tab, Navigation, helps customize the appearance of navigation bars and is discussed in "Navigation Bars," page 202.

Planning and Managing Folders

Other than the hidden folders used by FrontPage, there are no requirements and no limits on the number of folders your Web can use. Most sites use folders to segregate and categorize their content, but the extent of such use is a matter of judgment and preference.

When a FrontPage wizard or template creates a site, it normally places all HTML files in the root folder of the current Web and all images in an /images folder. There are several good reasons for having an /images folder.

1   At most sites, HTML files require more structure and management than image files. Keeping all the images in one folder reduces clutter and makes it easier to manage folders of Web pages.

2   Many images are stock items used on several pages. Keeping all images in one folder makes it easy to locate and use stock images when creating new Web pages.

3   Most browsers cache Web files to eliminate unnecessary downloads. If you store the same image in two different folders,

III

Building Your Site

however, the browser has no way of knowing the two images are identical and it downloads them *both*. Keeping all images in one folder eliminates duplicate downloads.

It's often a good idea to put all pages for a given topic in one folder, and to name the topic's home page with the server's default page name. Subtopics can then be nested in subordinate folders to form a topical tree. This keeps individual folders small enough to be reviewed at a glance and also provides a navigational aid for users. When users see a URL like

```
http://www.wizards.com/products/magic/wands.htm
```

they expect that shortening it to

```
http://www.wizards.com/products/magic/
```

will bring up a Magic Products home page, and that shortening this further to

```
http://www.wizards.com/products/
```

will produce a Products home page.

This isn't to say that every page—or even every menu page—should reside in its own folder. This is poor practice. It's also poor practice, however, to locate all pages in a large site in a single folder. The organization you choose depends on the structure of your content, but there *should* be organization of some kind.

Folder names are again a matter of preference, but long dual-case names containing special characters usually create more problems than clarity.

- Users do sometimes type URLs by hand—perhaps copying them out of magazines—and long names are simply hard to type. Folder names are limited to 32 characters on Unix Web servers, and to 8 on Windows 3.1 systems.

- Dual-case names create confusion because some systems (particularly Unix) are case-sensitive and others (such as Windows) are not. To Unix, /Potions and /potions are two completely different folders: as different as /potions and /notions. To a Windows Web server, however, /Potions and /potions mean the same thing. Always using lowercase avoids such confusion.

- Many special characters, even though acceptable as folder names, require special encoding when used in URLs. The coding consists of a percent sign followed by the hexadecimal value of the character's ASCII code. If you create a folder name containing a space, for example, you'll have to represent the space as %20 in all URLs—ungainly and hard to fathom.

Viewing and Organizing a FrontPage Web

FrontPage Explorer is the focal point for managing the files and folders that make up your Web site. In addition to showing you which files and folders exist, the Explorer shows hyperlink relationships and automatically updates them when you move, rename, or delete files. FrontPage Explorer also invokes editors for each type of file in your Web.

FrontPage Explorer is the entry point for managing your Web. From here you can create new Webs, delete old ones, import and export individual files, manage the Task list, and control global Web settings and options.

? SEE ALSO

For information about the following Front-Page commands on the Tools menu, refer to Chapter 14, "Keeping Your Site Up-to-Date": Recalculate Hyperlinks; Verify Hyperlinks; Spelling; Find; Replace.

The Explorer provides seven views of the currently open Web:

- **Folders.** Displays a tabular list of files in the Web organized by folder.

- **All Files.** Displays a tabular list of all files in a Web, regardless of folder.

- **Navigation.** Graphically displays the logical hierarchy of a Web.

- **Hyperlinks.** Graphically displays files in a Web, organized by hyperlink reference.

- **Hyperlink Status.** Displays the validity of all hyperlinks in a Web.

- **Themes.** Previews the appearance of all available themes and provides controls for applying them to the current Web.

- **Tasks.** Displays a list of reminders to complete or correct pages.

? SEE ALSO

For information on managing FrontPage security, refer to Chapter 15, "The FrontPage Security Model."

To select a particular view, click its icon in FrontPage Explorer's Views column or choose the View menu and select the view by name.

III

Building Your Site

Table 5-2 shows the toolbar buttons that appear in the different views within FrontPage Explorer and briefly describes their function. All the toolbar icons except Up One Level and Stop have equivalent menu commands. Most buttons appear in all Explorer views, but some appear only in the view for which they are relevant.

TABLE 5-2. The FrontPage Explorer Toolbar

Icon	Visible	Description	Function	Menu Command
New Page	Always	Create New Page	Creates a new, blank page in the current folder	File New Page
Publish	Always	Publish a Web	Copies the current Web to another Web or server	File Publish FrontPage Web
	Always	Open FrontPage Web	Loads an existing FrontPage Web into Explorer	File Open FrontPage Web
	Always	Print Navigation View	Prints the Navigation view	File Print Navigation View
	Always	Cross File Find	Searches multiple pages for a specified string	Tools Find
	Always	Cross File Spelling	Checks multiple pages for correct spelling	Tools Spelling
	Always	Cut	Copies the current selection to the Clipboard and mark s it for deletion	Edit Cut
	Always	Copy	Copies the current selection to the Clipboard	Edit Copy
	Always	Paste	Inserts the current Clipboard contents at the selection	Edit Paste
	Always	Delete	Deletes the current selection	Edit Delete
	Always	Show FrontPage Editor	Starts the FrontPage Editor	Tools Show FrontPage Editor

(continued)

TABLE 5-2. *continued*

Icon	Visible	Description	Function	Menu Command
	Always	Show Image Editor	Starts Microsoft Image Composer	Tools Show Image Editor
	Always	Stop	Interrupts operations in progress on the current Web—loading, checking, saving, and so forth	none
	Always	Help	Changes mouse pointer to Help pointer; clicking on any item then invokes help	Help Microsoft FrontPage Help
	Folders view	Up One Level	Displays the parent of the current folder	none
	Navigation view	Undo	Reverses the prior editing action	Edit Undo
	Navigation view	Redo	Cancels the effect of the previous undo action	Edit Redo
	Navigation view	Rotate	Toggles between horizontal and vertical Navigation view	View Rotate
	Navigation view	Size to Fit	Sizes the entire Web structure to fit in the current window	View Size to Fit
	Hyperlinks view	Hyperlinks to Images	Displays or hides hyperlinks to image files	View Hyperlinks to Images
	Hyperlinks view	Repeated Hyperlinks	Displays or hides multiple hyperlinks from one page to another	View Repeated Hyperlinks
	Hyperlinks view	Hyperlinks Inside Page	Displays or hides hyperlinks within the same page	View Hyperlinks Inside Page
	Hyperlink Status view	Verify Hyperlinks	Verifies external hyperlinks by attempting to connect with each one	Tools Verify Hyperlinks

The following sections explain each view and give examples of its use.

Working with Folders View

FrontPage Explorer provides Folders view, shown in Figure 5-23, on the next page, as a means to view or manage the physical arrangement of files and folders that make up your Web. It also displays properties such as file date and file size.

Folders view bears an obvious resemblance to Windows Explorer. As in Windows Explorer

- You can move and copy files by dragging and dropping.

- Right-clicking a file or folder brings up a context-sensitive menu.

- You can sort the listing in the right pane by clicking the column heading you want to sort by.

- Common keystroke conventions apply, such as using the F2 key to rename a file or the Delete key to delete a file.

- Double-clicking a file opens it, using the appropriate editor.

To change the view to another folder, single-click it in the left pane or double-click it in the right pane. If a folder is several levels deep, open each level sequentially. To create a new folder, first select its parent folder. Continue by choosing New from the File menu, selecting Folder, and then changing the folder's name from New Folder to whatever you desire.

FIGURE 5-23.
FrontPage Explorer Folders view displays the physical location of pages in a site.

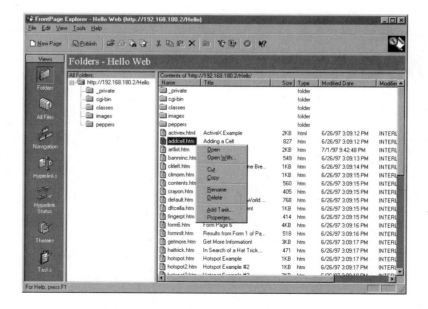

You can drag files and folders in either direction between Windows Explorer and FrontPage Explorer. Dragging a file or folder into FrontPage imports it into the current Web; dragging it into Windows Explorer creates a Windows shortcut. As usual, using the right mouse button for dragging into, out of, or within FrontPage Explorer results in a context-sensitive menu when the button is released. Figure 5-24 illustrates this.

FIGURE 5-24.
Dragging and dropping with the right mouse button opens a context-sensitive menu. Here, a file is right-dragged from Windows Explorer and dropped into FrontPage Explorer.

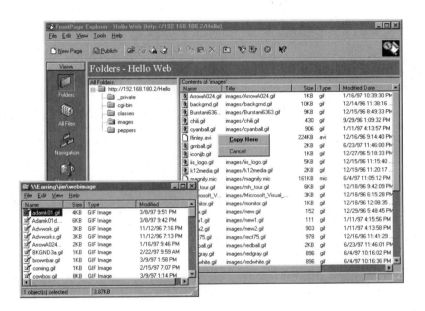

The Copy, Cut, Paste, Delete, and Rename commands on FrontPage Explorer's Edit menu work much as in Windows Explorer.

- **Copy** picks up selected files and folders with the intention of duplicating them elsewhere.

- **Cut** picks up selected files and folders with the intention of moving them elsewhere.

- **Paste** deposits the copied or cut items, presumably in another location.

- **Delete** erases any currently selected file or folders.

- **Rename** opens file and folder names to editing.

CAUTION

FrontPage can't automatically correct outside references to files within your Web. First, this would require searching the entire Internet. Second, even if FrontPage *could* locate such references, you probably wouldn't have authority to update them. You can minimize this problem by organizing related Web pages into the same Web.

Whenever you move or rename files in FrontPage Explorer, FrontPage will automatically correct all hyperlinks, image tags, and other references in the same FrontPage Web. Suppose, for example, that 23 pages in your Web use an image called cyanball.gif. For some reason, you decide to rename the file from cyanball.gif to cyandot.gif, and do so in FrontPage Explorer. FrontPage will update all 23 pages so that they reference cyandot.gif rather than cyanball.gif. FrontPage will also warn you before deleting a file used by other files in your Web.

FrontPage Explorer's Import command on the File menu adds an external file to the current FrontPage Web folder. If the FrontPage Web isn't on the local machine, the Import command will copy the file across the network. The Import command also updates FrontPage with appropriate file information, an operation that wouldn't occur if you simply copied the file to the Web's physical location by some other method.

The Export command on the File menu copies a file from the FrontPage Web to the local file system. This is no great feat if the Web is located on the local file system, yet it can be extremely useful for retrieving Web pages stored on remote systems.

SEE ALSO

For more information on using FrontPage Editor, see Chapter 6, "Getting Started with Web Pages."

Referring again to Figure 5-23, on page 176, note the Title column in the right pane. For Web pages, FrontPage obtains this automatically from the HTML itself. To update the title of a Web page, you must

1 Open the Web page with FrontPage Editor. (Double-click the filename, or right-click it and select Open, or select the filename and then choose Open from the Edit menu.)

2 Open FrontPage Editor's File menu.

3 Select Page Properties.

4 Choose the General tab.

5 Update the Title field.

6 Click OK.

7 Save the file.

To update the title of a non-HTML file, right-click it, choose Properties from the shortcut menu, choose the General tab, update the Title field, and click OK. Figure 5-25 illustrates this. You can bring up the same dialog box by right-clicking the file and choosing Properties from the Edit menu.

FIGURE 5-25.
For file types other than HTML, use the Properties command to update the file's title.

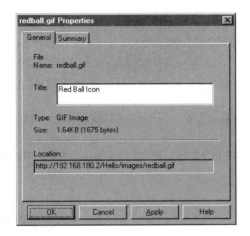

Working with All Files View

In terms of both appearance and operation, All Files view is very similar to Folders view. The primary differences are the following:

- All Files view is organized by filename only and not, as in Folders view, by filename within folder. In All Files view, the folder name is treated as descriptive data only.

- In All Files view you can't change the folder in which any file resides. You can rename files, but they remain in their original folder location. Likewise, you can't create folders in All Files view.

- Any files you create with the New Page command or that you import by dragging from Windows Explorer will reside in the Web's top-level folder.

- All Files view displays an Orphan column that indicates, for each file, whether any other pages in the same FrontPage Web have hyperlinks to it.

Figure 5-26, on the following page, illustrates All Files view.

III

Building Your Site

FIGURE 5-26.

All Files view provides a single, alphabetical list of all files in a Front-Page Web, regardless of folder.

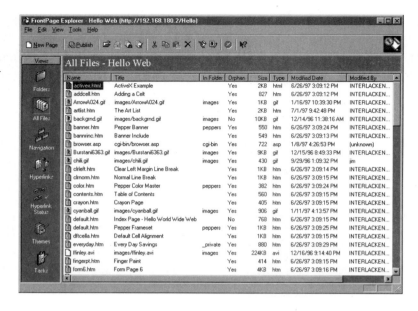

Working with Navigation View

Designers of most FrontPage Webs organize their pages in a logical hierarchy. The home page occupies the top position and presents several menu choices, each a Web page at the second level of the hierarchy. Pages at the second tier have child pages at the third, and so forth. As seen in Figure 5-27, Navigation view provides a way to record and organize this structure.

? SEE ALSO

To learn about navigation bars, see "Navigation Bars," page 202.

Using Navigation view has several advantages over other methods of drawing a site's logical structure.

- Navigation view, being electronic, is easier to revise than paper drawings.

- Integration with FrontPage means you can maintain content and structure seamlessly, using the same program.

- If you also use the Navigation Bar component of FrontPage Editor, FrontPage will automatically update the menus in your Web pages as you rearrange the view in FrontPage Explorer.

The first page you create in a FrontPage Web will become the top page in your Navigation view hierarchy. Its filename will be your Web

FIGURE 5-27.
Navigation view provides a way to record the logical structure of your Web.

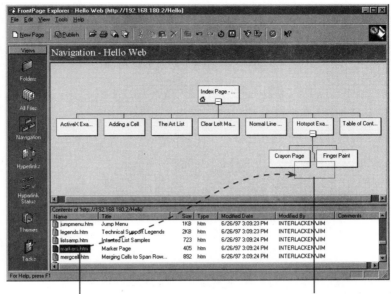

Add a file to the Navigation view by dragging it from here…

…and dropping it when it shows the position in the hierarchy that you want.

server's default page name, most often default.htm or index.htm. This is automatic for any new Web that FrontPage 98 creates. If FrontPage can't identify the home page, it might display the following message in the main Navigation view window.

```
To create a Home Page, click New Page on the toolbar.
```

If the Web doesn't contain a home page, the solution is simple: Click the New Page button on the toolbar and FrontPage will create one for you.

If the Web *does* contain a home page, try returning to Folders view and choosing Recalculate Hyperlinks from the Tools menu. Then, return to Navigation view. If a home page still doesn't appear, follow these steps:

1 Rename the existing home page file.

2 Create a new home page file by clicking New Page on the toolbar.

3 Open both pages in FrontPage Editor.

4 Copy the entire contents of the old home page file.

5 Paste the contents into the new home page file.

6 Close both files, saving the new home page file.

7 Return to Navigation view and test for proper operation.

8 Test the new home page file, using a Web browser.

9 Delete the old, renamed file.

? SEE ALSO

For information about creating redirection pages, see the sidebar "Taking Advantage of HTTP System Variables," page 230.

Confusion may result if your authoring and production Web servers have different default page names. For example, you might create Webs using a personal Web server whose default page name is default.htm, but publish them on a Unix Web server whose default page name is index.html. In such a case, create two home pages, one with each name, and redirect one to the other.

Once Navigation view displays a home page, adding child pages is easy. Simply drag them from the files list at the bottom of the window and drop them under the appropriate parent in the main window. As you drag files near prospective parents, FrontPage draws shaded lines suggesting a relationship. When the shaded line connects to the right parent, release the mouse button. If FrontPage won't draw shaded lines to a page you drag from the files list, it's because that file already appears in the hierarchy. Each page in a Web can appear in the hierarchy only once.

Orphan pages are perfectly valid in Navigation view. If your Web has pages that don't fall within the hierarchy—pages like Search, Send Mail, and Contact Webmaster—you can drag them to the left and right of the home page, and they'll remain there without links. You can then create navigation bars in FrontPage Editor that list all pages at the top level.

Unfortunately, there's no facility for adding pages outside the current Web to Navigation view. If you require this, consider adding a dummy page that contains a redirection to the desired page.

To create a new page and immediately define it as the child of another, right-click the parent page and then choose New Page from the pop-up menu. This is very handy when designing the initial structure of a Web. The new pages you create this way may not be immediately listed in the lower pane, but when the screen is updated by switching to another view, editing a page in FrontPage Editor, or closing the Web, the pages will be saved with filenames and titles similar to their Navigation view names.

Once the file appears in the lower pane you can select it and change its filename. However, if you want to change its title, you'll have to open it in FrontPage Editor and use the Page Properties command. To open the file from Navigation view, double-click its icon in the upper pane.

You may find it easier to create new pages from the bottom pane of Navigation view. First, click the New Page toolbar icon with anything in the lower pane highlighted, or right-click the lower pane and select New Page. Then rename the new page and drag it into position above.

 TIP

> To view the filename of a page displayed in Navigation view, right-click its icon and then choose Properties from the pop-up menu.

Rearranging pages is even simpler than adding them. In the main window, click the page you wish to move, hold down the mouse button while dragging, and then release it under the desired parent.

When you first add an existing page to Navigation view, FrontPage assigns a Navigation view name the same as the page's title. In many cases, however, you'll want to shorten the Navigation view name. Page titles—assigned in FrontPage Editor from the General tab of the Page Properties command—are the strings that search engines and browsers use to identify the page. You'll probably want page titles to be fully descriptive of each page, and possibly to contain your company or site name as well. The Navigation view name, by contrast, frequently becomes the menu text displayed in navigation bars, and you'll likely want to keep this short.

Changing the Navigation view name of a Web page is quite simple.

1   Highlight the page's icon by clicking it in the main Navigation view window.

2   Choose Rename from the Edit menu, press the F2 key, or click the name.

 TIP

> In place of steps 1 and 2, you can also right-click the page's icon and then choose Rename from the pop-up menu.

III

Building Your Site

3 Type or revise the page's Navigation view name.

4 Press Enter or click anywhere outside the Navigation view name text box.

To delete a page from Navigation view, do *one* of the following:

- Select the page and then choose Delete from the Edit menu.

- Select the page and press the Delete key.

- Right-click the page and choose Delete from the pop-up menu.

CAUTION

Deleting a file from the files list beneath the main window always removes it completely from the Web. You can't undo this action.

Following any of these actions, FrontPage will display a dialog box asking whether you want to remove the page just from Navigation view or to remove it completely from the Web. Make your choice and click OK.

To print a copy of the Navigation view structure, choose Print Navigation View from the File menu. To preview the printed appearance, choose Print Preview.

TIP

As the size of your structure grows, you might find it convenient to hide the parts you aren't working on. To hide the children of any page, click the minus icon on its lower edge. The children will disappear, but the icon will change to a plus. To display the children again, click the plus icon.

The View menu contains three commands to customize the appearance of Navigation view. These commands don't change any of the file relationships:

- **Expand All.** Enlarges the view so that all pages in the structure are displayed. This has the same effect as clicking all the plus icons to show all the child pages.

- **Rotate.** Toggles Navigation view between top-to-bottom and left-to-right display mode.

- **Size To Fit.** Toggles the size of the structure chart between normal view and a view that fits all visible pages into the main Navigation view window.

Working with Hyperlinks View

Hyperlinks view, illustrated in Figure 5-28, provides an excellent picture of the hyperlink relationships among pages. It can be quite useful for working with complex or unfamiliar sites.

FIGURE 5-28.
FrontPage Explorer's
Hyperlinks view charts
the hyperlink relation-
ships among the
pages in a site.

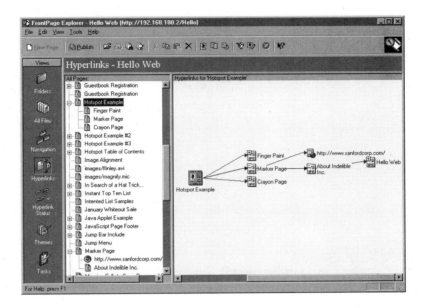

Hyperlinks view consists of two panes. The left pane displays the titles of all pages in the Web, regardless of folder, and the right pane displays a chart of hyperlinks to and from a so-called *center page*. You can specify the center page by double-clicking it in the left pane or by right-clicking a page in the right pane and choosing Move To Center on the pop-up menu.

Whenever FrontPage displays a new center page, it also displays

- All pages in the current Web with hyperlinks to the center page. These appear to the left of the center page, connected with arrows showing the direction of the link.

- All hyperlinks from the center page to any other page. These appear to the right of the center page, again connected by arrows.

Any page flagged with a plus icon has additional hyperlinks not displayed; this is true in both the left and right panes, and for pages

III

Building Your Site

pointing to and from the center page. Clicking the plus icon displays the additional links and changes the icon to a minus. Clicking a minus icon collapses the link display and changes the icon to a plus.

Hyperlinks view identifies items by their titles, not by their folder and filenames. You can view the complete path and filename of items in either pane by right-clicking an item and choosing Properties from the pop-up menu. To see the filename of any item in the right pane, rest the mouse pointer over it; FrontPage will briefly describe the type of item and display its name:

```
Internal Hyperlink: indelinc.htm
```

By default, Hyperlinks view displays only hyperlinks from one Web page to another, disregarding duplicates. To toggle display of additional items, use these commands on the View menu or their toolbar equivalents.

- **Hyperlinks To Images.** Activating this option adds image files to the Hyperlinks view display. Designating an image as the center of Hyperlinks view displays all pages using that image.

- **Repeated Hyperlinks.** Normally, if a page contains several links to the same target, Hyperlinks view displays only one of them. Activating this option shows all links, even duplicate ones.

- **Hyperlinks Inside Page.** Many Web pages contain hyperlinks to internal bookmarks, typically so that clicking a menu choice scrolls the browser to a particular spot within a page. Hyperlinks view normally doesn't display such links, but with this option activated it will.

Right-clicking a page in either pane produces a pop-up menu such as the following. Some choices might be dimmed or omitted, depending on the context.

- **Move To Center** designates the selected file as the center page in the right pane. This option doesn't appear for pages in the left pane, or when the selected page already occupies the center position.

- **Open** starts the appropriate program to edit the selected page or file. Double-clicking the item accomplishes the same thing, as does choosing Open from the Edit menu. This option and the next are dimmed for links to pages located outside the current Web.

- **Open With** presents a choice of command editors you can use to edit the selected file. The Open With command on the Edit menu is equivalent.

- **Verify Hyperlink** validates a file or hyperlink outside the current Web by attempting to retrieve it. This option is dimmed for locations inside the current Web because, in that case, FrontPage has other means of verification.

- **Delete** removes a page or file from the current Web. The Delete command on the Edit menu is equivalent.

- **Add Task** opens the New Task dialog box, where you can enter a Task that refers to the selected page.

- **Properties** displays information about the selected file, such as its title and filename. You can also enter summary information about the page that might help you plan or maintain your Web.

New users are frequently enamored of Hyperlinks view, especially if they have existing Webs. They can use this view to analyze the Web pages they've been tediously building and maintaining by hand, producing attractive diagrams as a result. This can be heady stuff, but most users find Folders view and Navigation view more valuable for day-to-day work. Still, hyperlink analysis remains much like milk: We never completely outgrow our need for it.

Working with Hyperlink Status View

Broken hyperlinks are living proof that, left to itself, the universe *does* revert to random bits. Even if nothing within your Web changes during a certain interval, hyperlinks outside your site are sure to change and require correction. Hyperlink Status view therefore provides a way to check and correct all the hyperlinks within your Web.

Figure 5-29 pictures a typical Hyperlink Status display. Links among pages in your own Web normally won't appear unless they're broken. To display all internal hyperlinks, choose the Show All Hyperlinks command either from the View menu or from the pop-up menu that appears if you right-click a blank area in the main Hyperlink Status window.

FIGURE 5-29.
Hyperlink Status view displays the last known status of all hyperlinks in a Web. To reduce clutter, valid internal links normally don't appear.

FrontPage uses internal indexes for verifying hyperlinks among pages in the same Web. If you suspect these indexes might be out-of-date, you can refresh them by choosing Recalculate Hyperlinks from the Tools menu. The number one cause of corrupt indexes is changing a Web through means other than FrontPage.

To verify hyperlinks outside your Web, FrontPage tries connecting to them. Therefore, make sure your connection to the Internet is working before you start the process. Once connected, choose Verify Hyperlinks from the Tools menu, right-click a blank area of the main window and choose Verify Hyperlinks, or click the Verify Hyperlinks toolbar button.

Verifying a long list of hyperlinks can take a long time, especially if your Internet connection is slow or you have many bad links. Bad links usually show up as timeouts, and a lot of timeouts can consume a lot of time. (You might want to make a sandwich here or visit your relatives in Madagascar.)

When Verify Hyperlinks ends, the good links will be flagged green and the broken ones flagged red. Right-clicking a failed link produces this pop-up menu.

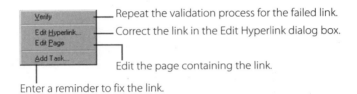

— Repeat the validation process for the failed link.
— Correct the link in the Edit Hyperlink dialog box.

Edit the page containing the link.

Enter a reminder to fix the link.

Figure 5-30 illustrates the dialog box for editing a hyperlink.

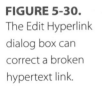

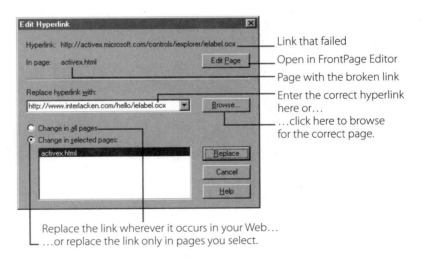

Link that failed
Open in FrontPage Editor
Page with the broken link
Enter the correct hyperlink here or...
...click here to browse for the correct page.

Replace the link wherever it occurs in your Web...
...or replace the link only in pages you select.

Working with Themes

FrontPage themes impart an attractive and consistent appearance to all the pages in a Web. Pages controlled by a theme surrender considerable flexibility in formatting options but gain cohesion and uniformity in return.

III

Building Your Site

⊗ CAUTION

Once you apply a theme, there's no Undo command that restores your Web to its prior appearance. Removing a theme returns pages to their default. Always back up your Web first or work from a copy.

FrontPage 98 provides a selection of good-looking, professionally designed themes you can use without further licensing or royalties. To modify or create themes requires utilities provided in the FrontPage Software Development Kit. Distributing themes requires installing them on each FrontPage editing machine. You can't modify or create themes within FrontPage, nor does FrontPage include features to distribute new or modified themes via the Web.

Figure 5-31 shows the Themes view in FrontPage Explorer. This view is the focal point for applying and removing themes at the Web level.

FIGURE 5-31.
The Themes view in FrontPage Explorer imparts a consistent, predesigned appearance to all pages in a Web.

1 Scroll through the list of themes.

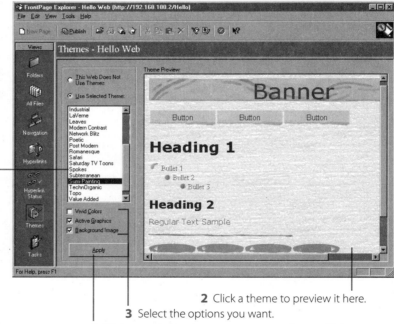

2 Click a theme to preview it here.

3 Select the options you want.

4 Click to apply the theme to every page in your Web.

The three check boxes below the list of themes have these effects:

■ **Vivid Colors.** Some themes provide two sets of colors: one muted and one vivid. Turning on this box selects and previews the vivid set.

■ **Active Graphics.** If a theme contains animated graphics, turning on this box will activate them. Tread carefully here; the novelty of flashing lights can wear off quickly.

- **Background Image.** This option determines whether a background image will be used. Most themes substitute a solid background color if this option is turned off.

After applying a theme and opening a Web page, you may be surprised to find it less elaborate than the preview. This happens because the preview includes page banners, navigation bars, hover buttons, dividers, and other FrontPage components your pages don't contain. Alas, there's no solution but to edit each page and insert the desired elements. FrontPage can't guess which text you intended to be the heading, for example, when you originally created each page.

To apply themes selectively to pages in a Web, you must apply them individually from FrontPage Editor. You can apply a theme to any page anytime, regardless of whether themes are in effect for the entire Web. Open the relevant page in FrontPage Editor and choose Theme from the Format menu. The Choose Theme dialog box provides these options:

- **This Page Does Not Use Themes.** This option removes any themes in effect for the current page and isolates the page from any future themes applied at the Web level.

- **Use Theme From Current Web.** Choosing this option links the current page to the theme in effect for its Web. In addition, the page will conform to any theme changes made in FrontPage Explorer—that is, at the Web level.

- **Use Selected Theme.** This option applies a selected theme to the current page and ignores any future changes made at the Web level.

Using the Task List

Developing and maintaining your site involves a multitude of small, interrelated tasks. Changes made to one page require updates on another. New pages require links from others. Errors in spelling, missing images, and hyperlinks to nowhere require follow-up and correction. In short, you need a task list.

As shown in Figure 5-32, on the following page, FrontPage provides an automated, highly integrated Task list. The FrontPage Task list provides several advantages over stand-alone follow-up systems.

III

Building Your Site

FIGURE 5-32.
The FrontPage Task
list helps you remem-
ber unfinished tasks
in a highly inte-
grated way.

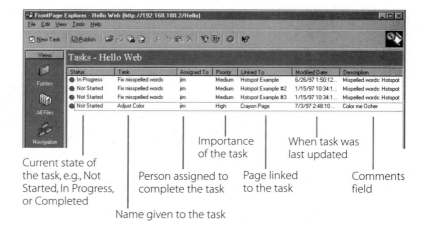

Current state of
the task, e.g., Not
Started, In Progress,
or Completed

Name given to the task

Person assigned to
complete the task

Importance
of the task

Page linked
to the task

When task was
last updated

Comments
field

■ FrontPage can add many tasks for you, automatically. These include

- Pages that contain spelling errors

- Pages with missing links

- New pages that need detail filled in

■ From the Task list, FrontPage can directly open pages associated
with each task.

■ When you open pages from the Task list and then save them,
FrontPage Editor will ask if those changes complete the task and,
if they do, FrontPage closes the item.

The Task list column headings are straightforward, as described in
Figure 5-32. Clicking any column heading sorts the list on that column.

FrontPage provides a variety of convenient ways to create tasks. You
can create tasks manually from Tasks view:

1 Click the New Task toolbar button, or right-click any blank area in
the main Tasks view window and choose New Task from the pop-
up menu, or choose New from the File menu and choose Task.

2 The New Task dialog box shown in Figure 5-33 appears.

FIGURE 5-33.
Use this dialog box to
create new tasks.

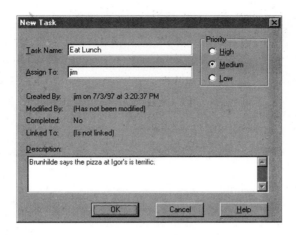

3   Enter a title in the Task Name box.

4   Select High, Medium, or Low Priority.

5   Verify the Assign To person.

6   Optionally, enter a comment in the Description box.

7   Click OK.

Note in Figure 5-33 that the Linked To field indicates no link. Creating a task directly from Tasks view has this effect. To manually create a task linked to a specific page, do *either* of the following:

■   Locate the page in another view, right-click it, and then choose Add Task from the pop-up menu. (To create a task linked to a hyperlink, create it from Hyperlinks view.)

■   Open the page in FrontPage Editor and choose Add Task from the Edit menu.

The following FrontPage options also create Task list items:

■   In FrontPage Explorer, choose Spelling from the Tools menu and then review the Spelling dialog box in Figure 5-34, on the next page. If you check Add A Task For Each Page With Misspellings, FrontPage will create a task for each page containing so much as a single misspelled word.

III

Building Your Site

FIGURE 5-34.
Explorer's Spelling function can add pages with misspelled words to the Task list.

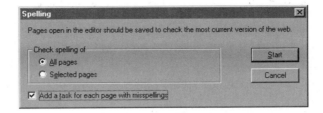

- When FrontPage Editor creates a new page, it can either open the page immediately or create a blank page and a task reminding you to edit the page later. Figure 5-35 shows how a user might create a hyperlink to a new page.

FIGURE 5-35.
FrontPage Editor uses the New dialog box to create new Web pages. The option Just Add Web Task adds an entry to the Task list rather than opening the new page.

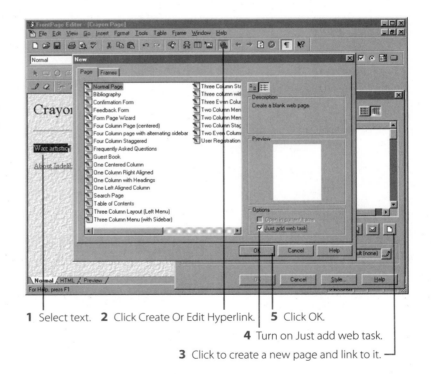

1 Select text.   **2** Click Create Or Edit Hyperlink.   **5** Click OK.

4 Turn on Just add web task.

3 Click to create a new page and link to it.

Right-clicking a task in Tasks view displays the pop-up menu shown below. These commands work as follows:

- **Edit Task** displays the Task Details dialog box, which is similar to the New Task dialog box shown in Figure 5-33, on page 193. Here you can modify the properties of a task. You can display the same dialog box by double-clicking the task you want to edit or by choosing Open from the Edit menu.

- **Do Task** opens the file with the appropriate editor, such as Front-Page Editor for an HTML page.

- **Mark Complete** changes the status of the task to Completed.

- **Delete** removes a task from the list after you confirm your choice. Pressing the Delete key accomplishes the same result.

Whenever you open a page using the Do Task command and then save it, Front-Page displays the message box shown in Figure 5-36 to ask if your changes satisfy the task's requirements. Clicking Yes indicates that your changes satisfy the task and instructs FrontPage to mark the task completed.

FIGURE 5-36.
This dialog box asks whether your changes to a Web page complete the page's remaining Task list items.

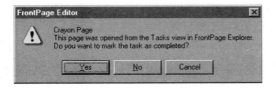

By default, the Task list displays only tasks that are Not Started or In Progress. To display completed tasks as well, choose Task History from the View menu or right-click a blank area in the main Task list window and select Task History from the pop-up menu.

Planning and Managing Reusable Components

This section presents a dilemma of book organization. It discusses a series of techniques you should be fully aware of as you plan and initialize your FrontPage Web—but these facilities exist primarily within the FrontPage Editor. Insofar as they involve planning issues, they belong in the current chapter; inasmuch as they involve FrontPage Editor, they belong in a later chapter.

Because you should consider creating reusable components before you start creating complete Web pages, the topics appear here.

Templates

Creating and using FrontPage templates is both easy and productive. Templates relieve page authors of repetitive tasks when creating new pages. Changing a template doesn't change pages previously created from it. However any variables, Include Page components, or color masters specified on a template will remain as such on created pages and provide global maintainability.

⊗ CAUTION

Templates are stored locally on each user's PC. FrontPage has no built-in features for distributing new or changed templates to a wide audience.

To create a template

1 Use any convenient method to create a Web page having the desired components and features. When in doubt, it's usually better to include optional page features than to omit them. Deleting features you don't need is easier than adding those you do.

2 Choose Save As from the File menu in FrontPage Editor.

3 Click the As Template button on the Save As dialog box—the middle dialog box shown in Figure 5-37.

4 Give the template a title, a filename, and a description, and then click OK on both dialog boxes.

To create a new page using the template

1 Start FrontPage Editor.

2 Choose New from the File menu.

3 When the New dialog box shown in Figure 5-38 appears, choose the desired template on the Page tab and click OK.

FIGURE 5-37.
FrontPage Editor is saving a page as a template named beachtem.

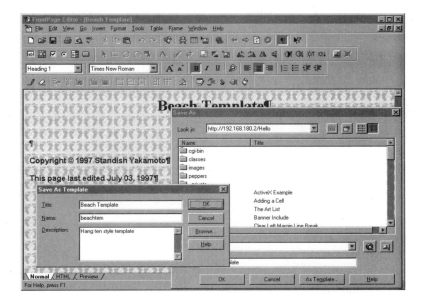

FIGURE 5-38.
FrontPage Editor prompts for a template when creating new Web pages.

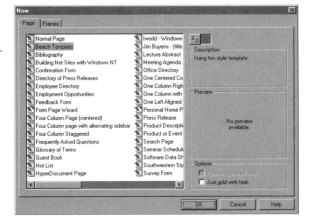

Themes

Earlier sections in this chapter have discussed themes in some detail, yet they're worth thinking about again. Taking maximum advantage of themes requires taking maximum advantage of other FrontPage components as well—components such as hover buttons, navigation bars, and page banners.

III

Building Your Site

The ability of a theme to modify hand-generated content is limited. Themes have much more control over HTML code that FrontPage itself generates: that is, HTML derived from FrontPage components. Planning effective use of themes up front is *much* easier than retrofitting them later.

Color Masters

FrontPage Editor can configure one Web page to use the background image and color scheme of another. If you key the backgrounds and color schemes of many pages off a single *color master* page, you can change those aspects of the whole set in one stroke, simply by updating the master. This is similar to the global style management provided by Microsoft Word's Normal.dot file.

The color master itself is just an ordinary Web page; don't bother looking for a Create Color Master command or option. The color master could be your home page or any other page in your site, but administration will be easiest if you dedicate a simple page to this purpose only.

To create a color master

1 In FrontPage Editor, choose New from the File menu.

2 Choose Normal Page and click OK.

3 Choose Page Properties from the File menu and select the Background tab.

4 Specify the background image, background color, and text colors you want the entire set of pages to have, and then click OK.

⭐ **TIP**

Refer to "Achieving Accurate Rendition—Safe Colors," page 124, for assistance in choosing colors that will display clearly and accurately.

5 Check the appearance of the page. If necessary, insert some text and a hyperlink so that you can see their colors.

6 Choose Save As from the File menu, specify a page title and a filename, and then click OK.

To have another page get its colors from the saved color master

1   Open the page in FrontPage Editor.

2   Choose Page Properties from the File menu and select the Background tab.

3   Choose the option Get Background And Colors From Page.

4   Enter the URL of the color master, or click Browse to select it from the current Web. Figure 5-39 shows browsing in progress.

5   Click OK in the Page Properties dialog box to apply the changes.

FIGURE 5-39.
You can control the appearance of many pages from one source by using the Get Background And Colors From Page option.

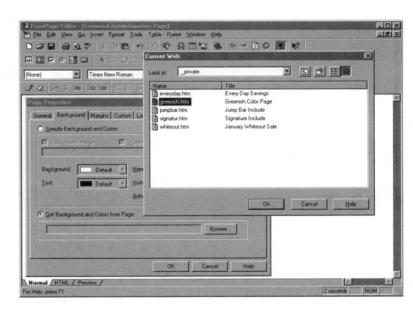

Converting a set of existing pages to use a color master is somewhat tedious the first time—but no more tedious than changing the colors on all the pages by hand. The next color or background change, however, will be a snap.

If you use a color master when you create a template (see "Templates," page 196), all pages created from that template will automatically use that color master as well.

III

Building Your Site

Shared Borders

This section discusses another facility FrontPage provides for stand-ardizing content and appearance across an entire Web. *Shared borders* provide a way to insert standard content at the top, bottom, left, or right edges of pages in the same Web.

As with themes, you can apply shared borders either at the Web level or at the individual page level. To apply borders at the Web level, choose Shared Borders from the Tools menu. The following dialog box results.

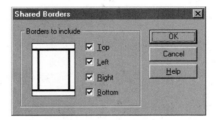

Turn on the check box for each border you want to appear, and then click OK. FrontPage will immediately

- Create a folder called _borders.

- Create Web pages called top.htm, left.htm, right.htm, and bot-tom.htm (or whichever of these you chose to use) within the _borders folder.

- Surround every page in the Web with an HTML table.

- Include the top.htm, left.htm, right.htm, and bottom.htm files within the appropriate borders cells.

Figure 5-40 shows FrontPage displaying a simple page that uses all four shared borders. The visible boundaries around each shared border dis-appear at browse time. You can edit information in the borders, but any changes will affect *every* page in the same Web that uses shared borders. That's the point of shared borders: to show zones of identical content on every page.

FIGURE 5-40.
Shared borders can provide standard content along the edge of any or all pages in a Web. The choice of edges is configurable.

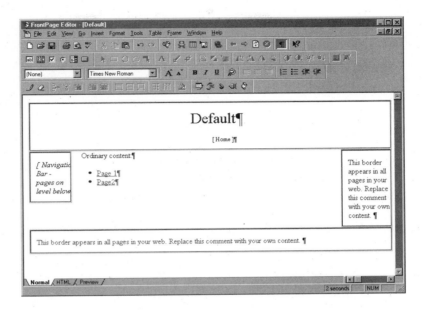

To override a Web's shared border settings for a specific page, open it in FrontPage Editor and choose Shared Borders from the Tools menu. The Page Borders dialog box appears:

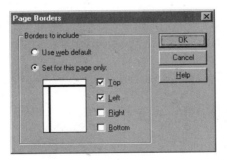

- Select **Use Web Default** to have the page use the default borders settings for the entire Web.

- Select **Set For This Page Only** to have the page use only the borders you specify here. If you clear all four check boxes, the page will use no shared borders.

Note that even when overriding Web settings for shared borders, the only choice is whether a particular shared border appears or not. You can't configure some pages to have different shared border content than others.

Shared borders are best used in conjunction with FrontPage components, such as the navigation bar, page banner, and timestamp, that configure themselves based on the page in which they appear.

Navigation Bars

This feature uses the information in Navigation view to construct menu bars on individual pages, ensuring that the user's view and the Navigation view are always in sync.

At first, navigation bars may seem to work backward. Most Web designers imagine a facility that draws structure charts based on hyperlinks, not a facility that creates hyperlinks from a structure chart. The problem with the first approach is that most Web pages contain too many convenience links. These are outside the Web's primary structure and their presence obscures the true structure of the site.

The first step in implementing navigation bars is to diagram your Web—or at least the main parts of it—in Navigation view. Once this is completed, you can add navigation bars in FrontPage Editor by doing the following:

1 Open a page and place the insertion point where you want the navigation bar to appear.

2 Choose Navigation Bar from the Insert menu.

3 Make your choices in the Navigation Bar Properties dialog box shown in Figure 5-41.

4 Click OK.

Setting Navigation Bar Properties

FrontPage provides the dialog box shown in Figure 5-41 for controlling the content and appearance of navigation bars. The same dialog box applies for both creating new navigation bars and modifying existing ones.

FIGURE 5-41.
This FrontPage Editor dialog box configures the contents of a page's navigation bar. The menu choices will come from the Web's Navigation view structure.

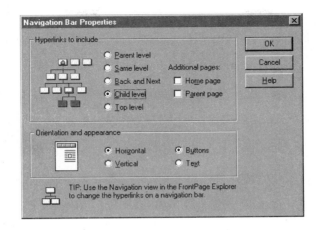

Hyperlinks To Include. You can apply only one of the following five choices to a single navigation bar. However, nothing prevents you from placing several navigation bars on the same page, each configured with different options.

- **Parent Level** specifies that the navigation bar will contain hyperlinks to all pages one level higher than the current page, as positioned in Navigation view.

- **Same Level** specifies that the navigation bar will list all pages at the same level as itself.

- **Back And Next** includes the two pages immediately left and right of the current page, and at the same level.

- **Child Level** includes all pages that have the current page as their parent.

- **Top Level** includes the home page and any others drawn at the same level.

Additional Pages. You can include either or both of the following pages regardless of the choice you made above.

- **Home Page** adds the home page to the navigation bar.

- **Parent Page** adds the parent of the current page.

Operation And Appearance. These options control the appearance of the navigation bar.

- **Horizontal** arranges the choices on the navigation bar as a single line of text.

- **Vertical** arranges the navigation bar choices vertically, with each choice on its own line. You can choose either Horizontal or Vertical, but not both.

- **Buttons** displays the navigation bar choices as graphical buttons.

- **Text** displays the navigation bar choices as text. You can choose Buttons or Text, but not both.

FrontPage labels each option on the navigation bar with the title of the target page as it appears in Navigation view. This provides an incentive to keep the Navigation view names short but descriptive. To change the label appearing on a navigation bar, change the title of the target page in FrontPage Explorer's Navigation view.

The Navigation tab of the Web Settings dialog box, shown in Figure 5-42, contains options for setting the labels displayed for the home, parent, previous, and next pages. The default labels are, respectively, Home, Up, Previous, and Next. To globally apply your own labels, select Web Settings from the Tools menu of FrontPage Explorer, select the Navigation tab, and then type the text you wish to have displayed.

FIGURE 5-42.

The default navigator bar names for the Home, Parent, Previous, and Next pages can be globally customized here.

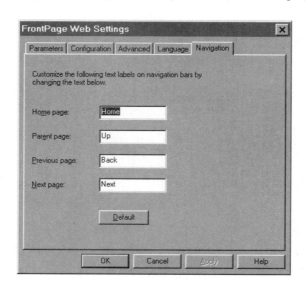

Figure 5-43 illustrates a horizontal text navigation bar. The bar appears between the two horizontal rules.

FIGURE 5-43.
This page includes a horizontal text navigation bar between two horizontal rules.

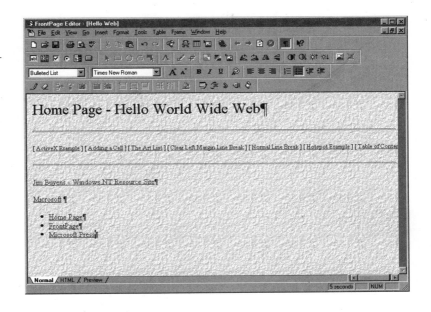

Site Parameters

A previous section, "Reviewing Web Settings" (page 166), described how to use the Parameters tab on the Web Settings dialog box to enter Web variables. Any text that will appear on multiple pages and be subject to occasional change is a candidate to become a variable. The variable names and values are completely at your discretion, but you should make the names easy to remember. Refer back to Figure 5-19, on page 167, for an example of typical variables.

Figure 5-44 and Figure 5-45, on the following page, show how to insert variables using FrontPage Editor.

FIGURE 5-44.
This is the FrontPage Editor dialog box that lets you choose which FrontPage component to insert.

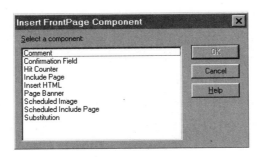

III

Building Your Site

To insert variables

1 Start FrontPage Editor and open a page.

2 Set the insertion marker where you'd like to insert some variable text.

3 Choose FrontPage Component from the Insert menu.

4 When the Insert FrontPage Component dialog box opens, as shown in Figure 5-44 (on the previous page), choose Substitution from the Select A Component list and click OK.

5 When the Substitution Component Properties dialog box appears, as shown in Figure 5-45, choose the variable you want to insert, and then click OK.

FIGURE 5-45.

The Substitution Component Properties dialog box lists all the variables you've defined in Explorer's Web Settings dialog box.

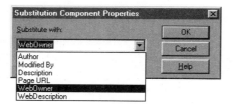

After you click OK in Figure 5-45, FrontPage Editor will insert a marker for the selected variable. If you redefine the variable later from the Parameters tab of the Web Settings dialog box in FrontPage Explorer, FrontPage will update the value displayed on your Web pages every-where the variable appears.

Note the four built-in variables shown in Figure 5-45: Author, Modified By, Description, and Page URL. FrontPage Explorer maintains these values on a page-by-page basis, as shown in Table 5-3. Only the Description field can be edited; it displays any comments entered on the Summary tab of a page's Properties dialog box in FrontPage Explorer. The variables WebOwner and WebDescription are user-defined.

TABLE 5-3. Substitution Variables Maintained by FrontPage

Substitution Name	Explorer Property	Description
Author	Created by	The username of the person who created the page
Modified By	Modified by	The username of the person who most recently modified the page
Description	Comment	Comments entered in a page's Properties dialog box in FrontPage Explorer
Page URL	Location	The location of the page, as seen from a browser

Figure 5-46 shows the result of inserting two site variables in a test page: Description and WebOwner.

■ Description is a system variable maintained by FrontPage. Inserting a system variable displays a placeholder in FrontPage Editor but displays the actual value in Internet Explorer.

■ WebOwner is a user-defined variable. FrontPage displays its value in both FrontPage Editor and Internet Explorer.

FIGURE 5-46.
FrontPage Editor shows system-maintained variables as placeholders, but displays user-defined variables as values. Browsers show the final values in either case.

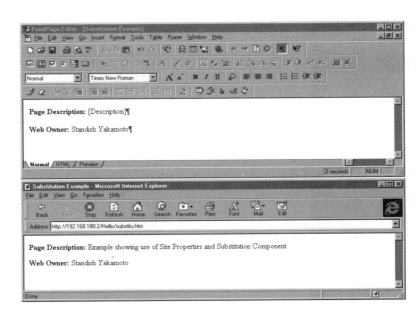

Include Page Components

The FrontPage Include Page component includes one Web page in another. This is a very useful feature for coding repetitive page segments once and using them on many pages. The concept is similar to that of boilerplate text in word processing.

Using Include Page components can improve your site's consistency and speed up initial development, though the real payback comes during ongoing maintenance. Collections of Web pages often contain repeating content such as standard menus, contact lists, and copyright notices that might change from time to time. Without Include Page components, you must locate each page containing a segment and update it by hand. With Include Page components, you only need to update each segment once.

Creating the segment to be included involves no special procedure; simply create a Web page containing only the desired content and save it as a normal file in your Web. To include the segment at any location on another page, do the following:

1 Use FrontPage Editor to Open the page that will contain the segment.

2 Position the cursor at the location where the segment should appear.

3 Choose FrontPage Component from the Insert menu.

4 Select Include Page from the list and click OK.

5 When the Include Page Component Properties dialog box appears, you can type the URL of the page, or you can click Browse and choose it from the current Web. Figure 5-47 shows the Current Web dialog box opened by clicking the Browse button.

6 Click OK after selecting the page you wish to include.

FIGURE 5-47.
The FrontPage Include Component Properties dialog box prompts for the page that should appear within the current Web page.

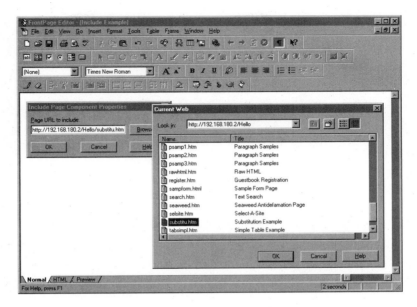

Your segment will now be included in the current page at the insertion marker. In the future, you can update the contents of the segment everywhere by opening its page in FrontPage Editor. When you save the segment, FrontPage will automatically update all pages in your Web that include it.

CHAPTER 6

Getting Started with Web Pages

A t some point the planning and background discussions stop and the actual work begins. In the case of this book, that point is here and now. The previous chapter described how to structure your FrontPage Web. In this chapter, we start filling it with pages.

Developing Web pages is, of course, an iterative process. No Web page is ever really finished; pages on the Web are either under construction or stale and outdated. Your proficiency as an author will no doubt progress as well, not only in content but also in style, appearance, tools, and technique.

This chapter covers the basics of creating, importing, opening, saving, and deleting Web pages, plus the essentials of modifying page-level properties. Subsequent chapters explain the processes of entering and formatting text, inserting images, adding hyperlinks, formatting tables, and so forth.

Creating a New Web Page

❓ SEE ALSO

For information about creating new Front-Page Webs, refer to "Initializing a FrontPage Web," page 147.

Figure 6-1 shows a new, blank FrontPage Web. FrontPage created the single Web page named default.htm and gave it the title Home Page (on some systems the file might be given a different name, such as index.htm). You can add pages to this or any other Web using either FrontPage Explorer or FrontPage Editor.

FIGURE 6-1.

This is a new, blank FrontPage Web ready for development.

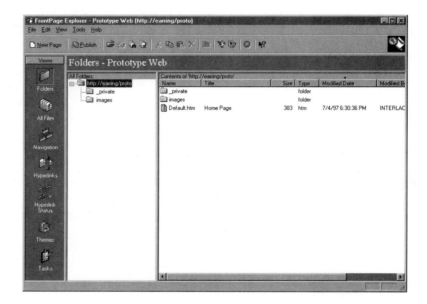

To create a new page in FrontPage Explorer

1 Select Folders view, All Files view, or Navigation view.

2 If using Folders view, select the folder where you want the file to reside.

3 Create the new page by taking *one* of these actions:

- Click the New Page toolbar icon.

- Choose New from the File menu and select Page.

- Press Ctrl+N.

- Right-click any blank area in the main window, and then choose New Page from the pop-up menu.

4 FrontPage will use the Normal template to create a home page and will name it with your server's default filename, usually default.htm or index.htm. If such a file already exists, FrontPage tries to create newpage.htm. If that exists, it tries to create newpage2.htm, and so forth.

5 FrontPage will display the new filename in Edit mode. This is an excellent time to rename it. Remember to give the file a more meaningful title when you open it in FrontPage Editor.

If you don't want the new page in the Web's root folder but you created it in All Files view or Navigation view, switch to Folders view at the next opportunity and move it.

To create a new page in FrontPage Editor

1 Choose New from the File menu. The New dialog box shown in Figure 6-2 appears.

FIGURE 6-2.
The New dialog box in FrontPage Editor initializes a new page.

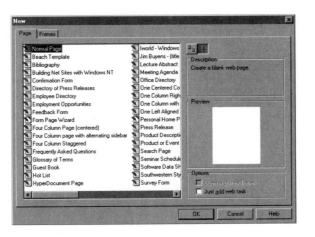

 SEE ALSO
For information about frames, refer to "Creating and Editing Frames," page 338.

2 Choose the Page tab to create a normal Web page.

3 Choose the template or wizard that will create the new page. To change the format of the template list, click one of the two icon buttons near its upper-right corner.

⭐ **TIP**

If you don't know what template or wizard to choose, select Normal Page. This produces a blank page with no special features or attributes.

III

Building Your Site

4 Review the template's description and preview.

5 The Open In Current Frame option will be available only if the active document in FrontPage Editor is a frameset. Ignore this for now.

6 If you want to create a page and edit it later, turn on the Just Add Web Task option. This option displays the new page, prompts you for a filename and title, saves and closes the file, and adds a task to the Task list. If Just Add Web Task is unchecked, Front Page Editor will open the page and let you start editing immediately, naming it when you save and close the file.

7 Click OK to create the new page.

TIP

> If you want to quickly create a blank, Normal page, click the New button on the toolbar.

Importing Web Pages

Adding existing Web pages, images, and other files to a FrontPage Web is a common requirement. FrontPage calls this process *importing* and can perform it at the file or folder level. There are two methods: the menu method and the drag and drop method.

NOTE

> FrontPage Explorer can import pages accessible on a local disk or through Windows file sharing, but it can't import individual pages accessible only via HTTP. To import pages available from an intranet or the World Wide Web, open them in FrontPage Editor and then save them to the current Web.

Importing files with menus is a two-step process. First you must build a list of files to import, and second you must actually import them. To build the list

1 Open the receiving Web with FrontPage Explorer.

2 Select the Web folder you expect to receive the most files.

3 Choose Import from the File menu. This will display the Import File To FrontPage Web dialog box, shown in Figure 6-3.

FIGURE 6-3.
Use this dialog box to build a list of items to import.

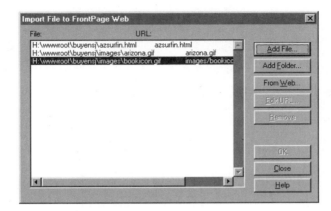

4 Depending on what you wish to import, choose *any* of these:

- To add individual files, click the Add File button. When the Add File To Import List dialog box appears, find the files you want to import and then click Open. FrontPage will add the selected files to the import list shown in Figure 6-3.

- To add all the files in a given folder (and all its subfolders), click the Add Folder button. When the Browse For Folder dialog box opens, locate the desired folder and click OK. FrontPage will add all the files in the selected folder, including subfolders, to the import list.

- To add the files from an intranet or World Wide Web site, click the From Web button. You will be prompted for the URL and will be able to select how many levels of the Web will be imported, limit the total size of pages imported, or choose to limit the import to text and image files.

5 Normally, FrontPage imports all files to the current folder in Front-Page Explorer. To change the destination of an individual file, select the file and click Edit URL. (You won't have this option if you're importing a Web.) When the Edit URL dialog box (shown in Figure 6-4, on the next page) appears, change the displayed destination and click OK.

III

Building Your Site

FIGURE 6-4.
Use the Edit URL dialog box to change the planned destination of an imported Web file.

Imported pages frequently contain incorrect or nonstandard HTML, especially if they were previously maintained by hand. FrontPage might interpret these questionable elements differently than a browser. Keep the original files until you view the imported versions in FrontPage Editor, save them, and review the results with your browser. If more than minor cleanup is needed, you might want to correct the originals and reimport them.

6 To remove a file you've placed on the import list, select it and click the Remove button.

When you're ready to import the files in the list, click OK. To abandon or postpone importing, click the Close button. FrontPage will remember the import list for this session. To import the list later in the same session, choose Import from the File menu.

To import Web files using drag and drop

1 Open the receiving Web with FrontPage Explorer.

2 Use Windows Explorer to locate the files or folders you want to import.

3 Drag the files or folders from Windows Explorer to the desired destination in FrontPage Explorer.

Importing Versus Copying—What's the Difference?

If your FrontPage Web resides on a local disk or file server, copying files into the Web file area with Windows Explorer or the command prompt might seem quicker and easier than importing them with FrontPage. The difference is this: When FrontPage imports a Web file, it copies the file into place and also updates all the necessary FrontPage indexes and cross-reference files. Externally copying the files into place *doesn't* perform the FrontPage updates. To restore a FrontPage Web to consistency after an external process has changed it

1 Open the Web with FrontPage Explorer.

2 Choose Recalculate Hyperlinks from the Tools menu.

Opening a Web Page for Editing

There are many ways to open a Web page for editing in the FrontPage Editor. If you're starting from FrontPage Explorer in Folders view, All Files view, Navigation view, or Hyperlinks view, do *any* of the following:

- Double-click the filename or icon.

- Right-click the filename or icon, and then choose Open from the resulting pop-up menu.

- Select the filename or icon and press Enter, press Ctrl+O, or choose Open from the Edit menu.

- Drag the filename or icon from FrontPage Explorer and drop it on a blank area of the main FrontPage Editor window.

    If a currently open page is maximized, you can click the Restore button to create a blank window area and drag another page to it in order to open more than one page.

CAUTION
You can't open a Web page by dragging it out of FrontPage Explorer and dropping it onto an open Web page in FrontPage Editor. That operation does something else: It modifies the open page by adding a hyperlink to the page you dragged.

If you're starting from Explorer's Hyperlink Status view, right-click the page and choose Edit Page from the pop-up menu.

If you're starting from Explorer's Task view, do *either* of the following:

- Right-click a task referencing the page and choose Do Task from the pop-up menu.

- Select a task referencing the page and choose Do Task from the Edit menu.

If you're starting from Front Page Editor, choose Open from the File menu, press Ctrl+O, or click the Open button on the Standard toolbar. Any one of these methods will display the Open dialog box shown in Figure 6-5, on the next page. From the Open dialog box you can select a Web page in any of the following five ways:

- Use the Look In drop-down list at the top of the dialog box, and then click the desired filename below.

- Click the Web browser button, and then locate the desired page with your browser.

III

Building Your Site

FIGURE 6-5.
Note that Front-Page Editor's Open dialog box opens a URL (a Web address) and not a traditional filename located by drive letter and folder.

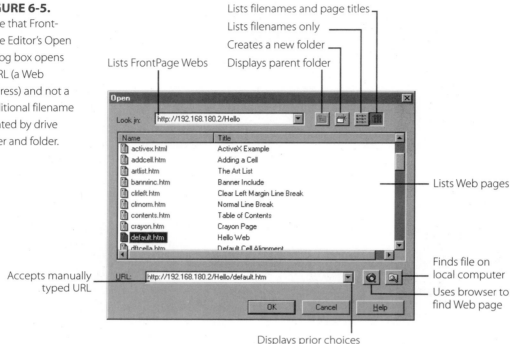

Lists filenames and page titles

Lists filenames only

Creates a new folder

Lists FrontPage Webs   Displays parent folder

Lists Web pages

Accepts manually typed URL

Finds file on local computer

Uses browser to find Web page

Displays prior choices

■ Click the Hyperlink File button to locate the desired file on your computer.

■ Click the drop-down arrow on the URL box, and then select from a list of your past choices.

■ Type or paste the Web address directly into the URL box.

Finally, if a hyperlink to the page you want to open is present on an open Web page, right-click the link and choose Follow Hyperlink from the pop-up menu.

Using the FrontPage Editor Standard Toolbar

In addition to commands for opening and creating Web pages, several other commands can be invoked directly from FrontPage Editor's Standard toolbar, as described in Table 6-1. Use the View menu to display or hide this and any other toolbars.

TABLE 6-1. FrontPage Editor Standard Toolbar

Icon	Description	Function	Menu Command
	New	Creates a new blank page	File New Normal Page
	Open	Opens a page from the current Web or the local file system	File Open
	Save	Saves the current page in HTML format	File Save
	Print	Prints the current page	File Print
	Preview in Browser	Launches a browser and sends it a command to open the current page	File Preview in Browser
	Check Spelling	Checks spelling of words in the current page	Tools Spelling
	Cut	Removes selected items from the page and stores them in the Clipboard	Edit Cut
	Copy	Copies selected items from the page and stores them in the Clipboard	Edit Copy
	Paste	Copies the contents of the Clipboard to the insertion point	Edit Paste
	Undo	Reverses the last change to a page	Edit Undo
	Redo	Reverses the last Undo command	Edit Redo
	Show FrontPage Explorer	Opens FrontPage Explorer and makes it the active window	Tools Show FrontPage Explorer
	Insert FrontPage Component	Opens the Insert FrontPage Component dialog box	Insert FrontPage Component
	Insert Table	Opens the Insert Table dialog box to create a new table	Table Insert Table
	Insert Image	Inserts an image at the insertion point	Insert Image

III

Building Your Site

(continued)

TABLE 6-1. *continued*

Icon	Description	Function	Menu Command
	Create or Edit Hyperlink	Creates or modifies a hyperlink from the currently selected text or image	Edit Hyperlink
	Back	Displays the previously displayed page	Tools Back
	Forward	Reverses the action of the previous Back command	Tools Forward
	Refresh	Reloads the current page from its source; if there are pending changes, FrontPage will prompt whether to save them	View Refresh
	Stop	Stops loading of files accessed via a hyperlink	none
	Show/Hide	Shows or hides hard line returns, bookmarks, and form outlines	View Format Marks
	Help	Displays Help on the next element click	Help Microsoft FrontPage Help

Saving Pages

If you fail to regularly save your files, all your hard work will be for naught. To save an open file in FrontPage Editor, choose the File menu and select Save. If the Web page or any of its components weren't previously saved in the current Web, FrontPage will generate Save As dialog boxes for them.

To save a page using another name, choose Save As from the File menu. The by-now familiar dialog box of Figure 6-6 will appear. Refer to the instruction for Figure 3-1 (page 68) if you need help understanding the controls.

This is essentially the same dialog box used for opening Web pages, with all the same options plus one:

- **Title.** Specify the name of the page in words. Although this is an optional field, for optimal user-friendliness don't omit it. A page's title appears whenever a user browses the page and in many FrontPage contexts.

FIGURE 6-6.
FrontPage Editor's
Save As dialog box.

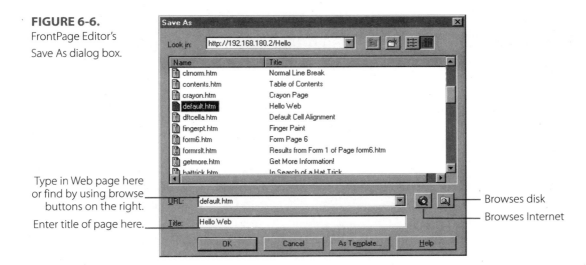

Type in Web page here
or find by using browse
buttons on the right.

Enter title of page here.

Browses disk
Browses Internet

Once you've specified a Web location, either by hand-typing or browsing, click OK. Be prepared to encounter additional security checks or denials when saving to locations outside the current Web or your file system.

 NOTE

You won't find a Save option in FrontPage Explorer, because there's nothing to save there. As you create, edit, and save files in the Editor, Explorer creates any necessary cross-referencing files in the background. Each time you run Explorer and open a Web, it reads those configuration files and assembles the Web from them.

Deleting an Existing Web Page

Along with the pages you create and add to your Web site will be the inevitable failures and the ones that become obsolete over time. There are four ways to delete a page, all involving FrontPage Explorer. You must be in Folders, All Files, Navigation, or Hyperlinks view.

1 Select the filename or icon by single-clicking it, and then press the Delete key.

2 Select the filename or icon, and then choose Delete from the Edit menu.

3 Right-click the filename or icon, and then select Delete from the pop-up menu.

4 Select the filename and click the Delete button on the Standard toolbar.

In each case you will be asked to confirm the deletion before the page is permanently erased.

Specifying Page-Level Attributes

Whether you start from a blank page, an existing page, or a page generated by a template or wizard, you no doubt have further changes in mind. These changes might affect not only content, but also the page's title, color scheme, or other general characteristics. Even for existing files, you may decide this is the time to standardize pages and apply uniform page attributes.

General Page Properties

FrontPage Editor provides the Page Properties dialog box to control the overall appearance of a page. It contains five tabs: General, Background, Margins, Custom, and Language. The General tab is shown in Figure 6-7.

FIGURE 6-7.
The General tab in FrontPage Editor's Page Properties dialog box.

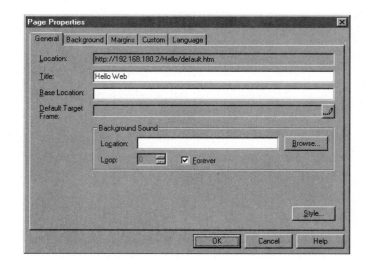

To open the Page Properties dialog box, choose Page Properties from the File menu or right-click anywhere on the FrontPage Editor window and choose Page Properties from the pop-up menu.

The data fields on the Page Properties General tab control the following characteristics. You should always specify a meaningful title, while use of the remaining fields is optional.

- **Location.** This is normally the Uniform Resource Locator of the page: the URL a browser would use to retrieve it. If FrontPage opened the page from a file, a URL beginning with file:// will appear. For new pages not yet saved, the location will be (New Page). You can't edit this field—it's for information only.

- **Title.** This is the name of the page in words. This is an often-overlooked but important attribute; it appears in many FrontPage windows and dialog boxes, as a page description in search results, and in the title bars of your visitors' browsers. Be certain that every page you maintain has a meaningful title suitable for public display.

- **Base Location.** Use of this field is rare; see the sidebar "Relative Addressing and Base URLs," on the next page, for an explanation of its use. You will usually leave this field blank.

SEE ALSO

For information on using frames, see "Creating and Editing Frames," page 338.

- **Default Target Frame.** If you've divided the browser window into frames, this field specifies in which frame, by default, hyperlinks from the current page will appear.

- **Background Sound.** These three fields select and control a sound file that the user's browser will play when it displays your page.

  - **Location.** Enter the name of the sound file. This can be a local file location or a URL. To browse the local file system or current FrontPage Web, click the Browse button.

  - **Loop.** Enter the number of times the specified file should play.

  - **Forever.** Turn on this box to have the sound file play indefinitely. This overrides the Loop setting.

III

Building Your Site

TIP

Avoid specifying large sound files or files in platform-specific formats. In general, MIDI files are the smallest and most widely supported.

? SEE ALSO
For information about cascading style sheets, see "Managing Page-Level Cascading Style Sheets," page 232.

- **Style.** This button opens a dialog box that specifies cascading style sheet information for the body of the current page.

Relative Addressing and Base URLs

Hyperlinks on Web pages needn't reference complete URLs. If a hyperlink doesn't include a host name, a browser uses the host that delivered the current page. If a hyperlink also contains no folder location, the browser uses the same folder as the current page. This is called *relative addressing* because hyperlink locations are relative to the current page unless a full and explicit path is included. Below are two examples.

```
Current Page:    http://www.pfew.com/info/default.htm
Hyperlink:                        /products/toasters.htm
Jump Location:   http://www.pfew.com/products/toasters.htm

Current Page:    http://www.pfew.com/info/default.htm
Hyperlink:                              contact.htm
Jump Location:   http://www.pfew.com/info/contact.htm
```

In general, it's best to use relative addressing wherever possible. This makes it very easy to move groups of pages from one Web server or folder to another. By contrast, specifying complete URLs means updating them whenever you move pages from one computer or Web to another.

Occasionally, you may find it convenient to base relative URLs not on the current page but on some other location. Specifying a base URL accomplishes this as follows.

```
Current Page:    http://www.pfew.com/info/default.htm
Base URL:        http://www.xxxx.com/info/
Hyperlink:                              contact.htm
Jump Location:   http://www.xxxx.com/info/contact.htm
```

Background Page Properties

Figure 6-8 illustrates the Background tab of the Page Properties dialog box. It controls most aspects of the page's overall color scheme.

FIGURE 6-8.
The Background tab of
the Page Properties
dialog box controls a
page's overall color
scheme.

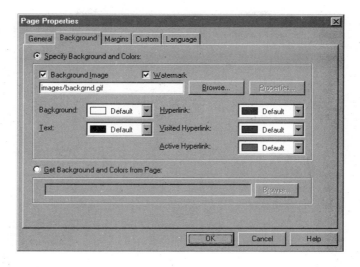

NOTE

The Background tab will be absent on any page controlled by a theme. The
theme takes over these attributes.

TIP

You can also access the Background tab by choosing Background from the
Format menu in FrontPage Editor.

Specify Background And Colors

Checking this option button indicates that you'll specify the color
scheme for this page explicitly, rather than getting the information from
another page. Selecting this option activates the following controls:

- **Background Image.** Turning on this box specifies that the page
  has a background image. The associated text box specifies the
  image file location. Rather than typing the file location, you can
  click the Browse button to locate it quickly.

- **Watermark.** Turning on this box indicates that when the user
  operates the browser's scroll bars, the background image is
  to remain fixed and not scroll with other content on the page.
  This feature is supported by Internet Explorer but might not be
  supported by other browsers. FrontPage itself doesn't exhibit the

> ### Using Background Images in Your Pages
>
> A background image appears behind any other images or text on the page. If the image is smaller than the page, the browser repeats it (called *tiling*) left to right and top to bottom. This allows a small image, which is fast to download, to fill the entire screen.
>
> To keep the background image from repeating left to right, make it wider than any typical computer screen display. A width of 1,200 pixels is usually sufficient. Most image editors have features called Add Margin or Extend Canvas that can widen images this way. Fill the added pixels with your background color, or make them transparent. Repeating pixels of the same color compress very well and add little to file size and download time.
>
> Wide images of this kind are often used to create border designs along the left margin. The design occupies the first 20 or 30 pixels at the left, and the rest of the image is a solid background color or transparent.
>
> Avoid strong colors or patterns in background images. These can easily obscure your text.

watermark behavior; it scrolls the background image even though watermarking is in effect. To see watermarking in action, browse the page with Internet Explorer.

? SEE ALSO

For an explanation of the Image Properties dialog box, refer to "Modifying Image Properties," page 284.

- **Properties.** Clicking this button takes you to a dialog box that displays or alters the properties of the specified background image.

- **Background.** This setting controls the background color of the page. This color appears if there's no background image, if any part of the background image is transparent, of if the browser is ready to start displaying the page before the background image arrives.

- **Text.** This setting controls the color of ordinary text.

- **Hyperlink.** This setting controls the color of hyperlinked text.

- **Visited Hyperlink.** This setting controls the color of hyperlinked text whose target has recently been visited. The text reverts to named hyperlink color when the remote user fails to visit the hyperlink target within the browser's cache timeout setting.

- **Active Hyperlink.** This setting controls the color of hyperlinked text the user has just clicked.

SEE ALSO
For more information
on choosing color
schemes for the Web,
see "Color," page 89.

 SEE ALSO
For more information
on choosing colors
that Web browsers can
display accurately,
review "Achieving
Accurate Rendition—
Safe Colors," page 124.

Choosing Page Colors

The Page Properties dialog box of FrontPage Editor provides color list boxes for
selecting background, text, hyperlink, visited hyperlink, and active hyperlink colors for each page. These color boxes provide 18 choices: Default, the 16 original
VGA colors, and Custom.

As explained in Chapter 4, "Achieving Visual Impact—Graphic Communication," it's usually best to choose colors with RGB components of 0, 51, 102, 153,
204, and 255. Eight of the choices in these color drop-downs comply with this
advice and eight do not, as can be seen in the following table:

Compliant Colors			Noncompliant Colors		
Standard Name	FrontPage Name	RGB Values	Standard Name	FrontPage Name	RGB Values
Black	Black	0-0-0	Gray	Gray	128-128-128
White	White	255-255-255	Light Gray	Silver	192-192-192
Red	Red	255-0-0	Dark Red	Maroon	128-0-0
Green	Lime	0-255-0	Dark Green	Green	0-128-0
Blue	Blue	0-0-255	Dark Blue	Navy	0-0-128
Cyan	Aqua	0-255-255	Dark Cyan	Teal	0-128-128
Magenta	Fuchsia	255-0-255	Dark Magenta	Purple	128-0-128
Yellow	Yellow	255-255-0	Dark Yellow	Olive	128-128-0

Even the eight compliant colors are rather boring: black, white, the three primaries, and their complements. These are wonderful colors and, used properly,
they provide plenty of contrast. However, they're hardly intriguing. You'll produce
more subtle and interesting Web pages by choosing custom colors with RGB
components using combinations of 0, 51, 102, 153, 204, and 255.

Even a short course in color appreciation exceeds the scope of this book.
Nevertheless, here are some quick guidelines:

- Choose complementary colors: earth tones, sky tones, ocean colors, and
  so forth. Colors that appear together in beautiful natural settings are likely
  to look good in other settings as well.

- Coordinate colors with those in any Web page images you plan to use.

- Ensure there's sufficient contrast between the various text colors and the
  background.

- Use dark text on a light background, which is easier to read than light text
  on a dark background.

III

Building Your Site

Choosing Page Colors   *continued*

- Strive for colors that contrast but don't clash.

- Avoid using background images that overpower normal text. The best background images are very light with low contrast.

Get Background And Colors From Page

Turning on this button deactivates the settings in the Specify Background And Colors area and obtains instead the color scheme of another page. Having groups of related pages obtain the same color scheme ensures uniformity and reduces maintenance. To obtain colors from another page, enter its location in the text box or use the Browse button to locate it.

Margin Page Properties

The Margins tab of the Page Properties dialog box appears in Figure 6-9. This tab controls the *x-y* coordinates of the first object displayed on the page, measured from the upper-left corner.

- To specify the top margin for a Web page, turn on the box captioned Specify Top Margin and enter the number of pixels.

- To specify the left margin for a Web page, turn on the box captioned Specify Left Margin and enter the number of pixels.

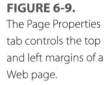

FIGURE 6-9.
The Page Properties tab controls the top and left margins of a Web page.

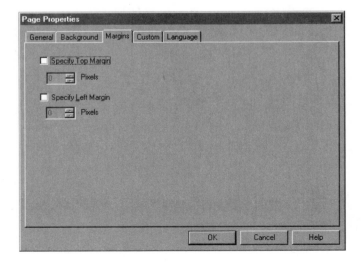

Figure 6-10 shows how a Web page set to zero top and left margins appears in three different applications. Note the amount of space between the window border and the capital *I* in the word *Index*. FrontPage Editor and Internet Explorer illustrate a zero margin in effect. Netscape Navigator 3, which sets margins using different commands, ignores these settings and applies its default margins.

FIGURE 6-10.
FrontPage Editor and Internet Explorer display a page with zero top and left margins. Netscape Navigator 3 ignores this method of setting margins.

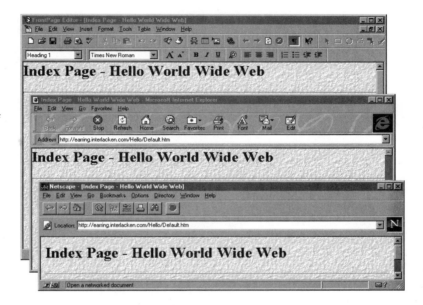

Custom Page Properties

Figure 6-11, on the next page, displays the Custom tab of the Page Properties dialog box, which maintains two categories of variables.

System variables are those defined as official HTTP headers, while user variables are any others you wish to specify. To add a variable, click the appropriate Add button and then type the variable name and its initial value into the dialog box shown in Figure 6-12, on the following page.

To change the value of a variable, select the variable, click the Modify button, and replace the value. To delete a variable, select it and then click Delete.

III

Building Your Site

FIGURE 6-11.
The Custom Page Properties tab specifies HTTP header field equivalents and user variables. These appear in the HEAD section of the HTML.

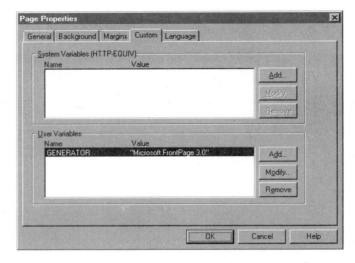

FIGURE 6-12.
This dialog box adds a variable to the System Variables list shown in Figure 6-11.

Taking Advantage of HTTP System Variables

The Refresh system variable illustrated in Figure 6-12 is a useful one. It instructs the browser to wait a specified number of seconds—5, in the example—and then automatically jump to the specified URL. This is how some sites introduce themselves with a timed series of pages. If you move a page to another location, you may wish to leave in its old location a blank or informative page with a Refresh system variable. This will automatically jump users to the page's new location. An informative page should display for a few seconds, at least. If you decide to use a blank page, you can set the number of seconds to zero.

Some additional system variables appear below. If present in your pages, they're used by the large Internet search engines (such as Yahoo, Lycos, AltaVista, and InfoSeek) to narrow the search and improve the accuracy of their search results.

- **Copyright.** Any copyright statement.
- **Description.** A sentence that describes the page's content.
- **Distribution.** One of two words: global or local. Local indicates pages of little or no interest to users outside a Web site's own organization.

Taking Advantage of HTTP System Variables *continued*

- **Expires.** A date after which the page will no longer be relevant. Use this format:

  `Tue, 02 Dec 1997 21:29:02 GMT`

- **Keywords.** Words that a prospective visitor might search for. Separate multiple keywords with commas.

- **Robots.** Instructions to control the actions of Web search "robots" such as the large search engines. Compliance is voluntary; some searching robots honor these commands, and some don't. Defined values are:

  - **None.** Tells robots to ignore this page. This is equivalent to Noindex, Nofollow.

  - **All.** Indicates that there are no restrictions on indexing this page or pages referenced in its hyperlinks. This is equivalent to Index, Follow.

  - **Index.** Welcomes all robots to include this page in search results.

  - **Noindex.** Indicates that this page might not be indexed by search engines.

  - **Follow.** Allows robots to follow hyperlinks from this page to other pages.

  - **Nofollow.** Asks robots not to follow hyperlinks from this page.

SEE ALSO
For more information about the Robot Exclusion Standard, browse *http://www. kollar.com/robots.html*.

SEE ALSO
For more information on HTML encoding, refer to "Reviewing Web Settings," page 166.

Language Page Properties

Figure 6-13, on the following page, displays the Language tab, which controls the HTML character encoding for the current page: that is, the international character set. The choices available depend on the languages installed with your copy of FrontPage. The default is US/Western European.

- **HTML Encoding For Saving This Page.** Select the character set FrontPage should use for saving the current page.

- **HTML Encoding For Displaying This Page.** Select the character set a browser should use to display the current page.

III

Building Your Site

FIGURE 6-13.
The Language tab of the Page Properties dialog box controls the international character set used for saving and loading a specific page.

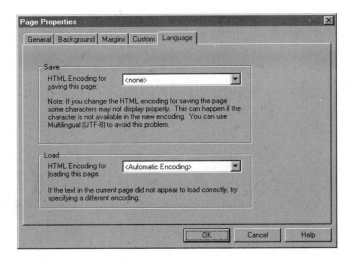

Managing Page-Level Cascading Style Sheets

As this book—and literally millions of HTML authors world-wide—have frequently mentioned, HTML is an extremely frustrating page description language.

- Its greatest strengths are simplicity and cross-platform portability.

- Its greatest weaknesses are crude control at authoring time (a consequence of simplicity) and incomplete control over the final formatting process (a consequence of portability).

The cascading style sheet (CSS) is a major advance that provides Web page authors more control at authoring time, yet maintains the portability of finished pages. As you might suspect, the resulting gains in capability come at the price of some complexity. Adding to the complexity, most current CSS implementations are incomplete—things that ought to work sometimes don't, and of course they don't fail in a consistent manner across platforms and software versions. Nevertheless, the promise of CSS is so great that the technology seems destined to grow, mature, and persist.

CSS provides precise control over more than 60 elements of style: typeface, font size, font weight, foreground colors, background colors, margins, borders, alignment, and dozens more. You can apply CSS style properties at various levels within HTML's hierarchy of objects.

- The highest, most general CSS properties are browser defaults. These are the properties in effect, as of today, in the absence of any other formatting options.

- In addition, each Web page can contain its own style sheet. Any properties specified here override the corresponding browser default settings.

- Within a Web page, properties specified for built-in styles and user-defined classes can override those otherwise in effect.

In CSS parlance, a *selector* is any name that denotes a collection of style properties. There are two major kinds of selectors: traditional HTML styles, such as H1
(Heading 1) and LI (List Item), and user-defined *classes*.

- Web authors can also define their own style codes, called *classes*, that incorporate settings for any number of properties. A page author could define a class called warning, for example, and then assign that class to various blocks of text. Later, changing the class definition would change the appearance of each use.

- Each instance of a built-in style or class can override its default. Establishing a new default appearance for bulleted list items, for example, doesn't prevent overriding the appearance of a *particular* bulleted list item.

- Finally, CSS formatting can override the appearance of any string of characters—that is, of a *span*.

The cascading part of cascading style sheets refers to the *inheritance* of properties. At each level in the list above, properties inherit their default values from the level above. Each succeeding level can override many, few, or no properties, but properties assigned at the lowest, most specific level always take precedence over higher-level settings. Starting at the top—from browser defaults—each property can be overridden many times, once, or not at all before final page formatting is determined.

III

Building Your Site

A complete discussion of cascading style sheets is well beyond the scope of this book; what's important to know for using them in Front-Page is the following:

- Cascading style sheets provide control over a rich selection of properties, some not previously available to Web page authors.

- Properties of cascading style sheets can be defined at the browser, page, selector, or span level. Properties specified at more specific levels individually override those defined at more general levels.

- FrontPage provides dialog boxes to guide you in adding CSS properties to your Web pages.

- The extent and consistency of CSS support varies greatly among different browsers, editors, and versions of each.

Managing CSS Selectors and Page Defaults

Figure 6-14 illustrates the dialog box obtained in FrontPage Editor by choosing Stylesheet from the Format menu. As you no doubt immediately noticed, it's a triumph of minimalist GUI design. This dialog box will no doubt improve as FrontPage develops better support for CSS, but for now, at least, it does the job.

The code in Figure 6-14 is shown below, with line numbers assigned for this discussion. Lines 1 and 7 mark the beginning and end of the stylesheet in typical HTML syntax. Lines 2 and 6 are comment delimiters, inserted to ensure that a browser that doesn't understand the `<style>` tag will see it as a comment and ignore the intervening data. Lines 3, 4, and 5 are the CSS definitions.

```
1 <style>
2 <!--
3 { font-family: Arial, sans-serif; }
4 H1 { font-style: italic; }
5 LI { color: red; font-family: "Comic Sans MS, ↵
   sans-serif"; }
6 -->
7 </style>
```

Curly braces ({}) mark the beginning and end of each CSS definition. Semicolons denote the end of each property setting within a style. If

FIGURE 6-14.

Format Stylesheet manages CSS page defaults and style definitions. The syntax is an extension of HTML language. If a string appears without an identifier, the setting becomes a page default.

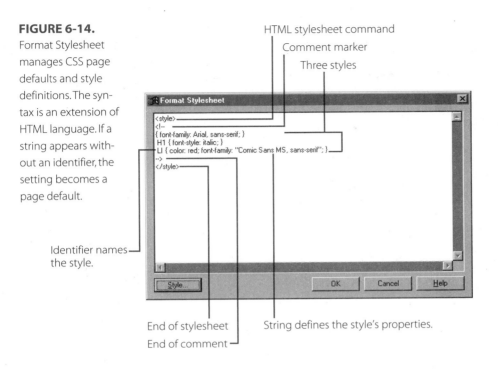

HTML stylesheet command

Comment marker

Three styles

Identifier names the style.

End of stylesheet
End of comment

String defines the style's properties.

no selector appears just before an opening curly brace, the style properties apply to the entire page. If a selector does appear, the property settings apply to that style only.

Line 3 assigns two font families to the entire page: Arial and sans serif. The browser will search for these fonts in left to right order on the remote user's computer. Thus, if Arial is available the browser will use it; otherwise, the browser will use whatever sans serif font is assigned as a default.

Line 4 assigns the italic property to all text designated with the HTML tag H1. This is the style FrontPage identifies as Heading 1 on its format toolbar. This line could contain additional property specifications, such as a font-family setting different from that on line 3. Because line 4 contains no font-family settings, the H1 style will inherit the font-family defined for the entire page—the font family defined on line 3. If line 3 were deleted, H1 text would appear in the browser's default font, but still italicized.

III

Building Your Site

Line 5 assigns the color red and the font-family Comic Sans MS (second choice sans serif) to all list items in the current page. This will affect all text appearing in conventional bulleted and numbered lists. (FrontPage actually uses HTML tables rather than HTML lists when formatting lists with graphic bullets.)

? SEE ALSO

For guidance in using the FrontPage CSS Style dialog box, jump ahead to "Assigning CSS Properties," page 239.

FrontPage provides lines 1 and 2 plus 6 and 7 automatically; you must provide at least a skeleton of the rest if you want to take advantage of cascading style sheets.

You can specify properties for more than one selector at a time by separating them with commas, as shown below.

```
H1, H2, H3, B { color: blue; }
```

This specifies that any text marked as a Heading 1, Heading 2, Heading 3, or as Bold should be blue. If this makes bold text in a Heading 3 paragraph hard to recognize, you can change its color by entering another line:

```
H3 B { color: green; }
```

Note the lack of a comma between H3 and B. This means the style applies *only* if the selectors H3 and B are *both* in effect: that is, for bold text in a Heading 3 paragraph.

Creating and Modifying CSS Styles

In order to work with the Format Stylesheet dialog box and add or modify a CSS style, you need to follow one of the three procedures below *before* you click on the Style button and open the Style dialog box, where you will actually select or modify a style. Pick the procedure below that suits your need.

To create a style that will apply globally to the page

1 Create a blank line.

2 Position the cursor in it.

To start a selector entry

1 Create a blank line.

2 Position the cursor in it and type the selector name.

To modify either a global style or a selector entry

1 Click anywhere *inside* the appropriate pair of curly braces.

Now click the Style button to open the Style dialog box and display its five tabs: Alignment, Borders, Font, Colors, and Text. The five sections starting with Assigning CSS Alignment later in this chapter describe these tabs and their properties in detail. If you want to experiment now, specify some properties for the style you're working with.

When you're done, click the OK button. The properties you specified in the GUI should now appear between the curly braces.

In Figure 6-15 FrontPage is displaying a Web page that uses the style sheet shown in Figure 6-14, on page 235. The italicized Heading 1 is displayed correctly, as is the color red for bulleted list items. (You'll have to trust me about the color!) Note that the fonts specified in the CSS dialog box are not displayed in true WYSIWYG fashion.

FIGURE 6-15.

FrontPage Editor displays a Web page that uses the style sheet of Figure 6-14, on page 235. Not all features appear in WYSIWYG mode; compare this figure to Figure 6-16, on the next page.

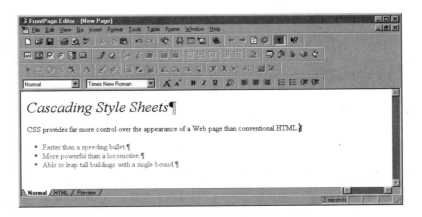

In Figure 6-16, on the next page, the Preview tab is selected at the bottom of the window pane, and now the same Web page is displayed with all CSS attributes appearing correctly.

Microsoft Internet Explorer has provided CSS support since version 3. Figure 6-17, on the following page, demonstrates the same page as it appears in Explorer version 3.

III

Building Your Site

FIGURE 6-16.
FrontPage Editor's Preview mode displays correctly the Web page of Figure 6-15 (on the previous page).

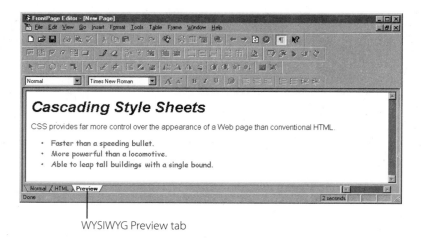

WYSIWYG Preview tab

FIGURE 6-17.
Internet Explorer also displays correctly the page of Figure 6-15 (on the previous page).

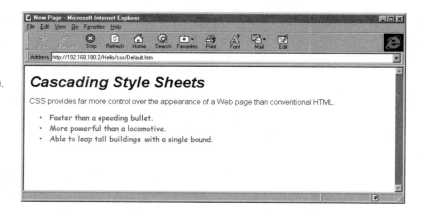

Netscape browsers prior to version 4 didn't support cascading style sheets. Web visitors using it would see the page as displayed in Figure 6-18.

In addition to noting the differences seen above, you should realize that support for CSS isn't an all-or-nothing proposition. More so than with conventional HTML, different software will continue to display CSS-enhanced pages with subtle or perhaps major differences. In the short term, and especially while the installed base of older Netscape browsers persists, it's probably best to use conventional HTML formatting whenever possible. If you *do* use CSS, test your pages thoroughly.

FIGURE 6-18.
Netscape Navigator versions through version 3 didn't provide CSS support.

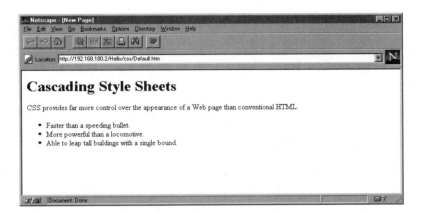

Assigning CSS Properties

The previous section discussed building style sheets that apply globally to an entire Web page. You learned how to specify default properties for the entire page, and how to override these for specific selectors—that is, for built-in styles and for user-defined classes.

Establishing page defaults and predefined styles for use throughout a Web page are valuable operations, but CSS can assign properties to more specific objects as well. In almost every FrontPage property dialog box, you'll notice a Style button that, if clicked, permits entering CSS properties. The Style button in the Page Properties dialog box sets CSS properties for the entire page body. The Style button in Paragraph properties sets CSS properties for the current paragraph, in Table Properties for the current table, in Image properties for the current image, and so forth.

With one exception, clicking any Style button displays the six-tabbed dialog box shown in Figures 6-19 through 6-25 (starting on page 240). The exception is the Format Stylesheet dialog box of Figure 6-14 (page 235), which defines global page defaults and selectors. Because that dialog box *defines* selectors, its Style button doesn't display the Class tab of Figure 6-19, on the next page (which *uses* selectors).

The following six sections describe the CSS propoerties and settings available on the six Style dialog tabs. You can apply these properties and settings to any object that has a Style button on its property dialog box—only the range of effect will change.

III

Building Your Site

Assigning CSS Classes

As shown in Figure 6-19, the Class tab of the Style dialog box provides two input fields: Class and ID.

- **Class** specifies the name of a style class you defined under Format: Stylesheet. The object you selected before invoking the Style dialog box will inherit whatever properties you assigned to the specified class.

- **ID** works like Class, except that ID selectors can be used only once on the same Web page. (Some browsers seem to allow multiple use, however.)

FIGURE 6-19.
Alignment is the first tab of the FrontPage CSS Style dialog box.

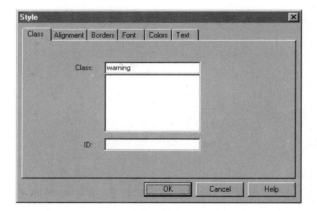

The following code defines a class named warning and an ID called flag. This is how it would appear on the Stylesheet dialog box:

```
1 <style>
2 <!--
3 { font-family: Arial, sans-serif; }
4 H1 { font-style: italic; }
5 LI { color: red; font-family: "Comic Sans MS, ⤶
     sans-serif"; }
6 .warning { color: #339900; font-style: italic; ⤶
     font-weight: bold; }
7 #flag { font-family: "Boulevard, fantasy"; ⤶
     font-size: "large"; }
8 -->
9 </style>
```

Note the period preceding `warning` on line 6 and the pound sign preceding `flag` on line 7. The period signifies that a class is being defined, and the pound sign an ID. Don't include the period or pound sign when entering the class or ID on the Class tab.

Remember, this dialog box tab doesn't appear when you invoke the Style dialog box from Format: Stylesheet, because in that context you're defining classes and IDs, not applying them.

Assigning CSS Alignment

Figure 6-20 shows the second tab of the CSS Style dialog box, which controls alignment.

FIGURE 6-20.
You can set the alignment properties of the current CSS object using this dialog box tab.

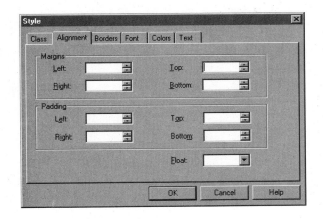

- **Margins.** These four settings control the amount of white space reserved around each edge of the object, plus a small buffer zone, called padding. Figure 6-21, on the next page, illustrates the concepts of margins and padding.

  - The *content area* is the space where an image would appear, where text could appear, the space occupied by a table, and so forth, depending on the kind of content.

  - *Padding* surrounds the content area, matching its background color and certain other properties.

  - If there's a visible *border*, it surrounds the padding area and not just the content area.

- *Margins* surround the padding area and borders, if there are any. Unlike padding—which matches the background of what it contains—margins match the background of whatever surrounds them.

FIGURE 6-21.
Padding surrounds a Web page object and matches its background. Margins surround the padding and match the exterior background. Borders, if specified, appear where the two meet.

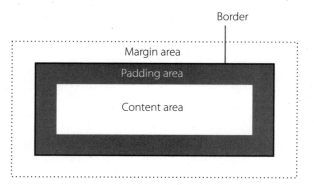

FrontPage assigns margins and padding in terms of pixels, although the CSS specification permits additional units of measure such as cm (centimeters), em (ems), pt (points), and % (percent).

The meaning of percentage measurements varies with the type of object. For most types, it's a percentage of the measurement the object would otherwise inherit. For example, a paragraph width of 80% would make the paragraph 80% as wide as it otherwise would be. The following are typical exceptions to this rule:

- For colors, the range 0% to 100% corresponds to the normal RGB values 0 through 255.

- For line height, the percentage value is applied to the surrounding text's point size.

In the context of CSS, an em is a unit of distance equal to the point size of text. Thus, within 12-point text, one em equals 12 points—1/6 inch. The advantage of using ems as a unit of measure is that your other measurements change proportionately when the point size changes.

- **Padding.** These four settings control the amount of white space reserved around each edge of the object.

■ **Float.** This property specifies whether an object should be left-aligned, centered, or right-aligned. Text will flow around left-aligned or right-aligned objects, but not around centered ones. If the property is blank, the object either flows in-line with text or is left-aligned with text not flowing around it, depending on the type of object.

Assigning CSS Borders

Figure 6-22 illustrates the Border tab for the CSS Style dialog box. For each of the four sides of an object, you can specify the following:

■ **Style.** Specify the type of line used to draw the border—none, solid, dotted, double, and so on.

■ **Color.** Indicate the color you want the border line to be with this property.

■ **Width.** Specify the thickness of the borders here. You can specify width using generic values of thick, medium, or thin, or as a specific number of pixels. As before, additional units of measure are supported by the CSS specification.

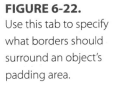

FIGURE 6-22.
Use this tab to specify what borders should surround an object's padding area.

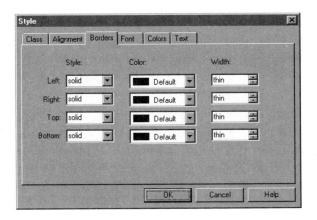

Assigning CSS Fonts

The dialog box tab for assigning CSS fonts appears in Figure 6-23, on the following page. Note that you can actually specify two fonts, which the browser will try in order. It's usually a good practice to specify one of the generic fonts listed in all lowercase letters as the Secondary

FIGURE 6-23.
This tab specifies fonts for a CSS style. The browser will first try to use the primary font, and then the secondary.

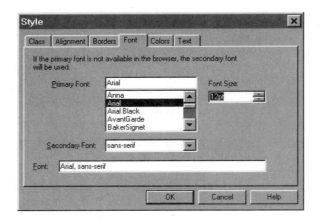

Font, because all browsers are supposed to have a reasonable default for each kind. The Font Size control sets the font in absolute point sizes or more traditional browser sizes such as small, medium, or large.

Assigning CSS Colors

The Color tab of the Style dialog box provides options for controlling colors within CSS styles, as shown in Figure 6-24.

FIGURE 6-24.
Colors defined within CSS styles are configurable using this dialog box.

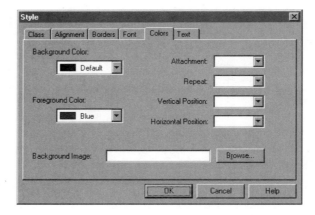

- **Background Color** specifies the default color used for filling unused portions of a text area, table cell, image, or other object.

- **Foreground Color** specifies the color used for presenting an object's contents. For many objects, this is the color in which text will appear.

■ **Background Image** specifies an image used for filling unused portions of an object.

■ **Attachment** scrolls the background image or keeps it fixed.

- **Scroll.** The browser will scroll the background image along with other content. This is the default.

- **Fixed.** The browser will keep the background image stationary, even when other content scrolls.

■ **Repeat** controls the repetitive tiling of a background image.

- **Repeat.** The browser repeats the background image both vertically and horizontally to fill the entire available area.

- **Repeat-x.** The browser repeats the image horizontally only.

- **Repeat-y.** The browser repeats the image vertically only.

- **No-repeat.** The browser displays the image in one location and will not repeat it.

■ **Vertical Position** specifies Top, Center, or Bottom, depending on where you want the background image to start appearing. Top is the default; center and bottom probably make sense only if Repeat is set to Repeat-x.

■ **Horizontal Position** specifies Left, Center, or Right, depending on where you want the background image to start appearing. Left is the default; center and bottom probably make sense only if Repeat is set to Repeat-y.

Assigning CSS Text Properties

Cascading style sheets provide amazing control over the appearance of text. The Style dialog box provides access to some of these through its Text tab, which appears in Figure 6-25, on the next page.

■ **Weight.** This property controls the thickness of the strokes making up a font. You can specify

- A numeric weight from 100 to 900.

- The keywords *normal* (=400) or *bold* (=700).

FIGURE 6-25.
To configure text properties using CSS, select the Text tab of the Style dialog box.

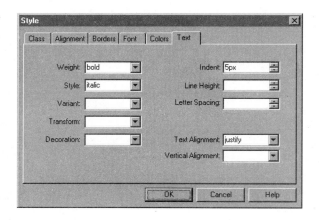

- The keywords *bolder* or *lighter*, which thicken or weaken strokes compared to the object's parent. The following example would produce a thinner than usual stroke for Heading 1 text.

```
H1 { font-weight: lighter }
```

- **Style.** This property's valid settings are Normal, Italic, and Oblique. Typically, normal text is upright, while italic text is slanted, thinned, and more curved. Oblique text is slanted but otherwise resembles normal.

- **Variant.** This property can be Normal or Small Caps. Small Caps replaces lowercase letters with reduced-sized capital letters.

> Using normal 12-point characters for capitals and substituting 9-point capitals for lowercase doesn't produce completely satisfactory results, because 9-point capitals have thinner strokes than 12-point characters of either case. A true Small Caps font has equal stroke thickness for both the large and small capitals.

- **Transform.** This property presents text in a certain case, regardless of how it was entered. The options are:

  - **Capitalize.** The browser capitalizes the first letter of each word and presents all others as lowercase.

  - **Uppercase.** The text is presented as all uppercase.

- **Lowercase.** The text is presented as all lowercase.

- **None.** The browser presents the text as is. This is the default.

■ **Decoration.** This property controls the following modifications to normal text: underline, overline, line-through, and blink. The default is none.

■ **Indent.** This property specifies first-line paragraph indentation. Negative numbers produce outdents (where the first line extends to the left of second and subsequent lines).

■ **Line Height.** This property controls the height of lines in a paragraph. FrontPage suggests measurements in pixels, but the CSS standard also provides for specifying a percentage or ratio of font size (for example, either 120% or 1.2).

When you specify the line height property (or most other text measurements) as a percentage, other objects will inherit not the percentage itself, but the result of multiplying. Consider the following example.

```
{ font-size: 12pt ; line-height: 120% ; }
fineprint { font-size: 10pt ; }
```

The default style's line height property will be 120%×12 points = 14.4 points. Because the default style's line height is a percentage, the fineprint class inherits the multiplied result—14.4 points—as its line height.

```
{ font-size: 12pt ; line-eight: 1.2 ; }
fineprint { font-size: 10pt ; }
```

In the second example, the default style's line height would again be 14.4 points—1.2×12 points. Because the default style's line hieght is a ratio, the fineprint class inherits the ratio and recalculates the effective line height as 1.2×10 points = 12 points. This will result in a more attractive display of 10-point text.

■ **Letter Spacing.** This property expands or tightens the spacing between letters. The default measurement is in pixels.

III

Building Your Site

■ **Text Alignment.** This property specifies one of these values:

- **Left.** The browser aligns text to the left margin (left-aligned, flush-left).

- **Right.** The browser aligns text to the right margin (right-aligned, flush-right).

- **Center.** The browser aligns the center of each line with the center of the available area (usually the width of the browser window).

- **Justify.** The browser aligns text to both the left and right margins, spreading the required space as evenly as possible between words in the line.

■ **Vertical Alignment.** This property specifies the alignment of an in-line object relative to the surrounding text. The permissible values are the following:

- **Baseline.** The baseline of the child (surrounded) object aligns with the baseline of the parent (surrounding) text.

> **NOTE**
>
> The baseline is the imaginary straight line on which letters in a line of text sit. (The lowercase descenders of letters such as *j* and *g* extend *below* the baseline.)

- **Sub.** The baseline of the child object aligns with the parent's preferred baseline for subscripts.

- **Super.** The baseline of the child object aligns with the parent's preferred baseline for superscripts.

- **Text-top.** The top of the child object aligns with the top of the surrounding text.

- **Middle.** The object's vertical midpoint aligns with the parent's baseline raised by one-half the x-height (the height of a lowercase letter with no ascenders or descenders, such as *a, e, o,* and, well, *x*). That is, the midpoint of the object would align with the midpoint of such letters as *a, e, o,* or *x* in the surrounding text.

- **Text-bottom.** The bottom of the child object aligns with the bottom of the parent.

- **Percentage.** If vertical alignment is a percentage, this value raises or lowers the child's position by that fraction of the parent's line height. The 50% setting raises the child object half a line.

Shared Cascading Style Sheets

CSS provides two ways for groups of Web pages to share one set of styles. The first method requires placing a line such as the following in the Head section of each page that will use the shared styles, where *styleset* is the URL of a master document containing the desired styles.

```
<link rel="StyleSheet" href="sharecss.css" ↵
type="text/css">
```

To insert this statement, select the HTML tab in FrontPage Editor. Place this line on a new line immediately after the <head> tag. The file sharecss.css must contain only CSS statements—such as those shown on lines 3, 4, and 5 on page 234.

This method is subject to these restrictions: you can only include one such statement in a file, and you cannot specify any other CSS styles in the same document. If you violate either rule, the browser is supposed to ask the user which set of styles to use. In fact, there seems to be little uniformity in the way this feature is implemented.

The second method involves adding @import statements to a normal style sheet. For example:

```
<STYLE type="text/css">
@import "styleset";
H1 { font-style: Arial, sans-serif; }
</STYLE>
```

This method avoids the restrictions present in the Link statement, but support for it is even less consistent.

Additional CSS Advice

The CSS properties described in this chapter are actually just a subset of the complete cascading style sheet specification; the full spec is an

III

Building Your Site

amazing achievement, an embarrassment of riches, an impossibility to implement, or Pandora's box, depending on your perspective.

An excellent reference to CSS is the book *Cascading Style Sheets: Designing for the Web*, by Hakon Wium Lie and Bert Bos, ISBN 0-201-41998-X.

For online information, review the World Wide Web Consortium's document "Cascading Style Sheets, level 1" at

http://www.w3.org/pub/WWW/TR/REC-CSS1

Support for CSS will undoubtedly improve over time—not only in browsers but also in editors like FrontPage and other Web-design tools. For now, caution and thorough page testing on relevant browsers are your best bet.

Adding and Formatting Text

The origin of the World Wide Web was text-based, and text still predominates it today. As much as graphics, moving images, and interactive controls can enhance a Web page, natural language text remains the workhorse for presenting information. This chapter describes the FrontPage commands for entering, modifying, cutting, pasting, moving, and formatting text.

Wherever possible, FrontPage follows the same text entry conventions as other Microsoft Office applications, especially Microsoft Word. This is hardly unexpected, considering FrontPage's status as a member of the Office family, and indeed it's very likely a major reason you or your company bought FrontPage. Despite its family resemblance to Word, FrontPage necessarily remains bound to the unique eccentricities and limitations of HTML.

It's *critical* to remember that the remote user's browser, not FrontPage, controls the final appearance of text and other objects on a Web page. FrontPage saves text with rather imprecise formatting instructions that the remote user's browser will interpret—or ignore—as it chooses. Therefore, the final display differs for each remote user, depending on the capabilities and settings of their browser. Differences in the browser software itself, its version, the size of the user's browser window, the availability of fonts on the remote user's system, monitor resolution and color depth, and other factors will *all* cause variations in output. Keep this in mind as you design your page: What you see is only approximately what the remote user will get.

Word Processing Conventions Used by FrontPage

Entering text in FrontPage is very much like typing into a word processor. In FrontPage Editor

1 Set an insertion point anywhere on the page by clicking the mouse on the desired spot.

The insertion point will jump to the nearest location where text can be entered.

> FrontPage accepts input like a word processor, and not like some graphics and publishing programs. You can't just click in the middle of some white space and locate objects there.

2 Start typing.

You cut, copy, paste, and clear work in standard fashion, as shown in Table 7-1. In addition, you can drag selected text anywhere on the page that text can normally appear. Simply dragging text moves it, and holding down the Ctrl key and dragging copies it. The Paste Special command provides choices to paste text as one paragraph or several, and to preserve or ignore the formatting in the pasted text. Paste Special is particularly useful when bringing in text from other applications like databases and spreadsheets.

TABLE 7-1.   Copying, Moving, and Deleting Text

Operation	Preparation	Menu Command	Drag and Drop	Keystroke
Cut	Select source text	Edit Cut	N/A	Press Ctrl+X or Shift+Del

Move	Select source text	Edit
		  Cut
		Edit
		  Paste
			Drag to new
			location
				(Cut and Paste)

Copy	Select source text	Edit Copy	Hold down Ctrl and drag to additional location	Press Ctrl+C or Shift+Ins
Paste	Set insertion point	Edit Paste	N/A	Press Ctrl+V or Ctrl+Ins
Paste Special	Set insertion poin	Edit Paste Special	N/A	N/A
Clear	Select source text	Edit Clear	N/A	Press Del

Table 7-2 lists the commands for selecting text.

TABLE 7-2.   Text Selection Commands

Operation	Command

Select range	Drag mouse across range, or
	From insertion point, hold down Shift and
	  click at end of range, or
	Hold down Shift and use arrow keys to
	  highlight desired selection

Select word	Double-click word
Select paragraph	Hold down Alt and click anywhere in paragraph
Select entire document	Choose Select All from the Edit menu, or Press Ctrl+A

Table 7-3, on the next page, lists the keyboard commands for changing the insertion point. Again, these are much the same as those in any word processor. Holding down Shift while changing the insertion point extends the current selection.

TABLE 7-3. Keyboard Commands for Changing the Insertion Point

Operation	Keystroke
Move one character right or left	Right or left arrow
Move one word right or left	Ctrl+Right arrow or Ctrl+Left arrow
Move to start of line	Home
Move to end of line	End
Move up or down one line	Up or Down arrow
Move up or down one paragraph	Ctrl+Up arrow or Ctrl+Down arrow
Move to top of page	Ctrl+Home
Move to bottom of page	Ctrl+End

To end a paragraph and start another, press the Enter key. To begin a new line within the same paragraph, press Shift+Enter.

Importing Text

FrontPage Editor is remarkably capable of accepting whole files or selected portions—in almost any format—and converting them to reasonably effective HTML. To add such content to a Web page, open the page in FrontPage Editor and take the following steps:

- To insert an entire file using the drag and drop method

    1 Locate the file's icon in Windows Explorer.

    2 Drag it to the desired location in FrontPage Editor.

    3 Drop it in place.

- To insert an entire file using commands

    1 Place the insertion point where you want the file to appear in FrontPage Editor.

    2 Choose File from the Insert menu and locate the file you want to insert.

    3 Double-click the filename or select it and click the Open button.

How FrontPage Interprets Text and Graphics

When asked to incorporate content that isn't in HTML format, FrontPage first determines whether the data is character-based or graphic.

If the data is character-based,

- FrontPage consults the table of standard file translators installed on the local machine.

- FrontPage translates the data to RTF (Rich Text Format).

- FrontPage translates the RTF to HTML.

Tabular data such as a spreadsheet becomes an HTML table. Other data becomes free-flowing text. FrontPage attempts to retain formatting instructions in the original data.

If the data is graphic,

- FrontPage converts the data to a Windows bitmap for display.

- When you save your Web page, FrontPage identifies images that originated outside the current Web and displays a Save As dialog box for each one.

- If an image uses transparency or contains no more than 256 colors, FrontPage saves it, by default, as a GIF file. If the image contains more than 256 colors and no transparency, it's saved in JPEG format.

SEE ALSO

For more information on HTML tables, see "Creating and Editing Tables," page 313.

SEE ALSO

For more information on using graphics in Web pages, see Chapter 8, "Incorporating Graphics."

- To insert less than an entire file using drag and drop

  1 Open the file in its normal application.

  2 Select the desired content.

  3 Drag the selection to the desired location in FrontPage Editor.

  4 Drag it in place.

- To insert part of a file using commands

  1 Open the file in its normal application.

  2 Select the desired content.

  3 Copy the selection to the Clipboard.

III

Building Your Site

4 In FrontPage Editor, set the insertion point where you want the content to appear.

5 Choose Paste from the Edit menu, or press Ctrl+V.

Text Conventions Unique to HTML

? SEE ALSO
For more information on HTML tables, see "Creating and Editing Tables," page 313.

The preceding section may have convinced you that entering text in FrontPage is no different than using virtually any word processor. This is no accident, and in fact it's a unique strength of FrontPage. Nevertheless, the nature of HTML introduces a number of unique restrictions.

- HTML considers tab characters the same as wordspaces. There's no facility for setting tab stops to line up text in columns.

- HTML treats all strings of white-space characters as a single space. White-space characters are wordspaces, tabs, line feeds, carriage returns, and so forth. FrontPage detects any repeating spaces you enter and replaces all but the last with nonbreaking spaces—that is, spaces neither FrontPage nor the browser will suppress.

- HTML provides no direct control over first-line indentation, paragraph indentation, line length, or line spacing.

When You Really Want Extra Spaces . . .

The practice of inserting two spaces between each pair of sentences is a carry-over from the days of typewriters when, because of monospaced fonts, letter spacing within words tended to be wide. Nowadays, with proportional fonts, letter spacing is narrower, and one space provides plenty of separation between sentences.

If you really want to insert extra spaces—for instance, if you want to present program code and line up levels of indentation—you have several options:

- Use the Formatted paragraph style, which provides an exception to HTML's normal handling of white space. Using the HTML *<pre>* command, paragraphs assigned this style display with an unattractive monospaced font and with all spaces and carriage returns honored, as if you were using a typewriter. You can't, however, use heading levels or

---

When You Really Want Extra Spaces . . . *continued*

other elements with a formatted paragraph; and you should avoid tabs, because different browsers might assign different numbers of spaces to them. But if you don't mind the monospaced font, if you stick to using spaces rather than tabs, and if you want to control the alignment of each character on a line, the Formatted style may be acceptable.

■ If you feel the need to add spaces in normal paragraphs of proportional type, you can press Tab, which generates five spaces: four nonbreaking spaces and one regular space. A nonbreaking space is considered a special character by HTML and is coded as * *. If you want to insert these nonbreaking spaces one at a time, press Ctrl+Shift+Spacebar and the space will be preserved even in normal paragraphs.

Using either of these features, however, constitutes bad style. Repeating spaces will seldom produce the results you want, given HTML's use of proportional fonts, variable page width, and automatic line wrapping.

Inserting Special Text Elements

The Insert menu in FrontPage Editor can add four kinds of special text elements: line breaks, horizontal lines, symbols, and comments.

Inserting a Line Break

Choosing Break from the Insert menu displays the dialog box shown in Figure 7-1, on the next page. This dialog box inserts four different kinds of line breaks.

■ **Normal Line Break.** This is an ordinary line break, just as you would create by pressing Shift+Enter. Text resumes flowing at the left margin exactly one line below the line containing the break.

SEE ALSO

For information on inserting and aligning images, refer to Chapter 8, "Incorporating Graphics."

■ **Clear Left Margin.** If this break occurs in text flowing around an image or other object aligned at the left margin, text following the break will start flowing immediately below that object.

■ **Clear Right Margin.** If this break occurs in text flowing around an object aligned at the right margin, text following the break will start flowing immediately below that object.

III

Building Your Site

FIGURE 7-1.

The Break Properties dialog box inserts a line break at the current insertion point. Clearing a margin means resuming text flow just beyond any nontext objects aligned at that margin.

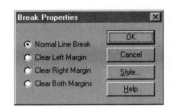

■ **Clear Both Margins.** If this break occurs in text flowing around objects aligned at either or both margins, text following the break will start flowing immediately below them.

? SEE ALSO

For a discussion of cascading style sheets, "Managing Page-Level Cascading Style Sheets," page 232.

Clicking the Style button on the right of the dialog box displays the standard FrontPage CSS Property dialog box. Any cascading style sheet properties you specify will be included with the Line Break tag.

Figure 7-2 shows a normal line break. Figure 7-3 shows a Clear Left Margin break for clearing an object on the left margin.

FIGURE 7-2.

This page illustrates a normal line break.

Inserting a Normal line break here...

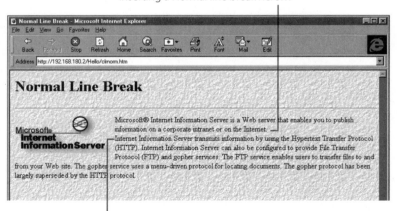

...forces a new line, but allows text to continue wrapping around image.

FIGURE 7-3.
Text following a Clear Left Margin line break jumps around any object on its left and resumes flowing at the true left margin below the object.

Inserting a Clear Left Margin line break here...

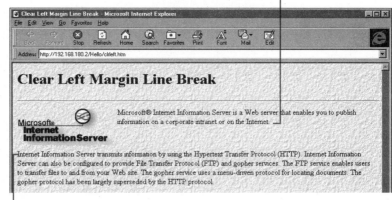

...causes remaining text to wrap to left margin below left-aligned image.

Inserting Horizontal Lines

Choosing Horizontal Line from the Insert menu places a variable-width horizontal line at the current insertion point. The horizontal line normally occupies the entire width of the browser window and forces line breaks before and after itself. Figure 7-2 and Figure 7-3 each contain a horizontal line; it appears just above the graphic and extends across the entire page.

If you right-click a horizontal line and choose Horizontal Line Properties from the pop-up menu, you can set the properties of the horizontal line. See Figure 7-4, on the following page.

- **Width.** Specifies the width of the horizontal line in pixels or as a percentage of available display width.

- **Height.** Specifies the height or thickness of the line in pixels.

- **Alignment.** Sets the line's alignment to the left, to the right, or in the center.

- **Color.** Selects the line's color. A drop-down list displays 18 possibilities: Default, the 16 original VGA colors, and Custom.

III

Building Your Site

For considerations related to choosing text colors, see the sidebar "Choosing Page Colors," page 227.

■ **Solid Line (No Shading).** Eliminates the normal three-dimensional effect along the edges of the line.

■ **Style.** Opens the Style dialog box where you can select any applicable CSS (cascading style sheet) properties for the horizontal line.

FIGURE 7-4.
This dialog box sets the properties of a horizontal line.

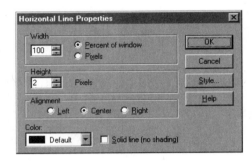

Inserting Symbols

You can easily insert special characters—those that don't appear on your keyboard—using the Symbol dialog box shown in Figure 7-5. To insert a special character

1 Place the insertion point where you want to insert the symbol.

2 Choose Symbol from the Insert menu.

3 Double-click the desired character, or select the desired character and click Insert.

4 Close the dialog box.

FIGURE 7-5.
To insert characters not on the keyboard, choose Symbol from the Insert dialog box.

Inserting Comments

Comments are text that appears in FrontPage Editor but that won't be seen by viewers of your Web pages. As shown in Figure 7-6, comments typically contain notes (preferably the scrutable kind) about the page for yourself or others on your team. To add comments to a Web page

1 Set the insertion point where you want the comment to appear.

2 Choose FrontPage Component from the Insert menu.

3 Double-click Comment, or select it and click OK.

4 Enter your comments in the Comment dialog box and click OK when done.

FIGURE 7-6.
Comments inserted here won't be visible to viewers of your Web site.

In FrontPage Editor, comments appear as purple text. To modify a comment, either double-click it or right-click and select Comment Properties. To delete a comment, click it and then press the Delete key.

Formatting Paragraphs

FrontPage supports the 15 basic HTML paragraph styles shown in Figure 7-7, on the next page. These are paragraph styles and not font styles; they modify the appearance of an entire paragraph and not of any specific text. HTML was designed to specify the structure of a document's elements, not the explicit formatting of a given element; therefore, each browser will display these according to its settings and the system configuration on which it's running.

III

Building Your Site

Heading 1 through Heading 6 are for successively lower-level titles. In practice, any page with six levels of titles is probably too long and an excellent candidate for separation into multiple pages. Nevertheless, the availability of six styles provides more flexibility in selecting sizes (you might, for example, choose to use Headings 1 through 3, or 4 through 6). Heading 1 generally uses the largest font and Heading 6 the smallest.

FIGURE 7-7.

FrontPage supports these standard HTML paragraph styles.

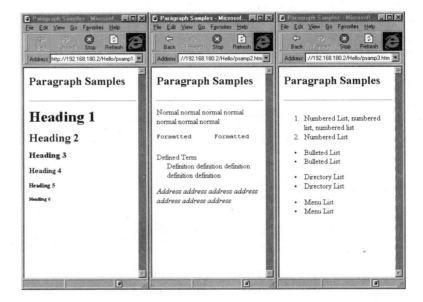

The Normal style is designated for most ordinary text. Like the heading styles and most of the others, it specifies no fixed line width but instead wraps within the current browser window.

The Formatted style is unique in three respects: it uses a monospaced font; it preserves and displays multiple spaces; and it doesn't wrap within the browser window. Because of these characteristics, the Formatted style is useful for applications like tabular data and program code listings, where preservation of columns and letter spaces is vital.

The Address style is designated to identify Web addresses. Its most common use is making e-mail hyperlinks stand out from ordinary text. Web address paragraphs frequently, though not always, appear in an italic font.

To assign the Heading, Normal, Formatted, or Address styles to a paragraph, set the insertion point in the paragraph or select any part of it. Then do *either* of the following:

- Select the desired style from the Change Style list in the Formatting toolbar. Table 7-4, shown on the next page, explains the Formatting toolbar.

- Choose Paragraph from the Format menu, and select the desired style from the Paragraph Properties dialog box. Figure 7-8 illustrates this dialog box.

To assign a paragraph style quickly, simply right-click in a paragraph and then choose Paragraph Properties from the pop-up menu.

FIGURE 7-8.
Use the Paragraph Properties dialog box to choose paragraph styles.

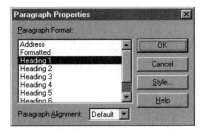

The Paragraph Properties dialog box contains two additional options:

- **Paragraph Alignment** specifies that the style will use its default setting for alignment; or you can select left, right, or center.

- **Style** invokes the FrontPage Style dialog box, allowing you to set additional CSS properties for the current paragraph *only* (not for all paragraphs of the same style).

III

Building Your Site

TABLE 7-4. Using FrontPage Editor's Formatting Toolbar

Icon	Description	Function	Menu Command
Normal ▼	Change Style	Modifies the HTML style of selected paragraphs	Format Paragraph

Times New Roman ▼	Change Font	Modifies the font of selected text	Format
			  Font
			    Font tab
			      Font List

A▲	Increase Text Size	Increases the size of selected text	Format
			  Font
			    Font tab
			      Size

A▼	Decrease Text Size	Decreases the size of selected text	Format
			  Font
			    Font tab
			      Size

B	Bold	Toggles bold attribute of selected text	Format
			  Font
			    Font tab
			      Font Style

I	Italic	Toggles italic attribute of selected text	Format
			  Font
			    Font tab
			      Font Style

U	Underline	Toggles underline attribute of selected text	Format
			  Font
			    Font tab
			      Font Style

A	Text Color	Changes the color of selected text	Format
			  Font
			    Font tab
			      Color

≡	Align Left	Left-aligns text in selected paragraphs	Format
			  Paragraph
			    Paragraph Alignment
			      Left

(continued)

TABLE 7-4. *continued*

Icon	Description	Function	Menu Command
	Center	Centers text in selected paragraphs	Format Paragraph Paragraph Alignment Center
	Align Right	Right-aligns text in selected paragraphs	Format Paragraph Paragraph Alignment Right
	Numbered List	Creates a numbered list	Format Bullets and Numbering Numbered
	Bulleted List	Creates a bulleted list	Format Bullets and Numbering Plain Bullets
	Decrease Indent	Decreases paragraph indentation on nesting level of selected list items	none
	Increase Indent	Increases paragraph indentation on nesting level of selected list items	none

Formatting Lists

As shown in Figure 7-9 (next page), Figure 7-10 (page 268), and Figure 7-11 (page 268), FrontPage supports three kinds of lists:

- **Image Bullets.** FrontPage uses a graphic image that you select as the item identifier.

- **Plain Bullets.** FrontPage instructs the browser to display a standard bullet character.

- **Numbered Bullets.** FrontPage instructs the browser to sequentially number the list items.

To convert existing paragraphs to a list

1 Select the desired paragraphs.

2 Do *one* of the following:

- Choose Numbered List or Bulleted List from the Change Style list on the Formating toolbar.

- Click the Numbered List or Bulleted List icon on the Formatting toolbar.

- Choose Bullets And Numbering from the Format menu.

You can't create an Image Bullet list from the Formatting toolbar. To create an Image Bullet list, choose the Bullets And Numbering command from the Format menu, and then select the Image Bullets tab, as shown in Figure 7-9. You can also select the Image Bullets tab by right-clicking an existing plain-bullets list and then choosing List Properties from the pop-up menu.

FIGURE 7-9.
If you choose Bullets and Numbering from the Format menu, you can insert image bullets from this dialog box.

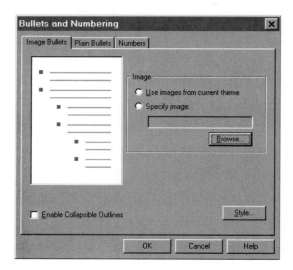

Internet Explorer 4 can selectively display or hide levels of an indented list. To activate this feature, turn on the box titled Enable Collapsible Outlines from any tab of the Bullets and Numbering dialog box.

You can create a new list in two ways. The first is to create normal paragraphs and convert them as just described. The second is this:

1   Place the insertion point where the list should begin.

2   Do *one* of the following:

- Click either the Bulleted List or the Numbered List button on the Formatting toolbar.

- Choose Bullets And Numbering from the Format menu, select a style, and then click OK.

3   Enter the text for each item in the list, and press Enter to continue to the next item.

4   To end the list and return to Normal paragraph style, press Enter twice. (If you don't want an extra line of space, press Backspace to delete it.)

> **NOTE**
>
> Remember the convention that two consecutive paragraph endings denote the end of a list. This explains many otherwise curious behaviors that occur around the end of lists.

From the Image Bullets tab, you can select images for your bullets in two ways:

- If the current Web or page uses themes, choose the option Use Images From Current Theme to use the bullet images supplied with the theme.

- Choose the Specify Image option if there's no theme in effect or if you don't want the standard theme bullets. Continue by hand-typing the image's URL or by using the Browse button to locate one. Browsing for an image is identical to browsing for any other file, except for the addition of the Clip Art button, described in "Adding Images to a Page," page 278.

> **NOTE**
>
> Image bullet lists aren't lists in an HTML sense. Rather, they're tables that Front-Page builds and maintains, using the same commands it uses for true HTML lists.

III

Building Your Site

Figure 7-10 shows the Plain Bullets tab of the Bullets And Numbering dialog box, from which you can select any one of several bullet styles that use text symbols rather than images. Click the style you want, and then click OK. Click the Style button to set CSS properties.

FIGURE 7-10.
FrontPage assigns the properties of normal bulleted lists according to the settings made here.

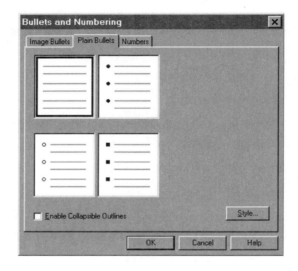

Figure 7-11 shows the Numbers tab of the Bullets And Numbering dialog box. Click the numbering style you want, verify or change the Start At value for the first paragraph in the list, and then click OK. Click the Style button to set cascading style sheet properties.

FIGURE 7-11.
The Numbers tab of the Bullets and Numbering dialog box controls the properties of numbered lists.

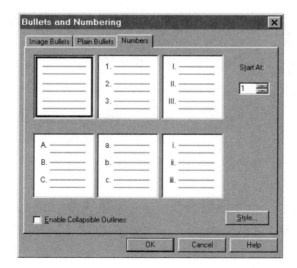

Figure 7-12 shows examples of indented lists using plain bullets, numbered lists, and image bullets. These are actually lists inside of lists; the entire sublist is part of the text for the item just above it. To begin a sublist

1 Place the insertion point at the end of the bullet that will precede the first indented bullet.

2 Press Enter to create a new list item.

3 Click the Increase Indent icon on the Formatting toolbar twice. The first click creates a Normal style paragraph, and the second click creates a sublist bullet.

To convert any item in a list to a normal paragraph, first select it and then click the Decrease Indent icon on the Formatting toolbar. More than one click might be necessary, depending on the original indentation. If you experiment with successive clicks of the Increase Indent and Decrease Indent buttons, you'll see that you can move from level to level, passing through a Normal style level in between list levels.

To continue adding new items at the current list level, simply press Enter at the end of each preceding item.

FIGURE 7-12.
Notice that each sublist is included within a parent list.

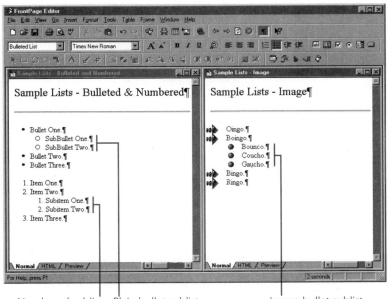

Numbered sublist   Plain bullet sublist   Image bullet sublist

To change the properties of an existing list, right-click anywhere in the list and choose List Properties from the pop-up menu, as shown in Figure 7-13.

FIGURE 7-13.
The Other tab of the List Properties dialog box contains additional list choices..

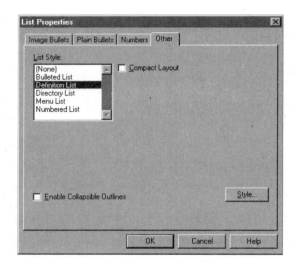

Other List Types

While the Other tab of the List Properties dialog box lists (among others) directory lists and menu lists, current browsers seem to display these identically to bulleted lists. Nevertheless, you can use this tab to assign the directory or menu list types to be used if the need arises. Bulleted lists are by far the most common of the three and therefore the most universally supported.

The Definition List option on the Other tab combines two HTML styles, Defined Term and Definition, to create a special type of list. The browser displays a Defined Term paragraph flush left followed by an indented Definition paragraph. Glance back at Figure 7-7, page 262, to see how the Definition appears in the middle window. To create a Defined Term and its Definition

1   Type the term you plan to define on its own line.

2   Select Defined Term from the Change Style list on the Formatting toolbar. The paragraph will format as a Defined Term.

3 Set the insertion point at the end of the Defined Term paragraph, and then press Enter. FrontPage will start a new line and apply the Definition style, indenting the new line.

4 Type the definition of the term.

5 Press Enter. FrontPage will start a new line and begin a new defined term so that you can type a list of terms and definitions without interruption.

6 When you're done with the entire definition list, terminate the list by pressing Enter twice at the end of the final definition line.

The Style button is present on the various list dialog boxes and will invoke the Syle dialog box, where you attach CSS attributes. These attributes might or might not have the effect you want, depending on where you use them and how well each viewer's browser supports them. They're yours to experiment with.

Formatting Text Fonts

Controlling fonts on Web pages presents unique difficulties. For one, there's no way of knowing what fonts or font technologies a given remote user will have available. For another, it's unlikely that all the same fonts will be available to any two users. Finally, even fonts that appear to be identical, down to their names, may have subtle differences when obtained from different vendors or even from the same vendor when used on different platforms.

? SEE ALSO

For information on how to format small amounts of text as images, refer to "Adding Text to Images," page 295.

The HTML specification tries to avoid font confusion by avoiding fonts. That is, instead of providing a way to specify fonts by name, it provides ways to flag blocks of text by their structural use in the document. Responsibility for assigning specific fonts then falls to the user's browser.

Some newer versions of HTML *do* support specific font name assignments, as does FrontPage. However, just because FrontPage lets you specify font names such as DomCasual BT and Elephant doesn't mean those fonts are available to your Web visitors. If the remote system doesn't have a font with the name you specify, it will substitute another font—usually the default browser font, which generally is adequate.

III

Building Your Site

SEE ALSO
for more guidance
on using fonts,
see "Typography,"
page 127.

Five Recommendations for Using Fonts on the Web

Consider these five common-sense suggestions for using font attributes effectively in your Web pages.

1 Use fonts large enough to read. Small print is for lawyers. If the verbiage isn't important enough to present legibly, omit it.

2 Don't waste space with large fonts. Large amounts of text in a large font slow down the reader and lead to excessive scrolling. In addition, they have far less impact than a pleasing and effective page design.

3 Stick to mainstream fonts. If remote users don't have the artistic font you want, their browser will probably substitute an ugly one.

4 Avoid ransom notes. Stick to a few well-chosen sizes and styles of type.

5 Aim for contrast, not clash. Achieve a pleasing contrast between background and text.

NOTE

Most browsers correctly substitute a local version of Arial, Helvetica, or Times Roman for any known variation of those names. Font substitution for less common names, however, can be problematic.

FrontPage provides seven font-related icons on the Formatting toolbar. Each icon applies an attribute to the currently selected text, or removes an attribute previously applied. Refer back to Table 7-4 (page 264) for help in identifying buttons you're not already familiar with:

- **Change Font.** Applies a selected font name.

- **Increase Text Size.** Increases font size.

- **Decrease Text Size.** Decreases font size.

- **Bold.** Toggles boldfacing on and off.

- **Italic.** Toggles italicizing on and off.

- **Underline.** Toggles underlining on and off.

- **Text Color.** Displays a standard color selection dialog box, and then applies the selected color.

TIP

You can also toggle boldfacing, italicizing, and underlining of selected words on and off by pressing Ctrl+B, Ctrl+I, and Ctrl+U, respectively.

Press Ctrl+Shift+> to increase font size of selected words, Ctrl+Shift+< to decrease it.

Ctrl+= flags text as a superscript and Ctrl+- as a subscript.

For maximum control of font settings, select the text you want to modify and then choose Font from the Format menu. The resulting dialog box contains the Font tab shown in Figure 7-14 and the Special Styles tab shown in Figure 7-15, on the following page.

 TIP

You can obtain the same dialog box by right-clicking a block of text and choosing Font Properties on the pop-up menu.

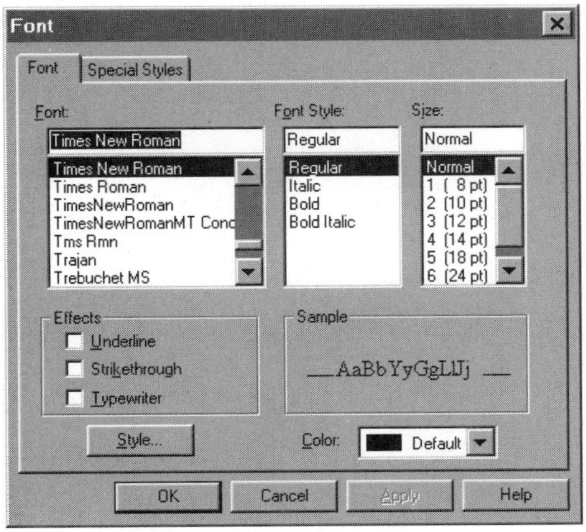

FIGURE 7-14.
The Font tab of the Font dialog box provides controls similar to those of any word processor.

The Font tab controls the following settings:

- **Font.** Selects a specific font name.

- **Font Style.** Controls the following effects: regular, italic, bold, bold italic.

Building Your Site

III

- **Size.** Specifies a relative size code from 1 to 7. The dialog box lists typical point-size equivalents for convenience, although these can vary by browser and system configuration.

- **Underline.** Underlines text.

> The underline setting has no effect on underlining of hyperlinks.

- **Strikethrough.** Draws a horizontal line through the selected text.

- **Typewriter.** Spaces text as if the font were monospaced.

- **Color.** Provides a drop-down list with 18 color selections: Default, the 16 original VGA colors, and Custom.

- **Style.** Opens the Style dialog box for using CSS attributes.

To preview the results of setting the various Font controls, refer to the Sample section.

FIGURE 7-15.
The Special Styles tab assigns text formatting as originally envisioned for HTML.

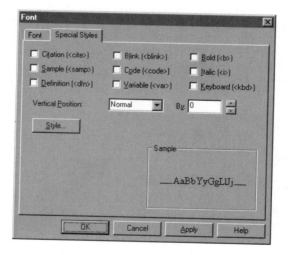

The Special Styles tab specifies a variety of text styles defined in early versions of HTML. The appearance of these styles is completely determined by the user's browser.

- **Citation.** A style designed to be assigned to a manual, section, or book, typically displayed in italics.

- **Sample.** A sequence of literal characters. This is similar to the typewriter font on the Font tab.

- **Definition.** A definition, typically in italics.

- **Blink.** Flashing text. Web browsers that can't display blinking text will ignore this setting.

- **Code.** A code sample. This is usually similar to the typewriter font.

- **Variable.** A variable name, typically in italics.

- **Bold.** Boldfaced text.

- **Italic.** Italicized text.

- **Keyboard.** Indicates typing by a user, as when following a procedure. This is usually similar to the typewriter font.

- **Vertical Position.** A style that sets text to Superscript, Subscript, or Normal (the default).

- **By.** In conjunction with Vertical Position, indicates the number of points by which the text should be raised or lowered from the baseline (the imaginary line on which letters such as *a, e,* and *o* rest).

- **Style.** An option that displays the FrontPage Style dialog box.

To preview the results of setting Special Styles controls, refer to the Sample section in the Font dialog box.

Aligning Text

HTML provides only four settings for aligning paragraph text: Default, Left, Center, and Right. There are three ways to apply these settings.

- Use the Align Left, Center, and Align Right icons on the Formatting toolbar, as described in Table 7-4 (page 264). Once an alignment is in effect, its button will remain pressed in. To specify default alignment, no alignment button should be pressed in.

- Choose Paragraph from the Format menu, and set the Paragraph Alignment control. See Figure 7-8 (page 263).

- Right-click the paragraph, choose Paragraph Properties from the pop-up menu, and then set the Paragraph Alignment control.

The following keystrokes also align text: Ctrl+R toggles right alignment; Ctrl+L toggles left alignment; Ctrl+E toggles centering.

In the next chapter, we'll complement the formatting of text covered in this chapter with information on how to incorporate graphics and format them for the best possible effect.

CHAPTER 8

Incorporating Graphics

M ost observers credit in-line graphics as the feature that transformed the World Wide Web from a curiosity of academic interest and a means of technical interchange to an amazingly pervasive icon of pop culture. Today, while excessive use of graphics slows download times and keeps users away, the lack of graphics drives them away at least as rapidly.

Strictly speaking, HTML is incapable of containing images. Instead, HTML contains the names of image files and some accompanying format codes. On receiving an HTML file, the user's browser notes the names of any required image files, retrieves them from the Web server, and displays them as specified in the HTML. Nevertheless, Web pages and the images they contain must work together and, therefore, be designed together too.

FrontPage not only supports the full capabilities of HTML for adding graphic images to Web pages, but also permits integrated graphical display and, to a limited extent, graphics editing. This chapter describes these facilities.

Adding Images to a Page

With FrontPage, adding graphics to a Web page is as easy as drag and drop. Figure 8-1 shows how you can drag images from FrontPage Explorer to an open page in FrontPage Editor. As you drag over the open Web page, the insertion point shows where the graphic will appear. You can also

- Drag images from Windows Explorer into Web pages

- Drag images from Internet Explorer into Web pages

- Copy images from other programs to the Clipboard, and then paste them into FrontPage

- Drag images from one open Web page to another

- Drag images from one location to another on the same Web page

 TIP

> When dragging images from the same or another Web page, the default operation is Move. That is, the images disappear from the source location and appear at the drop location. To create a second copy of the source image, either hold down the Ctrl key while dragging or drag with the right mouse button and choose Copy Here from the pop-up menu that appears after releasing it.
>
> Copying an image this way doesn't create a new image file, it simply loads the same file into two different locations on the same Web page.

You can also insert images by choosing Image from the Insert menu in FrontPage Editor. This produces the Image dialog box shown in Figure 8-2.

Initially, the Image dialog box displays files in the starting folder of the current FrontPage Web. To view contents of another folder in the Web, double-click it. To view the parent of the current folder, click the Up One Level button.

The list in the center of the dialog box displays all image files in the current folder. To select one, single-click it. The preview window to the right of the selection list will display the corresponding image.

FIGURE 8-1.
FrontPage Editor can accept images dropped from FrontPage Explorer, Windows Explorer, or Internet Explorer.

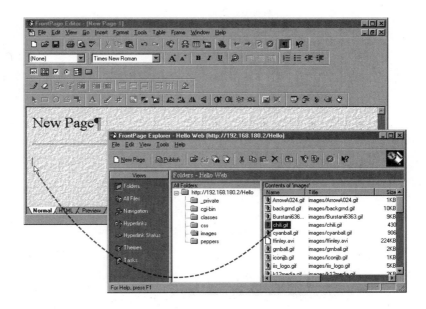

FIGURE 8-2.
Use this FrontPage Editor dialog box to locate a desired image.

Shows current folder or location

Lists files, folders, and page titles

Lists files and folders

Creates a new folder

Displays parent folder

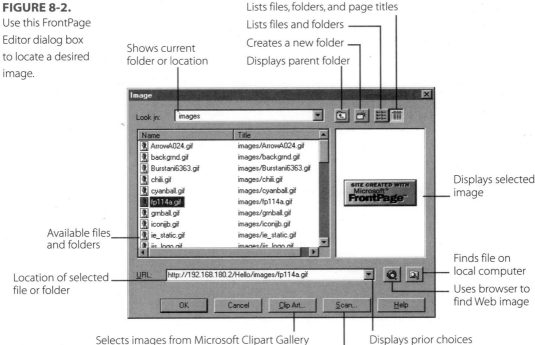

Displays selected image

Available files and folders

Finds file on local computer

Location of selected file or folder

Uses browser to find Web image

Selects images from Microsoft Clipart Gallery

Displays prior choices

Brings in image from scanner or digital camera

III

Building Your Site

Selecting Images with Your Web Browser

After clicking the Image dialog box's Use Your Web Browser To Select A Page button and waiting for the browser to appear, you can retrieve any Web image by displaying it in the browser and then switching back to FrontPage Editor. The image's Web location will automatically appear in the URL field of the Image dialog box.

This technique requires getting your browser to display just the image file, however, and *not* a Web page that contains the image file. That is, the Web address displayed in the browser's Location box must end in JPG, JPEG, or GIF. When a site provides direct hyperlinks to images, typically through thumbnail previews, this is easy to arrange. If the image you want isn't available this way, follow this procedure using Internet Explorer:

1 Locate a Web page containing the image you want.

2 Right-click the image and choose Properties from the pop-up menu.

3 When the Properties dialog box shown in Figure 8-3 appears, highlight the contents of the Address (URL) field by double-clicking its value.

4 Press Ctrl+C to copy the address, or right-click the Address (URL) field and choose Copy from the pop-up menu.

5 Click OK to close the dialog box.

6 Click the contents of the Location field in the Internet Explorer toolbar to highlight the entire URL.

7 Press Ctrl+V to paste the image's Address (URL) field copied in step 4.

8 Press Enter to display just the image in Internet Explorer.

9 Return to FrontPage Editor. The address you copied in step 4 should now appear in the URL field of the Image dialog box.

You don't actually have to complete steps 6, 7, and 8. Instead, once you've copied the image's URL in step 4, you can return directly to FrontPage Editor and simply paste the image URL into the URL field of the Image dialog box.

The Look In and URL fields in combination show the current location. Note that a Web address appears and not a local filename; thus, you can use this dialog box to retrieve any image on your personal Web

FIGURE 8-3.
This dialog box results from right-clicking an image in Internet Explorer and choosing Properties.

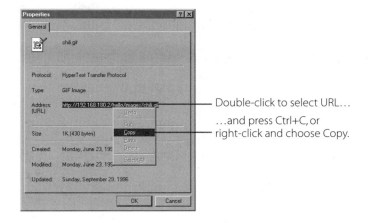

Double-click to select URL…

…and press Ctrl+C, or right-click and choose Copy.

server, your intranet, or the World Wide Web. To view your recent selections, click the drop-down arrow at the right of the URL field.

The Browser button uses your Web browser to find an image.

The Local File button selects an image from your local disk or network. After you've located the file, FrontPage converts its location to a *file://* URL and enters it in the URL field.

 TIP

> You can also insert image files—or, for that matter, any other type of file—by choosing File from the Insert menu.

FrontPage comes with a handy collection of Web clip art, plus it offers access to any clip art received with other applications in the Microsoft Office family. To select an image from the clip art library, click the Clip Art button in the Image dialog box shown in Figure 8-2, page 279, and the Microsoft Clip Gallery dialog box shown in Figure 8-4, on the next page, will appear.

 TIP

> To insert clip art directly, without going through the Image dialog box, choose Clipart from the Insert menu.

III

Building Your Site

FIGURE 8-4.

This dialog box lets you select images and pictures from the FrontPage clip art library.

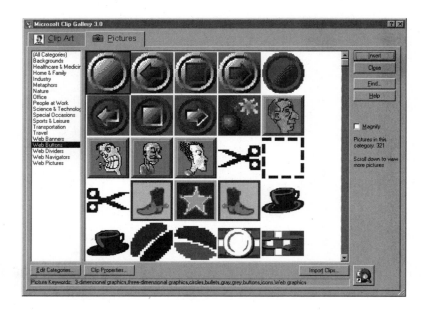

To add a clip art image to your Web page

1 Choose either the Clip Art or the Pictures tab. The Clip Art tab lists scalable drawings that you can resize without loss of image quality. The Pictures tab lists bitmapped images that resizing will generally degrade.

2 Choose a category from the category list box.

3 Choose an image by clicking it.

4 Click the Insert button.

> When you add a scalable drawing to FrontPage Editor, it remains scalable only until you save the page, when FrontPage saves it as a bitmap. It's best to rescale such drawings soon after inserting them, and certainly before the first Save.

To record an image directly from a scanner or digital image to a Web page, click the Scan button in the Image dialog box. This invokes Twain-compliant camera, scanner, or other device software and directly passes any image you capture to FrontPage.

When you insert an image not from the current Web, FrontPage holds the image in memory until you save the page, and then suggests adding the image to your Web. Figure 8-5 illustrates this prompt. In almost every case, you should consent.

FIGURE 8-5.
When saving a Web page, FrontPage suggests saving foreign images to the local Web.

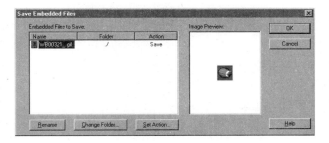

The dialog box shown in Figure 8-5 might also appear when you modify an existing object in your Web—such as an image—as part of another operation. This might result from changing the contrast of an image, for example. FrontPage presents the dialog box so that you can save the modified image under a different filename or in a different folder than the original.

■ To choose a different filename, click the name of the file you want to change, and then click the Rename button. Type a new name directly in place of the current name, and then press Enter. FrontPage usually remembers the filenames of any external files it adds during an editing session and proposes using the same names within the current Web. If FrontPage doesn't know the original filename—perhaps because the image came from the Clipboard or a clip art library—FrontPage internally generates an arbitrary filename. However, you can override either type of name.

■ To choose a different folder, single-click the file whose destination you want to change, and then click the Change Folder button. In the resulting Current Web dialog box, double-click your way to the folder you want, making sure any files in that folder are displayed, and then click OK.

■ The Set Action button permits saving the file now as part of the overall page save or *not* saving the file and leaving its definition unchanged in FrontPage Editor. The latter choice basically postpones saving until the next time you save the entire page. Saving immediately is the default.

To minimize download time for large images, it's common practice to display a small preview image (a thumbnail) on the Web page a remote user would first encounter, and display the full-size image only if the user clicks the thumbnail. To do this in FrontPage

1 Insert the full-size image where you want its thumbnail to appear.

2 Select the large image.

3 Select AutoThumbnail from the Tools menu. In one operation FrontPage will remove the large image, create the thumbnail in its place, and set up a hyperlink from the thumbnail to the large image.

4 Use the thumbnail's handles to resize it, if desired.

5 When you save the Web page, FrontPage will use a dialog box resembling Figure 8-5 (on the previous page) to prompt for the thumbnail's filename.

Adding Multimedia Formats

To add a video clip to a Web page, choose Active Elements from the Insert menu and select Video. The Video dialog box appears and is similar to the Image dialog box shown in Figure 8-2, page 279, except that it searches by default for video (AVI) files rather than still images, and it lacks the scanner button.

Page-level settings for a background sound are set in the Page Properties dialog box as described in "General Page Properties," page 222.

Animated GIF files don't qualify here as multimedia. Insert animated GIFs using the Image dialog box, as you would for any other GIF or JPG image.

Modifying Image Properties

Very often, making an image appear on a Web page is only half the job; the remainder involves details of placement and presentation. HTML, and therefore FrontPage, provides a variety of settings for this purpose.

To open the Image Properties dialog box, do *one* of the following:

- Click the image and choose Image Properties from the Edit menu.

- Right-click the image and choose Image Properties from the pop-up menu.

- Click the image and press Alt+Enter.

The three tabs of the Image Properties dialog box are shown in Figure 8-6 (on the next page), Figure 8-7 (page 288), and Figure 8-9 (page 290).

General Image Properties

You can use the General tab of the Image Properties dialog box shown in Figure 8-6, on the next page, to modify the properties of an image. Certain options might be unavailable (dimmed), depending on the context. The full complement of fields includes the following.

- **Image Source.** This text box specifies the full or relative URL of the image file being modified. It might be read-only, depending on the context.

- **Browse.** If Image Source is modifiable, clicking this button permits browsing the current Web or local file system to locate an image.

- **Edit.** Clicking this button invokes the default FrontPage editor for the image. Normally, this is Microsoft Image Composer.

For an explanation of the GIF and JPEG file types, refer to "Graphic File Formats," page 122.

- **Type.** This section initially displays the current image type—GIF or JPEG—and permits changing it.

  - **GIF.** If turned on, this option button instructs FrontPage to save the image as a GIF file.

  - **Transparent.** This box activates or inhibits the GIF transparency feature.

FIGURE 8-6.

This is the first of three tabs in FrontPage Editor's Image properties dialog box.

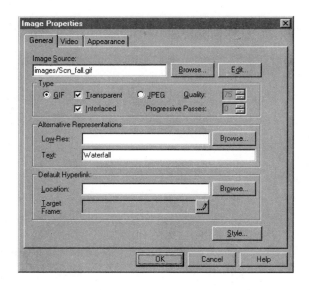

 **TIP**

Activating transparency accomplishes nothing unless you also designate a transparent color with the Make Transparent tool in the Image toolbar.

 CAUTION

Increasing the JPEG compression of a file (by *lowering* the Quality number) discards information that can't be restored later. What's gone is gone. To be safe, save a full-resolution version of any file *before* experimenting with its JPEG quality setting.

- **Interlaced.** If turned on, this box instructs FrontPage to save a GIF file with interlacing. Interlaced images appear first in coarse resolution, and then with increasing fineness.

- **JPEG.** If turned on, this option button instructs FrontPage to save the image as a JPEG file.

- **Quality.** This is an integer from 1 to 99. Lower numbers increase compression and decrease file size, but permanently decrease image quality. The default is 75.

- **Progressive Passes.** This is similar to the Interlaced feature for GIF images, but with more control. Specify the number of steps in which the JPEG image will appear.

TIP

Interlaced GIF and progressive JPEG formats provide viewers with coarse images early and full resolution later. This avoids waiting for a complete, full-resolution display.

- **Alternative Representation.** The fields in this section control alternate views of an image.

  - **Low-Res.** This specifies a low-resolution image the browser will display while downloading the larger image file. You can use the Browse button to find such an image file.

  - **Text.** This line of text will appear in browsers that can't display the image. Some browsers that *can* display images will also display this text while the image is downloading, or when the user pauses the mouse over the image.

? SEE ALSO

For information on hotspots, also called clickable image maps, see "Establishing Hotspots," page 292. For information on hyperlinks, see "Creating and Managing Hypertext Links," page 308.

- **Default Hyperlink.** This section establishes a hyperlink to another location from any part of the current image that has no hotspot defined. The command isn't available for background images.

  - **Location.** This field contains the URL the browser should retrieve if the user clicks the current image. You can use the Browse button to locate it.

  - **Target Frame.** This field specifies the frame in which the Location page will appear.

- **Style.** This button accesses the Style dialog box where you can apply cascading style sheet formats to the current image.

Video Properties

The Video tab of the Image Properties dialog box, shown in Figure 8-7, on the following page, controls the display and playback of digitized video such as AVI files.

- **Video Source.** Here you specify the location of the file containing digitized video. It can be in the current Web, on your local hard disk, on a file server, or on the World Wide Web. You can use the Browse button to locate the file.

> NOTE

If the Image Properties dialog box contains both an Image Source and a Video Source entry, the browser will first display the static image and then, when possible, replace it with the first frame of the video.

FIGURE 8-7.
The Video tab of the
Image Properties
dialog box controls
presentation of full-
motion video files.

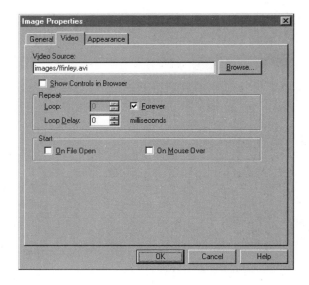

■ **Show Controls In Browser.** If this box is turned on, the
browser displays a button for starting and stopping the video and
a slide control for positioning replays. Figure 8-8 illustrates this.

FIGURE 8-8.
FrontPage can con-
figure video clips
to appear with play-
back controls.

Play button (toggles
to a Stop button)
Progress indicator
and slider

 TIP

You might need to manually increase the Height field on the Appearance tab
(discussed next) to accommodate browser video controls.

■ **Repeat.** Settings in this section control the replaying of the video.

• **Loop.** Controls the number of times the browser should
replay the video.

- **Forever.** Overrides the Loop setting and repeats the video continuously.

- **Loop Delay.** Causes a delay between repeat playings. The default is zero; any other value is milliseconds. A five-second delay, for example, would be specified as 5000.

■ **Start.** This section controls when the browser plays the video.

- **On File Open.** This setting plays the video as soon as the browser opens the file.

- **On Mouse Over.** This choice plays the video when the mouse passes over the display area.

Size and Placement Properties

The Appearance tab of the Image Properties dialog box controls image layout and size. Figure 8-9, on the next page, illustrates this. The dialog box's controls have the following effects.

■ **Layout.** This section positions the image on the page.

- **Alignment** controls vertical positioning of an image and text in the same line. See Table 8-1, on the next page, for a listing and description of each option.

- **Border Thickness**, if nonzero, surrounds the image with a border. The specified integer controls the border's thickness in pixels. Hyperlinked images have blue borders; others have black borders.

- **Horizontal Spacing** controls the separation, in pixels, between the image and other elements on the same line.

- **Vertical Spacing** controls separation between the image and any text or images in lines above or below.

■ **Size.** This frame controls the displayed size of an image.

- **Specify Size**, if turned on, indicates you wish to override the natural size of the image.

FIGURE 8-9.

The Image Properties Appearance tab controls page positioning and displayed image size.

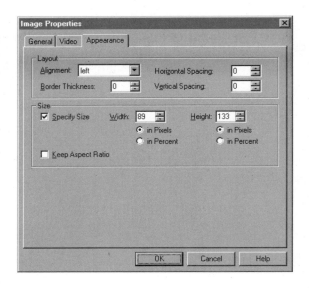

- **Width** sets the amount of horizontal space the browser should reserve for the image. Use the In Pixels or the In Percent buttons to denote the units of width.

- **Height** sets the amount of vertical space the browser should reserve for the image. Use the In Pixels or the In Percent buttons to denote the units of height.

- **Keep Aspect Ratio** specifies that changing either the image's height or its width changes the other dimension proportionally.

TABLE 8-1. HTML Image Alignment Settings

Alignment	Description
Left	Floats the image down and left to the next spot available at the left margin; wraps subsequent text around the right side of that image
Right	Aligns image with the right margin; wraps subsequent text around the left
Bottom	Aligns the bottom of the image with the baseline of the current line; see Figure 8-10 (on the next page) for illustrations of this and the following settings

(continued)

TABLE 8-1. *continued*

Alignment	Description
Baseline	Aligns the bottom of the image with the baseline of the current line
Absbottom	Aligns the bottom of the image with the bottom of the current line
Middle	Aligns the baseline of the current line with the middle of the image
Absmiddle	Aligns the middle of the current line with the middle of the image
Top	Aligns the image with the top of the tallest item in the line
Texttop	Aligns the image with the top of the tallest text in the line (this is usually, but not always, the same as top)

As HTML page design has evolved, most Web designers want more control over image placement than in-line images provide. Of the nine image alignment settings, Left and Right are probably the most often used. As Figure 8-10 illustrates, in-line images also result in uneven, distracting line spacing. The Left and Right settings provide at least some absolute positioning—the margins—while they also maintain uniform line spacing.

FIGURE 8-10.
This page illustrates various HTML Image Alignment settings.

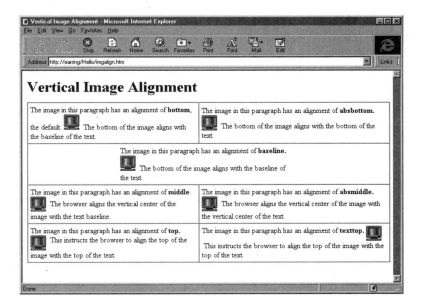

To center an image by itself, put it in its own paragraph. To center the paragraph, do *either* of the following:

- Select the paragraph and click the Center button on the Text toolbar.

- Right-click the paragraph, choose Paragraph Properties from the pop-up menu, and set the Paragraph Alignment control to Center.

By default, the user's browser will inspect all images on a page and allocate window space to display them at their natural size. For at least three reasons, you should consider overriding this behavior and setting an image size at authoring time.

1 Using the default behavior, the browser can't allocate window space to an image until it has received enough of the file to determine its dimensions. Not knowing the size of an image might also delay placement—and therefore display—of other page elements as well. Specifying sizes for all images on a page allows many page elements to display sooner than otherwise might be possible.

For more information on scripts, refer to "Script Languages," page 76, or "Incorporating Custom Script Code," page 510.

2 Browsers tend to have difficulty with pages containing both scripts embedded in the HTML and images with no preassigned Height and Width. These problems seem to arise from the scripts' starting to run before all page element locations are determined. Therefore, always specify dimensions—in pixels—for all images on pages that contain scripts.

3 Occasionally, you may wish to display an image larger or smaller than its natural size. This used to be rare because downloading a large image and having the browser reduce it takes more time than downloading a smaller one. By contrast, downloading a small image and having the browser expand it results in a loss of resolution. More recently, however, the practice of expanding small images has become surprisingly common. The sidebar "Using Transparent Images as White Space," page 299, will explain this.

Establishing Hotspots

Hotspots—also called image maps—are portions of an image that function as hyperlinks. The most common uses for hotspots are in menu bars and maps, though you can use hotspots for any application

(?) SEE ALSO

For an introductory discussion of hotspots, refer to "Image Maps and Hotspots," page 69.

(?) SEE ALSO

For a further discussion of hyperlinking, see "Creating and Managing Hypertext Links," page 308.

(?) SEE ALSO

For more information on handling hotspots on servers and browsers, review the material in "Reviewing Web Settings," page 166, and Figure 5-21, page 168.

that requires jumping to different locations in response to clicking different areas of an image.

To add hotspots to an image in FrontPage Editor

1 Single-click the image to select it.

2 Select the Rectangle, Circle, or Polygon tool from the Image toolbar described in Table 8-2, page 294.

3 Drag the mouse over the portion of the image that should define the hotspot. When using the Polygon tool, click the mouse at each corner. To close the polygon, double-click the next-to-last point and the final line will be drawn to the starting point.

4 When dragging is complete, FrontPage will open the Create Hyperlink dialog box. This is the same dialog box used for setting up hyperlinks both from text and from entire images. Define the hyperlink as described in the next section, and then click OK.

5 Repeat steps 2, 3, and 4 to define additional hotspots for the same image.

When you select an image that has hotspots, FrontPage displays the clickable areas as shown in Figure 8-11, on the next page. The figure shows a single image with three hotspots.

■ To modify a hotspot area, select it once by single-clicking, and then drag the edges or corner handles.

■ To modify a hotspot hyperlink, double-click the hotspot area, or right-click it and choose Image Hotspot Properties from the pop-up menu.

A frequent criticism of hotspots—and of image hyperlinks in general—is the lack of visual clues they provide. Users are reduced to moving the mouse pointer over an image and watching for the pointer to indicate a hyperlink, or to clicking images at random to discover what they do. If the image you're adding hyperlinks to lacks obvious visual clues, be sure to provide instructions in the surrounding text.

III

Building Your Site

FIGURE 8-11.
If an image's hotspots are difficult to see, the Highlight Hotspots button will toggle the Images to a solid white background.

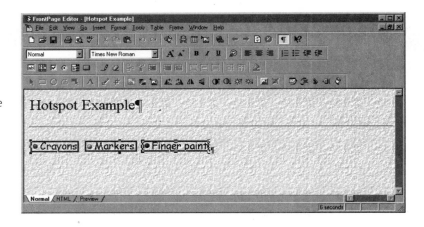

TABLE 8-2. **The FrontPage Editor Image Toolbar**

Icon	Description	Function
	Select	Readies the mouse pointer for selecting images or hotspots
	Rectangle	Readies the mouse pointer for marking rectangular hotspots
	Circle	Readies the mouse pointer for marking circular hotspots
	Polygon	Readies the mouse pointer for marking polygonal hotspots
	Highlight Hotspots	Displays hotspots on selected images against a solid white background so that you can review their positions
	Text	Superimposes formatted text over an image
	Make Transparent	Readies the mouse pointer to select a GIF image color and declare it transparent
	Crop	Readies the mouse pointer to select a portion of an image and discard the rest.
	Washout	Lightens an image so that it can be used as a background or so that text can be seen on top of it
	Black and White	Changes an image to monochrome

(continued)

TABLE 8-2. *continued*

Icon	Description	Function
	Restore	Restores an image to its last saved contents
	Rotate Left	Rotates an image 90 degrees counterclockwise
	Rotate Right	Rotates an image 90 degrees clockwise
	Reverse	Reverses an image right to left (mirror image)
	Flip	Flips an image top to bottom (inverted image)
	More Contrast	Darkens darks, whitens lights, and moves midtones toward dark and light extremes
	Less Contrast	Darkens lights and whitens darks, moving them closer to the midtone levels
	More Brightness	Adds white proportionally to every color in the image
	Less Brightness	Adds black proportionally to every color in the image
	Bevel	Adds a 3-D border around the edge of an image
	Resample	Physically converts an image (scaled only in memory) to its new size

Adding Text to Images

Web authors frequently need to add text, such as button titles, to graphics, such as buttons. FrontPage supports this operation completely within FrontPage Editor using a feature called Text On GIFs. Figure 8-12, on the next page, provides some examples.

Applying text to GIF files is quite simple:

1 Add the graphic to the Web page, if it isn't there already.

2 Select the graphic by clicking it.

3 Choose the Text tool on the Image toolbar.

III

Building Your Site

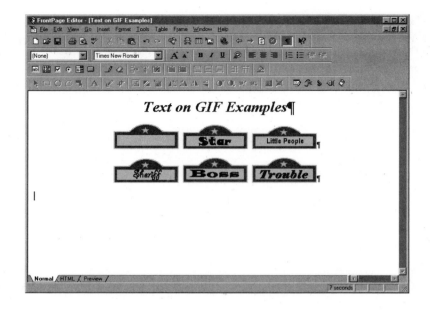

4 A second set of handles will appear within those surrounding the image. Click the mouse inside the inner handles to place an insertion marker, and then type your text. If the text doesn't fit, enlarge the text area by dragging its handles.

5 Set font, point size, alignment, color, and other attributes by either selecting the text and then choosing Font from the Format menu or using the buttons on the Format toolbar.

6 When you're done, click outside the graphic to stop text entry and editing.

To create headings, titles, and other small amounts of text using special fonts and colors, first use your image editor to create a completely transparent GIF file. Add this file to your Web page, and then use the Text button to add and format the text. The main advantage of this method, compared to just entering the text in your image editor, is having Text On GIFs readily available as you develop other parts of your page.

Many Web page creators keep a collection of transparent GIF files on hand to use for reserving white space or guaranteeing table widths. It's very tempting to stretch a small transparent GIF out to the size of a heading and then use the Text On GIFs feature to display the heading with full control over font and color. First, however, make sure that the GIF file's transparent color isn't the same as the color of your text; otherwise, the text will disappear along with the transparent GIF.

Then follow these steps to ensure the Text On GIF feature will work correctly:

1 Resize the GIF file by dragging its handles or entering dimensions in the Image Properties dialog box.

2 Resample the transparent file.

3 Save the Web page.

4 Give the transparent file a descriptive name when prompted.

> **NOTE**
>
> FrontPage can't save text on a small image you've merely resized on screen. Such resizing changes only the display size and not the number of pixels stored on disk. Resampling (described in "Cropping and Resizing Images," page 300) creates an image permanently sized to the dimensions that appear on your screen.

Setting Transparency

All GIF and JPEG images are rectangular. Most real-life objects aren't. One solution to this dilemma, though a poor one, is to enclose all images in picture frames. This often produces unattractive results. A second and better approach is coloring the unused portions of the image to match it's surroundings—the Web page background. However, this solution also has drawbacks:

■ It requires a different image version for each background color.

■ Smoothly matching a textured background image generally isn't possible.

■ Remote users can instruct their browser to ignore background images, to ignore background colors, or to ignore both.

The best solution is to make portions of the image transparent, as if they were printed on a sheet of clear plastic. Figure 8-13, on the next page, provides an example of this technique. The image on the left, with a white background, doesn't blend with the textured background.

III

Building Your Site

How Transparency Works

Of 16,777,216 possible colors, only 256 can exist within any given GIF file. These 256 are the GIF file's *palette*. Transparency works by designating one palette entry—out of the 256—as transparent. When the browser encounters this palette entry color, it displays whatever lies behind the GIF image instead of the palette entry color.

If two palette entries represent the same color, only one of them can indicate transparency. This may explain why you occasionally get incomplete results setting transparency on the basis of color.

The JPEG file format doesn't support transparency.

The image on the right has a transparent background that lets the page's background image show through. Take care, however, that the background's texture doesn't cause legibility problems for the text font, size, and attributes.

FIGURE 8-13.
The image on the left has a white background; that on the right is transparent.

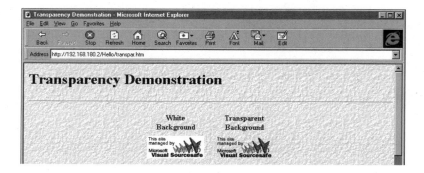

Most GIF file editors have features for handling transparency, though you can also control transparency from within FrontPage. The FrontPage procedure is as follows:

1 Add the image to your Web page (if not already present).

2 Make sure the Image toolbar is displayed. This is the toolbar described in Table 8-2, page 294.

 **TIP**

To toggle display of any toolbar, choose its entry from the View menu in Front-Page Editor.

3 Single-click the image to select it.

4 Click the Make Transparent button, shown in Table 8-2, page 294.

5 Move the mouse over the selected image and click any pixel of the color that should become transparent. All pixels matching that color in the image will immediately become transparent.

6 To make a different color transparent, repeat steps 4 and 5. FrontPage Editor can make only one color at a time transparent.

7 To turn off transparency for an image, go to the General tab of the Image Properties dialog box, shown in Figure 8-6, page 286, and turn off the Transparent box.

Using Transparent Images as White Space

In an effort to keep Web pages device-independent, HTML provides very little support for absolute positioning. HTML "thinks" in terms of flowing text, not in terms of objects placed on an *x-y* grid. This is greatly frustrating when presenting commercial art rather than, say, a research paper.

Tables and frames, discussed in Chapter 9, "Hyperlinks and Page Layout," provide page designers with a coarse measure of *x-y* positioning, but for fine control many designers have adopted the use of transparent GIF images. Anywhere they want some blank space on the page, they simply locate a completely transparent GIF image. Some cases where this works extremely well include

- Indenting the first line of a paragraph

- Spacing fractional lines between paragraphs

- Indenting objects from a window, frame, or table margin

- Guaranteeing a minimum width for a table column

Note that in a completely transparent GIF image, every pixel is the same color—the transparent color. Clever designers therefore keep a one-pixel by one-pixel transparent GIF file in their bag of tricks. This is the smallest possible file to download, and specifying an appropriate height and width for it (in the Appearance tab of the Image Properties dialog box shown in Figure 8-9, page 290) will stretch the file to any required size. Remember to turn off the Keep Aspect Ratio feature so that you can independently set the width and height. The same file can be used over and over again in different locations, simply by specifying different sizes of it each time.

Using Transparent Images as White Space *continued*

Working with one-pixel transparent GIF images presents a unique problem with WYSIWYG editors such as FrontPage; such images are quite difficult to locate, select, and modify. For this reason you may find it easier to work with slightly larger files. The accompanying CD contains these transparent GIF files for your use:

Filename	Pixels	File Size (Bytes)
trans1x1.gif	1×1	42
trans5x5.gif	5×5	45
trans9x9.gif	9×9	49

Cropping and Resizing Images

Cropping is the process of choosing part of an image and discarding the rest. The image becomes smaller in the process. To crop an image in FrontPage

1 Select the Image.

2 Select the Crop tool from FrontPage Editor's Image toolbar, shown in Table 8-2, page 294.

3 Within the selected image, FrontPage will draw a bounding box with handles. Move the handles so that the bounding box encloses the part of the image you want to retain.

4 Click the Crop tool again or press Enter. FrontPage will discard any pixels outside the bounding box.

When you save the Web page, FrontPage will consider the cropped image a new, unsaved file and present the Save Embedded Files dialog box, shown in Figure 8-5, page 283. By default, the dialog box will suggest saving the file in the root directory of your Web with the same filename as the original, uncropped file. Unless you want to overwrite the original file, it's best to rename the cropped file. And, as discussed in Chapter 5, "Structuring Your Web," it's best to keep all your images in an /images folder rather than the root.

To resize an image, simply select it and drag its handles. Dragging the corner handles resizes the image proportionately; the height and width are forced to change by the same percentages. Dragging the top or bottom handle changes only the height, while dragging the left or right handle changes only the width.

Resizing a file with its handles doesn't alter the size of the image file itself; it changes only the amount of screen space the browser must fill. The actual resizing occurs not when you save your Web page, but after it gets delivered to the user's browser. Therefore, reducing the size of an image this way saves the remote user nothing in download time.

To physically resize an image, you must both resize *and* resample it in FrontPage. First resize the file, and then click the Resample button on the Image toolbar. Resampling creates a larger or smaller file than the original, rescaled by mathematically averaging pixels.

Unlike resizing, resampling *does* change the file stored on your Web. When you save the Web page, FrontPage presents the Save Embedded Files dialog box of Figure 8-5, page 283, to suggest giving the modified file a new filename and location.

Applying Washouts and Monochrome

To wash out an image, select it and then click the Washout button on the Image toolbar. You can only wash out an image once per save. To avoid accidentally overwriting the original image file when you save the Web page, FrontPage will prompt you for a new filename and location.

To doubly wash out an image, wash it, save it, and then wash it again.

The Black And White toolbar button removes all color from an image; that is, it converts it to monochrome. You can undo this operation by clicking the button again, but not after the monochrome image is saved.

Figure 8-14, on the next page, illustrates these and other image effects.

FIGURE 8-14.
This page displays various image transformations you can apply directly within FrontPage Editor.

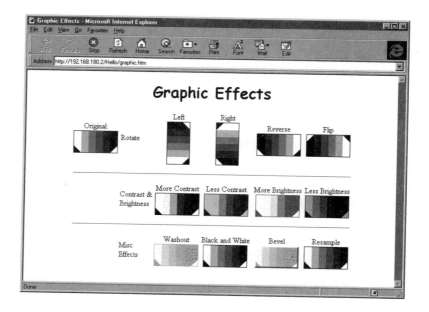

Rotating and Flipping Images

FrontPage provides four toolbar icons for rotating images (shown in Table 8-2, page 294): two to rotate right or left in 90-degree increments, and two more for flipping top-to-bottom and right-to-left. To see their effects, look at the top set of images in Figure 8-14.

FrontPage permits flipping and rotating the same image any number of times. As with other operations that modify the saved file, rotating and flipping open the Save Embedded Images dialog box when you save the Web page, giving you a chance to save it under a new name, thus preserving the original file.

Controlling Brightness and Contrast

The Image toolbar contains four buttons for modifying brightness and contrast: one each for increasing and decreasing, shown in the second set of images in Figure 8-14. Pressing these buttons repeatedly will intensify their effect.

- Increasing contrast makes high intensities higher and low intensities lower. That is, it pushes each color in an image closer to either black or white, whichever is closer.

- Decreasing contrast makes high intensities lower and low intensities higher. In short, it pushes your image in the direction of Seattle weather—all gray.

- Increasing brightness adds white to every color in the image; the darker the color, the more white added. Eventually, the image would become pure white.

- Decreasing brightness adds black to every color in the image; the lighter the color, the more black added. Eventually, the image would become completely black.

Brightness and contrast changes are saved in the image, so for any image you thus modify, FrontPage gives you the opportunity to save the file under a new name.

Beveling Edges

This effect lightens the top and left edges of an image while also darkening the bottom and right edges. This creates the effect of a three-dimensional button. After beveling an image and saving the page, you'll once again be prompted for a filename and folder.

Restoring Images

Until you save an image file, FrontPage can always revert to the version it originally loaded from your Web or other location. To return to this version, click the Restore button on the Images toolbar. Don't use Restore to reverse only the most recent of several changes; if you wish to do that, instead choose Undo from the Edit menu.

Managing Image Download Time

A constant concern for all Web users is the time required to download and view a given page. This is less a concern for users on local intranets or with high-speed connections than it is for dial-up modem users, but a concern nonetheless. As a Web provider, you should also be concerned with outbound bandwidth. The larger your pages, the fewer pages your server and your Internet connection can deliver per second (or minute).

In general, the time required to download a page is the combined size of all constituent files divided by the bytes per second of available bandwidth. Managing download time thus becomes an issue of managing download bytes. And, because most download bytes occur in image files rather than the HTML, managing download bytes becomes an issue of managing image file size.

FrontPage Editor estimates each page's download time for a typical modem user and displays it in the status bar; for example, the "6 Seconds" showing in the bottom-right corner of Figure 8-11, page 294. This feature permits monitoring the effect of images you add to a page. There are, however, three mitigating factors:

■ Most current browsers cache images and other files. That is, they keep local copies of recently used files. Before downloading any file, the browser checks for a local copy; if one exists, the browser, depending on its configuration, does *either* of the following:

- Uses it without question, subject to certain timing constraints.

- Transmits the local copy's date stamp to the server. If the cached copy is outdated, the Web server transmits a new version. If the cached copy is current, the Web server responds with a status code instructing the browser to use the cached version.

You can maximize the benefits of caching by using stock images and not storing them redundantly on your server. The use of stock images increases caching by reducing the number of different images. Storing all images in, say, an /images folder ensures that the same image has the same URL for all pages on your site. Storing the same image in two different server locations forces the browser to download and cache each copy separately.

■ Reducing total image bytes on a Web page suggests using many small image files rather than one large or medium file. This process can go too far, however, because of a factor called *connection overhead*.

Unless both the browser and the Web server support a feature called *persistent connections*, the HTTP protocol forces the browser to open a new connection for every file it downloads. Thus, a Web page containing 10 images forces the browser to open and close 11 server connections: 1 for the HTML page and 1 for each image. Each of these connections requires processing time on both the browser and server—time that might exceed what's required to download a smaller number of slightly larger files.

Stringent balancing of download bytes versus required connections is seldom warranted, given the number of other variables in effect. Nevertheless, it's good practice to avoid large numbers of very small files.

- GIF image compression works mainly by consolidating horizontal pixels. That is, rather than sequentially storing 100 white pixels on the same line, the file stores a single instruction to display 100 consecutive pixels, all white.

  You can use this information to create images that compress well. Just remember that flat, horizontal areas compress well but complex horizontal areas don't.

  JPEG compression is more two-dimensional and thus is less affected by the nature of the image. Flat areas still compress better than highly variegated ones, however. With JPEG files you can also balance quality against image size. To do this, vary the Quality setting in the Image Properties dialog box, Figure 8-6, page 286.

The next chapter deals with how to create and manage hypertext links, bookmarks, tables, and frames. It also discusses HTML markup commands, extended attributes, and ways to view commands in hypertext markup language.

III

Building Your Site

Hyperlinks
and Page Layout

This chapter describes the most common Web mechanisms for connecting and formatting Web pages, and discusses how to employ these mechanisms using FrontPage:

- hyperlinks

- bookmarks

- tables

- frames

Hyperlinks are the essence of the Web. Without hyperlinks, there would be no point and click navigation among Web pages—and without point and click the Web would be dead. Every time you click some underlined text or an image area and thereby jump to another page, you're using a hyperlink. A Web page lacking hyperlinks is truly a Web page going nowhere.

Bookmarks provide a means for jumping into a Web page not at its top, but at some point further within the page.

Essentially, they associate a name with a spot on a Web page and provide a way of jumping to that name.

Originally designed for displaying simple text in rows and columns, HTML tables have grown to become an important layout technique for Web pages. Tables are among the most flexible means for arranging page elements spatially and maintaining their proper appearance as the remote user resizes the page.

Frames are another popular way to subdivide the browser window into rectangular, functionally distinct areas. A *frameset* defines the size, location, and name of each area, while ordinary Web pages provide content for each frame. A hyperlink in one frame can change the Web page displayed in another.

The last section in this chapter describes how FrontPage supports access to the raw HTML for a page, as well as how it accommodates HTML features that FrontPage doesn't support directly.

Creating and Managing Hypertext Links

To review the format of URLs, read "Uniform Resource Locators," page 65.

Despite their impact, hyperlinks are extremely simple mechanisms. Associated with a given string of text or image is the address of another Web page. When the user clicks on that string of text or that image, the browser retrieves the associated page location.

Building a hyperlink in FrontPage is almost as simple.

1 Select the text or image you wish to hyperlink.

2 Choose Hyperlink from the Edit menu or click the Create Or Edit Hyperlink button on the Standard toolbar. The Create Hyperlink dialog box of Figure 9-1 will appear.

3 Specify the hyperlink's target location in the URL field.

4 Click OK.

All other options in the Create Hyperlink dialog box are variations on this pattern. For example, there are six ways to accomplish step 3 above.

■ Click any entry in the large list box in the center of the dialog box. FrontPage will enter its location in the URL box.

? SEE ALSO

If windows like Figure 9-1 are starting to look familiar, you're paying attention. The dialog boxes shown in Figure 3-2 (page 70) and Figure 8-2 (page 279) are quite similar.

- Click the browser button (the globe with the spyglass) and locate the target page with your browser. When you switch back to FrontPage Editor, FrontPage will get the current page from the browser and enter it in the URL box.

- Click the local file button (the folder with the spyglass) and locate a file on your computer. FrontPage will enter this filename in the URL box for you.

- Click the mail icon (the envelope) and type an Internet e-mail address. FrontPage will enter a URL that launches the remote user's e-mail program and creates a message sent to that address.

- Click the new page button (the blank document) to create a new page and link to it. FrontPage will enter the new file's name. The resulting New dialog box is the one that appeared previously in Figure 1-14 (page 26) and Figure 5-38 (page 197).

- Enter the target location by hand, either by typing or by pasting with the Ctrl+V or Shift+Ins keystrokes.

FIGURE 9-1.
FrontPage uses this dialog box to hyperlink a selected text string or image to another page in the current Web.

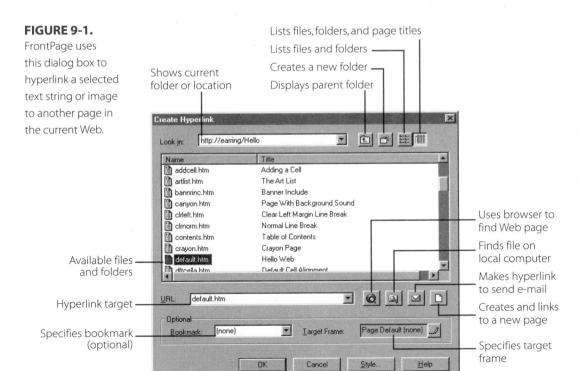

Lists files, folders, and page titles
Lists files and folders
Creates a new folder
Displays parent folder
Shows current folder or location

Uses browser to find Web page
Finds file on local computer
Makes hyperlink to send e-mail
Creates and links to a new page
Specifies target frame

Available files and folders
Hyperlink target
Specifies bookmark (optional)

Building Your Site

The large selection list in the center of Figure 9-1 (on the previous page) pertains to the current Web. As usual, you can open a folder by double-clicking it. To revert to a parent folder, click the Up One Level button. Clicking the List and Details buttons toggles the list between displaying files and displaying detailed file information.

The Bookmark control at the bottom of Figure 9-1 permits jumping not only to a particular page, but even to a particular location within that page. The next section in this chapter discusses bookmarks.

? SEE ALSO

For more information on using frames, see "Creating and Editing Frames," page 338.

The Target Frame control specifies which frame the results of the hyperlink should appear in. This presumes that the current Web page will appear within a frameset.

The Style button permits assigning cascading style sheet (CSS) properties to the hyperlink. Those properties affect only the current hyperlink.

Clicking the OK button will establish a link from the text or image you selected in FrontPage Editor to the location specified in the URL box.

To remove hyperlinking from a given text string or image, right-click the hyperlink and select Hyperlink Properties from the pop-up menu. The hyperlink's URL will be highlighted. Press the Backspace key to erase it, and then click OK.

Setting and Using Bookmarks

Sometimes, especially when a Web page is long, it's desirable for hyperlinks to point somewhere other than the top of a page. Bookmarks provide this handy function. They allow hyperlinks to jump from one location to another within the same page, or even from one page to any location in another page. To define a bookmark

1 Open the target page in FrontPage Editor.

2 Set the insertion point where you want the hyperlink to jump to. This is where you'll insert the bookmark.

3 Choose Bookmark from the Edit menu. The Bookmark dialog box shown in Figure 9-2 will appear.

FIGURE 9-2.
Bookmarks move viewers to specific page locations.

4   Type the name of the bookmark in the field titled Bookmark Name.

5   Click the OK button. A flag, as pictured in Figure 9-3, on the next page, will denote the bookmark's location.

The other buttons in Figure 9-2 perform the following functions.

■   **Clear.** To delete a bookmark, double-click its name in the list titled Other Bookmarks On This Page, and then click the Clear button after it appears in the Bookmark Name field.

You can also delete bookmarks by first selecting them and then pressing the Delete key or choosing Cut from the Edit menu. Selecting a bookmark means dragging the insertion pointer across the flag until it's highlighted—you can't just click it.

To move a bookmark, first select it, and then either drag it or use the cut and paste commands.

■   **Goto.** To move the insertion point to an existing bookmark, select its name in the list titled Other Bookmarks On This Page, and then click the Goto button.

To set up a hyperlink that jumps to the bookmark

1   Open the page that will contain the hyperlink.

2   Specify the hyperlink's target URL in the normal way.

III

Building Your Site

3 If the FrontPage dialog box has a Bookmark field, enter the book-mark's name there. Otherwise, append a pound sign (#) and the bookmark's name to the URL.

Figure 9-3 shows adding a hyperlink from one spot in a page to another. The flag in front of the heading Backup indicates the presence of a bookmark. The bookmark's name is backup, a fact you could confirm by right-clicking the left edge or the center of the flag and selecting Bookmark properties.

FIGURE 9-3.
A hyperlink is being added from the Backup menu bar text to the Backup heading on the same page.

Hyperlink

Backup bookmark

Other bookmarks

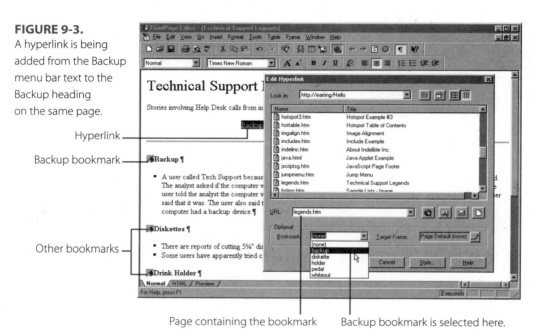

Page containing the bookmark   Backup bookmark is selected here.

To establish the hyperlink, the page creator took these steps:

1 Highlighted the word Backup in the menu bar at the top of the page.

2 Clicked the Create Or Edit Hyperlink toolbar button.

3 Selected the page containing the bookmark.

4 Dropped down the Bookmark list.

5 Selected backup.

The page creator will finish by clicking the OK button.

If the page containing the bookmark isn't in the current Web, the drop-down list of bookmarks might not be available. In this case, simply type the bookmark name.

Creating and Editing Tables

Tables are an incredibly useful addition to HTML. Before tables were available, HTML offered no practical means to organize content horizontally or in grids. The entire World Wide Web was left-justified.

For ease of learning, the following discussion will use very simple grids as examples. A later section titled "Using Tables for Page Layout" (page 333) will describe how to use tables for laying out more complex content. As each feature is introduced, refer to Table 9-1 to identify the relevant toolbar buttons.

TABLE 9-1. The FrontPage Editor Table Toolbar

Icon	Description	Function	Menu Command
	Draw Table	Creates a new table sized in accordance with mouse dragging	Table Draw Table
	Eraser	Erases any cell walls the mouse is dragged across; merges affected cells	Table Merge Cells
	Insert Rows	Inserts rows above the current selection	Table Insert Rows or Columns
	Insert Columns	Inserts columns left of the current selection	Table Insert Rows or Columns
	Delete Cells	Deletes currently selected cells	Table Delete Cells
	Merge Cells	Combines two or more cells into one cell that spans multiple rows or columns	Table Merge Cells
	Split Cells	Divides one cell into several (opposite of Merge Cells)	Table Split Cells

III

Building Your Site

(continued)

TABLE 9-1. *continued*

Icon	Description	Function	Menu Command
	Align Top	Aligns contents to the top of a cell	Table Cell Properties Vertical Alignment Top
	Center Vertically	Aligns contents to the middle of a cell	Table Cell Properties Vertical Alignment Middle
	Align Bottom	Aligns contents to the bottom of a cell	Table Cell Properties Vertical Alignment Bottom
	Distribute Rows Evenly	Fixes table height to its current value in pixels and row height to uniform values	Table Distribute Rows Evenly
	Distribute Columns Evenly	Fixes table width to its current value in pixels and column width to uniform values	Table Distribute Columns Evenly
	Background Color	Sets background color for the entire table, if selected, or for selected cells	Table Cell or Table Properties Background Color

Creating a New Table

FrontPage provides five distinct ways to create HTML tables. The method you choose depends on your preferences and the type of content you want to display. The five methods are

- drawing with the mouse

- using the Insert Table button

- inserting a table with menus

- converting text to a table

- pasting tabular data

The remainder of this section will provide step-by-step instructions for each of these methods.

Drawing a table. To create a table by drawing

1 Choose Draw from the Table menu or click the Draw Table button on the Table toolbar. The mouse pointer will take on the shape of a pencil.

2 Click the mouse where you want one corner of the table to appear, hold down the mouse button, and then drag it to the table's opposite corner.

3 Release the mouse to create the table. Note the following:

- All such tables are sized in pixels.

- All such tables initially consist of one cell. You can create rows and columns within the table by drawing lines with the Draw Table button.

- FrontPage will do its best to position the table where you drew it, though the limitations of HTML still apply.

- If you draw two tables that overlap horizontally, FrontPage will locate the second inside the first. HTML doesn't allow horizontally overlapping tables.

4 Right-click the new table, and then choose Table Properties from the pop-up menu.

5 In the Table Properties dialog box, shown later as Figure 9-8 (page 321), specify additional properties as required, and then click OK.

Using the Insert Table button. The Insert Table button creates a table at the insertion point and, unlike the draw method, lets you choose the number of cells in the table.

1 Place the insertion point where the table should appear.

2 Click and hold the Insert Table button on the Standard toolbar. A small grid of table cells will appear.

3 Drag the mouse pointer to highlight the number of rows and columns you want, and then release it. The table will appear at the insertion marker. If you change your mind while selecting the cells, just move the mouse pointer back up to the Insert Table button and release it to cancel the operation.

III

Building Your Site

Inserting a table using menus. Inserting a table with menus offers more initial control than either method above. To insert a table using menus

1 Place the insertion point where the table should appear.

2 Choose Insert Table from the Table menu. The Insert Table dialog box shown in Figure 9-4 will appear.

3 Specify characteristics for the table.

4 Click the OK button.

FIGURE 9-4.

This dialog box adds a table to a Web page.

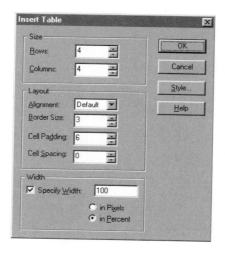

The available properties are described below. You can modify any of these properties later without re-creating the table.

- **Size** controls the dimensions of the table in terms of rows and columns.

  - **Rows** specifies the number of horizontal rows the table should have.

  - **Columns** specifies the desired number of vertical columns.

- **Layout** controls page positioning and appearance.

  - **Alignment** specifies where you want the table positioned on the page. Choices are Default, Left, Center, and Right. Default lets the browser do what it wants, which is normally to left-align tables. Left and Right align a table to the corresponding margins, while Center positions it in the center of the page.

TIP

> Text can't ever flow around left- or right-aligned tables as it does around left- and right-aligned images. Nothing ever appears to the left or right of a table.

- **Border Size** specifies the thickness in pixels of a border that will surround the table. A border size of zero specifies no such border and no interior gridlines.

- **Cell Padding** indicates the number of pixels to insert between the edges of a cell and its contents. Think of padding as a margin inserted just inside each edge of all cells in a table. In a table containing four columns, setting Cell Padding to 3 would consume a total of 24 pixels: 3 inside the left edge and 3 inside the right edge of the four cells in each column.

- **Cell Spacing** indicates the number of pixels to place between cells in a table. Spacing inserts white space only where two cells would otherwise touch. In a table containing four columns, setting Cell Spacing to 3 would consume 15 pixels: 3 to the left of column 1, 3 between each of the columns (9 pixels), and 3 to the right of column 4.

  Figure 9-5, on the following page, illustrates the difference between cell padding and cell spacing. Distinguishing cell padding from cell spacing is easier when cell borders are turned on. Figure 9-5 also illustrates tables within tables.

CAUTION
Most Web browsers treat design-time table measurements as first approximations and not as concrete specifications.

- **Width** controls the width of the table provided the check box is turned on. If the box is turned off, the browser sizes the table automatically.

  - **Specify Width** specifies the amount of horizontal space you want the table to consume. The next two settings control the units of measure.

  - **In Pixels** specifies the width of the table in pixels.

III

Building Your Site

- **In Percent** sizes the table as a percentage of available space at browse time. A table width of 100% stretches the table across all available space.

■ **Style.** Click this button to apply cascading style sheet properties to the table.

FIGURE 9-5.
This Web page illustrates the difference between cell spacing and cell padding. Note also that the four 3×3 tables are located within the cells of a 7×2 table.

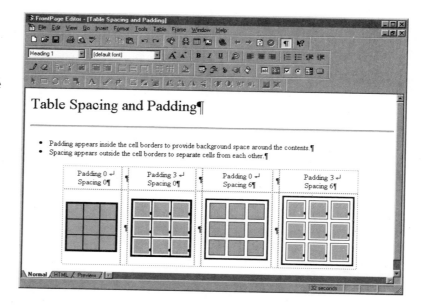

Figure 9-6 shows the result of inserting a table with the properties given in Figure 9-4 (page 316).

Creating a table from text. To convert existing text into a table

1 Select the text you want converted to a table by dragging the mouse across it.

2 Choose Convert Text To Table from the Table menu.

3 When the dialog box titled Convert Text To Table, shown in Figure 9-7, on page 320, appears, choose one of the following:

- To convert each paragraph in the text to a full row in the table, click Separate Text At Paragraphs.

- To divide each row's text into columns based on the presence of tab characters or commas, click Tabs or Commas, respectively.

- To divide each row's text into columns based on some other character, click Other and enter the character you wish in the space provided.

4 Click the OK button.

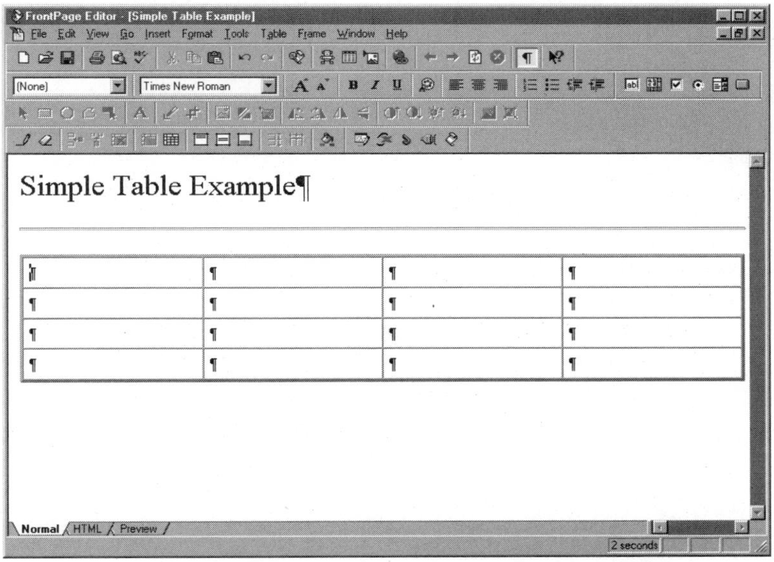

FIGURE 9-6.

This table was created from the Insert Table dialog box of Figure 9-4 (page 316).

Figure 9-7, on the following page, shows actual before and after results. After the user clicks the OK button, the selected text will become another table like the one already shown.

Pasting tabular data.   Another way to create a table in FrontPage is to paste tabular content from other programs, such as a table from a word processor or database, or cells from a spreadsheet. If FrontPage doesn't automatically create a table, use the Paste Special command from the Edit menu to format the text as you paste it. If necessary, then use the Convert Text to Table command just discussed to complete the table.

FIGURE 9-7.
The Convert Text To Table command builds a table from existing plain text.

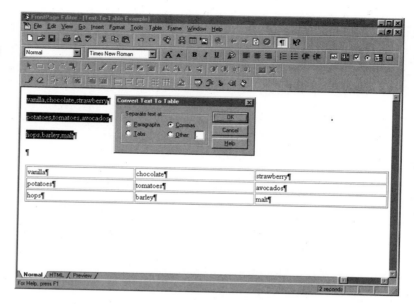

Modifying an Existing Table

Regardless of how you create a table, you probably won't get it exactly right on the first try. Most people spend considerably more time modifying and refining existing tables than creating new ones.

The Table Properties dialog box contains settings that affect an entire table. There are two ways to open this dialog box.

- Set the insertion point or selection anywhere in the table, and then choose Table Properties from the Table menu.

- Right-click anywhere in the table, and then choose Table Properties from the pop-up menu.

Either action displays the Table Properties dialog box shown in Figure 9-8. The following settings are available.

Layout.   This section controls page positioning and appearance.

- **Alignment** specifies the table's horizontal page positioning. Choices are

  - **Default** specifies no special alignment for the table. At display time, browser defaults will apply; this usually results in a left-aligned table with no text wrapping.

FIGURE 9-8.
This dialog box provides access to settings that affect an entire HTML table.

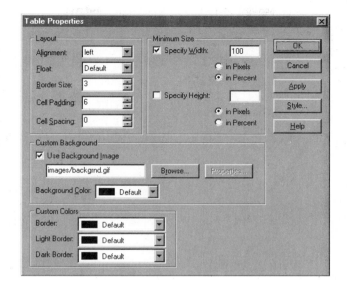

- **Left** and **Right** place the table in an HTML division that aligns its content to the specified margin. No text will wrap around the table.

- **Center** places the table in an HTML division that centers its content. No text will wrap around the table.

■ **Float** controls left and right positioning of the table. Choices are

- **Default** specifies no special alignment for the table. At display time, browser defaults will apply, usually producing a left-aligned table with no text wrapping.

- **Left** and **Right** align the table to the left or right margin, respectively; both allow text to flow around it.

Unfortunately, the Float setting is less useful than it might first appear. FrontPage always inserts a paragraph ending before a table, plus a paragraph start after the table. This prevents any text from coming close enough to a table to flow around it.

III

Building Your Site

- **Border Size** specifies the thickness of a border that surrounds the table. A size of zero suppresses both the border and interior grid.

- **Cell Padding** indicates the number of pixels between the edges of each cell and its contents.

- **Cell Spacing** indicates the number of pixels between adjacent cells.

Minimum Size. This area controls the width and height of the table, provided the corresponding check box is turned on. If either check box is turned off, the browser automatically sizes that dimension of the table.

- **Specify Width** controls the amount of horizontal space the table occupies. To apply this setting, you must turn on the check box, specify a value, and indicate a unit of measure.

  - **In Pixels** indicates the width value is specified in pixels.

  - **In Percent** indicates the width value is a percentage of available space at browse time.

TIP

When you specify the dimensions of any Web page object as a percentage, that percentage is relative to the object's immediate container. Thus, depending on where it appears, an object sized at 50 percent might occupy 50 percent of the browser window, 50 percent of a frame, or 50 percent of a table cell, whichever is most specific.

- **Specify Height** controls the amount of vertical space the table occupies. To apply this setting, you must turn on the check box, specify a value, and indicate a unit of measure.

  - **In Pixels** indicates the height value is specified in pixels.

  - **In Percent** indicates the height value is a percentage of available space at browse time.

Custom Background. These options control the table's background image or color.

- **Use Background Image** gives the table a background image. To use this feature, turn on the check box and specify the background image's filename and location in the current Web.

⑦ SEE ALSO
Refer to the sidebar "Choosing Page Colors," page 227, for advice on selecting colors.

- **Browse** displays the Select Background Image dialog box for finding a background image. It looks through the current Web, the local file system, or the FrontPage clip art library.

- **Properties** displays the Image Properties dialog box shown in Figure 8-6 (page 286), which alters the properties of the specified background image.

- **Background Color** controls the table's background color.

Custom Colors. This section provides control over the table's border colors.

- **Border** specifies a solid color for drawing the border that surrounds the table.

- **Light Border** overrides the color of the top and left table borders.

- **Dark Border** overrides the color of the right and bottom table borders.

▷ NOTE

According to common GUI guidelines, the light source for three-dimensional images is above and to the left. Thus, to make a raised object look three-dimensional

- Make the top and left edges light, as if catching light directly.

- Make the bottom and right edges dark, as if in shadow.

Pages take on a very confusing perspective if different objects appear lighted from different directions.

Adding Rows and Columns to a Table

Two methods are available for adding rows or columns to a table: menus and the toolbar. To add rows or columns using menus

1 Click any cell that will adjoin the new row or column.

2 Choose Insert Rows Or Columns from the Table menu.

3 In the resulting dialog box, click either the Columns or Rows option button, indicating what to insert.

III

Building Your Site

4 Indicate the number of rows or columns to insert. If you choose to insert columns, the text label changes from Number Of Rows to Number Of Columns.

5 For rows, indicate whether to insert above or below the current selection. For columns, specify right or left.

6 ·Click OK.

Here's the toolbar procedure for adding rows to a table.

1 Select one or more existing rows that will appear *under* the new row. See the sidebar opposite, "Selecting Table Cells."

2 Click the Insert Rows button on the Table toolbar.

3 FrontPage will insert an equal number of rows just above your selection.

TIP

> When you insert rows or columns using toolbar buttons, FrontPage makes room for them by pushing the rows (or columns) you select down (or to the right).

To add columns to a table via the toolbar

1 Select one or more existing columns that will appear *to the right of* the new column or columns.

2 Click the Insert Columns button on the Table toolbar.

3 FrontPage will insert an equal number of columns just left of your selection.

HTML tables are quite flexible and don't require all rows to have the same number of cells. To add cells to a single row

1 Click inside the cell just left of where you want the new cell inserted.

2 Choose Insert Cell from the Table menu.

Selecting Table Cells

There are three approaches to selecting cells, rows, columns, or an entire table.

Using Menus

Click any cell in the desired range, and then choose one of the following commands from the Table menu.

- Select Cell
- Select Row
- Select Column
- Select Table

Using Mouse Movements at the Table Margins

- To select columns or rows, move the mouse over the top margin (to select columns) or over the left margin (to select rows). Click when the mouse pointer changes to a thick arrow.
- To select multiple columns or rows, proceed as above but drag.

Clicking Cells

- To select a single cell, press Alt and click the cell.
- To select a range of cells one cell at a time, hold down the Alt key and drag the mouse pointer across each one. As an alternative to dragging, click each cell you want to select while pressing the Alt key.
- To select a contiguous range of cells, click and drag from one corner of the selection to the opposite corner. You can also click one corner cell and then click the opposite corner while pressing the Shift key.
- To add cells to a selection, hold down Shift while clicking the additional cells.
- To deselect cells from a group of selected cells, click the cells while pressing the Ctrl+Alt key combination.
- To select the entire table, click the top or left table border while pressing the Alt key.

III

Building Your Site

In Figure 9-9 the insertion point was in the cell numbered 3 when the FrontPage user inserted a cell. The new cell appeared between existing cells 3 and 4.

FIGURE 9-9.
A user added one cell to this table between cells 3 and 4 of the second row.

Setting the insertion marker in this cell and choosing Insert Cell...

...inserts the new cell here...
...and pushes the existing cell to the right.

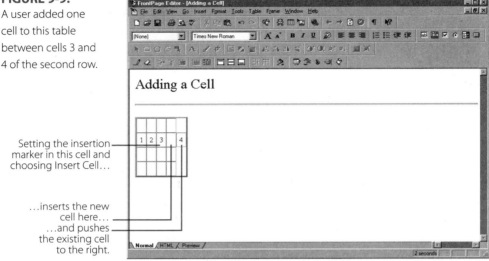

⊗ CAUTION
Merging two cells into one produces quite a different result than deleting one of them. *Merged* cells span multiple rows or columns—whatever space the individual cells occupied before the merge. *Deleting* a cell forces adjacent cells to move in from below or from the right.

FrontPage can also merge adjacent cells to span several rows or columns. Figure 9-10 illustrates this concept; note the large cells in each corner that occupy the space normally occupied by two. The procedure for merging cells is

1 Select the cells you want to merge. They must be contiguous and form a rectangular block—no L-shapes or other irregular shapes.

2 Choose Merge Cells from either the Table menu or the Table toolbar.

The only tricky part of this procedure is selecting the cells. Refer to the sidebar "Selecting Table Cells" (previous page) for details.

To split cells already merged, select them, and then either click the Split Cells toolbar button or choose the Split Cells command from the Table menu.

FIGURE 9-10.
The oversized cells in the corner of this table resulted from merging cells in a 4x4 table.

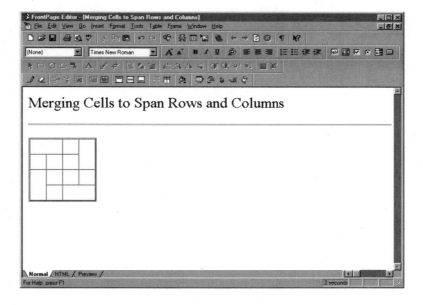

Adding a Table Caption

To give the table a caption, click anywhere in the table, and then choose Insert Caption from the Table menu. FrontPage will create a blank caption above the table and set the insertion point there. Type the caption wording you want. To move the caption below the table

1   Click the caption, and then choose Caption Properties from the Table menu. (Alternatively, right-click and choose Caption Properties from the pop-up menu.)

2   Choose the caption position you prefer: Top Of Table or Bottom Of Table.

3   Click OK.

Figure 9-11, on the following page, shows a simple 4×4 table containing some data. Inserting the text was a simple matter of placing the insertion point inside each cell, and then typing. The same approach works for inserting images and other objects—even additional tables!—into a cell. You can set the same properties for items within a cell that you can set for them elsewhere on the page.

III

Building Your Site

FIGURE 9-11.

Like a browser, Front-Page automatically adjusts default column height and row width, based on cell contents and window size.

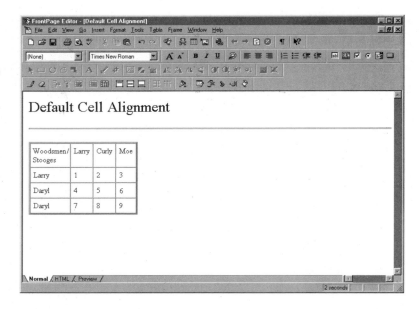

By default, the rows and columns in a table grow automatically in height and width to accommodate cell content. Browsers—and Front-Page as well—normally try to minimize white space by widening columns whose cells contain a lot of text. At the same time, they try to keep columns wide enough not to truncate any images or other fixed-width objects. If possible, the table formatter sizes the table horizontally to fit within the available display area.

Adjusting Cell Properties

Although the table layout in Figure 9-11 looks generally pleasing, several aspects beg improvement. The numeric entries should allow for two-digit numbers and therefore should be right-justified, for example, and the column headings might look better bottom-aligned. You can make these kind of adjustments in the Cell Properties dialog box. To specify cell properties

1 Select one or more cells using *one* of these methods:

- Set the insertion point in a cell.

- Select content in one or more cells.

- Use any of the methods cited in the sidebar "Selecting Table Cells," on page 325.

2 Choose Cell Properties from the Table menu or right-click and choose it from the pop-up menu.

Step 2 will display the Cell Properties dialog box shown in Figure 9-12. This controls the following properties for the selected cells.

FIGURE 9-12.
The Cell Properties dialog box exposes settings for any number of selected table cells.

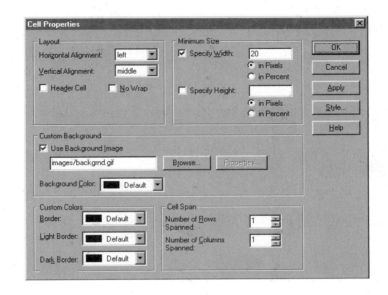

Layout. These four controls determine how objects in the selected table cell are displayed. Note that all the following properties can be applied to a single cell or a block of cells.

- **Horizontal Alignment** controls lateral positioning of the cell's contents. There are three possibilities.

  - **Left** aligns the cell's contents to the left border. This is the default.

  - **Center** places the cell's contents between the cell borders.

  - **Right** aligns the cell's contents to the right border.

- **Vertical Alignment** controls vertical positioning of the cell's contents. Again, there are three possibilities.

  - **Top** aligns the cell's contents to the top of the cell. Any white space appears at the bottom.

III

Building Your Site

- **Middle** distributes any vertical white space half above and half below the cell's contents. This is the default.

- **Bottom** aligns the cell's contents to the bottom of the cell. Any white space appears at the top.

- **Header Cell** indicates, if turned on, that the selected cell contains headings. This normally causes any text to appear in bold.

- **No Wrap** indicates, if turned on, that the browser mustn't wrap text in the selected cell.

Minimum Size. The next group of options sets a lower boundary on the size of a cell.

> HTML provides no definitive way to size either cells or entire tables. Any dimensions you specify are merely suggestions that the browser might override. Inserting a transparent image often provides better control of minimum cell dimensions than do the settings in the Cell Properties dialog box.
>
> For more information about this technique, refer to the sidebar "Using Transparent Images as White Space," page 299.

- **Specify Width** signifies that a minimum width is in effect. To use this setting, you must turn on the check box, specify a value, and indicate a unit of measure.

  - **In Pixels** indicates that the Specify Width text box contains a value in pixels.

  - **In Percent** indicates that the Specify Width text box specifies a percentage of table size.

- **Specify Height** signifies that a minimum height is in effect. To use this setting, you must turn on the check box, specify a value, and indicate a unit of measure.

  - **In Pixels** indicates that the Specify Height text box contains a value in pixels.

  - **In Percent** indicates that the Specify Height text box specifies a percentage of table size.

Custom Background. This section controls the background image or color for the selected cell.

- **Use Background Image** indicates, if turned on, that the cell will have a background image. The associated text box specifies a location and filename in the current Web.

- **Browse** presents a dialog box that browses the current Web, the local file system, or the FrontPage clip art library for a background image.

- **Properties** displays the Image Properties dialog box, shown in Figure 8-6 (page 286), which alters the properties of the specified background image.

- **Background Color** controls the color of the cell's background.

Custom Colors. This section controls the colors of the selected cell.

(?) SEE ALSO

Refer to the sidebar "Choosing Page Colors," page 227, for advice on selecting colors.

- **Border** specifies a solid color for drawing the cell border.

- **Light Border** specifies a color for drawing the top and left cell borders.

- **Dark Border** specifies a color for drawing the right and bottom cell borders.

Cell Span. These two settings expand the range of a cell. Values greater than one make a cell occupy the vertical or horizontal space of several ordinary cells.

- **Number Of Rows Spanned** indicates the height of the cell, in terms of normal table rows.

- **Number Of Columns Spanned** indicates the width of a cell, in terms of normal table columns.

> NOTE

Merging cells and setting a span accomplish similar end results, but they aren't the same. *Merging* combines two or more cells into one wider cell that spans multiple rows or columns; cells not involved in the merge retain their former positions. *Setting a span* widens one cell to cover multiple rows or columns, pushing any following cells down or to the right.

III

Building Your Site

Compare Figure 9-11 (page 328) and Figure 9-13. The latter figure reflects the following edits.

- The cells in the top row have a background color of 204-204-204.

- The text in the top row of cells is bold.

- The cells in the top row have a vertical alignment of Bottom.

- The cells containing numbers have a horizontal alignment of Right.

FIGURE 9-13.
Although still simple, this table is considerably enhanced from that in Figure 9-11 (page 328).

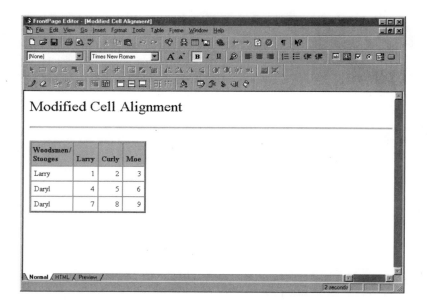

FrontPage provides two commands that attempt to produce uniform row and column sizes. Each appears in FrontPage Editor on the Table menu as well as on the Table toolbar.

- **Distribute Rows Evenly** sets the height of the currently selected table to its present value in pixels, divides this value by the current number of rows, and sets the height of each cell to the resulting value.

- **Distribute Columns Evenly** sets the width of the currently selected table to its present value in pixels, divides this value by the current number of columns, and sets the width of each cell to the resulting value.

Unfortunately, the power of these commands is greatly diminished by HTML's weak control over the dimensions of table cells. Browsers consider cell dimensions specified in the HTML as initial suggestions only. You can specify all the cell dimensions you want—but the browser, reacting to the user's current display window, will *still* apply its cell-sizing logic.

Using Tables for Page Layout

It bears repeating that, despite its popularity, HTML is one of the *worst* page description languages in use. Its inventors, in the interest of device independence, stripped HTML of virtually all capabilities to control page appearance. And page authors, in the interest of visual communication, have tried to regain page control ever since.

Tables constitute a major weapon in the battle to control page layout. They provide a way to split the page into horizontal and vertical sections, and thus to lay out page elements spatially. Whoever invented HTML tables may have imagined simple grids like that shown in Figure 9-11 (on page 328), but what has evolved are some of the most attractive and complex pages seen today on the World Wide Web.

Figure 9-14, on the next page, illustrates a Web page laid out with HTML tables. The page is a prototype for some Web pages designed about this book. The concept is simple: Emulate the familiar look of a daily newspaper's front page. The top of the page resembles a masthead, the articles are set with headlines, and the text is in columns. An index points to features located elsewhere. Stripes, indicating the newspaper's edition, run down the left side of the page. Text, naturally, is black on white. The first line of each paragraph is indented. There's no extra spacing between paragraphs. Layout elements such as headlines, bylines, and captions employ a variety of fonts.

The edition stripes are a background image 20 pixels high by 1,200 pixels wide. The image is wide enough not to repeat horizontally on any normal display and yet is only 1,123 bytes in size.

Figure 9-15, on the following page, shows the same page in FrontPage Editor. Each table is indicated by a large number in Figure 9-16, on page 335.

III

Building Your Site

FIGURE 9-14.
HTML tables make possible the layout of this newspaper-style Web page.

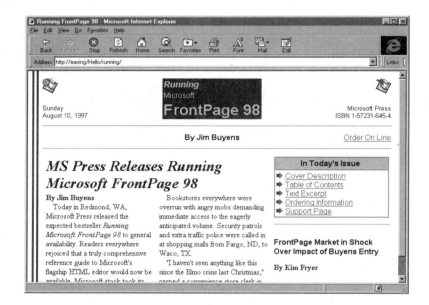

FIGURE 9-15.
Here is the Web page of Figure 9-14, displayed in FrontPage Editor.

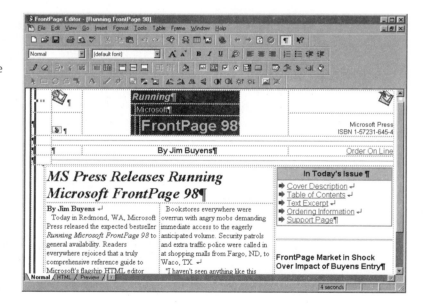

FIGURE 9-16.
This page uses five HTML tables for page layout. The page is shown twice and lightened so the tables, numbered 1 through 5, can be more easily seen.

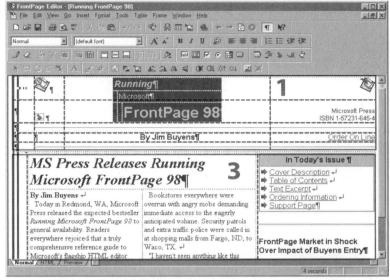

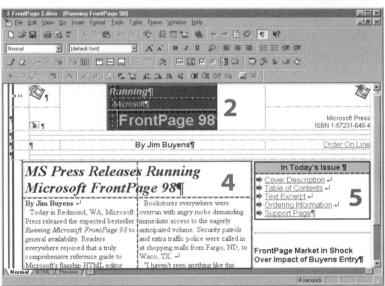

1 A table with five rows and four columns constitutes the masthead. The four columns include

- A spacer column that overlays the edition stripes. The cell at row 1, column 1 contains a transparent GIF image 20 pixels wide to ensure that the second column never encroaches upon the stripes.

- The second column contains the FrontPage Explorer icon and the J icon. The J icon contains some JavaScript code that displays the current day and date whenever the page is displayed.

- The third column contains the book logo and the phrase *By Jim Buyens*.

- The fourth column contains the FrontPage Editor icon, the phrase *Microsoft Press*, the book's ISBN number for ordering purposes, and the hyperlink *Order On Line*.

Note that rows 1 and 2 in column 3 are merged. This permits the following alignments in columns 2 and 4.

- The cell that contains the FrontPage Explorer icon (row 1, column 2) has alignment Left, Top.

- The cell just below, containing the J icon, has alignment Left, Bottom.

- The cell with the FrontPage Editor icon (row 1, column 4) has alignment Right, Top.

- The cell with the phrase *Microsoft Press* is aligned Right, Bottom, as is the cell containing *Order On Line*.

Columns 2, 3, and 4 are merged in rows 3 and 5. This allows an unbroken horizontal line. The white space above and below the horizontal lines is a bit excessive but can't be reconfigured. A GIF image of a black line wouldn't have a variable width.

The merged cells in rows 1 and 2 of column 3 and the corresponding cell in row 4 are aligned Center. These contain the Running Microsoft FrontPage 98 logo and the byline *By Jim*

? SEE ALSO

For more information on scripts, refer to "Script Languages," page 76, or "Incorporating Custom Script Code," page 510.

Buyens. This arrangement doesn't precisely center the items on the page, but it does center them with respect to each other.

Note that columns 2 and 4 will, in general, be different widths. The browser sizes each column to accommodate its widest cell, and the data output by the JavaScript routine and the phrase *ISBN 1-57231-645-4* will usually be different widths.

Better centering would result from including a transparent GIF file in columns 2 and 4 and setting their widths to make each the widest item in its respective column. However, it's very difficult to know how long such a GIF should be, because the end user can adjust font sizes at the browser. Forcing columns too wide constrains other columns awkwardly if the user selects a small browser window.

2   A second table with three rows and three columns forms the *Running Microsoft FrontPage 98* logo. This table is entirely contained within rows 1 and 2 (merged), column 3, of the first table.

- The first row has all three columns merged.

- The second row has columns 2 and 3 merged. Row 2, column 1 is blank to achieve an indented effect.

- The third row has no merged cells. Columns 1 and 2 are blank for additional indenting.

3   The third table has only one row and three columns, but it covers the bottom two-thirds of the page. There's no vertical space between tables 1 and 3, but a new table was needed to establish a new set of column widths.

- Column 1 is again a spacer that overlays the edition stripes. Like the first table, it contains a 20-pixel-wide transparent GIF image.

- Column 2 contains the fourth table, described next, which contains the large headline and two-column story.

- Column 3 contains the fifth table, headed *In Today's Issue*, a horizontal line, and the beginning of the one-column story.

III

Building Your Site

4 The fourth table is entirely contained in row 1, column 2 of table 3. It consists of two rows and two columns.

- The two cells in the first row are merged and contain the headline *MS Press Releases Running Microsoft FrontPage 98*.

- The two cells in row 2 contain the two columns of text. HTML has no facility for specifying paragraph indents, so a 10-pixel-wide transparent GIF appears at the beginning of each paragraph. Line breaks rather than paragraph marks separate paragraphs.

5 The fifth table has one column and two rows; it contains the index box titled *In Today's Issue*, located halfway down the right margin. The upper row of this table contains the heading while the lower row contains five hyperlinks with large bold arrows pointing to them.

If the use of tables, as described above in some detail, seems convoluted compared to other page-layout techniques, you're right! HTML itself was never designed for this kind of work—nor, most likely, were tables. Nevertheless, advanced use of tables permits a degree of layout control impossible using any other technique. Fortunately, FrontPage can make creating and formatting complex tables easier by reducing the need for arcane syntax and HTML tags.

Creating and Editing Frames

Whether arranging simple columns of data or complex page layouts, tables are among the most powerful page composition tools on the Web. A major shortcoming, however, is that tables aren't dynamic. The browser can't replace the contents of a table or cell without redisplaying the entire Web page.

Another approach divides the browser window into zones called *frames*. A special Web page called a *frameset* defines the overall frame layout but provides no actual content. Instead, each frame displays a self-sufficient Web page. The frameset tells the browser what pages to load initially; later, hyperlinks reload individual frames in response to user selections.

Understanding Frame Fundamentals

Figure 9-17 shows a Web display that uses frames. Creating this display requires four HTML files:

- One HTML file to define the frame areas, giving each frame a position, name, and frame source. This file is called a *frameset*, and it contains no visible content of its own.

- Each frame has a property, called its *frame source*, that specifies the URL of the Web page that provides its content. The frameset specifies an initial frame source for each frame.

FIGURE 9-17.
This display involves use of four HTML files: one to define the three frame areas, and one per frame to provide content.

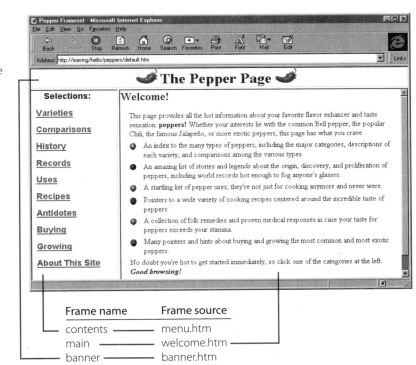

The labels in Figure 9-17 show the frame names and sources for each of the three frames that make up the frameset. The fact that Figure 9-17 displays four HTML files *at once* is a key concept. The browser's Location line shows only one URL, but three more are hidden. To see the other URLs, right-click the content area of a frame and choose Properties from the pop-up menu. Figure 9-18, on the next page, illustrates this.

FIGURE 9-18.

The Page Properties dialog box for the main "Welcome!" frame shows a URL different from that of the frameset.

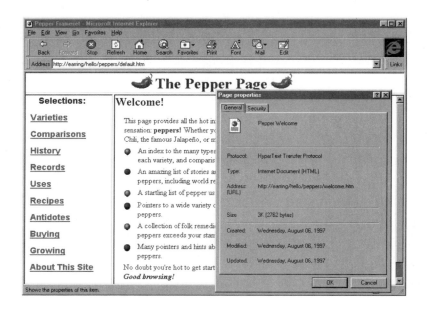

A frameset can also be the source of another frame; that is, you can have framesets within frames. This can fast become extremely confusing, but it works.

Once a frameset and its frame sources are on display, hyperlinks in any frame can display new content in the same frame, a different frame, or a different window. A link property called the *target frame* specifies—by name—which frame a given hyperlink should affect. The browser looks for the target frame in three locations. In order, these are

1 **The hyperlink itself.** Dialog boxes like that in Figure 9-1 (page 309) specify the target frame for an individual hyperlink.

2 **A default target frame.** The Web page containing the hyperlink can specify a default target frame. This applies to all hyperlinks on that page that don't specify an explicit target frame. Figure 6-6 (page 221) shows the Page Properties dialog box, where a default frame can be specified.

3 **The current frame.** If the hyperlink target frame and the default target frame are both absent, hyperlinks display their contents in the frame in which they occur, just as you'd expect on a page with no frames.

If you specify a target frame that doesn't exist, the browser will usually display the named HTML file in a new window. This could happen to you! Always double-check frame name spellings, especially if a frameset isn't working properly.

The most frequent use of the target frame on today's Web pages can be seen in Figure 9-17. Note the menu of hyperlinks in the left frame. When the viewer clicks one of these hyperlinks, the page appears in the main frame to the right—you wouldn't want the content to appear in the menu frame, making further menu choices unavailable. By setting each hyperlink's target frame (or the menu page's default target frame) to Main, you ensure that the menu remains visible in the left frame (as does the banner in the top frame) even as the content displayed in the right frame changes.

In addition to the frame names you create as part of a frameset, the four built-in target frame names listed in Table 9-2 may be useful. FrontPage sometimes identifies these by the Common Target names listed in column 2.

TABLE 9-2. Built-in Frame Names (No User Definition Required)

HTML Code	Common Target Name	Browser Action
_new	New Window	Loads the hyperlink target into a new window.
_self	Same Frame	Loads the hyperlink target into the frame that contains the hyperlink. This is useful for overriding a page's default target frame on selected hyperlinks.
_parent	Parent	Loads the hyperlink target into the parent of the frame that contains the hyperlink. That is, the hyperlink target will replace the entire frameset that defines the frame containing the hyperlink.
_top	Whole Page	Loads the hyperlink target into the full window of the Web browser, replacing all prior framesets. This is commonly used as the exit door from a framed page back to a single-HTML, full-page display.

Frames provide a certain (and welcome) continuity as users traverse your site. An arrangement such as that shown in Figure 9-17 (page 339) constantly displays your site's banner in the top frame and a menu of common hyperlinks in the left frame, no matter which page users browse in the main window. However, this structure has disadvantages as well.

- Managing frame names is a manual process, by nature tedious.

- Hyperlinking to specific frameset combinations can be difficult. When another hyperlink loads the entire frameset, the default frame sources will always load. To load the frameset with a different combination of sources, you'll have to create (and perpetually maintain) a second version of the frameset.

Creating and Modifying Framesets with FrontPage

Creating a new frameset in FrontPage 98 is fairly simple. As with tables, you'll spend far more time modifying than creating.

1   Choose New from the File menu in FrontPage Editor. Then, when the New Page dialog appears, click the Frames tab. The New dialog box shown in Figure 9-19 will result.

Alternatively, choose New Frames Page from the Frame menu in FrontPage Editor. This will produce a dialog box very similar to Figure 9-19, but minus the Page tab.

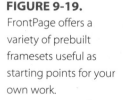

FIGURE 9-19.
FrontPage offers a variety of prebuilt framesets useful as starting points for your own work.

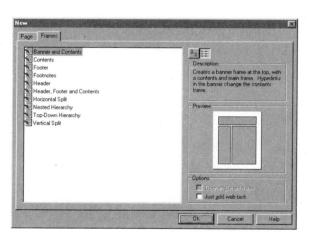

2   Single-click the listed framesets until you find the one closest to your needs. The description and preview boxes display information about each selection and an image of it.

3   Click OK. FrontPage will display the new frameset as shown in Figure 9-20.

FIGURE 9-20.

This is a new frameset, ready for content in each frame.

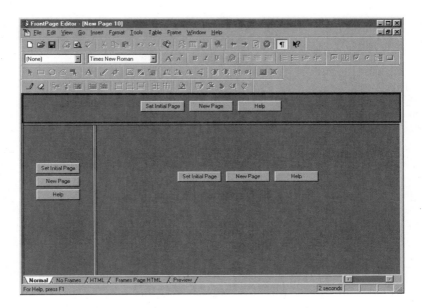

In and of itself, a frameset contains no content. A new frameset is much like a picture frame with no picture. In place of content, Front-Page therefore displays three buttons in each new frame.

- **Set Initial Page.** This button displays the Create Hyperlink dialog box from Figure 9-1 (page 309). To initialize the frame with an existing Web page, use this dialog box to find it, and then click OK.

- **New Page.** Click this button to create a new Web page whose content will fill the frame when the frameset opens. No templates are offered for new pages used as frame targets; instead, Front-Page Editor fills the frame with a blank page and prompts you for a name and title when you first save the frameset.

- **Help.** Click this button for more information.

When displaying a frameset, FrontPage Editor displays not only the frame positions but also their default targets in fully editable, WYSIWYG mode. Clicking each of the New Page buttons in the frameset of Figure 9-20 (on the previous page) and supplying preliminary content thus produces the results shown in Figure 9-21.

FIGURE 9-21.
Now the frameset of Figure 9-20 (page 343) is populated with new target pages and some initial content. Saving this view saves four files: the frameset itself, and each of three target Web pages. The dark line around the large frame indicates the active frame.

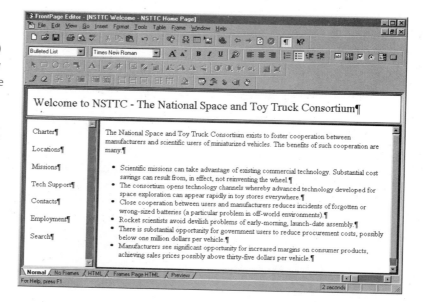

When you first save the frameset, FrontPage will prompt not only for the frameset filename but also, in turn, for the filename of each new target. Subsequently, when you save the frameset, FrontPage also saves any open target pages you've modified.

- To save a specific target page, select its frame, and then choose Save Page from the Frame menu.

- To save the page under another name, select its frame, and then choose Save Page As from the Frame menu.

To change the default target for a frame, select the frame, and then choose Set Initial Page from the Frame menu. The Edit Hyperlink dialog box appears, shown earlier in Figure 9-3 (page 312), letting you choose a new target.

Saving Individual Frames

The Save Page As command on the Frame menu saves the contents of the current frame using a new filename. However, it *doesn't* automatically update the frame's Initial Page setting. This means FrontPage Editor temporarily displays the *wrong* Web page in the saved frame. FrontPage recovers by reloading the last-saved version of the frame's Initial Page when you switch to another frame or, if you immediately close the frameset, the next time you open it.

Suppose, for example, that a frame's Initial Page is apples.htm. You modify the frame's content and save the results as oranges.htm. FrontPage will temporarily display the contents of oranges.htm even though the frame's Initial Page remains apples.htm. FrontPage loads the last-saved version of apples.htm when you switch to another frame.

The behavior just described is perfect if you wanted to open the frameset, save a modified version of one source page, and leave the original frameset and source page unchanged. Obviously, your assessment of perfection will differ if you intended something else.

To save a frame's content as a new Web page *and* point the frame's Initial Page setting to it, first use the Frame menu's Save Page As command; then, with the same frame displayed, use the Frame Properties dialog box to update the Initial Page field.

To change a frame's content and save it under *both* the existing name *and* a new one, you'll have to save the target twice—first using the Frame menu's Save Page command, and then using its Save Page As command.

Frames are always tiled in a window. This means frames never overlap each other and the complete frameset always fills the entire browser window. The only way to add a frame, therefore, is to split an existing one. To do so

1 Select the frame you want to split.

2 Choose Split Frame from the Frame menu. The following dialog box will result.

- Select Split Into Columns to divide the frame vertically.

- Select Split Into Rows to divide the frame horizontally.

3 Click OK.

4 FrontPage will display a new frame containing the same three buttons it displays in new framesets. Click one.

- **Set Initial Page** specifies an existing page.

- **New Page** creates a new blank page.

- **Help** displays additional information.

To delete a frame, first select it, and then choose Delete Frame from the Frame menu. This deletes only the frame and *not* the Web page configured as its default target.

You can specify the dimensions of a frame in three ways: by percentage, by relative sizing, or by pixels.

- Percentage states what fraction of the frameset's available height or width a given frame will occupy. This has the advantage of changing proportionately, depending on the size of the remote user's browser window.

- Relative sizing assigns a sizing factor to each frame, and then divides the available space proportionately. For example, if the frameset consisted of three horizontal frames with relative heights of 10, 20, and 30, the three frames would receive 10/60, 20/60, and 30/60 of the browser window, respectively. (To calculate the denominator, just add the values.)

- Specifying frame sizes in pixels seems at first to offer more absolute control, but only if you know in advance the size of all objects in the frame. Remember, for example, that in most cases you won't know the actual font sizes the user has chosen for various kinds of text.

To resize a frame, you can use two methods. First, to resize a frame visually in FrontPage Editor, move the mouse over the frame border until it becomes a double-headed arrow, and then hold down the mouse button and drag the border to the desired position.

Second, using menus, you can resize frames relative to each other, as a percentage of available space, or as a specific number of pixels. These settings are part of the Frame menu, which you can display *either* of two ways.

- Left-click the frame, and then choose Frame Properties from the Frame menu.

- Right-click the frame, and then choose Frame Properties from the pop-up menu.

Either method displays the Frame Properties dialog box shown in Figure 9-22, on the following page. It controls the following settings for the current frame.

- **Name.** Enter the name that hyperlinks will specify to load their contents into the selected frame.

- **Options.** Two frame properties are controlled by these settings.

  - **Resizable In Browser.** If this box is turned on, the browser can resize the frame based on the size of the window.

  - **Show Scrollbars.** The choices in this list box control when the browser will display scroll bars for the frame.

    If Needed. The browser will display scroll bars whenever the frame's contents are larger than the current window.

    Never. The browser never displays scroll bars for the frame.

    Always. The browser always displays scroll bars for the frame, even if the entire contents of the page fit within it.

- **Frame Size.** The fields here control the frame's display size. There are three units of measure: Relative, Percent, and Pixels.

  - **Relative** units specify frame sizes relative to each other. If the frameset is divided horizontally into two frames with relative sizes of 1 and 4, the frame will occupy 1/5 and 4/5 of the available window space, respectively. Relative sizes of 2 and 8 would produce identical results, as would 5 and 20.

- **Percent** units allocate portions of the frameset. A frame sized at 33 percent would occupy 1/3 of the horizontal or vertical space available to the frameset.

- **Pixel** dimensions are straightforward. The frame will occupy the specified number of pixels or dots on the user's monitor.

FIGURE 9-22.
The Frame Properties dialog box controls the name, size, and other settings pertinent to a frame.

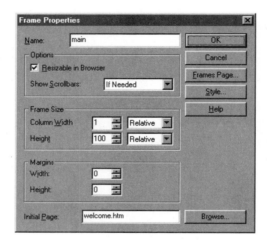

As you might expect, frames have two dimensions.

- **Width/Column Width.** This setting normally controls the width of a frame. However, if the frame resides in a column with other frames of uniform width, the caption will be Column Width (as it is in Figure 9-22) and the setting will control all frames in the column.

  In either case, specify both a width and the corresponding unit of measure.

- **Height/Row Height.** This setting normally controls the height of a frame. However, if the frame resides in a row with other frames of uniform height, the caption will be Row Height and the setting will control all frames in the row.

  In either case, specify both a height and the corresponding unit of measure.

- ■ **Margins.** These options control the size of margins within the selected frame.

  - • **Width.** Specify the number of pixels you want between the frame contents and the left and right borders. The number applies to both the left border and the right border.

  - • **Height.** Specify the number of pixels you want between the frame contents and the top and bottom borders. This value applies to both the top and bottom borders.

- ■ **Initial Page.** Specify the URL of the Web page that will initially appear in the frame (that is, when the browser first loads the frameset). The Browse button can be used to locate the page.

- ■ **Style.** Clicking this button displays the standard FrontPage CSS Style dialog box. Any cascading style sheet properties you specify will become defaults for the current frame.

SEE ALSO

For descriptions of the first five tabs in the Frame Page dialog box, refer to "Specifying Page-Level Attributes," page 222.

- ■ **Frames Page.** Clicking this button displays the Page Properties dialog box for the frameset that contains the current frame.

The Page Properties dialog box for a frameset is quite similar to that of a normal page; it consists of the five tabs shown in Figures 6-6, 6-7, 6-8, 6-10, and 6-12 (starting on page 221), plus the Frames tab shown here in Figure 9-23.

FIGURE 9-23.
The Frames Page button on the Frame Properties dialog box opens this version of the Page Properties dialog box, which contains an additional tab: Frames.

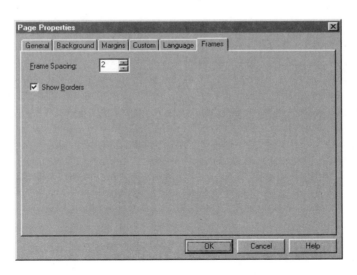

Building Your Site

The Frames tab contains two settings.

- **Frame Spacing** specifies the number of pixels the browser will insert between frames. If Show Borders is also turned on, the space will display as a border; otherwise, the frame contents will appear to be separated by this amount of neutral space.

- **Show Borders** specifies, if turned on, that the browser should display visible borders between frames, of the thickness specified in Frame Spacing.

NOTE

FrontPage Editor will display borders even if Show Borders is turned off. To view the page without frame borders, click the Preview tab at the bottom of the Front-Page Editor window, or preview the page in your browser.

To open a normal editing window for a page already open in a frame, click anywhere in that frame, and then choose Open Page In New Window from the Frame menu. You can edit in the larger window and switch back to the framed page (use the Ctrl+F6 shortcut) to check its appearance there.

Today most browsers support frames, but this obviously wasn't true when frames were first introduced. The frames specification therefore provides a way to embed an ordinary Web page in a frameset. A frames-capable browser will ignore the ordinary Web page, while a frames-deficient browser will ignore the frameset information.

NOTE

A major tenet of HTML is that browsers should silently ignore anything they don't understand. This smoothes adoption of new HTML features by allowing older browsers to run as they always have—though the lack of error messages can make debugging maddeningly difficult.

To display the page a frames-deficient browser will display, open the frameset and then click the No Frames tab at the bottom of the window. This tab is visible in Figure 9-21, on page 344. FrontPage initializes the No Frames page with a message stating *This page uses frames, but your browser doesn't support them,* but you can replace this with a complete Web page if you want.

When designing a frame-based site, keep in mind that not all users have frames-capable browsers, and that other users simply don't like frames. This means you should either provide a parallel set of non-frames pages or include adequate hyperlinks on a single set of pages so that non-frame users can also navigate your site.

Framesets appear in Navigation view as ordinary Web pages. A frameset's default target pages aren't automatically made children in Navigation view, nor are Navigation view children automatically designated default target pages.

Great care is necessary when using themes and frames in the same Web. Backgrounds, color schemes, and graphic elements that look good on single Web pages are often distracting when displayed multiple times, once in each frame.

Combining shared borders and frames is almost never a good idea, because the shared border content will appear redundantly in every frame of a frameset.

Incorporating Additional HTML Tags

FrontPage 98 includes support for unsupported HTML features. This isn't as crazy as it sounds, for the following reasons:

- Keeping up-to-date with every new HTML feature is an extremely difficult task, especially given the constant succession of browser upgrades.

- Accommodating obsolete features is difficult as well.

- Pages newly imported into FrontPage might contain syntax errors or incorrect codes, particularly if previously maintained by hand.

FrontPage includes two features to accommodate any HTML that it doesn't support directly. These are

- The Insert HTML component

- HTML view in FrontPage Editor

The following sections will describe these facilities in detail.

III

Building Your Site

The Insert HTML Component

This FrontPage component inserts a block of HTML directly into your Web page. FrontPage doesn't check this HTML at all, doesn't display it, and doesn't integrate the HTML with neighboring objects.

Figure 9-24 shows the Insert HTML component in use. The small icon with the question mark shows where the HTML resides; double-clicking it displays the illustrated foreground window. Enter or correct any required HTML, and then click the OK button.

FIGURE 9-24.

The Insert HTML component inserts and modifies HTML outside the control of FrontPage.

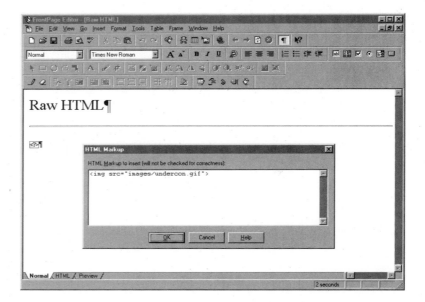

To insert new HTML, set the insertion point, choose FrontPage Component from the Insert menu, then select Insert HTML.

To modify such HTML, double-click the question mark icon, or select it and then choose FrontPage Component Properties from the Edit menu.

To delete an Insert HTML component, select it and then either press the Delete key or choose Clear from the Edit menu.

It's not unusual to find question mark icons in newly imported HTML code. These often reflect marginal or incorrect syntax in HTML that was previously maintained by hand. You can view the incorrect code by double-clicking the icon. In many cases you might choose to delete the bad HTML and re-create it using FrontPage tools, but you can also decide to correct the bad HTML in place. Once corrected, there are two ways to merge HTML markup code with regular FrontPage HTML. To use the first method

1 View the HTML markup as shown in Figure 9-24.

2 Select all or part of the HTML code (as desired).

3 Copy the selected HTML with Ctrl+C or Ctrl+Ins.

4 Close the HTML Markup window.

5 Delete the question mark icon. (Don't use the cut command!)

6 Use the View HTML command to display the page's remaining HTML.

7 Paste in the desired HTML using Ctrl+V or Shift-Ins.

8 Click OK.

To use the second method

1 If the page is open in FrontPage Editor, close it.

2 Locate the page in FrontPage Explorer, and then choose Open With from either the Edit menu or the right-click pop-up menu.

3 When the Open With Editor dialog box appears, choose Text Editor (notepad.exe) and click OK.

4 After Notepad opens the page, locate the HTML Markup code and remove the FrontPage component tags surrounding it. These tags are

```
<!--webbot bot="HTMLMarkup" startspan -->
<!--webbot bot="HTMLMarkup" endspan -->
```

5 Choose Save from Notepad's File menu.

6 Exit Notepad.

III

Building Your Site

Viewing HTML

One of the principal reasons FrontPage was developed was to free users from ever having to look at sometimes inscrutable HTML strings. Occasionally, however, people who know HTML decide they're doing a certain task the hard way and scream, "Just let me see the blasted code and I'll fix it!" FrontPage Editor *can* look under the hood; simply select the HTML tab at the bottom of the FrontPage Editor window. A display like that of Figure 9-25 will result.

FIGURE 9-25.

FrontPage readily displays the HTML it originally opened, or a version including current modifications. Changes take effect on closing the window.

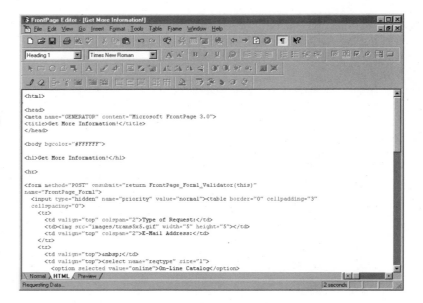

The display in Figure 9-25 is fully editable as text. You can cut, copy, paste, delete, find, replace, undo, open, and save using the normal FrontPage commands and keystrokes. Most other commands, however, are disabled.

If you're accustomed to maintaining HTML by hand, you've probably developed indentation styles and other conventions to make the HTML more readable. FrontPage makes some effort to format readable HTML, but don't expect it to preserve your original coding style. FrontPage

CAUTION
If you decide to edit HTML or images outside FrontPage, be sure to run Recalculate Hyperlinks (on the Tools menu) in Front-Page Explorer the next time you open the Web. Otherwise, Front-Page might use outdated information when updating hyperlinks, setting image sizes, and performing various other tasks.

reads all your HTML into an internal format, and then writes it back out just as FrontPage pleases. Thus, when using the View HTML command, you'll see FrontPage's formatting conventions in use, not your own.

If you choose HTML view while editing a frameset, FrontPage will display the HTML for all open target pages, using the same frame arrangement as Normal view in FrontPage Editor. To view the frameset HTML, choose the Frames Page HTML tab as shown at the bottom of Figure 9-21, on page 344.

Using FrontPage Components

FrontPage provides a number of intelligent objects called FrontPage Components that add function to your site and ease maintenance by performing tasks automatically. Once configured, these components run automatically whenever an author saves a page or, in some cases, whenever a user browses it.

When you add a FrontPage component to a page, FrontPage inserts a number of hidden commands and settings. When FrontPage saves the page, the commands generate HTML based on these hidden settings. The HTML is visible to the end user yet the commands and settings are not.

Some FrontPage components require the presence of the FrontPage Server Extensions at browse time. The Search Form component, for example, obviously requires a server-based program to satisfy interactive user queries; the searching occurs at browse time and not at authoring time. If you're using FrontPage to create Web pages for a server that lacks the FrontPage extensions, you'll need to avoid these components.

This chapter will discuss the following FrontPage components.

- **Banner Ad Manager** continuously displays a series of images, based on a time interval you specify. The images continue to change as long as the remote user keeps your Web page on display.

- **Comment** inserts text visible in FrontPage Editor but not in a browser.

- **Confirmation Field** identifies where in a response page certain FrontPage components should echo input received from an HTML form.

- **Hit Counter** tabulates and displays how many times Web visitors access a page.

- **Hover Button** displays a graphic button that changes appearance when a Web visitor's mouse passes over it. Clicking the button activates a hyperlink.

- **Include Page** displays the contents of one Web page within another. Included pages typically contain blocks of content that appear repetitively throughout a site. Including this content many times from one master copy ensures uniformity and eliminates the need for redundant maintenance.

- **Insert HTML** adds hypertext markup language to a Web page, keeping that code outside the control of FrontPage. This is useful for preserving obsolete, innovative, or marginal HTML that FrontPage might not support.

- **Marquee** scrolls one line of text across an area of the screen.

- **Navigation Bar** automatically constructs menus that link pages within a site. The structure entered in FrontPage Explorer's Navigation view provides the menu content.

- **Page Banner** displays the title of the current page as text.

For introductory material on FrontPage components, refer to "FrontPage Components," page 31.

- **Scheduled Include Page** works like the Include Page component, but only between two given dates. Outside those dates, the Include Page component will display a different page or nothing.

- **Scheduled Image** works like Scheduled Include Page but displays an image rather than another Web page. Turning icons on and off automatically is a common use.

- **Search Form** adds an HTML form to the current Web page for entering and submitting text search queries. At browse time, the form submits these queries and the Web server returns a clickable list of matching pages.

- **Substitution** displays the value of a FrontPage variable. Like the Include Page component, Substitution ensures uniformity and eliminates redundant maintenance.

- **Table of Contents** creates an indented, clickable table of contents based on hyperlink analysis, starting from a given page in the local Web.

- **Timestamp** displays the date a page was last edited or updated.

Banner Ad Manager

This FrontPage component displays a series of images, one at a time, at a particular location on your Web page. Clicking any image in the series can jump the user to another Web location. The list of images, the time interval and transition among them, and the hyperlink location are all under your control.

Many ad rotators on the World Wide Web rotate images only once, when a user requests a certain Web page. The FrontPage rotator, by contrast, continuously rotates images even if the user doesn't reload the Web page. Figure 10-1, on the next page, illustrates a page containing a Banner Ad Manager.

FIGURE 10-1.

The Banner Ad Manager component replaces an image at timed intervals. The image on this page changes every five seconds.

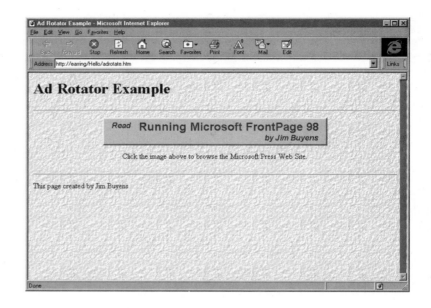

Three images are involved in the rotation of Figure 10-1: the one in the figure plus the two shown below.

To insert a Banner Ad Manager you must first, of course, obtain or prepare the images. It's best but not required that all the images be the same size. When you specify a list of differently sized images, the browser pads or crops them; this might not give the effect you want.

 TIP

The most common size for advertising images on the World Wide Web is 468 pixels wide by 60 pixels high.

To insert a Banner Ad Manager, first create or open the Web page in FrontPage Editor. Choose Active Elements from the Insert menu, and then select Banner Ad Manager. The Banner Ad Manager dialog box shown in Figure 10-2 will appear.

FIGURE 10-2.
This dialog box is set to cycle through each of three images at five-second intervals.

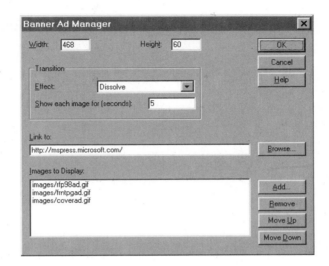

- **Width** and **Height** control the amount of space available for displaying the images. If an image is smaller than specified here, FrontPage will surround it with neutral space (gray). If an image is larger, FrontPage crops the excess height or width.

- **Effect** controls the way each image transitions into the next. The choices are

    - **None** switches directly from one image to another with no special effect.

    - **Blinds Horizontal** replaces each existing image with successively wider horizontal strips of its replacement.

    - **Blinds Vertical** replaces each existing image with successively wider vertical strips of its replacement.

III

Building Your Site

- **Dissolve** fades out existing images until only a new image remains.

- **Box In** displays new images in a rectangle that grows inward from the edges of the existing image.

- **Box Out** displays new images in a rectangle that grows outward from the center of the existing image.

- **Show Each Image For (Seconds)** specifies the number of seconds each image will remain on display before transitioning to the next image.

- **Link To** specifies where the browser will jump if the user clicks any image in the rotation. A single Banner Ad Manager jumps to a single location, no matter which image the user clicks.

- **Browse** displays the Select Banner Ad Hyperlink dialog box. You can browse the current Web, your local file system, or the World Wide Web to select the Link To location.

- **Images To Display** lists the images the Banner Ad Manager will rotate. FrontPage displays the listed images in order, from top to bottom, and then restarts at the top.

- **Add** inserts an image at the bottom of the list. FrontPage displays its normal image browsing dialog box so that you can search the FrontPage Web, the World Wide Web, your local disk, or the clip art library.

- **Remove** deletes the currently selected item from the Images To Display list.

- **Move Up** moves the currently selected image one position higher in the Images to Display list.

- **Move Down** moves the currently selected image one position lower in the Images to Display list.

> ### Whatever Happened to WebBots?
>
> As you may have noticed, FrontPage 98 has no components called WebBots and no menus or dialogs that refer to that term. This may cause a shock, given that WebBots were a heavily promoted feature of FrontPage 97.
>
> WebBots still exist; they're just called FrontPage components now. If you look at the raw HTML for a Web page featuring a FrontPage component, you'll still see information coded with "webbot" comments. The WebBot mechanism is a way to collect properties using dialog boxes in FrontPage Editor and then save the information in two forms for the Web page—as properties and as the HTML necessary to implement them.
>
> FrontPage stores WebBot properties as special HTML comments. This ensures that browsers will ignore the original property information, which they may not understand. The generated HTML, which the browser *does* understand, can consist of any valid statements. It can, for example, be ordinary content, JavaScript code, VBScript programming, code that invokes Java applets or ActiveX controls, or HTML that sends transactions back to the Web server.
>
> As the range of technologies used by FrontPage components has grown, the original term *WebBot* has become too narrow. Thus, the more general term *Front-Page component* is now more appropriate, even though FrontPage still uses the WebBot approach internally.

> **NOTE**
>
> FrontPage will automatically add Java applets to your Web for any FrontPage components that require them, when you first use the component. If prompted whether to add the applet, you should normally respond Yes.

After you click OK to add the Banner Ad Manager, FrontPage will display it as shown in Figure 10-3, on the following page. As you'll learn in Chapter 13, "More Ways to Activate Your Site," inserting a Banner Ad Manager in FrontPage Editor actually creates HTML that invokes a Java applet. When a remote user browses the page, the Java applet does the work of retrieving and displaying the images. FrontPage stores a copy of this Java applet in your Web; it's in a hidden folder named _fpclass. This also explains why, if you right-click a Banner Ad Manager in FrontPage Editor, you'll see the choice Java Applet Properties rather than Banner Ad Manager Properties.

III

Building Your Site

FIGURE 10-3.
FrontPage Editor displays Banner Ad Manager components as Java applets. This is, after all, their true nature.

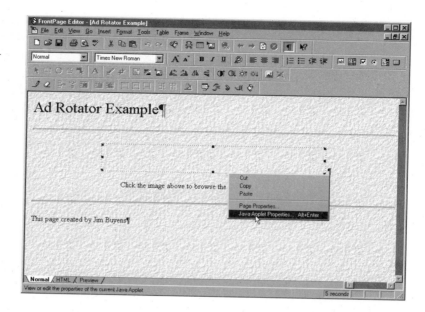

Comment

The Comment component adds hidden text to a Web page. You can use Comment components to makes notes to yourself, to plant short explanations for others using your Web, or to associate any other textual information with a Web page. Be aware, however, that comments consume download time and that remote users can see them by using the View Source command in their browser.

"Inserting Comments," page 261, describes the procedure for entering comments in FrontPage.

Confirmation Field

Certain FrontPage components prompt your Web visitors for data, and then submit the data to a Web server for processing by the FrontPage Server Extensions. Three of these components—Save Results, Registration, and Discussion—confirm successful server-side processing by echoing the data back to the person who entered it. A Web page that echoes user-entered data this way is called a *confirmation page*.

You can design a confirmation page like any other, but some means is obviously needed to tell the server extensions where to put the user-submitted data values. The Confirmation Field component provides this. Each such component contains the name of one data field. The server extensions replace each component with its named data value during transmission to the remote user.

A full discussion of the Confirmation Field component appears in Chapter 11, "Using HTML Forms and FrontPage Form Handlers," which also describes the Save Results, Registration, and Discussion components. See "Using the Confirmation Field Component," page 459.

Hit Counter

Popularity is a common measure of success on the Web. The more often people on the Web visit your page, the more successful you're deemed to be. Most Web servers keep detailed activity logs that, in batch mode, permit intricate analysis of access patterns. Nevertheless, simple "hit counters" are a favorite way to measure activity against a given Web page—and to publicly brag (or moan) about the results. Hit counters involve three components.

- A count kept in a small file on the Web server. For FrontPage, this is a file in the _private folder of your Web.

- A program on the Web server that (1) increments the count and (2) creates a displayable version for output. For FrontPage, this is part of the FrontPage Server Extensions.

- HTML that triggers the server-side program and indicates where to insert the displayable output. This is what the Hit Counter component in FrontPage Editor creates.

Figure 10-4, on the next page, shows a page displaying a typical Front-Page hit counter. The displayed count is actually an image whose source—rather than being a GIF or JPEG file—is a program that increments a count and generates data in GIF format. Each execution of the program increments the count by 1, until you reset the counter.

FIGURE 10-4.

It's easy to create a hit counter for your Web page using one of FrontPage Editor's active elements.

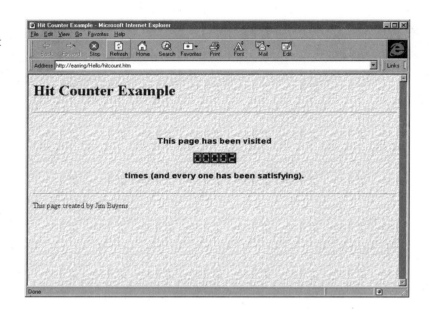

Adding a hit counter to your page is simplicity itself. Open the page in FrontPage Editor, choose Active Elements from the Insert menu, and then select Hit Counter. The Hit Counter Properties dialog box shown in Figure 10-5 will result.

The fields on the Hit Counter Properties dialog box work as described below.

- **Counter Style** controls the style of digits that displays the hit count. Select the option button of the style you prefer.

- **Custom Image** specifies a digit style you designed or obtained yourself. Specify a file location relative to the root of your FrontPage Web, such as images/snapcnt.gif. This should be an image file containing the digits 0 through 9, in left to right order. The hit counter will use the leftmost 10 percent of this image to represent 0, the next 10 percent to represent 1, and so forth. Obviously, the width of the image should be a multiple of 10 pixels.

- **Reset Counter To** sets the hit counter's starting value. To set a new start value, turn this check box on, specify the new starting count, and then save the Web page.

TIP

After resetting the counter to a new value, save the page, turn off Reset Counter To, and save again. Otherwise, FrontPage will keep resetting the counter every time the page is saved.

- **Fixed Number Of Digits** controls how many digits are displayed in the count. If the check box is turned off, FrontPage displays as many digits as necessary to represent the count without leading zeros. If the box is turned on, FrontPage always displays the number of digits you specify.

FrontPage Editor doesn't display hit counters interactively in FrontPage Editor; instead, as you can see in Figure 10-5, it simply displays the text *Hit Counter*. To see the hit counter in action, preview the page with your browser.

To display the Hit Counter Properties dialog box for an existing hit counter, first select the counter and then choose FrontPage Component Properties from either the Edit menu or the right-click pop-up menu. You can also use the Alt+Enter keyboard shortcut.

FIGURE 10-5.
Use the dialog box shown here to create or configure your hit counter.

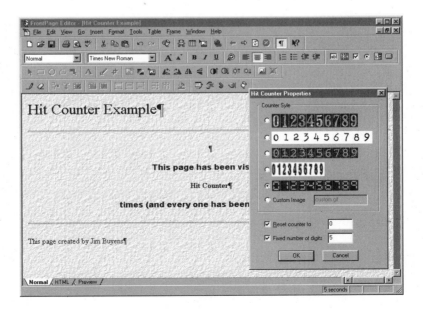

III

Building Your Site

? SEE ALSO

For more information about installing and configuring the Front-Page Server Extensions, see "Installing the FrontPage Server Extensions Under Windows," page 597.

? SEE ALSO

For more information about FrontPage Security, refer to "Administering Security for an Existing FrontPage Web," page 571.

If the hit counter doesn't work, the problem usually lies on the Web server. Verify that *both* of the following are true:

- The FrontPage Server Extensions are installed. If they aren't, ask your server administrator to install them. If you administer the Web server yourself—perhaps because you have a Personal Web server on your PC—try using the Check And Fix function in FrontPage Server Administrator or reinstalling the FrontPage Server Extensions.

- Anonymous users have security permission to execute the server extensions, as well as to update the _private directory in your Web.

Hover Button

Hyperlinked text, images, and push buttons are well-established fixtures on the Web, though they're hardly original. Some links undoubtedly deserve something that gains more attention, and this is what the hover button component can provide.

A hover button is another small Java applet supplied with FrontPage. The applet displays a button—actually just a mouse-sensitive rectangle—with a solid-color background and a text caption. The applet changes appearance when the mouse moves over it, and jumps to a hyperlink location when the remote user clicks it.

Figure 10-6 shows a Web page with seven hover buttons, one for each background effect. Because the mouse pointer is positioned on the button with the Glow effect, it displays a gradient background while all the others are solid. The gradient remains in effect only while the mouse pointer is over the button; otherwise, the button's background is solid like all the others.

To create a hover button, open the Web page in FrontPage Editor, choose Active Elements from the Insert menu, and then select Hover Button. The Hover Button dialog box shown in Figure 10-7 will appear, prompting for the following settings.

FIGURE 10-6.
These buttons demonstrate all seven background effects available to hover buttons. Only the Glow effect is visible here, because that's where the mouse is positioned.

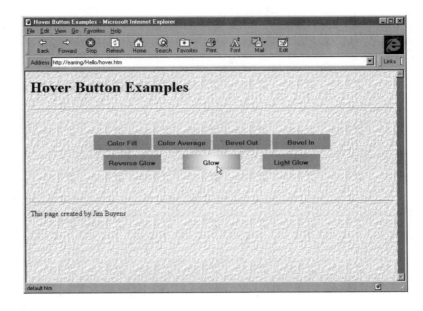

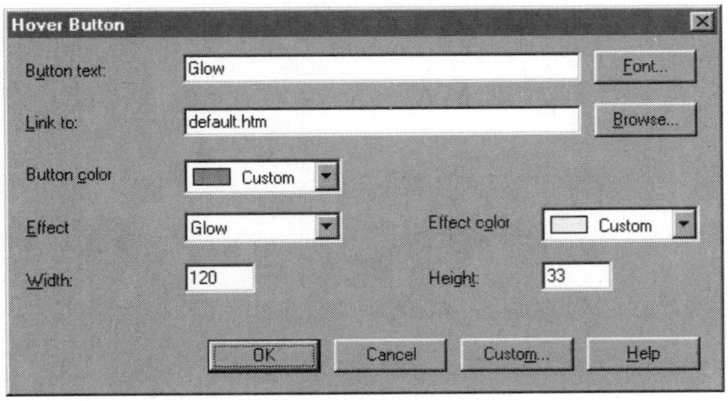

FIGURE 10-7.
This is the dialog box for configuring hover buttons.

- **Button Text** specifies the text the button will display.

- **Link To** controls the jump taken when the button is clicked. Clicking the Browse button displays the standard Browse Hyperlink dialog box.

- **Button Color** specifies the button's normal background color. This displays the usual 16 boring and somewhat inappropriate color choices from the original VGA card. As usual, it's best to choose Custom and specify RGB values having some combination of 0, 51, 102, 153, 204, and 255.

■ **Effect** determines how the button will appear when the mouse passes over it. The available choices and their effects are

- **Color Fill** means the effect color will replace the background color.

- **Color Average** means the background color will change to the average of its red, green, and blue components combined with those of the effect color.

- **Glow** means the button's center will take on the effect color, its left and right edges will retain the background color, and areas in between will display a gradient. This is the effect shown in Figure 10-6 (on the previous page).

- **Reverse Glow** means the button's center will retain the background color, the edges will take on the effect color, and areas in between will display a gradient.

- **Light Glow** means the button's left and right edges will retain the background color, its center will display a lighter tint of the same hue, and areas in between will display a gradient. The Effect Color is ignored with this setting.

- **Bevel Out** gives the effect of popping up the button by lightening the top and left edges, darkening the bottom and right, and lifting the text slightly up and to the left.

- **Bevel In** gives the effect of pressing the button by darkening the top and left edges, lightening the bottom and right, and moving the text slightly down and to the right.

■ **Effect Color** specifies an accent color to display when the mouse is over the button.

■ **Width** and **Height** determine the button's size, in pixels. After selecting a hover button, you can also resize it by dragging its handles. (These are the eight small squares that appear around the edges.)

■ **Font** and **Custom** open additional dialog boxes for setting more hover button options.

FIGURE 10-8.
The Font dialog box
appears when you
click the Font button
in Figure 10-7 (page
369) and controls the
font, style, color, and
size of a hover
button's label.

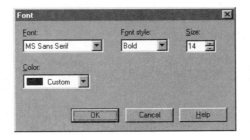

The Font button displays the Font dialog box shown in Figure 10-8. This dialog box controls the appearance of the button's label.

- **Font** sets the label's typeface. For maximum portability across systems, the list of typeface choices is limited.

- **Font Style** selects normal, bold, italic, or bold italic type.

- **Size** controls the font size, in points.

- **Color** determines the color of the text. Choices, as usual, include the boring and inappropriate 16 VGA colors, plus default and custom.

The Custom button in Figure 10-7 (page 369) opens the Custom dialog box shown in Figure 10-9. Four settings are available for creating additional special button effects.

FIGURE 10-9.
This Custom dialog
box controls additional
hover button effects.

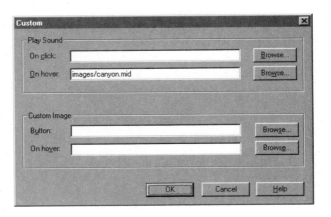

- **Play Sound** specifies sound files the browser will play under certain conditions. It's best to use small, brief sound files. Both settings are optional.

  - **On Click** specifies a sound that will play when the Web visitor clicks the button.

  - **On Hover** specifies a sound that will play when the Web visitor moves the mouse over the button.

- **Custom Image** identifies image files that display within the hover button. Both settings are optional. If you specify both an image in this dialog box and a text caption in the main Hover Button dialog box, the caption will appear superimposed over the image.

  - **Button** names an image that will appear inside the hover button when the mouse isn't over it.

  - **On Hover** names an image that will appear when the mouse passes over the hover button.

> To avoid alignment problems, it's best if the hover button and any custom images are the same size.

You can use the Browse buttons near each choice to locate files in the current Web, on the World Wide Web, or on the local file system.

To modify an existing hover button, select it and then choose Java Applet Properties from the Edit menu. You can also right-click the button and choose Java Applet Properties from the pop-up menu.

Include Page

FrontPage's Include Page component merges the content of one Web page into another. Included pages usually contain page segments rather than full-blown page layouts—segments that appear on several or all pages in a site. Including the same segment on several pages guarantees that it will look the same everywhere. Later, if a change to the segment is required, only one location needs updating.

Figure 10-10 shows two typical candidates for the Include Page component. The upper segment is an image with hotspots and the lower one is a plain-text copyright notice. Each segment is an ordinary, freestanding Web page but consists entirely of content to be included as part of other pages. The filenames are jumpbar.htm and signatur.htm, respectively. To include these segments in another Web page:

1 Construct the segment to be included on its own page, just as you would any other Web page.

> The _private folder in a FrontPage Web is an excellent place to keep Web page segments used by the Include Page component. This folder (thanks to the leading underscore in its name) is accessible to you while editing but not to remote users when browsing.

2 Use FrontPage Editor to open the page that will include the segment.

3 Set the insertion point where the included content should appear (that is, click that spot).

FIGURE 10-10.
FrontPage Editor displays two pages suitable for inclusion in other pages.

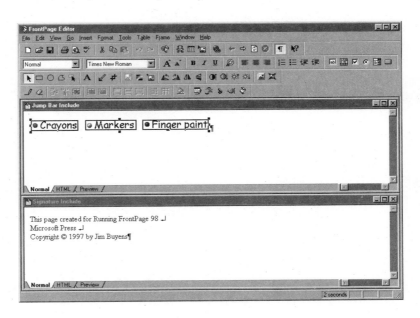

4 Choose FrontPage Component from the Insert menu or use the Insert FrontPage Component button on the Standard toolbar (it resembles a robot).

5 When the Insert FrontPage Component dialog box shown in Figure 10-11 appears, select Include Page and click OK. Double-clicking Include Page accomplishes the same results.

FIGURE 10-11.
Select Include Page from this dialog box to include a page segment in the current page.

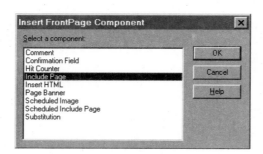

6 The Include Page Component Properties dialog box shown in Figure 10-12 appears next. Click the Browse button, locate the page you wish to include, and then click OK. You can also type the Web path and filename directly in the text box. The page you choose to include must already reside in the current Web.

FIGURE 10-12.
Specify the page segment to be displayed at the insertion point in your currently open page.

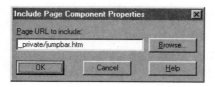

Figure 10-13 shows a Web page that includes both files shown in Figure 10-10 (previous page). Note that included content takes on the properties of the page that includes them—background, color scheme, and so forth. The included portions look no different than if they'd been cut and pasted into the parent page.

There's an implied line break before and after every Include Page component. That is, the included content occupies the entire display width and doesn't flow continuously with surrounding content. If this presents a problem, expand the amount of included content. Include

FIGURE 10-13.
Included portions of a
Web page take on the
appearance of the par-
ent page.

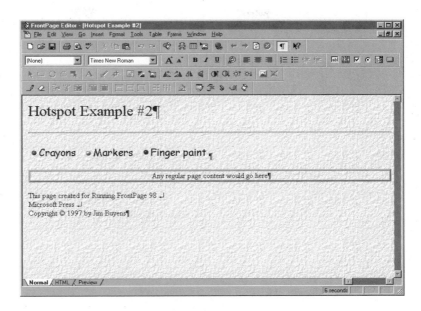

entire paragraphs, for example, and not single words. Alternatively, use
the Substitution component for words or phrases.

To change the included content, edit the source page. To change the
properties of this or any FrontPage component, do *any* of the following:

- Double-click any area it occupies.

- Right-click the area and choose FrontPage Component Properties
  from the pop-up menu.

- Select the area that contains the FrontPage component, and then
  choose FrontPage Component Properties from the Edit menu.

The Include Page component places a full copy of the included content in each Web page that uses it, for two reasons. First, merging
content at browse time would consume more resources on the Web
server. Second, merging content at authoring time produces pages that
display correctly even on Web servers that don't have the FrontPage
Server Extensions installed.

Whenever FrontPage updates a Web page, it consults its cross-references,
identifies other pages that include the current page, and updates those
pages as well, keeping all copies of the included content up-to-date.
Changing your Web with editors other than FrontPage, however, *won't*

propagate changes to included files and *won't* update FrontPage's cross-references tables. If you don't use FrontPage for all changes to your Web, run the Recalculate Hyperlinks command (on the Tools menu) in Front-Page Explorer after using other editors.

Insert HTML

? **SEE ALSO**
For additional information regarding the Insert HTML component, refer to "The Insert HTML Component," page 352.

FrontPage makes every effort to support every feature of HTML, and to save Web pages with all formatting and features they had when opened. Occasionally, however, it might be necessary to insert pieces of HTML that FrontPage absolutely won't touch. The Insert HTML component provides this function. The procedure is as follows:

1 Open the Web page in FrontPage Editor.

2 Set the insertion point where you want the new HTML to be placed.

3 Choose FrontPage Component from the Insert menu or click the Insert FrontPage Component button on the Standard toolbar.

4 Select Insert HTML from the resulting dialog box and click OK.

5 When the HTML Markup window shown in Figure 10-14 appears, enter the HTML and then click OK.

FIGURE 10-14.
You can add custom HTML to a Web page, but FrontPage won't review or alter it.

Insert HTML components appear as question mark icons in FrontPage Editor; three of them are visible in Figure 10-15.

FrontPage 97 required use of the Insert HTML component to flow text around a captioned picture. The table and caption occupy the top and bottom cells in a one-column, two-row table, and it seems natural for other text to flow around this combination. Unfortunately, FrontPage

FIGURE 10-15.
FrontPage Editor doesn't try to interpret the content of Insert HTML components. Instead, it displays them as question mark icons.

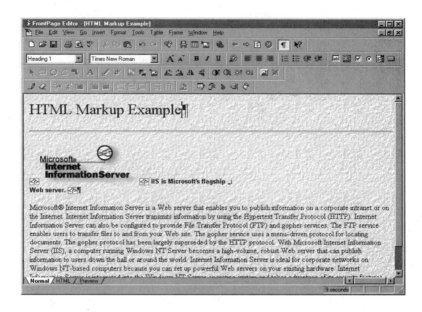

would always end a paragraph before every HTML table and begin a new paragraph just after it. This behavior made it impossible to wrap text around tables.

To prevent FrontPage 97 from inserting the hated paragraph marks, some users resorted to adding table codes with the Insert HTML component. This technique is reflected in Figure 10-15.

- The first HTML insertion contains code that starts the table, the first row, and the first column.

  ```
  <table align=left><tr><td>
  ```

- The contents of the first row and column appear normally on the Web page. This is the image "Microsoft Internet Information Server."

- A second HTML insertion terminates the first table row and column, and then starts row 2, column 1.

  ```
  </td></tr><tr><td align=center>
  ```

- The content of the second row appears directly on the page.

- A third HTML insertion ends the last table row and column, and terminates the table itself.

  ```
  </td></tr></table>
  ```

III

Building Your Site

Figure 10-16 shows the same page as Figure 10-15 (on the previous page), this time in Preview mode in FrontPage 98. FrontPage Editor can't show this formatting in Normal view because, by design, it doesn't look at the HTML placed inside the HTML components.

FIGURE 10-16.
FrontPage Editor previews the Web page that Figure 10-15 (page 377) shows in Normal view. Code within the HTML Insert components is interpreted at browse time, but not during edit.

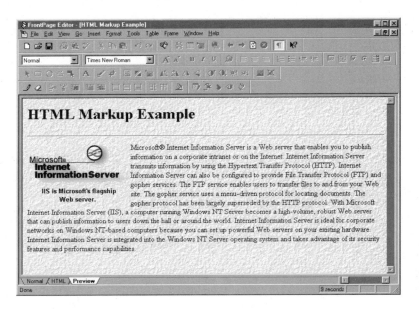

Overuse of the Insert HTML component generally indicates a problem. Except in rare cases, FrontPage should handle your HTML well enough that the "hands-off" aspect of Insert HTML isn't necessary.

If someone gives you a piece of HTML code, such as the code to use a non-FrontPage hit counter or mailer, first try pasting it into FrontPage Editor's HTML view. If this works, it permits a much better WYSIWYG display than using the Insert HTML component; it also greatly facilitates editing and provides much better integration with your other content.

Finding the correct location to insert HTML can be difficult in FrontPage Editor's HTML mode, especially if you're not a whiz at HTML. To make this job easier, set the insertion point in FrontPage Editor's Normal view before switching to HTML view. FrontPage will usually highlight the same general area in HTML view.

Marquee

The Marquee component displays a line of text that scrolls automatically across the browser window. It uses a facility introduced in Internet Explorer 3, but not available in Netscape Navigator 3. Browsers lacking built-in marquee support display the marquee text statically.

To add a marquee to your Web page

1   Open the page in FrontPage Editor.

2   To convert existing text to a marquee, select it. To create a marquee that uses new text, just set the insertion point where you want the marquee to appear.

3   Choose Active Elements from the Insert menu, and then choose Marquee. The Marquee Properties dialog box shown in Figure 10-17 will appear.

FIGURE 10-17.
This dialog box configures a FrontPage marquee.

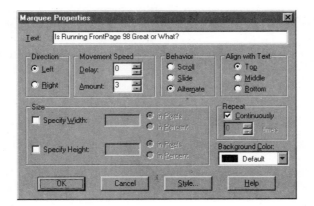

4   Configure the marquee by setting the dialog box options as described below, and then click OK.

The Marquee Properties dialog box provides the following options:

- **Text** specifies the verbiage the marquee will animate. Any text you selected before starting the marquee command will appear here.

III

- **Direction** controls how the marquee text will move—toward the left (the usual choice) or toward the right.

- **Movement Speed** controls how quickly the marquee will move.

  - **Delay** specifies the number of milliseconds between each motion of the marquee.

  - **Amount** specifies how many pixels the marquee will shift in each step.

- **Behavior** determines the type of motion.

  - **Scroll** advances the marquee continuously across the screen in accordance with the Direction setting. Motion continues until the *trailing* edge of text reaches the end of the marquee area.

  - **Slide,** like scroll, advances the marquee continuously across the screen. Motion continues until the *leading* edge of text reaches the end of the marquee area, where it stops.

  - **Alternate** moves the marquee text back and forth within the available area. In this method the marquee text is always completely visible, for maximum impact.

- **Align With Text** specifies how the marquee should align with surrounding text.

  - **Top** aligns the marquee with the top of normal text.

  - **Middle** aligns the marquee with the middle of normal text.

  - **Bottom** aligns the marquee with the bottom of normal text.

- **Size** determines the screen area occupied by the marquee.

  - **Specify Width** controls the marquee's horizontal dimension. The default is to occupy all available width: the entire browser window, table cell, frame, or other container.

To choose a specific width, turn on the check box, enter a value, and then indicate unit of measure as either pixels or percent.

- **Specify Height** controls the marquee's vertical dimension. The default is to accommodate only the marquee text, including its formatting.

  To choose a specific height, turn on the check box, enter a value, and then indicate unit of measure as either pixels or percent.

- **Repeat** controls how often the marquee will redisplay the moving text.

  - **Continuously** means the marquee will continue moving text as long as the remote user's browser displays the Web page.

  - **Times** specifies how many times the marquee effect will repeat.

- **Background Color** gives the marquee its own background color. The default is the Web page's background color.

- **Style** lets you assign cascading style sheet attributes to the marquee.

⊗ CAUTION

If you specify Movement as Scroll and then set Repeat to a specific number of times, movement will stop with little or nothing visible in the marquee area.

To modify an existing marquee, either select it and choose Marquee Properties from the Edit menu, or right-click and choose Marquee Properties from the pop-up menu.

To change a marquee's font, font size, text color, or other text properties, either select the marquee and use the normal format menus, or open the Marquee Properties dialog box and click Style to apply cascading style sheet attributes.

Figure 10-18, on the following page, shows a marquee in FrontPage Editor's Preview mode. Assigning a behavior of Alternate makes the text bounce back and forth between the two icons. This effect is achieved by placing the two icons and the marquee in the left, right, and center cells of a one-row, three-column table.

FIGURE 10-18.
The marquee in this Web page continuously bounces the text left and right between the two icons.

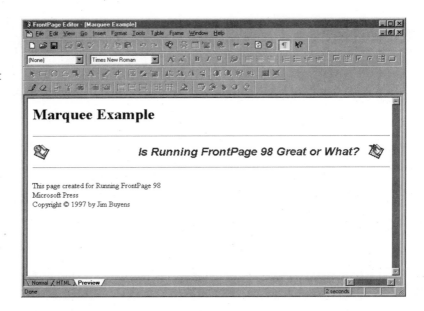

Navigation Bar

This component automatically creates and maintains menu bars (often called jump bars) that unify the pages in your Web. Using navigation bars requires first entering structure information in FrontPage Explorer's Navigation view, and then inserting and configuring a navigation bar in FrontPage Editor.

"Working with Navigation View," page 180, describes how to enter the structure information FrontPage uses to construct navigation bars.

"Navigation Bars," page 202, describes using FrontPage Explorer to customize menu labels and using FrontPage Editor to add navigation bars to pages in your Web.

Page Banner

The Page Banner component performs a single function requiring very little configuration: It displays a page's title as text. This is handy if you follow the wise practice of giving Web pages the same title and heading text.

NOTE

> The title of a Web page is its official name. You enter the title when first saving the Web page, or later in the Page Properties dialog box. The title appears in the title bar of the browser window and in various FrontPage dialog boxes.
>
> A Web page heading, by contrast, is much less formally defined. In general it's an identification that appears in large type at the top of the page.
>
> Navigation view assigns yet another name for each page in your Web's structure. If you have trouble getting Page Banner to display the heading you want, correct it in Navigation view.

The true power of the Page Banner component lies not in reducing typing, but rather in permitting reusable components to obtain a different title for each page where used. It's very efficient, for example, to design an attractive heading format *once* and then use the Include Page component to place it on many pages throughout your Web. The problem with this, in previous versions of FrontPage, has been lack of a means to provide different heading text on every page. The Page Banner component now provides that means. It is also used heavily by shared borders and themes.

Adding a page banner is a snap.

1 Open the Web page in FrontPage Editor.

2 Set the insertion point where you want the banner to appear, most frequently at the top of the page.

3 Choose FrontPage Component from the Insert menu.

4 Choose Page Banner when the FrontPage Component dialog box appears.

5 Select Image or Text from the Page Banner Properties dialog box.

6 Click OK.

If your Web page uses themes, the difference between an image banner and a text banner will be quite apparent. In Figure 10-19, the upper banner is an image while the lower one is text. Both banners display the title *Page Banner Example*.

FIGURE 10-19.
Page Banner Example
appears first as an
image and then as text.

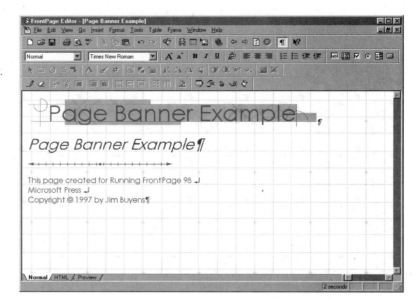

On pages not controlled by a theme, image banners appear as placeholders titled *[Page Banner]*. Text banners more logically display the current page title in large text. You can modify the final appearance of either type by selecting it and applying font properties in the usual way. In the absence of themes, however, both types of page banner display exactly the same at the browser—as text.

Scheduled Include Page

As often as content on the Web changes, it's not surprising that the need to make scheduled changes is a common requirement. Figure 10-20, for example, shows two Web page segments that might appear on the same page at different times—the upper during January and the lower during other months.

FIGURE 10-20.

Here are two segments that might appear on the same Web page at different times.

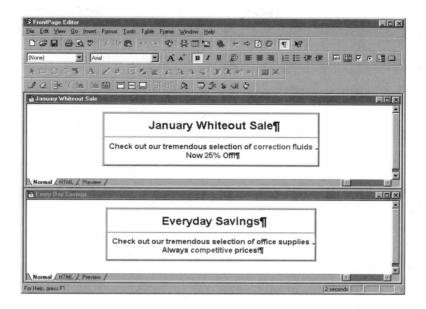

FrontPage supports scheduled changes with the Scheduled Include Page component. This component works much like the Include Page component described earlier, but adds three features:

- A start date

- A stop date

- An optional URL

Inserting a Scheduled Include Page component is much like inserting an ordinary Include Page component: Set the insertion point, choose FrontPage Component from the Insert menu, select Scheduled Include Page, and click OK. The dialog box for the Scheduled Include Page component appears in Figure 10-21 (on the next page). The available settings are

- **Page URL To Include.** Enter the Web location of the content you want Web visitors to see during the scheduled period. Type the Web path and filename directly or click the Browse button to locate the file.

III

Building Your Site

- **Starting Date And Time.** Specify the year, month, day, and time Web visitors should begin seeing the scheduled content. To begin showing the new content immediately, enter a past date.

- **Ending Date And Time.** Specify the year, month, day, and time Web visitors should stop seeing the scheduled content. To keep showing the new content indefinitely, enter a date far in the future.

- **Optional Page URL To Include Before Or After The Given Dates.** Enter the Web location of the content you want Web visitors to see before and after the scheduled period. If you leave this field blank, nothing will display. Click Browse to locate the page in the current Web.

FIGURE 10-21.
This dialog box controls the properties of a Scheduled Include Page component.

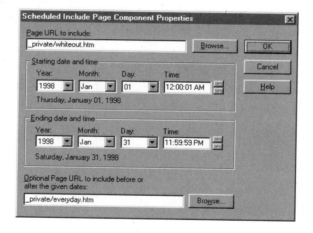

? SEE ALSO

The fpsrvadm.exe program described in "Installing the Front-Page Server Extensions from the Command Line," page 599, can be run from a scheduled batch file to recalculate hyperlinks.

Figure 10-22 shows Internet Explorer displaying the Scheduled Include Page component configured in Figure 10-21. The current month isn't January 1998.

The Scheduled Include Page component, like the Scheduled Image Front-Page component described next, suffers one nagging flaw: The scheduled change isn't completely automatic. Even on a Web server running the FrontPage extensions, there's no automatic process for the scheduled

FIGURE 10-22.
This is the Web page configured in Figure 10-21. The everyday.htm segment appears because the current date isn't January 1998.

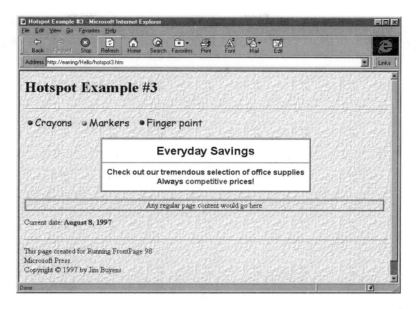

content to be inserted, replaced, or removed at the specified time. To ensure proper timing of Scheduled Include Page components, you must do *either* of the following:

- Make some change to your FrontPage Web every day. (For example, change the value of some configuration variable.)

- Arrange with your server administrator to recalculate hyperlinks in batch mode on a nightly basis.

Scheduled Image

The Scheduled Image component works almost exactly like a Scheduled Include Page component. The differences are

- The Scheduled Image component conditionally displays a single image rather than an arbitrary block of content.

- Conditionally displayed images flow in-line with text. There are no automatic paragraph breaks before and after a scheduled image.

Figure 10-23 shows the Scheduled Image Properties dialog box. This dialog box and the procedure for invoking it parallel those for the Scheduled Include Page component exactly; refer to the previous section for details.

Scheduled images suffer the same timing nuisance as scheduled include pages; for date changes to take effect, you must somehow initiate a hyperlink recalculation.

FIGURE 10-23.
This dialog box sets the properties of a Scheduled Image component.

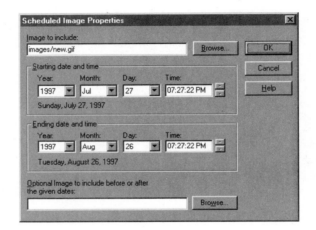

Search Form

Text searching is one of the most common and popular means for users to find content on the Web. No matter how well organized a site's Web pages and menus, some visitors will always prefer entering a few keywords, reviewing a list of matching pages, and cutting to the chase. The FrontPage Search Form component provides a text search capability for FrontPage Webs.

The Search Form component searches only the local Web server, the current FrontPage Web, or one folder tree within a FrontPage Web. These restrictions aren't such a disadvantage as they might appear. First, if you've done a good job of organizing your Webs and servers, each Web represents a specific body of knowledge; searching that realm may well be a reasonable thing to do. Second, if the Webs belong to different clients, each client may prefer or even demand that search results stay within the client's own pages. Finally, if you want to search an entire group of servers, many other tools are available for that purpose.

There are two ways to provide search capability for a Web.

- Add a Search Form component to any new or existing page. The process is much the same as for other FrontPage components.

    1   Set the insertion point.

    2   Choose Active Elements from the Insert menu.

    3   Select Search Form.

- Create a new page using the Search Page template.

    1   Choose New from the File menu.

    2   Locate Search Page in the list of templates and wizards.

    3   Double-click Search Page, or select it and click OK.

    4   When the new page appears in FrontPage Editor, locate the FrontPage component (an HTML form with a text box labeled Search For, like that shown in Figure 10-24) and double-click it.

FIGURE 10-24.
The Search Page template produces a Web page like this. The Search Form component is the HTML form containing the Search For text box.

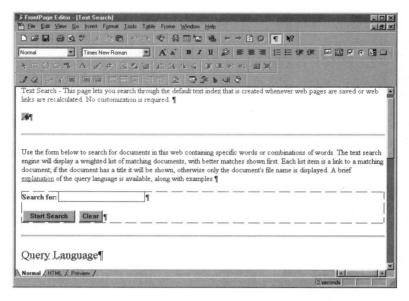

Following either procedure will open the two-tabbed Search Form Properties dialog box shown in Figures 10-25 and 10-26. The options shown here are for a FrontPage Web residing on a Windows NT Server with Microsoft Index Server installed. Fewer options may appear in other, less capable environments.

FIGURE 10-25.

This dialog box controls properties of the FrontPage Search Input Form.

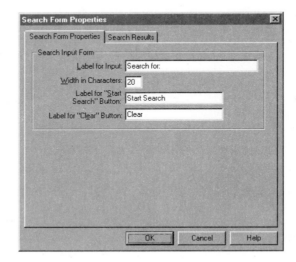

FIGURE 10-26.

This dialog box controls the properties of FrontPage Search Results.

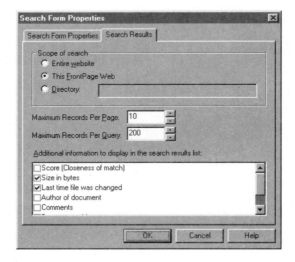

Entries on the Search Form Properties tab control the appearance of the input form.

- **Label For Input** supplies the phrase that prompts for the keywords to locate.

- **Width In Characters** specifies the width, in typical characters, of the text box provided for entering search terms.

- **Label For "Start Search" Button** supplies a caption for the button that initiates the search.

- **Label For "Clear" Button** supplies a caption for the button that reinitializes the search form.

Settings on the Search Results tab control the presentation of items found in the search.

- **Scope Of Search** sets the range of Web pages to search.

  - **Entire Web** requests a search of the entire Web server on which the FrontPage Web resides, including the Root Web and all other Webs on the same server.

  - **This FrontPage Web** requests a search of the current FrontPage Web only.

  - **Directory** requests a search of a single folder (plus its subfolders) in the current FrontPage Web. Specify the folder in the text box provided.

- **Maximum Records Per Page** limits the number of matching pages reported on one page of search output. The remote user must click a Next button to see each additional page of results.

> **NOTE**
>
> Regardless of other settings, searches configured in FrontPage don't search hidden folders—those whose names begin with an underscore. Such folders aren't available for normal Web browsing.

III

Building Your Site

- **Maximum Records Per Query** limits the number of matching pages reported by an entire search.

- **Additional Information To Display In The Search Results List** controls information presented with search results. Scroll down for more selections.

  - **Score** displays a number indicating match quality.

  - **Size In Bytes** displays the size in bytes of each matching page.

  - **Last Time File Was Changed** displays the date and time that matched pages were last modified.

  - **Author Of Document** displays the name of the person who created the document (if known).

  - **Comments** reports any notes recorded with each matching file.

  - **Document Subject** reports the name of matched documents in words. For Web pages, this is the title field.

  - **Hit Count** reports the number of matching documents found.

Virtually all full-text search engines use a text index—a database of word locations—to satisfy queries. Scanning large numbers of files for every query would simply consume too much time. With one exception, the Search Form component searches the same text index FrontPage creates when it saves Web pages or recalculates hyperlinks. Changing a Front-Page Web with tools other than FrontPage might therefore result in incorrect search results until someone recalculates the hyperlinks.

The one exception is this: If the Web server is Microsoft Peer Web Server or Internet Information Server—the Web servers supplied with Windows NT Workstation and Server—and if Microsoft Index Server is installed, then the FrontPage Search Form component will use Microsoft Index Server instead of the FrontPage search engine. Microsoft Index Server detects *all* file changes—whether made by FrontPage or other means—and updates its indexes as soon as the Web server has processing time available.

Substitution

For details on setting up Web variables, consult "Reviewing Web Settings," page 166. To review the Substitution component, refer to "Site Parameters," page 205.

Web variables are commonly occurring character strings you can establish centrally and then reference by name throughout a Web. Like included page segments, Web variables provide uniformity and eliminate redundant maintenance. If the value of a site parameter changes, you only need to update one place.

The Substitution component provides a way to insert site parameter values into a Web page. The component's properties specify the site parameter's name, though the Web page itself displays its value.

Table of Contents

The Table of Contents component generates a clickable table of contents based on any starting page in your Web. The first level of entries consists of all hyperlink targets referenced in the starting page. Below each of these page entries, indented, are it's hyperlink targets. This process continues through any number of levels. Each entry is a hyperlink to the page it represents.

The Table of Contents component lists only pages in the current Web. Hyperlinks to locations outside the current Web don't appear. Pages are identified by their titles, not by the hyperlink text nor by their filenames. To change a page's title, open it with FrontPage Editor, open the Page Properties dialog box, and update the Title field.

As with the Search Form component, you can create a table of contents *either* of two ways:

- Add a table of contents to any new or existing page. The process should by now be familiar.

    1   Set the insertion point.

    2   Choose Table of Contents from the Insert menu.

- Create a new page using the Table of Contents template.

    1   Choose New from the File Menu.

    2   Select the Table of Contents template.

3 Locate the table of contents in the new page, and then double-click it.

Both procedures display the Table of Contents Properties dialog box shown in Figure 10-27. The settings in this dialog box work as follows.

- **Page URL For Starting Point Of Table.** Identify the page whose hyperlinks will become first-level entries in the table of contents. To display the entire FrontPage Web, specify its home page.

- **Heading Size.** Specify a heading style for the table of contents heading. Selecting 1 specifies the Heading 1 style, selecting 2 specifies the Heading 2 style, and so on. To omit the heading, specify None. The title of the starting point page provides the heading text.

- **Show Each Page Only Once.** Turn this box on to prevent pages from appearing more than once in the table of contents. Turn it off if you want each page to appear under each page that has hyperlinks to it.

- **Show Pages With No Incoming Hyperlinks.** Turn this box on to display any *orphan pages* at the end of the table of contents. An orphan is a page that can't be reached by clicking any combination of your site's hyperlinks. If this check box is turned off, no orphan pages will appear.

- **Recompute Table Of Contents When Any Other Page Is Edited.** Turn this box on to make FrontPage re-create the table of contents every time a page in the Web changes. This can be time-consuming. To re-create the table manually—by opening and saving the table of contents page—leave this box turned off.

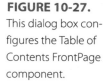

FIGURE 10-27.
This dialog box configures the Table of Contents FrontPage component.

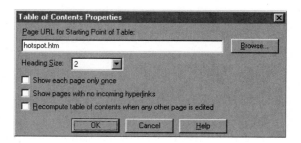

A page containing the Table of Contents component appears twice in Figure 10-28—first in FrontPage Editor and again in Internet Explorer. FrontPage Editor shows only a mock-up of the actual table; to see the actual table, you must open the page using your browser.

FIGURE 10-28.

The Table of Contents FrontPage component appears in FrontPage Editor as a mock-up. Browsing the page displays the actual content.

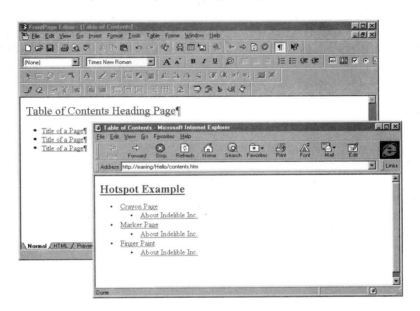

Figure 10-28 reflects the Table of Contents settings shown in Figure 10-27. The page About Indelible Inc. appears three times because each of the other three pages hyperlink to it. Choosing Show Each Page Only Once would eliminate all but the first reference to About Indelible Inc. Turning on Show Pages With No Incoming Hyperlinks would extend the table with hyperlinks to all remaining files in the Web.

Not only are recursive hyperlinks possible on the Web, they're common. A *recursive hyperlink* is any pair of pages with links to each other, such as a home page hyperlinking to a topic page and that topic page hyperlinking back to the home page. To avoid infinitely nested entries, the Table of Contents FrontPage component stops expanding hyperlinks for any page found subordinate to itself.

Approach this FrontPage component realistically. The concept of automatically creating a site table of contents is appealing, but few sites have pages so tightly organized that they automatically produce a well-organized table of contents. You may find that constructing a table of contents manually is easier than reorganizing your site so the Table of Contents component produces satisfactory results.

Timestamp

The Timestamp component displays the date a page was saved manually or updated by any means. Such dates are maintained by FrontPage Editor, and don't necessarily correspond to the page's file system date.

Insert a Timestamp component in the normal way. Set the insertion point and choose Timestamp from the Insert menu. Figure 10-29 shows the Timestamp Properties dialog box that appears.

⊗ CAUTION

Avoid date formats that use numbers for months. The expression 2/10/98 means February 10 in some parts of the world and October 2 in others.

- **Display** controls the significance of the displayed date.

  - **Date This Page Was Last Edited** displays the date someone last saved the page with FrontPage Editor.

  - **Date This Page Was Last Automatically Updated** displays the date a page last changed because of (1) manual editing or (2) automatic updating caused by a change elsewhere in the FrontPage Web.

- **Date Format** selects a date format or (None) from the list provided.

- **Time Format** selects a time format or (None) from the list provided.

A common use for the Timestamp FrontPage component is indicating a version date at the bottom of a Web page.

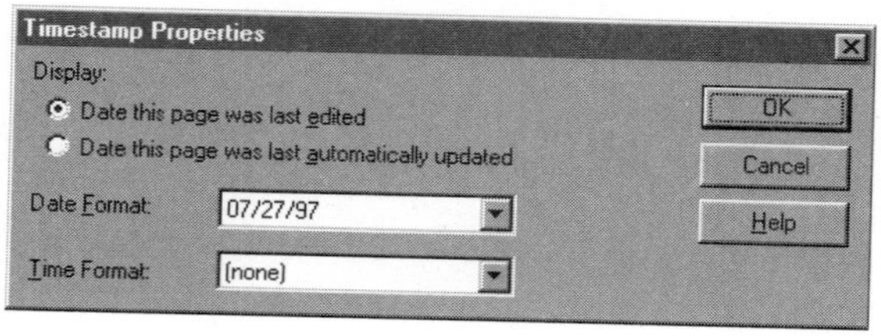

FIGURE 10-29.
This dialog box configures the Timestamp component.

PART IV

Activating Your Site

Using HTML Forms and FrontPage Form Handlers

The vast majority of current Web pages consist of text, images, and hyperlinks. Such pages are relatively easy to create and deliver, and they provide a valuable electronic publication service. Still, regardless of visual appearance, so-called *flat* Web pages eventually run out of function. Simple hyperlinks can't provide the full-function interface required for data entry, data retrieval, and a rich user experience.

This chapter first describes HTML forms, which add text boxes, radio buttons, check boxes, push buttons, and other user interface controls to your Web pages. Programs run on a Web server or on the user's browser can process information collected from such forms.

The chapter continues by describing four services—provided by the FrontPage Server Extensions—that process data from forms. Although these components reside and execute on the server, you configure them in FrontPage Editor.

- **Save Results** converts data entered on an HTML form to a sequential file on the server or to electronic mail. The server-side file can be a text file suitable for input to a database or spreadsheet, Web pages available for immediate viewing, or both.

- **Registration** allows users to create their own accounts for access to FrontPage Webs.

- **Discussion Site** maintains a list of comments or messages about a certain topic and makes it available for browsing or searching.

- **Confirmation Page** verifies successful processing of submitted data by displaying the results back to the originator.

Because these components use services of the FrontPage Server Extensions, they won't work unless the extensions are installed on your Web server. In addition, for reasons explained later, the Registration component doesn't work with Internet Information Server for Windows NT Server, Peer Web Server for Windows NT Workstation, or Microsoft Personal Web Server.

Chapter 12, "Accessing Databases with FrontPage," will describe how to create server-based database applications with FrontPage, and Chapter 13, "More Ways to Activate Your Site," will discuss the use of scripts, ActiveX controls, and Java applets. In many cases, using these techniques involves using HTML forms as well.

HTML Forms

Pages that collect input data are a familiar feature of the Web. Figure 11-1 provides an example. Such pages contain one or more *HTML forms* that operate in a relatively simple way.

- Each form occupies a specific area on a Web page. A single Web page can contain one or more forms.

- Within each form are one or more *form elements*. Table 11-1, on page 402, lists the available types.

- Each element on the form has a name and a value. The name internally identifies the input field, while the value reflects its current value.

- One element in the form—either a push button or image form field—must act as the *submit button*. When the user clicks this element, the browser

    - Encodes all the element names and values in the form, *and*

    - Transmits the data to a Web server for processing. The form's *action* property contains a URL that starts the necessary program on the server.

SEE ALSO

For more information about using browser scripts, see "Incorporating Custom Script Code," page 510.

The idea of HTML forms submitting data to programs running on a Web server is the original—and still most common—approach. More recently, script languages like VBScript and JavaScript have also gained access to form elements. Script code can respond to form element events such as gaining focus, losing focus, mouse movements, and clicking.

NOTE

> *Browser scripts* are small blocks of program code that appear within HTML and execute on the remote user's computer. The capabilities of browser scripts are intentionally limited for security reasons, but two capabilities they retain are setting form element properties and responding to form element events.

FIGURE 11-1.
This page shows a typical HTML form. It collects data from the remote user and submits it to some process.

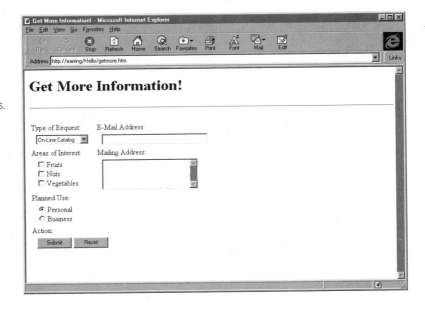

TABLE 11-1. Form Element Types

Appearance	Description	Typical Uses
Text Box	One-Line Text Box	Short, one-line text strings.
Scrolling Text Box	Scrolling Text Box	Multiple-line text such as suggestions or comments.
Check Box	Check Box	Independent fields having only two values, such as yes/no or true/false.
Radio Button	Radio Button	A list of choices where only one at a time can be selected.
Drop-Down Menu	Drop Down Menu	A list of choices. A user can select one listed item or several, depending on restrictions set by the page creator. If sized so that only one choice is visible, a button at the right drops it down to permit selection. If sized so that two or more choices are visible, a scroll bar replaces the drop-down button.
Push Button	Push Button	A button that transmits the form contents to the Action URL, clears the form, or invokes a script.
(Any chosen image)	Image Form Field	An image that, when clicked, transmits the form contents to the Action URL.
(Invisible)	Hidden	An invisible element the browser transmits with the Action URL.

Drawing Forms in FrontPage Editor

FrontPage Editor can easily add forms and form elements to your Web pages. This is the procedure:

1 Set the insertion point where you want the first form element to appear.

2 Use the Forms toolbar or choose Form Field from the Insert menu to insert the type of form element you want. Table 11-2 lists the Form toolbar buttons, functions, and equivalent menu commands.

3 For each additional element you want in the same form, set the insertion point inside the form, and then repeat step 2.

TABLE 11-2.   The FrontPage Editor Forms Toolbar

Button	Description	Function	Menu Command
[abl]	One-Line Text Box	Inserts a one-line text box at the insertion point.	Insert 　Form Field 　　One-Line Text Box
[grid icon]	Scrolling Text Box	Inserts a scrolling text box at the insertion point	Insert 　Form Field 　　Scrolling Text Box
[✓]	Check Box	Inserts a check box at the insertion point	Insert 　Form Field 　　Check Box
[◉]	Radio Button	Inserts a radio button at the insertion point	Insert 　Form Field 　　Radio Button
[menu icon]	Drop-Down Menu	Inserts a drop-down menu at the insertion point	Insert 　Form Field 　　Drop-Down Menu
[button icon]	Push Button	Inserts a push button at the insertion point	Insert 　Form Field 　　Push Button
(none)	Image Form Field	Inserts an image form field at the insertion point	Insert 　Form Field 　　Image

Form elements appear in-line with text. Thus, to put two form elements on different lines, you'd have to insert a paragraph ending or line break between them. To line up form elements horizontally or vertically with others—or with surrounding HTML objects—organize them into a table. One common approach is to place field captions and corresponding form elements in consecutive columns. Another is to place each caption and field element pair within a single cell.

Instead of explicitly designating part of a Web page as a form, Front-Page draws a form border around the first form element you insert. To expand the form, simply add more content—whether it's text, images, tables, more form elements, or any other valid objects. You can add content by direct insertion, by dragging, or by cutting and pasting. To create a second, separate form, insert a form element *outside* the boundaries of the existing form.

Arranging Form Elements

Some general guidelines will help you choose form element types and arrange them effectively.

- Place required fields, key fields, and other important fields near the upper-left area of the form to give them top prominence.

- Group fields in naturally expected sequences such as Name, Address, City, State/Province, ZIP Code/Postal Code.

- Group related fields by placing them close together. Make the groups distinct by using white space, indentation, or graphic elements.

- Put lengthy fields—such as comments or special instructions—at the bottom of the form.

- Use ordinary HTML text for field captions.

- Use one-line text boxes for single fields consisting of plain text.

- Use scrolling text boxes for multiple lines of free-form text, such as comments.

- Use check boxes for yes/no or true/false choices. Checked means Yes or True. For a list of yes/no items, use a series of check boxes.

- Use radio buttons for lists where only one item at a time can be selected.

- Use drop-down menus with multiple selections as a substitute for check boxes.

- Use drop-down menus with a single selection as a substitute for radio buttons.

- Use HTML tables to align captions and form elements horizontally and vertically.

- If groupings appear repeatedly—such as an order requiring multiple lines for each item ordered—create an HTML table with a row for each grouping and a column for each field.

- Put the Submit and Reset buttons at the bottom of the form. This provides some assurance that the user has reviewed the entire form before submitting it.

Creating an HTML form visually is only part of the job. You must also configure the properties of both the form itself and each form element. Finally, collecting data from the Web visitor is only half the battle; you also need to provide a way to process it. Subsequent sections in this chapter will discuss these tasks.

Setting HTML Form Properties

? SEE ALSO

For more information about using browser scripts, see "Incorporating Custom Script Code," page 510.

An HTML form is only a data entry template and does no processing on its own. To process or save data entered on HTML forms, you'll need to follow *one* of these approaches:

- Correctly invoke features of the FrontPage Server Extensions.

- Obtain server-side programs or scripts from another vendor and correctly invoke them.

- Arrange for custom script or server-side programming.

In any event, your form will need to use the element names and values these methods expect.

Figure 11-2 shows the form of Figure 11-1 (page 401) open in Front-Page Editor. The heavy dashed lines show the form's boundaries.

FIGURE 11-2.
FrontPage Editor created the form pictured in Figure 11-1 (page 401).

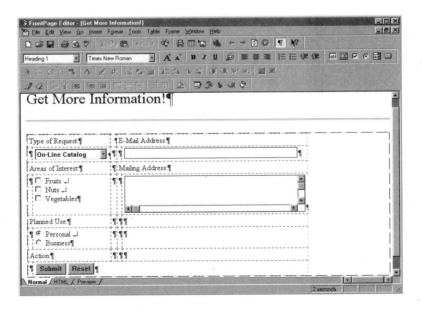

An HTML table keeps the various form elements aligned horizontally and vertically.

To view or modify the form's properties, right-click anywhere in the form and choose Form Properties from the pop-up menu. This displays the Form Properties dialog box shown in Figure 11-3, which controls the following properties.

- **What To Do With Form Results?** indicates the type of action that will process data entered in the form.

  - **Send To File Name** adds data in the form to a file on the Web server. This file can be either a Web page that gets longer and longer with each submission, or a data file suitable for later processing in Excel, Access, or some other off-line program. The associated text box specifies the name of the file—on the Web server—that will receive the data.

  - **Send To E-Mail Address** sends an electronic mail message containing the data in the form. Each time a user clicks the form's Submit button, it generates one message. Enter the receiving e-mail address in the associated text box.

  - **Send to Other: Custom ISAPI, NSAPI, CGI, Or ASP Script** sends the form data to a server-based program that's not part of FrontPage. You must consult the program's documentation or designer to determine what input it requires for proper operation.

FIGURE 11-3.
The Form Properties dialog box in Front-Page Editor.

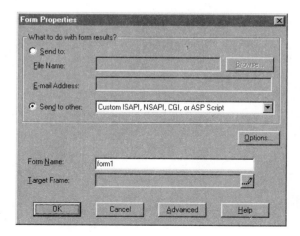

- **Send To Other: Discussion Form Handler** places the information entered into the form onto a discussion-type site. It's discussed later, in "Creating and Managing Discussion Sites," page 442.

- **Send To Other: Registration Form Handler** is used to collect registration data from users of a site. See "Enabling User Self-Registration," page 437.

■ **Options** displays different dialog boxes, depending on what you chose to do with the form results. Two are discussed here.

- If you chose either of the Send To options, the Options button invokes the form handler dialog box titled Options For Saving Results Of Form. Refer to "Saving Form Results for Later Use," page 429, for information on completing this dialog box.

- If you chose Custom ISAPI, NSAPI, CGI, Or ASP Script, the Options button displays the Options For Custom Form Handler dialog box of Figure 11-4, with these settings:

  Action must contain the URL of the server-side program. It's your responsibility to provide this program or ensure that it exists.

  Method specifies POST or GET, whichever the server-side program requires. These are two different ways of transmitting form data to a Web server program. POST, which transmits data in the HTTP headers, is newer, less restrictive, and generally preferred. GET is subject to length and other restrictions because it transmits form data as part of the URL.

  Encoding Type indicates the encoding method used for passing form data to a server-side program. This method permits transmission of reserved characters such as carriage returns and slashes. The only valid entries are blank and *application/x-www-form-urlencoded,* which mean the same thing.

FIGURE 11-4.
Use this dialog box to specify a custom program for processing form data.

- **Form Name** gives the form a name. This field is optional unless needed by a script or custom form handler.

- **Target Frame** specifies the name of a frame where output from the server-based program should appear. This field is optional.

- **Advanced** displays the Advanced Form Properties dialog box of Figure 11-5, which controls hidden form fields.

FIGURE 11-5.
This dialog box maintains hidden fields on an HTML form.

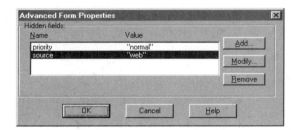

The Advanced Form Properties dialog box controls *hidden fields*—fields whose names and values are both coded into the HTML. The Web visitor can neither see nor alter these fields; they're totally under control of the page creator. Hidden fields usually contain application data that's constant or parameters that control the actions of a server-side program. This permits changing the behavior of the server-side program through changes to the HTML—a much easier process than changing the program itself.

To add a hidden field

1 Click the Add button in the Hidden Fields section.

2 In the resulting dialog box, enter the hidden field's name and value in the respective text boxes.

3 Click OK.

To change a hidden field

   1 Select the field to change.

   2 Click the Modify button.

   3 Correct the field value.

   4 Click OK.

To delete a hidden field, select it and click the Remove button.

Setting Form Element Properties

You can modify the basic properties of any form element in any of four ways.

- *Using menus*—Select the form element you want to modify, and then choose Form Field Properties from the Edit menu.

- *Using keystrokes*—Select the form element you want to modify, and then hold down the Alt key while pressing Enter.

- *Using the mouse*—Right-click the element you want to modify, and then choose Form Field Properties from the pop-up menu.

- *Double-clicking*—Double-click the element you want to modify.

The dialog box you see will depend on the type of form element. A series of sections later in this chapter, beginning with "One-Line Text Box Properties," on page 411, will discuss the dialog boxes for each type of form element.

Validating Form Input

Most applications involving HTML forms require constraints on form input. Certain fields are generally required, for example—meaning it's an error to leave them blank. Other fields must conform to certain patterns; such as ZIP or postal codes consisting of five numeric digits.

FrontPage supports these requirements with a feature called *validation*. Using FrontPage Editor, the page designer specifies value constraints using convenient dialog boxes. FrontPage then enforces these constraints by adding JavaScript or VBScript code to the Web page. If the

⊗ CAUTION

Specifying a Validation Script Language of <None> doesn't inhibit validation dialog boxes in FrontPage Editor. If you find your validation rules aren't being enforced, make sure the Validation Script Language is one your browser supports.

user violates the constraints, the browser transmits no data to the server but instead displays an error message. Figure 11-6 provides an example of this.

Validation is available for text boxes, drop-down menus, and radio buttons. Check boxes have only two values, both presumably valid, and therefore need no validation. Similarly, there's no validation for either push buttons or submit images because there's no wrong way to click them.

The Web Settings Advanced dialog box pictured in Figure 5-21, on page 168, controls the language used for all validation scripts in a Web. Choosing JavaScript or VBScript instructs FrontPage to create validation scripts in those languages. Choosing <None> instructs FrontPage not to create validation scripts.

⊗ CAUTION

VBScript validation scripts won't work in Netscape Navigator versions 3 and earlier. Check later versions for compatibility.

There are two ways to specify validation rules for form elements that support them.

■ Open the element's Properties dialog box and click the Validate button.

■ Right-click the element you wish to modify and choose Form Field Validation from the pop-up menu.

FIGURE 11-6.
Validation code in this page's HTML displayed an error message when the user clicked the Submit button.

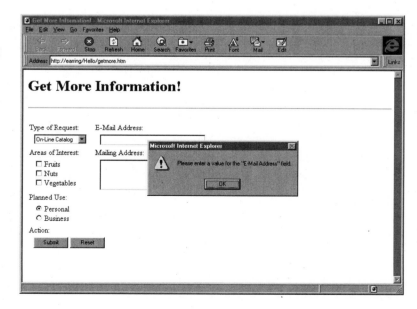

The following sections on each form element will discuss the applicable validation rule settings.

One-Line Text Box Properties

You can change the position of an existing one-line text box by dragging or by cutting and pasting. In addition, you can change its width by selecting the element and then dragging its left or right handles. For other kinds of changes, however, you'll need to display the element's property sheet. Figure 11-7 displays the property sheet for a one-line text box. It provides the following entries.

FIGURE 11-7.
Use this dialog box to modify the properties of a one-line text box.

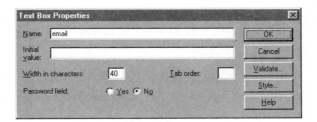

- **Name** designates an internal name for the field. For a given field to be processed, you must give it the name expected by the script or server-side form handler. If you—rather than the form handling programmer—get to name the field, use short, lower-case names with no special characters or hyphens.

- **Initial Value** optionally supplies a data value that appears when the browser initially displays the form or when the user clicks the Reset button.

- **Width In Characters** specifies the width of the field in typical display characters.

- **Tab Order** controls the order in which fields receive the focus when the user presses the Tab key. The current field receives the focus after any fields with lower tab order values, but before any fields with higher values.

NOTE

Receiving the focus means that a text box or other control is highlighted and will receive any keystrokes the user generates. Fields gain focus and lose focus as the user presses the Tab key or clicks different fields with the mouse.

- **Password Field,** if turned on, instructs the browser to display asterisks in place of whatever characters the user actually types.

Clicking the Validate button in Figure 11-7 displays the Text Box Validation menu shown in Figure 11-8. The latter figure is actually a *composite* shown with all fields active, for clarity; in practice, one or more fields will be disabled, depending on the Data Type selected.

FIGURE 11-8.
This dialog box sets constraints on values entered in a one-line text box.

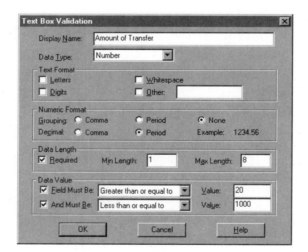

These are the available properties:

- **Display Name.** Give the field a name that will appear in error messages. Normally, this should agree with the field's caption on the Web page. If you don't specify a display name, error messages will use the internal name from the element's property sheet.

- **Data Type.** Specify the type of data the field can contain.

  - **No Constraints** indicates that the field can contain any type of data.

- **Text** indicates that the field can contain alphanumeric or linguistic expressions.

- **Integer** means that the field can contain only whole numbers.

- **Number** means that the field can contain only whole or decimal numbers.

■ **Text Format.** Indicate what kinds of text characters are valid. FrontPage enables this section only if Data Type is Text.

- **Letters** indicates that alphabetic characters are valid.

- **Digits** indicates that numeric characters are valid.

- **Whitespace** means that spaces, tabs, carriage returns, and line feeds are acceptable.

- **Other** indicates that additional characters are acceptable. Enter the acceptable characters in the text box provided.

■ **Numeric Format.** Set the format of numbers. FrontPage enables this section only if Data Type is Integer or Number.

- **Grouping** indicates which characters, in addition to numeric digits, are valid in a numeric field.

  Comma means the comma character is permissible, as in 12,345,678.

  None means that no punctuation is permissible, as in 12345678.

  Period means the period character is permissible, as in 12.345.678.

- **Decimal** indicates which character is acceptable as a decimal point. This field is disabled if Data Type is Integer. Note that the grouping character and the decimal character can't be the same.

  Comma means that the comma is acceptable as a decimal point.

  Period means the period is acceptable as a decimal point.

- **Data Length.** Set the length restrictions on data entered in the field.

  - **Required,** if turned on, indicates that the field can't be left blank.

  - **Min Length** indicates the fewest characters the field can contain.

  - **Max Length** indicates the most characters the field can contain.

- **Data Value.** These properties set range constraints on values entered in the text box. If the data type is Number or Integer, FrontPage will use numeric comparisons. If the data type is Text or No Constraints, FrontPage will use alphabetic comparisons.

  - **Field Must Be.** To set a range limit on the value the user enters, check this box and then specify a comparison and a boundary value. The available comparisons are Less Than, Greater Than, Less Than Or Equal To, Greater Than Or Equal To, Equal To, and Not Equal To.

  - **Value.** Specify the boundary value. Comparison against this value must be true or an error will occur. If, for example, Field Must Be reads *Greater Than 10* and the user enters *9,* the user will get an error message.

  - **And Must Be.** Check this box and specify a comparison to enforce a second range limit on the value in the one-line text box. The Value property on this line works as above.

Scrolling Text Box Properties

The dialog box for changing the properties of a scrolling text box appears in Figure 11-9. The available properties are the following.

FIGURE 11-9.
This dialog box sets constraints on values entered in a one-line text box.

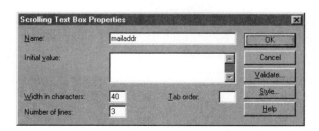

For information on CSS, see "Managing Page-Level Cascading Style Sheets," page 232.

- **Name** designates an internal name for the field. This name must be known to the script or server-side form handler.

- **Initial Value** optionally supplies a data value that appears when the browser first displays the form or when the user clicks the Reset button.

- **Width In Characters** sets the width of the box in units of typical display characters.

- **Tab Order** controls the order in which fields receive the focus when the user presses the Tab key.

- **Number Of Lines** sets the height of the box in lines.

- **Validate** displays the same validation dialog box as for one-line text boxes. Refer to the previous section for details.

- **Style** sets cascading style sheet properties for the text box.

Check Box Properties

The dialog box shown in Figure 11-10 controls the properties of a check box. The following properties are available:

- **Name** gives the field an internal name. This must be the name the script or server-side form handler expects.

- **Value** specifies a string the browser will transmit to the server or script if the box is checked. If the box configured in Figure 11-10 is turned on when the user clicks Submit, the browser will transmit *fruits=on*. If the box isn't checked when the user clicks Submit, the browser sends neither the name nor the value.

- **Initial State** specifies how the browser initializes the check box—on or off—when it first displays the form or later responds to the press of a Reset button.

- **Tab Order** controls the sequence, as the user presses the Tab key, in which this control receives the focus, compared to other controls.

- **Style** specifies cascading style sheet properties for this element.

IV

Activating Your Site

There's no Validation for check boxes—it's hard to imagine what an invalid check box entry would be.

Radio Button Properties

Like lobbyists, heartaches, and rock-band aficionados, radio buttons appear in groups. Of all radio buttons in a group, only one at a time can be turned on. No other HTML form elements interact this way.

The grouping mechanism for radio buttons within a form is quite simple: All buttons with the same name are in the same group. Conversely, to group a set of radio buttons, give them all the same name.

Assigning duplicate names to form elements is usually an error, but in the case of radio buttons it's a necessity. Each like-named radio button, however, must have a different value so the server can determine which button was selected when the user clicked Submit. The browser transmits the clicked radio button's value and no others.

Figure 11-11 shows the properties dialog box for radio buttons. It provides access to the following settings.

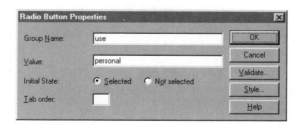

- **Group Name** supplies the internal name of all radio buttons in the same group as this button. This name must be known to the script or server-side form handler.

- **Value** designates a string the browser will transmit if this radio button is selected when the user clicks Submit. Be sure to give each radio button in the same group a different value.

- **Initial State** initializes the radio button—on or off—when first displayed or when the user clicks the Reset button.

> **NOTE**
>
> Setting the initial state of one radio button to Selected sets the initial state of all other buttons in the same group to Not Selected.

- **Tab Order** controls the order in which this element receives the focus when the user presses the Tab key. Radio buttons in the same group should almost always have consecutive Tab Order values.

- **Style** assigns cascading style sheet properties.

- **Validate** displays the Radio Button Validation dialog box that appears in Figure 11-12. The settings are

  - **Display Name** gives the button group a name that will appear in error messages. This field is disabled unless the following field is checked.

  - **Data Required,** if checked, displays an error if the user clicks Submit and no radio buttons in the group are selected.

FIGURE 11-12.
This is the validation dialog box for radio buttons.

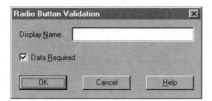

Normally, a user can't turn off all the radio buttons in a group. The only way to turn off a button is to turn on another button in the same group. It's possible, however, to have all radio buttons in a group turned off when first displayed. This, together with the Data Required validation rule, assures that the user made a conscious choice and didn't simply take the default.

Changing the validation rules for one radio button automatically changes them for all buttons in the same group.

Drop-Down Menu Properties

The property sheet for drop-down menus appears in Figure 11-13. It offers access to the following settings:

■ **Name** assigns an internal name to the menu. This name must be known to the script or server-side form handler.

■ **Choice - Selected - Value** contains a row for each entry in the drop-down list. Use the five buttons at the right to maintain this table.

- **Add** displays the Add Choice dialog box, with the same choices as the one in Figure 11-14. Enter the following fields:

  Choice specifies the text the browser will display to the user.

  Specify Value controls the value transmitted if this choice is selected when the user clicks the Submit button. If this setting is on, the browser transmits the value in the associated text box. Otherwise, it transmits the value in the Choice box.

  Initial State determines whether the current choice is selected when first displayed and when the user clicks Reset. There are two settings: Selected and Not Selected. If the Allow Multiple Selections option described below and shown in Figure 11-13 is No, setting the initial state of one

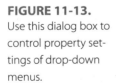

FIGURE 11-13.
Use this dialog box to control property settings of drop-down menus.

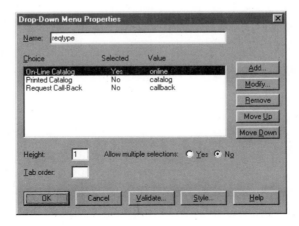

IV

FIGURE 11-14.

The Add Choice and Modify Choice dialog boxes contain identical fields for adding or modifying entries in a drop-down menu.

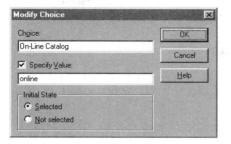

choice to Selected also sets the initial state of all other choices to Not Selected.

- **Modify** displays the dialog box shown in Figure 11-14 for the currently selected choice. Make any changes and then click OK.

- **Remove** deletes the currently selected choice.

- **Move Up** moves the currently selected choice one position higher in the list.

- **Move Down** moves the currently selected choice one position lower in the list.

■ **Height** specifies the height of the displayed list in lines. A one-line list has a drop-down button at the right. Lists two or more lines high have scroll bars at the right.

> **NOTE**
>
> A drop-down menu with a height of one displays in Windows as a drop-down list. Drop-down menus with height greater than one display as scrollable list boxes.

■ **Allow Multiple Selections** should be set to No if only one selection at a time can be selected. Specify Yes if two or more items can be selected simultaneously.

■ **Tab Order** controls the order in which fields on the same form receive the focus as the user presses the Tab key.

■ **Style** controls cascading style sheet properties.

- **Validate** displays the Drop-Down Menu Validation dialog box shown in Figure 11-15. The available entries are the following:

  - **Display Name** gives the drop-down menu a name that will appear in error messages.

  - **Data Required**, if turned on, displays an error if the user clicks Submit and no choices in the menu are selected.

  - **Disallow First Item** prevents submitting the form with the first choice of this menu still selected. In such cases, the first menu choice is typically a prompt to select a subsequent choice. This assures that the user makes a conscious choice and doesn't simply accept the default.

FIGURE 11-15.
This is the validation dialog box for drop-down menus.

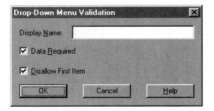

Push Button Properties

Figure 11-16 shows the dialog box for push buttons. The available fields are these:

- **Name** denotes the internal name of the field. This is optional for push buttons.

- **Value/Label**, if specified, serves two purposes.

  - It becomes the button's visible caption.

  - If the push button has both a Name and a Value/Label, the browser will transmit the *name=value* pair when the user clicks the button. This tells the server which of several buttons the user clicked.

- **Button Type** determines the type of push button.

  - **Submit** specifies that clicking this button submits the form. It also sets the default label to Submit.

- **Reset** indicates that clicking this button resets a form to its initial state. It also sets the default label to Reset.

- **Normal** assigns no predetermined action for the button. However, a script can respond to button clicks and perform any programmed action. Choosing button type Normal sets the default label to Button.

■ **Tab Order** determines the sequence in which the button receives the focus when the user presses the Tab key.

■ **Style** sets cascading style sheet properties for the button.

■ **Form** opens the Form Properties dialog box for specifying what to do with the form results once the push button submits them.

There are no validation features for push buttons—either you click a push button or you don't.

FIGURE 11-16.
This dialog box controls push button properties.

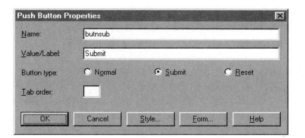

Image Form Field Properties

An image form field works much like a submit push button. Clicking an image form field submits the form's data using the form's Action URL.

To insert an image form field, choose Form Field from the Insert menu in FrontPage Editor, and then select Image. Using the Image command inserts only an ordinary image, even when inserting into a form area.

Figure 11-17, on the next page, shows the dialog box for setting the properties of an image form field. The single property—Name—identifies the image form field and gets transmitted to the server when the user clicks the image. No validation is available. Clicking image properties opens the Image Properties dialog box shown in Figure 8-6, page 286, and described in "Modifying Image Properties," page 285.

FIGURE 11-17.
This is the property
sheet for image
form fields.

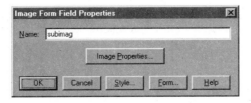

The Style button can be used to assign cascading style sheet properties
to the image. The Form button displays the Form Properties dialog
box, already shown in Figure 11-3, page 406.

Designating Form Element Labels

Normally, the text that visually identifies form elements to the user is just
that: ordinary text. Visual proximity associates the label with its control.

HTML now contains a tag that associates the label and its control internally as well. The use of this tag isn't yet well defined, but one possibility might involve a script modifying the prompt for a form element.
For example, a script could change a label to Dollars, Pounds, Marks,
Francs, or Yen based on a ship-to address.

Changing portions of a page already displayed requires Dynamic HTML—a feature of only the very latest browsers—as well as knowledge of scripting.

To "officially" designate text as the label of an HTML form element

1 Enter the label text inside the HTML form and directly adjacent to
   the form element.

2 Select both the text and the form element.

3 Choose Form Field from the Insert menu, and then select Label.

This will produce no visible change in the Web page, but the text will
be internally designated as the control's label and a thin dotted box
will surround the text in FrontPage Editor. HTML view will display a
label tag preceding the text you selected and referencing the internal
name of the form element.

To remove the label designation, select the label, choose Form Field from the Insert menu, and then select Remove Label.

Using the Form Page Wizard

FrontPage Editor provides a wizard to help you get started creating HTML forms. This wizard has so many options that only a representative sample appears here.

The Form Page Wizard is unlikely to produce a finished page tailored to your complete satisfaction, but it can give you a good starting point or at least some quick ideas. If you don't like the results you first achieve, keep rerunning the wizard with different options until results improve.

To run the wizard

1   Start FrontPage Editor.

2   Choose New from the File menu.

3   From the Page tab, choose Form Page Wizard and then click OK.

4   When the banner pictured in Figure 11-18 appears, click Next to continue.

FIGURE 11-18.
Click Next to proceed past the Form Page Wizard banner.

5   When the wizard displays the dialog box shown in Figure 11-19, on the following page, enter a title for the page and a filename in the current Web, and then click Next.

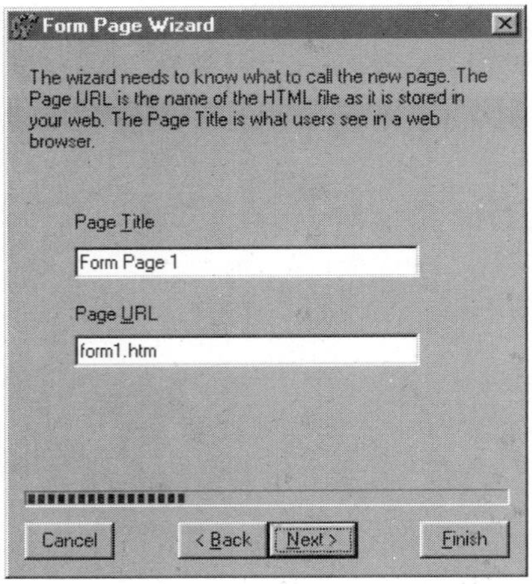

FIGURE 11-19.
Give the new form page a location in the current Web and a title.

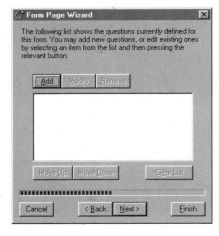

6 The wizard will next display the dialog box shown in Figure 11-20, which contains a list of the major questions the form will ask. To add questions, click the Add button to display the dialog box shown in Figure 11-21.

FIGURE 11-20.
This dialog box builds a list of major questions for the user.

7 From the list at the top of Figure 11-21, select the type of input to collect for the current question. In the text box at the bottom, review the suggested prompt and make any necessary changes. Click Next.

FIGURE 11-21.
This Form Page Wizard dialog box prompts for the type of input to collect for a question.

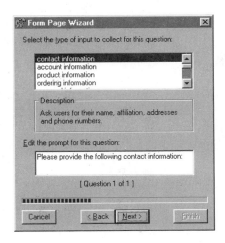

8 Figure 11-22 displays a typical dialog box the wizard might display next. Each type of input in the previous step results in a different dialog box, with different fields, in this step. Select the fields you want to collect, revise the base name for those fields if necessary, and then click Next.

FIGURE 11-22.
Choose the data elements you wish to collect from the user.

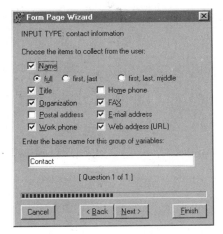

9 Repeat steps 6, 7, and 8 as often as necessary to collect all the input you need. To start over, click the Clear List button in Figure 11-20. When finished, click Next.

10 When the dialog box shown in Figure 11-23 appears, indicate how you want the list of questions presented, whether you want a table of contents, and whether to use tables for form field alignment. Click Next when finished.

FIGURE 11-23.
This dialog box from the Form Page Wizard controls high-level aspects of form page layout.

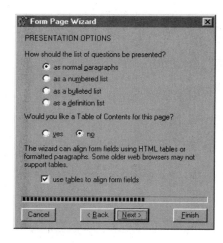

11 The next dialog box, pictured in Figure 11-24, controls how you want to capture the input fields you've specified. The options are described below the figure.

FIGURE 11-24.
This dialog box controls how form data is saved.

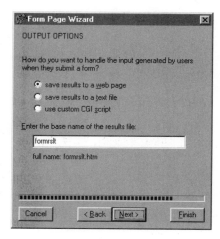

- **Save Results To A Web Page** creates a new Web page whenever a user submits the form.

? SEE ALSO

For details on saving form results, refer to "Saving Form Results for Later Use," page 429.

⊗ CAUTION

The options Save Results To A Web Page and Save Results To A Text File use facilities in the FrontPage Server Extensions. Make sure the extensions are installed on any Web servers you plan to use, and check that your application is properly configured.

- **Save Results To A Text File** saves submitted data in a text file on the server. Various programs can import data from such files at a later time.

- **Use Custom CGI Script** assumes a Web programmer will write a custom process to store the data.

- **Enter The Base Name Of The Results File** designates the name of the Web page or text file (minus the HTM or TXT extension) where the form results will be saved. This page or file will be located in your Web, on the server from which the remote users access the HTML forms page.

  If you choose Use Custom CGI Script, this field is disabled.

12 Figure 11-25 shows the final dialog box in the Form Page Wizard. You can use the Back and Next buttons to review and correct your work. When done, click Finish to create the page as specified.

Figure 11-26 and Figure 11-27 show typical results from running the Form Page Wizard. Rerun the wizard as often as necessary to optimize results, and then finalize layout and appearance by editing the page directly. It's a good idea to test data collection features often, to ensure any problems from changing the form manually show up right away and can be dealt with.

FIGURE 11-25.
This is the final confirmation dialog box in the Form Page Wizard. Click Finish to build the page.

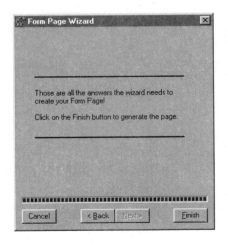

Form Page Wizard

Those are all the answers the wizard needs to create your Form Page!

Click on the Finish button to generate the page.

Cancel   < Back   Next >   Finish

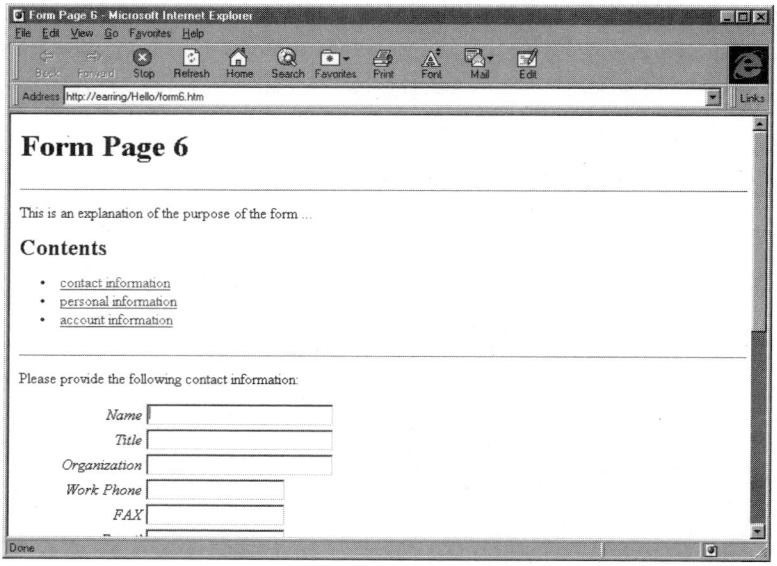

FIGURE 11-26.
This is the top half of a page generated by the Form Page Wizard.

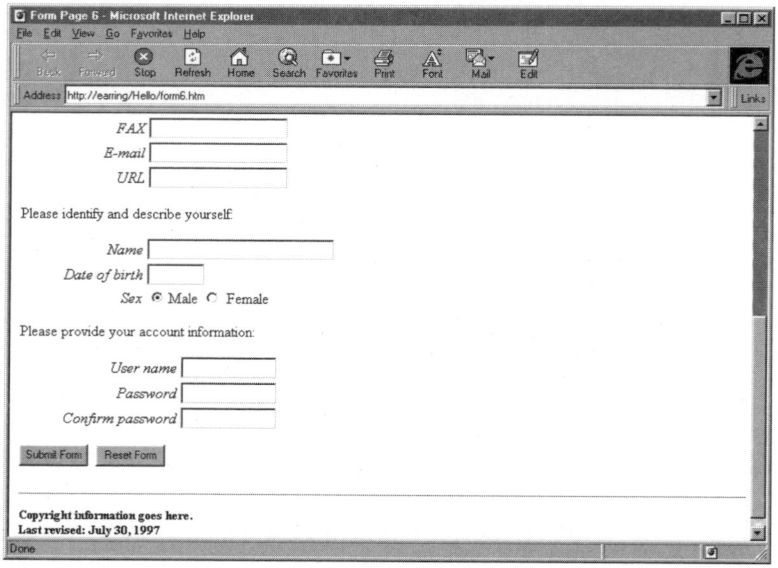

FIGURE 11-27.
This is the lower half of the page displayed in Figure 11-26.

Saving Form Results for Later Use

The FrontPage Save Results component receives data from an HTML form and then saves it on a Web server, sends it by electronic mail, or both. Save Results can format data as Web pages, simple ASCII text, or data files ready for importing into database or spreadsheet applications. Accumulating data in text files avoids the complexities of managing and configuring databases on the server, though it does require later retrieval and offline processing.

The Save Results component absolutely requires presence of the Front-Page Server Extensions, both on the Web server you'll use for testing and on the server remote users will use in production. If this is a problem, you'll have to get your system administrator to install the extensions, find another provider, or change your approach.

There are two ways to start using the Save Results component.

1   Create a new Web page in FrontPage Editor, specifying the Feedback Form template. This will create a working Save Results page you can modify to suit your requirements.

2   Create or modify your own form, choosing and configuring the Send To option in the What To Do With Form Results section of the Form Properties dialog box.

Figure 11-28, on the next page, shows a form created by the Feedback Form template and its form properties. The setting Send To File Name is the sole unique feature of pages created with this template; you can discard or modify anything else on the page. You can also choose this setting on existing forms or forms you create yourself.

 TIP

To display the Form Properties dialog box shown in Figure 11-28 (on the following page) right-click anywhere on the form and select Form Properties from the pop-up menu. Alternatively, open the properties of any push button in the form, and then click the Form button.

FIGURE 11-28.
The Feedback Form template creates a Web page that, using the Save Results component, accumulates data in files on the server.

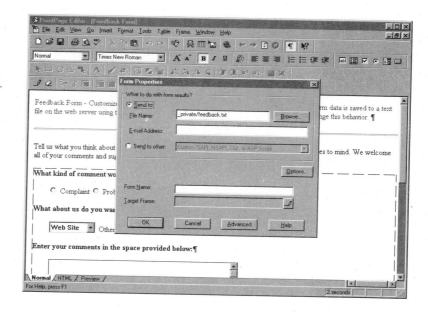

To configure the Save Results component, click the Options button shown in Figure 11-28. This will display the four-tabbed dialog box shown in Figure 11-29, Figure 11-31 (page 434), Figure 11-32 (page 435), and Figure 11-34 (page 436).

FIGURE 11-29.
This dialog box configures settings for the Save Results component.

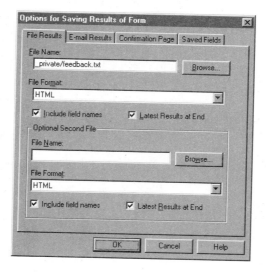

Set the fields on the File Results tab as follows:

- **File Name.** Specify the name and location of the data collection file.

  - For locations within the current Web, specify a relative URL.

  - For locations outside the current Web, specify a filename and folder in the server's file space. That is, specify a UNC or drive letter path. If the file doesn't exist, the FrontPage extensions will create it when the first data arrives.

    If File Format (the next field) specifies an HTML option, use an HTM filename extension and a folder location users can browse.

    If File Format specifies text, use a TXT or CSV filename extension and locate the file in the _private folder of your Web. Be aware that the _private folder is hidden from Web browsers.

- **File Format.** Choose a format for the results file. Table 11-3, on the following page, lists the choices.

- **Include Field Names.** Turn this box on to save both the name and value of each form field. If the box isn't checked, only the values are saved.

- **Latest Results At End.** Turn this box on to append data to the end of a Web page. Turning the box off adds new data at the top of the page. FrontPage ignores this setting if the File Format isn't one of the HTML types; new data in such cases always appears at the end of the file.

In the section titled **Optional Second File** specify the name, format, and other settings for a second file where the component will save results. This permits saving form results twice in different formats, such as HTML and comma-separated, or in two different file locations to reduce the risk of loss. Configure this section with the same four fields described above.

TABLE 11-3. Format Options for Save Results Component

File Format	Description
HTML	The component will append the data to a Web page, formatting the data as normal text with each field on a new line. This is the default.
HTML definition list	As above, but the component will format the *name=value* pairs as a definition list.
HTML bulleted list	As above, but the component will format the data as a bulleted list.
Formatted text within HTML	As above, but the component will format the data as Formatted (monospaced) text.
Formatted text	The component will save a plain text file formatted for easy reading.
Text database using comma as a separator	The component writes all data values on one line, separating them with commas. This is useful for databases, spreadsheets, and other programs that can import the comma-separated values (CSV) format.
Text database using tab as a separator	As above, but tab characters separate the data values.
Text database using space as a separator	As above, but spaces separate the data values.

Figure 11-30 shows the effects of saving results with the HTML file format setting. The Save Results component keeps appending form results to the same HTML page indefinitely in the manner shown. The identical data (numbered for clarity) appears below in the format Text Database Using Comma As A Separator. Note that the first data record contains field names rather than data; this is a common convention and very useful when performing spreadsheet and database imports.

```
1 "MessageType","Subject","SubjectOther","Comments",
  "Username","UserEmail","UserTel","UserFAX",
  "ContactRequested","Date","Time","Remote Name",
  "Remote User","HTTP User Agent"

2 "Praise","Web Site","","Visiting your Web site has
  produced an incredible improvement in my personal
  lifestyle. Before, I was despondent and suicidal.
  Now, I'm so charged with life that I've become
  president of several highly profitable
  corporations, six of which I started myself.",
  "Yu Forria","yforria@megacorp.com","800-555-9876",
```

"800-555-6789","ContactRequested","7/30/97",
"4:49:37 PM","192.168.180.23","","Mozilla/2.0
(compatible; MSIE 3.02; Update a; Windows 95)"

3 "Complaint","Store","","Your clerk overcharged me
on push pins last month. Please remit check for
$0.04 immediately.","Ishmael McTavish",
"mctavish@freenet.com","555-486-0050",
"555-486-1023","ContactRequested","7/30/97",
"4:57:49 PM","192.168.180.23","","Mozilla/2.0
(compatible; MSIE 3.02; Update a; Windows 95)"

4 "Suggestion","Employee","","Please get your
mechanic Otto to stop putting garlic by the
carburetor.","Vladimir Spinoza","vlad@casket.org",
"","","ContactRequested","7/30/97","5:09:44
PM","192.168.180.23","","Mozilla/2.0 (compatible;
MSIE 3.02; Update a; Windows 95)"

FIGURE 11-30.
Saving form results
as HTML produces an
ever-growing Web
page formatted
like this.

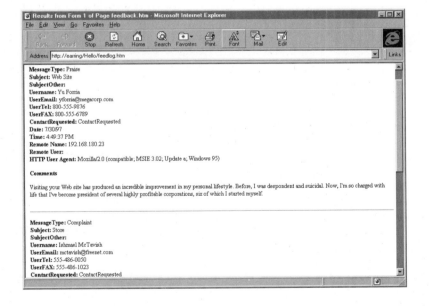

Figure 11-31, on the next page, shows the E-Mail Results tab on the Options For Saving Results Of Form dialog box. Set the options as follows.

■ **E-Mail Address To Receive Results.** Enter the electronic mail address that will receive the mailed data.

- **E-Mail Format.** Select a data format for the mailed data. Formatted text is the most universally readable and is the default.

- **Include Field Names.** Turn on this box if you want to include field names in the message as well as field values.

FIGURE 11-31.
Use this tab to send HTML form data as electronic mail.

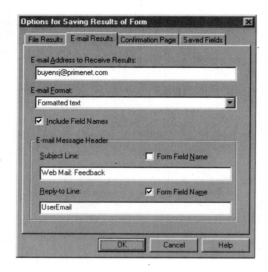

Fields in the **E-Mail Message Header** section control the subject line and Reply-to address of the mailed data.

- **Subject Line.** This field is optional but recommended.

  - If the associated **Form Field Name** box is turned off, enter some text that will become the message's Subject line.

  - If the box is on, enter the name of a form field; any data entered in that field then becomes the Subject of the message.

- **Reply-To Line.** This field is optional; it adds a Reply-To header to the message that transmits the form data. If the recipient of the form data replies to that message, the reply will be delivered to the address you specify here.

  - If the associated **Form Field Name** box is turned off, enter the E-Mail address of a person who will receive all such replies.

- If the box is on, enter the name of a form field. Any data entered in that field will then become the Reply-To address.

Saving results to a file and sending e-mail aren't mutually exclusive. If the need arises, the Save Results component can send mail as well as saving zero, one, or two result files.

❓ SEE ALSO
For advice in creating confirmation pages, refer to "Managing Confirmation Pages," page 458.

Figure 11-32 shows the third tab, labeled Confirmation Page, of the Options For Saving Results Of Form dialog box. If the URL Of Confirmation Page field is blank, the Save Results component will automatically generate a confirmation page like that shown in Figure 11-33, on the next page. If this format isn't acceptable, you can design your own page and specify its URL on the Confirmation Page tab.

FIGURE 11-32.
The Confirmation Page tab specifies the URL of a custom confirmation page.

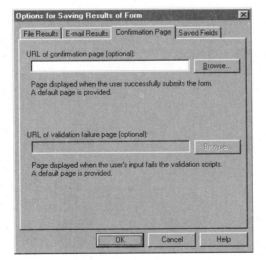

❓ SEE ALSO
For advice in creating validation failure pages, refer to "Managing Confirmation Page," page 458.

You can also specify the relative or absolute URL of a validation failure page. The Save Results component will display this page if any submitted fields fail validation. If you don't specify a validation failure page, the Save Results component creates one on the fly.

The fourth tab in the Options For Saving Results Of Form dialog box is titled Saved Fields and pictured in Figure 11-34, on the following page.

FIGURE 11-33.
By default, the Save Results component will generate form confirmation pages such as this.

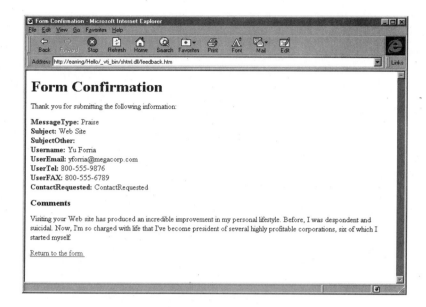

FIGURE 11-34.
Use the Saved Fields tab to control which HTML form fields and system fields the Save Results component will save.

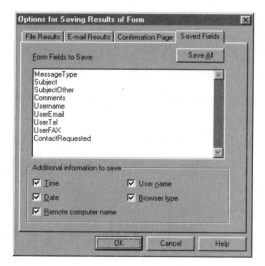

The upper half of the Saved Fields tab specifies which fields to save and in what order. Clicking the button Save All lists all fields defined in the current form. To remove a field, select it by dragging the mouse, and then press the Delete key.

To reposition a field

1 Select it (including the carriage return at the end), and then press Ctrl+X or Shift+Del to cut.

2 Set the insertion point at the beginning of a line elsewhere in the list.

3 Press Ctrl+V or Shift+Ins to paste.

The five check boxes in the Additional Information To Save section record additional data not derived from the form itself. Checking any of these boxes appends the relevant information to the form data.

■ **Time.** The time the user submitted the form.

■ **Date.** The date the user submitted the form.

■ **Remote Computer Name.** The name of the computer that submitted the form.

■ **User Name.** The name of the user who submitted the form. This data will be blank unless the Web page containing the form resides in a restricted Web and the user was prompted for both a name and a password.

■ **Browser Type.** The type of Web browser used to submit the form.

Enabling User Self-Registration

The FrontPage Registration component lets users create their own accounts for Browse access to a FrontPage Web. An HTML form gathers the new user's name and password, plus any other desirable fields. The Registration component adds the username and password to the Web's authentication database and additionally uses the Save Results component to store submitted data for other uses.

A common use for the Registration component is requiring users to identify themselves before granting them access to a given Web. This supports any later follow-up you wish to perform and, combined with a log analysis tool, supports analysis of usage by individual.

There are two major restrictions that affect use of the Registration component.

1 The Registration form must be created, stored, and maintained in the Root Web of the server that hosts the relevant FrontPage Web. Administrators of other FrontPage Webs can't configure the Registration component unless they're also administrators of the Root Web.

> A Registration form can't reside within the Web it provides access to. Before registering, users have no access there!

2 The Registration component isn't supported for the following Web servers:

- Microsoft Personal Web Server

- Microsoft Peer Web Server for Windows NT Workstation

- Microsoft Internet Information Server for Windows NT Server

The second restriction arises because the listed Web servers use a Windows NT User Account Database for user identification. Allowing unknown users to create their own Windows NT accounts would be a major security breach. If you need to offer user registration capability on these servers, consider the Microsoft Membership System, a product in the Microsoft Commercial Internet System.

To activate the registration component for a FrontPage Web on a supported server

1 Open the server's Root Web in FrontPage Explorer.

2 Start FrontPage Editor by choosing Show FrontPage Editor from the Tools menu.

3 Choose New from the File menu.

4 Select the User Registration template from the Page tab, and then click OK.

5 Choose Replace from the Edit menu, and then change all occurrences of *[OtherWeb]* to the name of the Web that will have self-registration (note there are no spaces in *[OtherWeb]*).

6 Scroll to the bottom of the page and locate the HTML form pictured in Figure 11-35.

FIGURE 11-35.
This HTML form is the significant part of the Web page produced by the User Registration template.

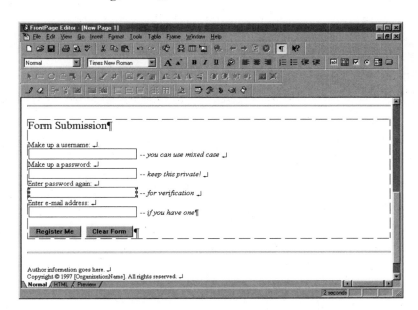

7 Right-click anywhere in the form and choose Form Properties. (Alternatively, double-click one of the push buttons, and then click the Form button.)

8 When the Form Properties dialog box appears, verify that the Send To Other option is turned on and set to Registration Form Handler. Clicking the Options button should then cause the dialog box shown in Figure 11-36, on the following page, to appear.

9 Enter or verify the following fields.

- **FrontPage Web Name.** Enter the name of the FrontPage Web users will register to use. This must consist of a leading slash followed by the internal (short) name of the Web. Don't use a trailing slash or the Web's name in words.

FIGURE 11-36.
This dialog box controls settings for the Registration form handler.

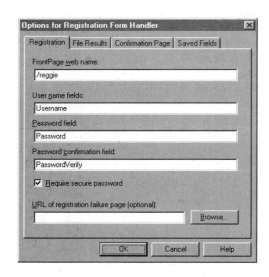

- **User Name Fields.** Enter the names of one or more form fields, separated by commas or spaces. The form handler will construct the username by joining these fields. By default, the User Registration template creates a one-line text box named Username for this purpose.

- **Password Field.** Name the form field where the user enters a new password. The default text box is named Password.

- **Password Confirmation Field.** Name the field where the user retypes the new password to confirm it. The default text box is named PasswordVerify.

- **Require Secure Password.** Turn on to require new passwords to be at least six characters long and not partially match the username.

- **URL Of Registration Failure Page.** Optionally, enter the relative or absolute URL of a page the form handler will display if it can't register the user for the FrontPage Web. You can hand-type the URL or click the Browse button to locate it.

10 If desired, use the File Results, Confirmation Page, and Saved Fields tabs to accumulate data about each registration in a Web page or text file. These tabs work exactly like the corresponding tabs in the Save Results component, described in the previous section.

TIP

If you want the Save Results component to save the registration information within the Web users are registering for, be sure to specify the file location as a local file such as D:\FrontPage Webs\Content\hello_private\regdb.txt and not a relative URL such as hello/_private/regdb.txt.

CAUTION

If you rename the Username, Password, or PasswordVerify form elements, be sure to adjust the field names in the Registration Form Handler dialog box (Figure 11-36) as well.

11 Add any additional fields or make any desired changes to the Registration form or Web page.

12 Save the Web page in the root folder of the Root Web. Each FrontPage Web supporting user registration will have its own registration page, so be sure to adopt a workable naming scheme such as *reg* followed by the Web name and then the HTM filename extension.

13 Quit FrontPage Editor.

14 In FrontPage Explorer, open the FrontPage Web users will register for, logging in as an administrator.

15 Choose Permissions from the Tools menu in FrontPage Explorer.

16 On the Settings tab, select Use Unique Permissions For This Web and click Apply.

17 On the Users tab, select Only Registered Users Have Browse Access and click OK.

NOTE

After you complete steps 16 and 17, every Web visitor will need to enter a valid username and password before accessing any page in the FrontPage Web.

SEE ALSO

For more information on security settings for FrontPage Webs, refer to Chapter 15, "The FrontPage Security Model."

Once you have Registration working, you can make further changes to the Registration page. However, you must have form elements for the username, password, and password confirmation fields, and you must also specify their names in the Registration Form Handler dialog box (Figure 11-36).

Creating and Managing Discussion Sites

A discussion site is a special FrontPage Web that accumulates messages users submit through a special HTML form. The FrontPage Server Extensions

- Save each message as a Web page

- Build Next and Previous hyperlinks between pages

- Maintain an index page of all articles

In some respects, Discussion Webs resemble Usenet newsgroups. Discussion Webs can also incorporate the Search component to locate articles containing specified text and the Registration component to identify users.

The primary restrictions on Discussion Webs are the following:

1 Each Discussion Web must be its own FrontPage Web.

2 Discussion Webs are an add-only facility. There's no mechanism to purge old articles or offensive postings; the Discussion Web simply grows forever. A Web administrator can replace the content of an article with *Expletive deleted* or some other phrase, but deleting an article results in broken links from the preceding and following articles.

To create a Discussion Web, you must be an administrator of the Root Web for the server. The steps required are these:

1 Use FrontPage Explorer to open the Root Web on the server where the Discussion Web will reside. Log in as an administrator.

2 Choose New from the File menu, and then select FrontPage Web.

3 When the dialog box shown in Figure 11-37 appears, specify Discussion Web Wizard, choose a title for the new Discussion Web, and click Change if necessary to specify a different Web server or folder name. When finished, click OK. The FrontPage Server Extensions must be installed on the server you specify.

FIGURE 11-37.
Use this dialog box to
specify the server
name and Web
name of a new
Discussion Web.

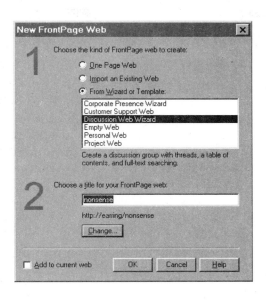

TIP

The short name of a Discussion Web must conform to the rules for naming folders on the system that hosts the Web. Pithy, intuitive names are usually better
than verbose ones. You can provide a more descriptive name later.

4 When the Discussion Web Wizard displays the banner page
shown in Figure 11-38, click Next.

FIGURE 11-38.
Click Next after read-
ing this banner page.

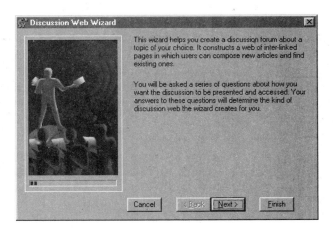

5 The second Discussion Web prompt appears in Figure 11-39. Select options for the discussion as follows.

- **Submission Form.** This option is mandatory. It provides the form for discussion participants to enter messages.

- **Table Of Contents.** Turn on this box if you want an index page containing hyperlinks to each message in the discussion.

- **Search Form.** Turn on this box to permit searching all messages for a word or phrase.

- **Threaded Replies.** Turn on to allow participants to create new top-level topics or replies to existing topics. Replies to a message will appear indented below it. Leaving this box turned off keeps messages in chronological sequence.

- **Confirmation Page.** Turn on this box if users should receive confirmation after posting discussion entries.

FIGURE 11-39.
Choose the major features of your Discussion Web using this dialog box.

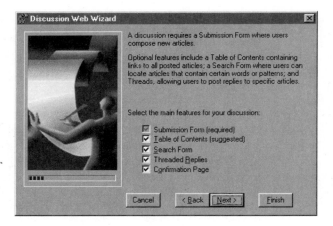

Click Next when your entries on this panel are complete.

6 In the next dialog box, Figure 11-40, specify

- A descriptive name for the Discussion—the name of the Web in words.

- A name for the folder that will contain the posted messages. This is a folder within the FrontPage Web, and not the Web's root folder. The name must be two to eight characters long and begin with an underscore.

FIGURE 11-40.
Give the Discussion
Web an external title
and an internal
folder name.

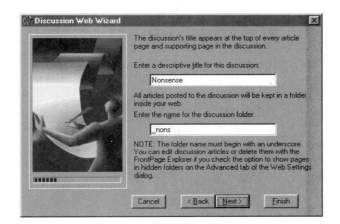

7 After clicking Next, use the prompt shown in Figure 11-41 to choose the fields you want on the input form. The Category and Product fields are drop-down list boxes. You can add additional fields later by editing the form directly in FrontPage Editor. When satisfied with your entry, click Next.

FIGURE 11-41.
Choose the fields you
want included in the
Discussion Web's mes-
sage posting form.

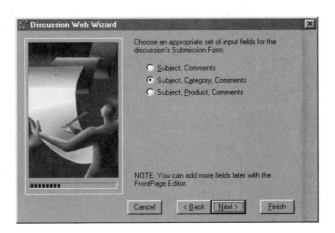

Before choosing this option, review the restrictions described in "Enabling User Self-Registration," page 437, regarding the Registration component.

8 Figure 11-42 shows the next prompt. To restrict discussion group posting to registered users, choose Yes. Click Next to continue.

9 The next dialog box controls the order for displaying posted articles. See Figure 11-43. After choosing oldest to newest or newest to oldest, click Next to continue.

10 When the dialog box shown in Figure 11-44 appears, specify whether you want the discussion's table of contents to be the home page for the Discussion Web, and then click next.

FIGURE 11-42.
Choose Yes to restrict the Discussion to registered users.

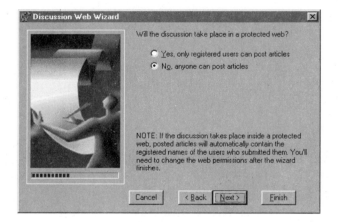

FIGURE 11-43.
Specify here the order in which posted articles should appear.

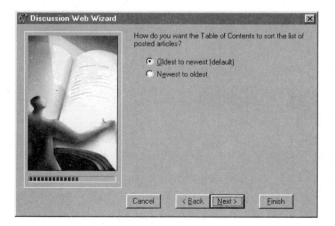

FIGURE 11-44.
Clicking Yes makes the table of contents the home page for the Discussion Web.

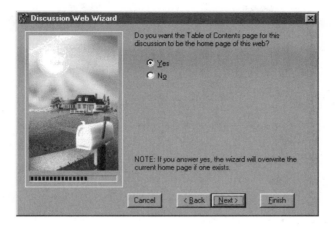

11 If you chose in step 5 to have a search form, the prompt shown in Figure 11-45 will appear next. Choose the combination of fields a search of the discussion should report, and then click Next.

FIGURE 11-45.
Specify the result fields a search of the discussion should display.

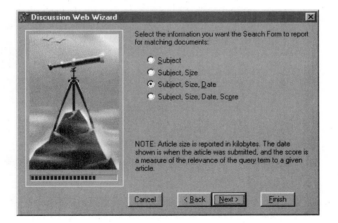

12 The Discussion Web Wizard uses the dialog box shown in Figure 11-46, on the next page, to prompt for a theme. Clicking the Choose Web Theme button displays a standard theme preview dialog box for selecting the theme you want.

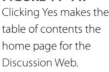

> **NOTE**

You can change the theme used by a Discussion Web anytime from Themes view in FrontPage Explorer.

FIGURE 11-46.
Optionally set the
color scheme for a
Discussion Web using
this dialog box.

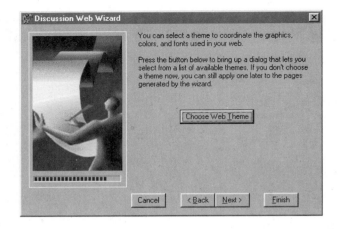

13 Use the dialog box shown in Figure 11-47 to control use of
frames. As you choose different settings in the Frame Options
section, the diagram in the left of the window will change to
show the resulting appearance. You can adjust the relative frame
sizes by dragging their borders with the mouse.

FIGURE 11-47.
Choose a frame
design, or none, for
the Discussion Web.

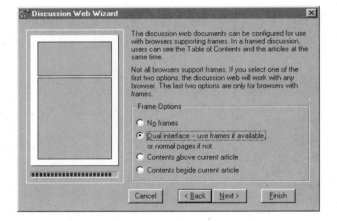

14 Figure 11-48 shows the final dialog box displayed by the Discussion Web Wizard. There are no input fields—just a reminder that
you can use the Back and Next buttons to review and modify any
settings. The wizard saves nothing until you click the Finish button. When satisfied with your entries, click Finish and let the wizard create your Discussion Web.

FIGURE 11-48.
Clicking the Finish button creates the Discussion Web. Use the Next and Back buttons to review your entries before clicking Finish.

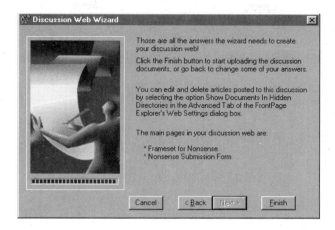

15   If you chose in step 8 to restrict the Web to registered users, FrontPage will create the Self-Registration Form shown in Figure 11-49. This form won't yet be saved.

FIGURE 11-49.
FrontPage creates this registration page if you chose to restrict the Discussion Web.

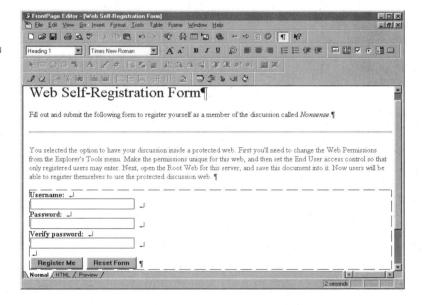

To complete settings for the restricted Web make FrontPage Explorer the active window.

a   Verify that the new Discussion Web is the current Web.

b   Choose Permissions from the Tools menu.

? SEE ALSO

To check configuration of the self-registration page, add additional fields, or enhance data gathering, refer to "Enabling User Self-Registration," page 437.

c Choose Use Unique Permissions For This Web, and then click Apply.

d Click the Users tab, select Only Registered Users Have Browse Access, and then click OK.

e Without closing FrontPage Editor, choose Open FrontPage Web from the File menu in FrontPage Explorer, and then select the Root Web of the server that hosts the new Discussion Web.

f Make FrontPage Editor the active window.

g Save the Web page shown in Figure 11-49, on the previous page, in the root folder of the Root Web.

h To resume work on the new Discussion Web, switch to FrontPage Explorer, choose Open FrontPage Web from the File Menu, and then select the new Discussion Web.

Figure 11-50 shows a newly created Discussion Web named Nonsense. The root folder contains the following folders and files. (The prefix nons_ will vary, depending on naming conventions within your Web.)

FIGURE 11-50.
FrontPage Explorer displays a newly created Discussion Web.

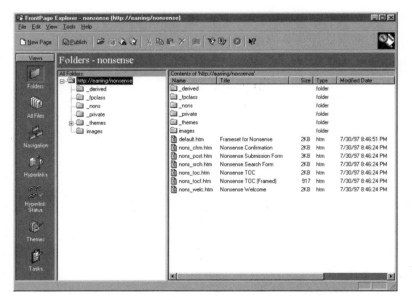

- **_derived** contains files created by FrontPage as a result of other operations. After you've used the Text command to place a label on an image, for example, FrontPage stores the composite image displayed to the user in this folder. Don't modify anything here.

TIP

Folders whose names begin with an underscore are normally hidden. To view documents in hidden folders, choose Web Settings from the Tools menu, choose the Advanced tab, and activate the setting Show Documents In Hidden Directories.

- **_fpclass** contains Microsoft-supplied Java applets that FrontPage uses on certain Web pages.

- **_nons** is the folder that contains all the submitted articles.

- **_private** contains headers and footers included on various pages.

- **_themes** contains the Web's current theme.

- **images** is a folder designated for storing any images used within this Web.

- **default.htm** is the home page for the Web. This is a frameset having the nons_tocf.htm table of contents page and the nons_welc.htm welcome page as frame sources. The name of the home page might vary, based on your Web server's configuration.

- **nons_cfrm.htm** is a confirmation page that provides feedback after a user contributes a message.

- **nons_post.htm** is the form used for posting messages.

- **nons_srch.htm** is the form that initiates a text search for messages.

- **nons_toc.htm** is a table of contents page formatted for freestanding use.

- **nons_tocf.htm** is a table of contents page formatted for use within the home page.

- **nons_welc.htm** is a welcome page formatted for use within the home page.

Figure 11-51 shows the default.htm frameset displaying the nons_tocf.htm table of contents page in the top frame and the nons_welc.htm Welcome page in the lower. Indentations in the table of contents indicate *threading;* that is, responses to an article are indented under it.

FIGURE 11-51.
The default frameset displays the discussion's contents at the top and a welcoming page below.

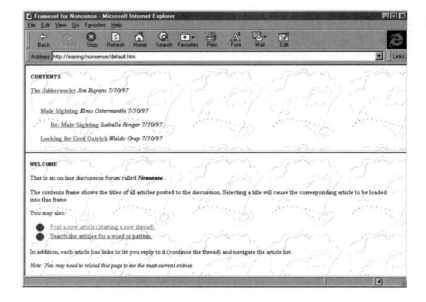

Clicking an article in the table of contents displays it as shown in Figure 11-52. The article frame includes a menu bar for displaying the table of contents, searching the entire discussions for words or phrases, posting a new article, posting a reply to the current article, jumping to the next or previous articles, or jumping to a higher article in the thread hierarchy. The discussion form handler constructs these pages from a combination of submitted data and included templates.

Figure 11-53 shows the discussion group submission form open in FrontPage Editor. This page, like the others, provides more function than style. You'll almost certainly want to update the Category drop-down menu with meaningful choices, include a site logo, add hyperlinks to other pages, and so forth.

FIGURE 11-52.
Displaying an article with frames combines the table of contents with the article text and details.

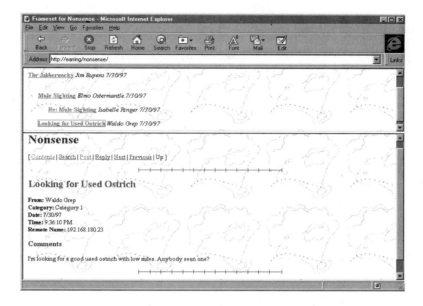

FIGURE 11-53.
FrontPage Editor displays a Discussion Web's submission form.

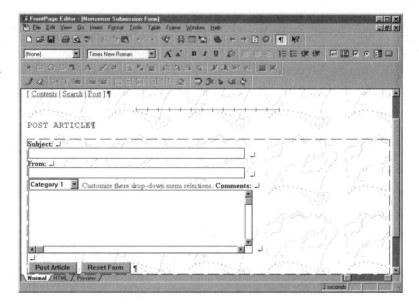

Enhancing Your Discussion Web's Appearance

The Discussion Web Wizard creates pages that—except for themes—are spartan at best. You'll almost certainly want to modify the styles, page layouts, and colors to make your Discussion Web distinctive and attractive. Be careful, though, to make *cosmetic* changes only.

- Take care not to delete or modify hyperlinks, form fields, or form properties involved in making the Discussion Web work. You can change the Category drop-down list to a radio button group, for example, but you must retain the element name Category.

- Don't delete any included sections. FrontPage will only include them again when it constructs future pages. Instead, change the content of the included sections.

- Because FrontPage makes frequent use of FrontPage components when constructing discussion group pages, view this as a help and work within the structure provided. The FrontPage components provide a degree of centralized control impossible with self-contained pages.

Like most pages in a FrontPage Discussion Web, the header and footer sections are included with the Include Page component. To modify these sections, *don't* delete the Include Page component and enter something in its place; instead, modify the included file.

The submission form stores most operational settings for a Discussion Web. Submissions are, after all, a Discussion Web's primary update transactions. So, to view or modify the properties of an existing Discussion Web

1 Open the Discussion Web's article submission page with Front-Page Editor. To find it, look in Explorer's Folders view for a file with the title *Submission Form*.

2 Right-click the HTML form on the submission page and choose Form Properties from the pop-up menu. Alternatively, double-click any push button in the form area, and then click the Form button on the Push Button Properties dialog box.

3 On the Form Properties dialog box, Send To Other should be turned on and the Discussion Form Handler should be specified as the location.

4 Click the Options button to display the properties of the Discussion Form Handler.

The dialog box for the Discussion Form Handler has three tabs. The first of these is the Discussion tab shown in Figure 11-54. Settings controlled by this tab include the following:

■ **Title.** Supply a textual name for the discussion group. It will appear on article pages.

■ **Directory.** Name the folder in the Discussion Web that will contain the article pages. This name must be two to eight characters long and begin with an underscore.

■ **Table Of Contents Layout.** Use this section to control which fields appear in the table of contents.

  • **Form Fields.** Enter the names of one or more form elements, separated by spaces. Together, the content of these fields will become the article's subject in the table of contents.

  • **Time.** Turn this option on if you want the table of contents to include the time the user submitted the article.

FIGURE 11-54.

This is the Discussion Form Handler's Discussion tab.

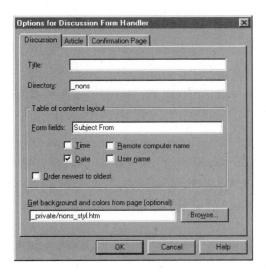

- **Date.** Turn this option on if you want the table of contents to include the date the user submitted the article.

- **Remote Computer Name.** Turn this option on if you want the table of contents to include the name or IP address of the submitting user's computer. Whether you get the computer's name or IP address depends on the configuration of your Web server. If you get the name, it may serve to identify the user's organization. IP addresses are considerably less interesting.

- **User Name.** Turn this option on if you want the table of contents to include the name of the user who submitted each article.

- **Order Newest To Oldest.** Turn on this option to make new postings appear at the beginning of the table of contents. If the option is off, new articles appear at the end.

■ **Get Background And Colors From Page.** Specify the location of a Web page whose background color, background image, and text colors will apply to all pages in the Discussion Web. This setting is optional.

■ **Browse.** Click to select the background and colors page from the current Web.

The Article tab of the Discussion Form Handler dialog box controls the page layout of discussion group articles. This tab, shown in Figure 11-55, has the following properties.

■ **URL Of Header To Include.** Specify the location of a page Front-Page will include as the header of each article, or click the Browse button to select the header page from the current Web.

■ **URL Of Footer To Include.** Specify the location of a page Front-Page will include as the footer of each article, or click the Browse button to select the footer page from the current Web.

■ **Additional Information To Include.** Turn on any of the boxes in this group to include the corresponding information on each article page.

FIGURE 11-55.
The Article tab controls the format of pages the Discussion Form Handler creates.

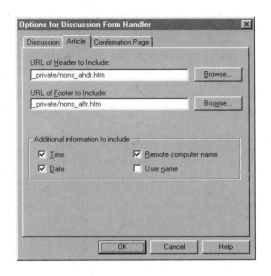

- **Time.** The time the user submitted the article.

- **Date.** The date the user submitted the article.

- **Remote Computer Name.** The name of the submitting user's computer.

- **User Name.** The name of the user who submitted the article.

For advice in creating Confirmation pages, read, "Managing Confirmation Pages, page 458."

Confirmation Page is the final tab of the Discussion Form Handler dialog box. It specifies the location of a page that will provide feedback to users who post articles.

The Search facility is optional. If included, it uses the same Search facilities as any other FrontPage Web—those described in Chapter 6, "Getting Started with Web Pages." Refer to Chapter 6 for information about configuring this component.

FrontPage Discussion Webs can be a useful and convenient tool, but their lack of a purge mechanism for old articles is a serious limitation. Discussion Webs are best suited to topics requiring permanent retention or topics where the entire Discussion Web can be deleted after some period.

IV

Activating Your Site

Managing Confirmation Pages

Several FrontPage components can display a custom Web page to echo input data and report successful completion. FrontPage calls these confirmation pages. The same components also support validation failure pages—pages that report failures caused by invalid input. The components that use confirmation pages are

- Save Results

- Registration

- Discussion

If you don't specify a confirmation or validation page, the component's form handler will generate default pages as required.

Enabling Custom Confirmation Pages

The dialog boxes for the Save Results, Registration, and Discussion components each contain a Confirmation Page tab as shown in Figure 11-56. The tab has these properties.

FIGURE 11-56.
The Confirmation tab controls feedback to users.

- **URL Of Confirmation Page.** Supply the location of a page Front-Page will use as a template in reporting successful processing. If this field is left blank, the form handler generates a default format on the fly. You can click the Browse button to select a confirmation page from the current Web.

■ **URL Of Validation Failure Page.** Specify the location of a page FrontPage will use to inform the user when it rejects input. This option is sometimes unavailable. If it's left blank, the form handler generates a default format on the fly. You can also use the Browse button to select a validation failure page from the current Web.

Using the Confirmation Field Component

The Confirmation Field component provides a way to include submitted input data with the form results. Figure 11-57, for example, shows a Confirmation page created for a FrontPage Discussion Web. The discussion form handler will send this form to the user whenever an article is submitted successfully. The visible text *[Subject]* is actually a FrontPage component that will, on output, be replaced by whatever the user typed in the form element named Subject.

FIGURE 11-57.
Confirmation pages generally contain confirmation field components the form handler replaces with user input values, such as *[Subject]* in this figure.

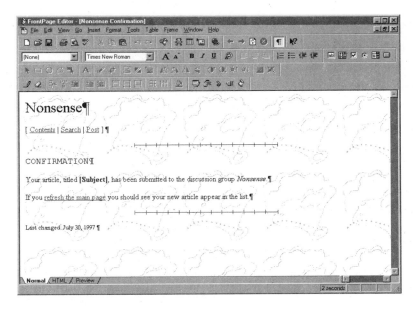

To create a new Confirmation page

1 Use FrontPage Explorer to open the Web where the Confirmation page will reside.

2 Start FrontPage Editor.

3 Choose New from the File menu.

4 Choose Confirmation Form from the Page tab.

5 Click OK.

There's nothing terribly unique about the Confirmation Form template except that it contains some sample text and a few sample Confirmation Field components. If you find creating something from something easier than creating something from nothing, go ahead and use it.

Format the page in any style and with any text or images you want. To add a Confirmation Field component—that is, an object the server will replace with a user-supplied data value—proceed as follows:

1 Set the insertion point where you want the component to appear.

2 Choose FrontPage Component from the Insert menu.

3 Select the Confirmation Field component and then click OK.

4 When the dialog box shown in Figure 11-58 appears, enter the name of the input field and click OK.

FIGURE 11-58.
Enter the name of the form element the Confirmation Field component should display.

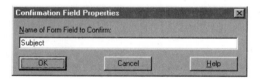

To find the name of a user input field, open the Web page containing the HTML form, and then double-click the form element. The Name field on the element's dialog box contains the name the Confirmation Field component expects.

Normally, the name you enter in the Confirmation Field Properties dialog box should be the name of an element on the form the user submits. However, for the registration component only, the following names are also valid.

- **Registration-Username.** The name of the user attempting to register.

- **Registration-Password.** The password the user requested.

- **Registration-Error.** A text explanation of a run-time error condition.

You can include any text, images, hyperlinks, or other Web page objects you want on a Confirmation page. Confirmation pages are normal Web pages in every way, except that a form handler will replace any Confirmation Field components you insert with user input data.

This chapter has explained how to capture data with HTML forms, and then store it in various ways on the Web server or send it as electronic mail. All these techniques, however, used simple text files. The next chapter explains how FrontPage works with databases.

CHAPTER 12

Accessing Databases with FrontPage

Database applications are among the fastest growing on the Web. As the Web progresses from passive viewing to interaction between user and server, databases are critical and inevitable building blocks. If your applications involve users querying, entering, or updating persistent data, you need Web access to database services.

FrontPage 98 isn't a full-blown client-server development system but—through *Database Regions*—it does provide a simple database query mechanism. A Database Region is simply a FrontPage component that displays information from a database on the Web server. Database Regions can often satisfy simple database inquiry requirements, though for such complex systems as online shopping and order entry you'll need a more advanced tool like Microsoft Visual InterDev.

FrontPage implements Database Regions by adding server-side VBScript code to your Web page. To execute these scripts, your Web server needs a feature called Active Server Pages. It's included with Microsoft Peer Web Server 3 (and above) for Windows NT Workstation and Microsoft Internet Information Server 3 (and above) for Windows NT Server. If you're using Microsoft Personal Web Server for Windows 95, read the sidebar below.

❌ CAUTION

Heavy use of Active Data Objects with Microsoft Personal Web Server may cause Windows 95 to stop. This is caused by a problem in the Windows 95 operating system that shows up when ADO receives multiple simultaneous requests. In short: Confine use of ADO on Windows 95 to light testing; save your work early; and save often.

The VBScript code FrontPage creates uses Active Data Objects—a component that comes standard with Active Server Pages—to query your database. Active Data Objects, in turn, access databases through Open Database Connectivity.

If this sounds like a lot of software and configuration, and hints at a lot of terms and acronyms to come, you're right. This chapter therefore begins with a general discussion of database use on the Web, followed by the specifics you'll need to get started with Database Regions.

Using Active Server Pages with Microsoft Personal Web Server

As delivered on the FrontPage 98 CD or downloaded from Microsoft's Web site, Microsoft Personal Web Server supports neither Active Server Pages nor Active Data Objects (ADO). To add these capabilities, you must download and install the Active Server Pages component from Microsoft's Web site.

1 Start your Web browser and connect to the following location: *http://www.microsoft.com/iis/*

2 Click the Get IIS button, and then click Download IIS 3.0. (Version 4 may be available by the time you read this.)

3 From the Internet Information Server 3.0 Download page, click the link titled Register To Download.

4 Fill out the Registration form, and then click the Submit User Info button.

5 On the page titled Choose The IIS 3.0 Features You Would Like To Download, turn off the check boxes for all components except Active Server Pages. Select the correct language version, and then click Next.

6 On the page titled Choose A Download Location, choose a location near you, and then click Download From This Site.

Using Active Server Pages with Microsoft Personal Web Server   *continued*

7   On the page titled Click On Each Item Below In Turn To Download, click the Active Server Pages link to download asp.exe. If prompted What Would You Like To Do With This File?, choose Save This Program To Disk.

8   On the computer where Microsoft Personal Web Server is installed, run asp.exe to install Active Server Page support.

The information above is based on two Microsoft Knowledge Base Articles.

■   Q164001 ACC97: How to Download Active Server Pages from the Internet

■   Q164479 PRB: Win95 Hangs When Using ADO with Active Server Pages

If you encounter difficulties, search the Microsoft Knowledge Base at *www.microsoft.com/kb* for updates to these articles.

Databases on the Web—An Overview

Despite the widespread use of databases and the long efforts of many smart people, using databases remains somewhat complex. Multiple layers of software are required, each with its own eccentricities and configuration requirements. Web server interfaces add yet another layer of complexity.

This section will explain, as simply as possible, what you need to know about database technology and configuration to create data access pages with FrontPage.

The FrontPage Database Environment

Figure 12-1, on the next page, is a simple block diagram illustrating how Database Regions work. The step-by-step process flow consists of this:

1   An ordinary HTML form, as described in the previous chapter, collects any required or optional input fields from the user. The form's Action property specifies the Web page containing the Database Region. This page will be an ASP (Active Server Page) file residing on the Web server.

FIGURE 12-1.
This diagram illustrates the operation of an Internet Database Connector.

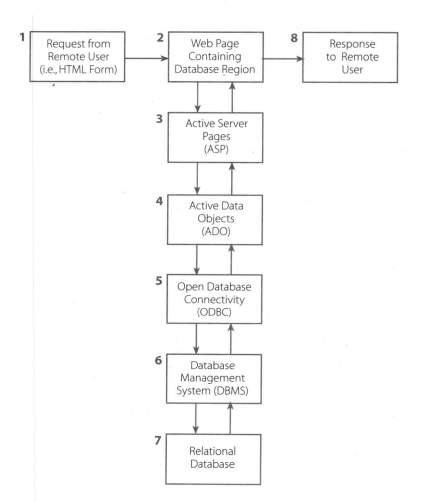

If a Database Region requires no user input, no HTML form is required. Instead, the ASP file that contains the Database Region is simply the target of a hyperlink.

2 As it delivers the requested ASP file, the Web server calls the ASP script processor into play. The script processor executes VBScript code FrontPage has placed in the HTML. This code performs three key functions.

- It merges any variable data into a SQL (pronounced *sequel*, short for Structured Query Language) statement that specifies what data to retrieve.

- It opens a connection to the database and sends the SQL statement.

- When Active Data Objects returns the data, VBScript code in the HTML reads each record and replaces itself with HTML that displays the results.

3 Active Server Pages (ASP) is an interpreter that executes specially marked lines of VBScript, JavaScript, or other languages embedded within HTML. Server-side script code isn't transmitted to the remote user, but the remote user *does* receive any HTML such scripts generate.

> **NOTE**

> If you look at an ASP file on the server, you'll see any server-side script code it contains. If you browse the same file—using an *http://* URL—and choose your browser's View Source command, you'll see either generated HTML or nothing where the script code resided.

4 Active Data Objects (ADO) provide database capability for server-side scripts. They are ActiveX objects without a user interface—they operate in background mode only.

5 Open Database Connectivity (ODBC) is a software component that provides a relatively standard interface for applications despite differences in database systems. It consists of general-purpose modules that make up ODBC itself, plus specific drivers for each database system. An initial set of ODBC drivers comes with the Windows operating system. Upgrades and additions typically come with various kinds of database software.

An ODBC Data Source is a definition, made through the ODBC Control Panel applet, that equates a Data Source Name (DSN) to a database driver, the name of a database, and other settings, depending on the database type.

6 A database management system (DBMS) accepts high-level transaction commands—usually SQL statements—and manipulates the physical files that constitute databases. Microsoft SQL Server and the Jet database engine in Microsoft Access are examples.

7 A relational database consists of data arranged in rows and columns—that is, in tables. Each row is in essence a record, each column a field. All records in the same table contain the same fields (but not, of course, the same values). If two tables have identifying fields in common, the DBMS can match rows having like values and present the results as a joined table. The DBMS can present any desired combination of columns to the user, and can select records based on data values.

8 The response delivered to the user consists of HTML only (including HTML for any browser-side scripts). Except for the ASP filename extension and the variability of output, the remote user won't be aware that a server-side script is involved.

Of the eight components shown in Figure 12-1 (page 466), FrontPage can create and maintain items 1 and 2: the submitted HTML form (if any) and the Web page containing the Database Region. These files must reside on the same Web server that accepts transactions from users, runs the database query, and returns the response. In addition, the page containing the Database Region must reside in an executable folder on that Web server.

Design and configuration of the databases, the database management system, and the ODBC interface all occur completely outside Front-Page. If these resources don't already exist, use standard database development tools such as Microsoft SQL Server or Microsoft Access to

? SEE ALSO
See Chapter 16, "Choosing and Configuring Your Web Server," for information on configuring Web folders as executable.

Executable Web Folders

Programs that run on Web servers present a significant security risk. Allowing users to store and execute programs on the server grants them capability to do *anything* a program can do. This could be useful work, certainly, but it could also interfere with normal server operation or invade the privacy of others. For this reason, most server administrators allow programs to execute solely if they reside in certain folders that only a few trusted individuals can update.

ASP files contain source code rather than executable programs but, because they trigger executable processes, they too must reside in an executable folder. For Database Region development, the executable folder can reside on any enterprise, workgroup, or personal Web server that has access to a test copy or production copy of the database.

develop and implement them. If they do exist, get the necessary file locations and record layouts from their owner or administrator.

Whatever Happened to Internet Database Connectors?

FrontPage 97 supported database access through a facility called Internet Database Connectors, which, like Active Server Pages, is available only on Microsoft Web servers. Using Internet Database Connectors required two special files—one with an IDC extension, to define the SQL statement; and another, with an HTX extension, that defined the output HTML page.

You can still open IDC and HTX files in FrontPage 98 and process them as you did with FrontPage 97. The facilities for creating new files of these types, however, are gone. Microsoft is phasing out the IDC/HTX approach in favor of Active Server Pages and Active Data Objects.

The difference in mind-set between Active Server Pages and Internet Database Connectors is a classic one: Active Server Pages are *procedural,* while Internet Database Connectors are *specification-oriented.*

- The procedural approach requires lines of program code that describe, stepwise, how to produce the desired result. Its statements are imperative (that is, they're commands).

- The specification-oriented approach involves describing what you want rather than how to produce it. Its statements are declarative (that is, they're descriptions).

Specification-oriented approaches may be easier for nonprogrammers to learn and use, but only for relatively simple and well-known problems. The specification approach deals poorly with both complex logic and conditions that require change to the specified output. When the output is too variable, specifying it declaratively becomes very awkward. This was the problem with Internet Database Connectors; they didn't accommodate the variable logic and variable presentation so often required when processing databases. Happily, FrontPage 98 doesn't have that problem to contend with.

Designing Active Pages in a Static Environment

It's worth noting, with the previous section in mind, that WYSIWYG editing of any kind is inherently specification-oriented. When you format content in any of the Microsoft Office applications, you specify what you want and *not* how to program the printer. When you write a SUM formula in Excel, you say what cells you want added and not how to loop through an array or increment an accumulator. Drawing Access forms, reports, and queries is specification-oriented as well.

True to its membership in the Microsoft Office family, FrontPage is also specification-oriented. You tell FrontPage what you want a Web page to look like and FrontPage does the work of writing the HTML. This is, after all, probably why you bought FrontPage.

FrontPage is also a *static* environment. Animated GIF files don't play, nor do video clips. Scripts don't run. ActiveX controls and Java applets don't start. The reason is that FrontPage displays a point in time, not an active environment. Editing a document that constantly changes itself would be an exercise in reflexes—perhaps an exercise in futility. The experience of playing a video game comes to mind.

? SEE ALSO

For more information about writing Active Server page scripts in FrontPage, see "Incorporating Server-Side Scripts," page 527.

Although Active Server Pages and Active Data Objects undoubtedly provide a richer and fuller-function approach than Internet Database Connectors, their procedural nature doesn't mesh as well with FrontPage. If your requirements go beyond simple queries, you'll have to create your own Active Server Page code, enter it, and debug it. FrontPage can insert such scripts with its Script Component, but it can't write them for you.

Locating a Web Database Facility

Running database applications on a Web server is more difficult than delivering simple Web pages, for two reasons: complexity and resource consumption.

- Complexity issues arise because database management systems require much more effort to install, configure, and manage than ordinary Web servers. In addition, DBMSs are usually administered at the system rather than the user level. Not many system administrators are willing to turn over administration of a DBMS to end users; the potential problems and the difficulty in analyzing them are simply too extreme. However, these same administrators frequently lack the time to do database administration for a large base of diverse users.

■ Issues of resource consumption arise because a database transaction can consume far more processor time, memory, and disk activity than delivering any simple Web page.

As a result of these issues, most Web-based database access occurs on intranets and public Web sites having dedicated communication lines and servers. Intranets usually have plentiful bandwidth and server capacity, together with a more homogeneous community of developers and users than, say, a public Internet service provider. Most public Web sites belonging to corporations, government agencies, and other organizations also enjoy adequate bandwidth and dedicated servers.

Holders of standard dial-up ISP accounts usually lack the flexibility to offer database services on their personal home pages because of the complexity and resource consumption issues just explained. For such users to provide their own database services will require either a new category of database management software with highly distributed management or cheap, permanent bandwidth supplied to homes and small offices.

Configuring a Web Database Environment

Table 12-1 lists the Web servers that support Active Server Pages, Active Data Objects, and Open Database Connectivity. You can use any database system that has thread-safe ODBC drivers, though the most common are Microsoft Access and Microsoft SQL Server.

TABLE 12-1.   Web Servers Supporting ASP, ADO, and ODBC

Web Server	Operating System
Microsoft Personal Web Server	Windows 95
Microsoft Peer Web Server	Windows NT Workstation
Microsoft Internet Information Server	Windows NT Server

The issue with thread-safe ODBC drivers is this: The ADO facility pushes database requests into ODBC as fast as they arrive, rather than waiting for one request to be completed before submitting another. Some ODBC drivers can cope with this and some can't; the ones that can't, malfunction or fail completely when two requests arrive too close together. The current drivers for Microsoft Access and SQL Server are thread-safe.

Microsoft's top-of-the-line, industrial-strength server components are Windows NT Server, Internet Information Server, and SQL Server. All three components are designed for high volume use. Extensive multi-threading ensures optimal performance under heavy load. Their system management and administration are also enterprise-strength.

The combination of Windows 95, Microsoft Personal Web Server, and Microsoft Access consists entirely of tools designed for individual desktop use. This is both its greatest strength and greatest weakness. In terms of strength, the Win 95/Microsoft Personal Web Server/Access combination is undoubtedly the easiest for new Web authors to learn and deal with. Its performance and stability as a production environment, however, are moderate at best.

Likewise, few production environments have such casual requirements that Windows 95 and Access can satisfy them. Windows NT Server and Access might be adequate for light database use, but NT Server and SQL Server are clearly optimal in most cases.

The best production and development environments for your project wil lie somewhere between Access on Windows 95 (at the low-end) and SQL Server on NT Server (at the high-end).

Choosing a Web Database Development Environment

Running NT Server, Internet Information Server (IIS), and a full-blown copy of SQL Server are probably overkill for any developer. NT Workstation, Microsoft Peer Web Server, and a developer version of SQL Server provide essentially the same software at a much lower price (albeit with license restrictions that prevent use as a production server).

The degree of separation between your test and development environments depends on their natures. For informal intranet applications with no critical service requirements, the development and production environments may be one and the same. For mission-critical and highly secure applications, elaborate implementation and quality assurance procedures will generally be necessary, and these will involve development and production environments that are quite distinct.

The risk of problems moving from your development environment to production environment is least if you develop on Windows NT Workstation and run on Windows NT Server. Transitioning from Windows 95 and Microsoft Personal Web Server might involve additional problems, because Windows 95 doesn't provide all of Windows NT Server's security features.

Moving from a Microsoft Access development environment over to a SQL Server production environment can also be difficult. These two database systems use different dialects of SQL, and at least some SQL statements will likely need adjustment. Copying database and table definitions from Access to SQL Server is more problematic than copying them between like systems. In short, whatever problems you sought to avoid by developing with Microsoft Access, you're likely to encounter anyway when you transfer the system to production.

If you decide on a development environment using SQL Server, remember that not every developer needs a private copy. In most cases, a single copy of SQL Server running on a local NT server or workstation can easily support an entire workgroup of developers.

Don't overlook the attractive possibility of running FrontPage in Windows 95 while locating your Web and database servers on Windows NT. Remember, FrontPage manages the files in your Web using HTTP and doesn't require local file access.

SQL

Virtually all modern relational databases use SQL as the means for accepting database commands.

? SEE ALSO

For more information about SQL statements, see the examples in this chapter, the documentation that came with your database application, or one of the many books available on SQL.

A typical SQL statement looks like this, with line numbers added to facilitate discussion. All fields named in the SQL statement must exist in the specified table.

```
1   SELECT <field>, <field>...
2     FROM <table>
3     GROUP BY <field>, <field>...
4     HAVING (<field><op><value>) AND/OR (<field><op>↵
          <value>)...
5     ORDER BY <field>, <field>...
```

1 The fields named after the SELECT keyword are the only fields returned. To return all fields in a table, specify an asterisk (*) rather than a field list.

2 The FROM clause specifies the table being queried.

3 The GROUP BY clause consolidates rows with equal values in the named fields.

4 The HAVING clause specifies one or more field comparisons that restrict the records returned.

5 The ORDER BY clause controls the order in which returned records appear.

Unfortunately, FrontPage doesn't provide a point and click means for generating SQL statements or for looking up the properties of a database. One approach is to get a listing of table names and field definitions from the owner or administrator of the database, and then to type the required SQL statement manually. However, another approach is as follows:

1 Open the database with Microsoft Access.

> NOTE

For SQL Server tables, open a new or existing Access database, and then connect to the SQL database (choose Get External Data from the File menu, select Link Tables, and select Files Of Type ODBC Databases). Then, select a Data Source Name created as described later in this chapter.

2 Create a new query, specifying any key values or selection criteria as constants.

3 Make the new query produce the output you want.

4 Have Access show you the SQL it generated.

NOTE

> To see the SQL statement for a Microsoft Access query, choose SQL from the View menu while viewing the query's output or design.

5 Copy the SQL out of Access and paste it into the Database Region Wizard described later in this chapter. Use the right mouse button or the usual keystroke commands for cutting and pasting.

6 Replace any key values or selection criteria with form parameters, as required.

Building Database Pages with FrontPage

Because of the nature of databases, providing access through Front-Page is a multistep process. This discussion assumes you've already designed the database, loaded it with data, and successfully queried it with a tool such as Microsoft Access. What remains is defining an ODBC Data Source for the database and creating a Database Region in FrontPage.

Configuring ODBC Data Sources

To access a database using the Active Server Page facility, you must first define it as an ODBC System Data Source on the same machine that runs the Web server software.

Think of ODBC (Open Database Connectivity) as a collection of definitions and software drivers that isolate applications from differences occurring among database systems. An ODBC Data Source, using a single name, identifies the type, location, and operating parameters of any database supporting ODBC. The procedures and dialog boxes needed to define ODBC Data Sources vary, depending on the operating system, the type of database, and the version of ODBC itself.

There are two kinds of ODBC Data Source Names (DSN): User and System. User Data Source Names are in effect only when a certain user is logged in to the local system. System Data Source Names are in effect for all users and background processes, even when no one's logged in. Active Server Pages require System Data Source Names.

Opening the ODBC Data Source Administrator

32bit ODBC

The process for defining a System Data Source Name is very similar for Windows 95 and Windows NT. To start, open the Control Panel and double-click the 32-bit ODBC icon, as shown on the left.

The dialog box shown in Figure 12-2 will appear. Selecting the System DSN tab displays these options.

- **Add** creates a new System Data Source Name.

- **Remove** deletes an existing System DSN. First select the System DSN you want to delete, and then click the Remove button.

- **Configure** displays (and optionally modifies) an existing System DSN. Select the System DSN you desire, and then click the Configure button. Double-clicking a listed System DSN has the same effect.

FIGURE 12-2.
This is the ODBC Data Source Administration dialog box.

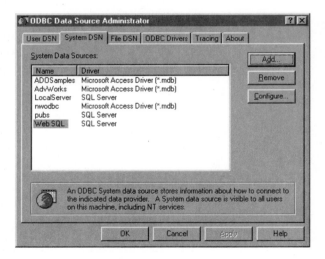

In the procedures described below, you'll click the Add button and then select a driver you wish to configure.

Defining a Data Source Name for SQL Server

To define a System DSN for a SQL Server database, proceed as follows:

1 Click the Add button on the System DSN tab of the ODBC Data Source Administrator dialog box shown in Figure 12-2.

2 The Create New Data Source dialog box shown in Figure 12-3 will appear next. Select the SQL Server entry from the list and then click the Finish button. (Alternatively, double-click the SQL Server entry.)

FIGURE 12-3.
This Windows NT dialog box specifies the driver for a new ODBC System DSN.

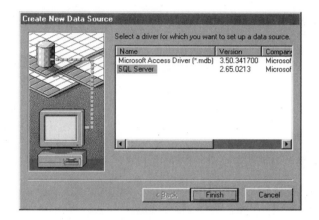

3 The ODBC SQL Server Setup dialog box shown in Figure 12-4, on the following page, will appear next. This is the dialog box where you actually define the SQL Server System DSN. Enter the following options:

- **Data Source Name** supplies the name that Active Server Pages and other processes will specify to access the database. Short, meaningful names are best.

- **Description** provides a brief text description. This entry is optional.

- **Server** identifies the name of the computer where SQL Server runs. Hand-type the computer name or select it from the drop-down list.

FIGURE 12-4.
This dialog box
defines a SQL Server
ODBC System Data
Source Name.

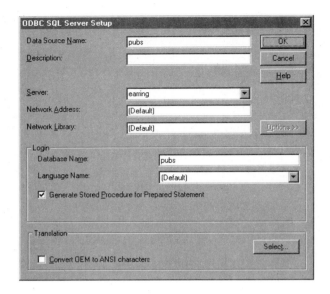

- **Network Address** gives the network location of the named SQL Server. Normally, this can be (Default).

- **Network Library** names the Net-Library DLL the SQL Server driver should use to communicate with the network software. Normally, this can be (Default).

Click the Options button to display the following data fields.

- **Login.** This section specifies information required for connecting to the database.

  Database Name gives the name of the SQL Server database you wish to access.

  Language Name sets SQL Server to use English or another available language. Typically this can be (Default).

  Generate Stored Procedure For Prepared Statement, if turned on, creates stored procedure code for common functions, saves it on the server, and compiles it. If the box is off, a prepared statement is stored and executed at execution time. On is the normal setting.

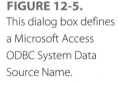

- **Translation.** This section controls translation between different character sets. Translation can also perform tasks like encryption/decryption and compression/decompression.

  Select provides a list of installed translators. However, usually no translation is required.

  Convert OEM To ANSI Characters should be turned off. Turn it on only if the SQL Server client and server use the same non-ANSI character set. When on, this converts extended database characters to ANSI for use by Windows applications.

4 When done, click the OK button.

Defining a Data Source Name for Microsoft Access

If the Data Source names a Microsoft Access database, proceed this way:

1 Click the Add button on the System DSN tab of the ODBC Data Source Administrator dialog box shown in Figure 12-2 (page 476).

2 Select Microsoft Access Driver from the list of ODBC Drivers displayed in the dialog box shown in Figure 12-3 (page 477), and then click the Finish button. (Alternatively, double-click the Microsoft Access Driver entry.)

3 The ODBC Microsoft Access Setup dialog box shown in Figure 12-5 will appear next.

FIGURE 12-5.
This dialog box defines a Microsoft Access ODBC System Data Source Name.

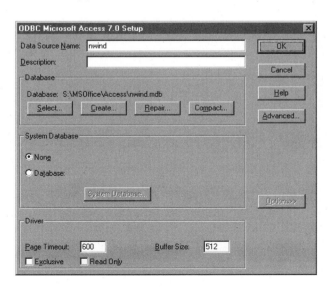

This is the dialog box where you actually define the Microsoft Access System DSN. Enter the following options:

- **Data Source Name** supplies the name that Active Server Pages and other processes will specify to access the database. Short, meaningful names are best.

- **Description** provides a brief text description. This entry is optional.

- **Database** specifies the name of the Access database and provides certain management functions.

  Select browses the local or network file system to locate and select the target Access database. An Access database normally has an MDB filename extension.

 TIP

> If an Access database isn't on the local system, specify a UNC (universal naming convention) name. Don't use mapped drive letters. Drive mappings change as different users log on and off the computer, and when no one's logged on there are no drive mappings in effect at all. UNC names have the form \\<computername>\<sharename>\<path>\<filename>.

  Create creates a new, empty database containing no tables.

  Repair performs consistency checks and attempts to repair structural problems in the database.

  Compact recovers unused space from the database file.

- **System Database** controls use of a system database in conjunction with the normal Access database. The system database stores security and option settings for Access databases.

  None signifies that the Access database isn't controlled through a system database.

  Database signifies that a system database controls the Access database. Click the System Database button to specify the system database's location.

4 Click the Options button to display the following data fields that control operating parameters specific to the Microsoft Access driver.

- **Page Timeout** specifies a time limit for completing ODBC operations. The default value is normally adequate.

- **Buffer Size** specifies the number of bytes available for ODBC buffering. The default value is normally adequate.

- **Exclusive,** if turned on, opens the database for exclusive use.

- **Read Only,** if turned on, opens the database for read-only use.

5 When done, click the OK button.

If the data source is intended for some other type of database, use the procedures above as a general guide. Also, consult the online help or documentation for the applicable ODBC driver.

Completing this process allows any ODBC application, including a Database Region, to open and manipulate the database in a uniform way based on a single identity—the System Data Source Name you assigned. ODBC determines the correct driver type, physical location, and name of the database from the information you supplied.

Be aware that ODBC drivers are updated frequently, and new versions tend to appear whenever you install database-related software. This might result in minor changes in the dialog box options and settings described above.

The number one cause of ODBC driver failure is mismatched versions. If you run into system-related problems, click the About button in the ODBC Data Source Administrator dialog box shown in Figure 12-2, page 476. If all the listed modules aren't the same version, replace them with a set that are the same.

Adding a Database Region

Proceed as follows to add a database query to your Web Page.

1 Define a System Data Source on the computer where your Web server is running. If your development and production Web servers are two different machines, you'll need system Data Source Names defined on both.

Although the System DSN and the Web server must be on the same machine, The System DSN and the database do not. This allows System DSNs on several machines to access the same physical database.

If you lack the necessary security authorizations, your system administrator, Webmaster, or database administrator may need to build the System Data Source Name for you.

2 Use FrontPage Editor to open the page that will display the query.

3 Set the insertion point where you want the query results to appear.

4 Choose Database from the Insert menu, and then select Database Region Wizard. The wizard dialog box shown in Figure 12-6 will appear.

- **ODBC Data Source Name (DSN)** identifies the database that will satisfy the query. The name you enter here should match the System DSN you assigned in the previous section.

- **Username**, if necessary, supplies a username with authority to access the database.

- **Password**, if necessary, supplies the password for the username immediately above.

5 Click the Next button to obtain the dialog box shown in Figure 12-7, which you must complete as follows.

- **Enter The SQL String For The Query** identifies a text box where you can type a SQL statement. Alternatively, you can paste a SQL statement from the Clipboard using the button provided or the keystrokes Ctrl+V or Shift+Ins.

FIGURE 12-6.
Use this dialog box to specify the ODBC data source for a Database Region.

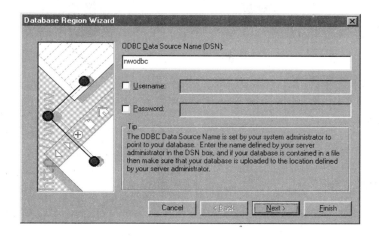

FIGURE 12-7.
Use this dialog box to specify the SQL statement for the query.

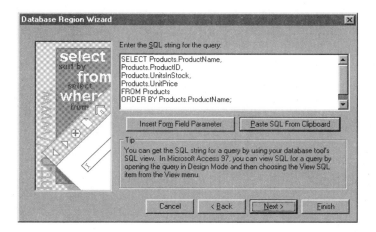

 TIP

The query builder in Microsoft Access provides an excellent way to develop and test SQL statements. Access can display the SQL for any query it builds, thus providing a source for pasting SQL into FrontPage.

SEE ALSO
Refer to "Modifying a Database Region," page 486, for more information about referencing form data within queries.

- **Insert Form Field Parameter** provides assistance referencing data a user entered on an HTML form. Set the insertion point inside the SQL statement where you want the form data to appear, click this button, and enter the name assigned on the form element's property dialog box. FrontPage will insert two percent signs (%%), the field name, and two more percent signs at the insertion point.

IV

Activating Your Site

- **Paste SQL From Clipboard** pastes text into the box titled Enter The SQL String For The Query.

6 The third and last dialog box of the Database Region Wizard appears in Figure 12-8. This dialog box builds a list of fields the Database Region will display.

- **Add Field** attaches a field to the list, positioning it just below the currently selected item. FrontPage displays a simple dialog box prompting you to type the field's name.

  The fields you list here needn't be the same as the SQL statement fields in the previous dialog box. There's no requirement to report all fields retrieved, for example, and SQL permits retrieving all the fields in a table by specifying an asterisk (*) rather than a list of field names. Specifying a nonexistent field, however, will produce an error at run time.

- **Remove Field** deletes the currently selected field from the list.

- **Show The Query In A Table,** if turned on, formats the database records by placing each field in one column of a table. If this box is turned off, FrontPage will display each field in a separate line of ordinary text.

  Unlike all the other fields in Figure 12-6 (page 483), Figure 12-7 (page 483), and Figure 12-8, this setting is available only when you create the Database Region and can't be changed later.

FIGURE 12-8.
This dialog box controls which database fields are available for viewing.

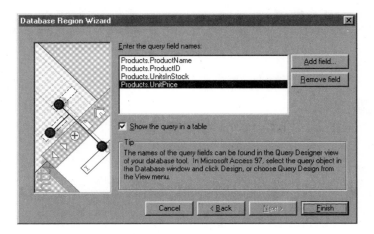

7 Click Finish when you're done.

Figure 12-9 shows Microsoft Access displaying the table structure used in the example above.

FIGURE 12-9.
Microsoft Access displays the structure of this section's example table.

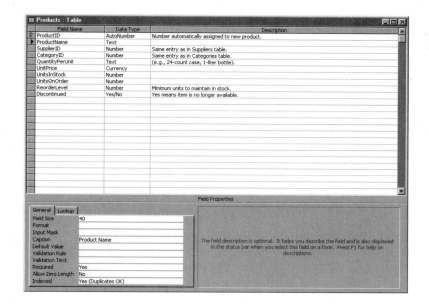

Figure 12-10, on the following page, shows Front Page displaying the Database Region created in Figure 12-6 (page 483), Figure 12-7 (page 483), and Figure 12-8. Some minor editing has removed the normal table borders, added column headings, and set column alignment.

Figure 12-11, on the following page, shows the Web page of Figure 12-10 (also on the next page) in Internet Explorer. Note the filename extension ASP in the Address field. The query has retrieved data and displayed it, repeating the Database Region once per record in the result set.

In database lingo, the outcome of a query is a *result set*—the group of records matching the given criteria.

FIGURE 12-10.
The Database Region in this Web page occupies row 2 of the table.

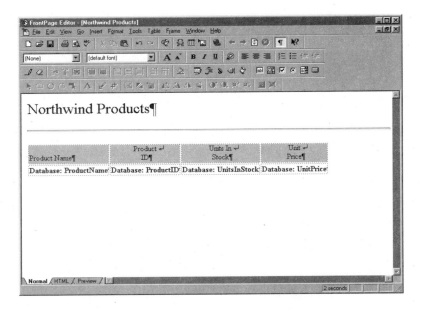

FIGURE 12-11.
Processing a Database Region replicates the database region for each record matching the query.

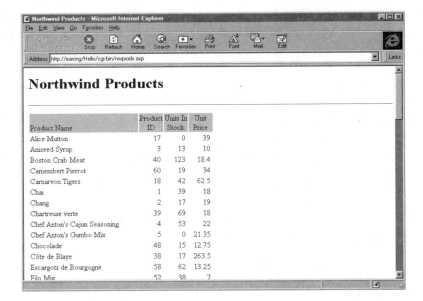

Modifying a Database Region

To change the overall properties of a Database Region, right-click anywhere in it and choose Database Region Properties from the pop-up menu. This will redisplay the wizard dialog boxes described in the previous section. Overtype the entries you want to change, and then click Finish.

 TIP

> The cursor in FrontPage Editor changes to a robot icon whenever it hovers over a FrontPage component. To determine the type of component, right-click it and examine the bottom choice on the pop-up menu.

Use normal FrontPage commands to change the visual properties of a Database Region: Use font commands to change fonts; table commands to change column widths, cell alignment, borders, and backgrounds; and so forth.

Adding header and footer rows to a Database Region table can be tricky. If you add them within the Database Region itself, they'll be repeated once for each record in the result set. If all else fails, switch to HTML view in FrontPage Editor, and then look for two lines of HTML (line numbers were added for discussion) such as the following:

```
1 <table border="0">
2 <!--webbot bot="DatabaseRegionStart" startspan
```

Line 1 marks the beginning of the table, and line 2 marks the beginning of the Database Region. To insert a heading row, insert a line as shown below.

```
1 <table border="0">
2 <tr><td></td></tr>
3 <!--webbot bot="DatabaseRegionStart" startspan
```

This will add a row containing one cell to the top of the table, above and not part of the Database Region. Use the Insert Columns toolbar button or the Insert Cell command on the Table menu to create additional cells. If you have difficulty adding a footer row, locate the `</table>` line that follows the Database Region and insert a line containing `<tr><td></td></tr>` just above it.

To display an additional database field, follow this procedure.

   1 Right-click anywhere in the Database Region and choose Database Region Properties.

2 If necessary, adjust the SQL statement in the dialog box shown in Figure 12-7 (page 483) so that the query returns values for the additional field.

3 Click Next to obtain the dialog box shown in Figure 12-8 (page 484), and then verify that the new field appears in the list titled Enter The Query Field Names. If not, add it.

4 Click Finish.

5 Create any necessary table cells, table columns, or titles, and then set the insertion point where you want the additional field displayed.

6 Choose Database from the Insert menu, and then select Column Value. A dialog box such as the following will appear.

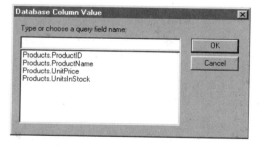

7 Click or retype one of the listed entries, and then click OK. If the field you want doesn't appear, go back to step 3.

To reposition a Column Value, cut, paste, or drag it just as you would any other FrontPage component. Don't move it outside the Database Region, however, or it won't work.

Using Form Data to Control Results

The query shown above displayed all records in the respective table. This is fine for tables of a few dozen records, but clearly it's inappropriate for enterprises whose normal applications contain hundreds, thousands, or even millions of records. Most applications display only portions of an entire table, limited by a key value the remote user specifies. For Database Regions, limiting the range of a query usually requires an HTML form. Figure 12-12 shows an example.

FIGURE 12-12.
This Web page contains both a Database Region to display possible values and an HTML form to request more detail.

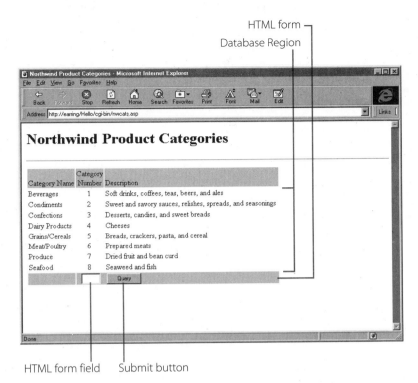

The upper portion of the Product Categories page displays a list of product categories. A Database Region obtains this data from a table named Categories in the Northwind database.

An HTML form occupies the cell spanning columns 2 and 3 in the bottom row of the table. This row lies outside the Database Region. To view products in a particular category, the remote user types the category number in the one-line text box, and then clicks the Query button to submit the request. The form's Action property requests a Web page that queries the Products table and displays any products in the given category.

FrontPage Editor displays the properties of the one-line text box in the dialog box of Figure 12-13, on the next page. The Name property is the most important to remember; you'll need this to build the products-within-category query. It's a good idea to set validation rules here as well. You might specify, for example, that the category value is

FIGURE 12-13.

FIGURE 12-13.
The one-line text box in Figure 12-12 (page 489) has these properties. The name *category* will identify the entered value in a later query against the Products table.

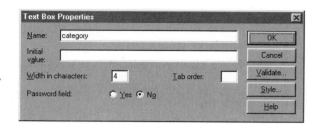

required, must be an integer, and must be greater than zero. Specifying an upper bound of 8 would be a bad idea, because someone could add categories 9 or above to the database anytime.

Figure 12-14 shows the properties of the HTML form that contains the one-line text box. Note the Form Properties entry sending form results to Custom ISAPI, NSAPI, CGI, Or ASP Script; the page containing the Products query will, of course, use ASP scripting and have an ASP filename extension. The Action field in the Options For Custom Form Handler dialog box specifies its URL.

FIGURE 12-14.
The HTML form of Figure 12-12 (page 489) has these properties. Submission invokes the ASP script whose URL appears in the Action property.

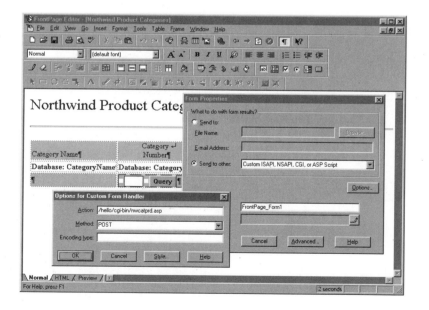

Figure 12-15 shows the page and the query that retrieve all products in the given category. Note the SQL clause repeated below, which limits the query to records whose CategoryID value equals that of the form field named *category*.

```
WHERE (((CategoryID) = %%category%%))
```

Surrounding the word *category* with double percent signs tells the Database Region to retrieve the named value from the form that initiated the request. You can enter the double percent signs and the field name yourself, or you can use the Insert Form Field Parameter button to insert them. Even using the button, though, you still have to type the field name.

? SEE ALSO
For more information about creating server-side scripts, see "Incorporating Server-Side Scripts," page 527.

The small Visual Basic icon just to the right of the page heading contains the following one-line script.

```
= Request.Form("category")
```

This displays the field *category* from the HTML form data that arrived with the request to display the Products In Category page. Displaying the category once is slightly more elegant than displaying it as a field in each row of query results.

FIGURE 12-15.
This is the Web page requested by the Action property of Figure 12-14. The category value entered on that form will replace the **%%category%%** string in the SQL statement.

Indicates the presence of Visual Basic script

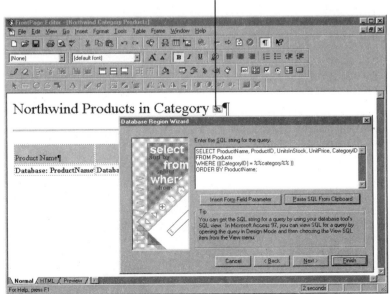

Figure 12-16 shows Internet Explorer displaying the Products in Category page. The remote user entered a *2* in the one-line text box of Figure 12-12 (page 489) and then clicked the Query button.

FIGURE 12-16.
This is the Web page requested by the Action property shown in Figure 12-14 (page 490).

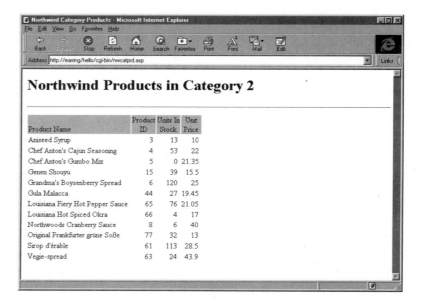

Assessing Database Regions

The Database Region facility makes no claim to being either a powerful or a complete database development environment. Still, Database Regions can develop simple queries in minimal time, and they have the added benefit of requiring little or no programming knowledge.

Even so, the simple pages shown in Figure 12-12 (page 489) and Figure 12-16 beg improvement. It's quite enticing to make each category name listed in Figure 12-12 a hyperlink, or to replace the one-line text box with a drop-down list of valid selections. The page in Figure 12-16 lacks a category lookup that displays the category name rather than the number, as well as hyperlinks to jump the user to more information about each product. You'll have gathered that Database Regions are designed for queries only; you can't use them for data entry or update.

For now, the ASP/ADO combination can easily support features like those described in the preceding paragraph, but developing such functions requires understanding HTML and writing VBScript code by hand. Typing SQL statements manually or copying them from Access is awkward at best; an integrated query builder and test facility would be far preferable. For an integrated query builder, investigate other products such as Microsoft Visual InterDev.

Don't overlook the ability of Microsoft Access to create dynamic Web pages. With its Save As HTML commands, Access can automatically create interactive Active Server Page files from Access datasheets and forms. You can then import these pages into your FrontPage Web to improve their appearance, fine tune their operation, and integrate them with the rest of your Web.

Over time, the database features in FrontPage may improve, products like Visual InterDev may proliferate, or prewritten ActiveX or Java components may provide higher-level functions. These are all areas to watch. In the meantime, despite the progress FrontPage has made toward easing the creation of Web pages, database management remains to a large extent a task for programmers and system managers.

CHAPTER 13

More Ways to Activate Your Site

This chapter describes seven ways to enhance your Web pages beyond the mundane dimensions of height and width and into the active dimension of time. These techniques range from the simple to the complex, but they all involve motion or interactivity.

- **Channels** provide a subscription service for all or part of your Web site. Once remote users subscribe to your site—by simply clicking a hyperlink—their browser will periodically check for updated pages, download them, and allow offline access through the browser's channel frame or screen saver.   .

- **Video** provides a way to play movies and other animations inside the browser window.

- **Page transitions** make Web pages appear or disappear with a series of fades, wipes, and other effects.

- **Animation** applies special effects as text, graphics, and other elements appear on a Web page. For example, you can make the page heading drop in from above and have section headings fly in from the left or right.

- **Scripts** supply simple blocks of program code embedded in Web pages. Scripts run on either the browser or the server.

- **ActiveX controls** are program modules that occupy space in a Web page and provide any function a Windows program can implement. However, their use of windows-specific technology limits their use on other platforms, and many people consider their free access to all system resources a security risk.

- **Java applets** are programmed objects that, like ActiveX controls, can occupy space on a Web page and respond to user input. Java applets can run on any computer that has a Java interpreter but, for security reasons, their capabilities on the local computer are severely limited.

This chapter will concentrate on using FrontPage Editor to enter, manage, and integrate these last three objects, rather than on programming them. Complete treatments of script languages, browser objects, server objects, and programming techniques require full-length books in themselves.

Defining Web Channels

As originally designed, the World Wide Web was demand-based; the browser retrieved each page at the moment the remote user wanted to view it. Over time this model evolved to include caching Web files on the local disk, but retrieval and cache refresh still occur on a demand basis. This is the *pull* model of Web delivery.

> **NOTE**

Caching is a feature of Web browsers that saves copies of all retrieved Web files on disk. If the user requests the same file again, the browser can avoid further downloading by using the disk copy.

Requesting a cached Web page makes the browser check the server for a new version at a set interval. Version checking typically occurs during the first access of a day, during the first access since the browser was started, or on every page request. The browser downloads a new copy of the file only if the version has changed.

Cached Web files remain on disk until they reach a specified age or until the sum of all cached files exceeds a configured limit.

More recently, various interests have promoted *push* models of Web delivery—approaches that deliver content with no user action required. All such approaches involve a subscription process whereby users elect to receive ongoing updates to a Web site. Thereafter, the user's browser receives new pages—and possibly displays them—automatically.

Web sites can't actually push content onto user disks. Instead, the browser periodically opens a connection to each subscribed site, checks for updates, and downloads whatever needs refreshing. Thus, *server push* is really *scheduled pull* performed by the browser.

Because retrieval occurs in the background, before the user asks to view the pages, there are no download times to endure. With pages downloaded in advance, the user can even view them when disconnected from the network. If displayed by a screen saver, pages can be refreshed in the background and displayed in the foreground without user intervention.

Microsoft calls its version of server push *Webcasting* and, continuing the analogy to television, defines *channels* as individual Web sites that support it. Figure 13-1, on the next page, shows Internet Explorer 4 displaying a channel. The content, which appears in the main part of the window, is an ordinary Web page. You can designate any page in your Web as the first page displayed in Channel view—your regular home page, as shown here, or any other.

A *channel definition file* (CDF) stored in your Web provides all the information a browser needs to initialize a subscription. Remote users subscribe by clicking a hyperlink that delivers a CDF. The browser responds to the CDF by setting up the subscription. The CDF specifies the name of the channel, its logo image (an 80×32 pixel GIF), its icon image (a 16×16 pixel GIF), the titles and URLs of published pages, suggested download frequencies, and so forth. The image captioned *Subscribe to this site* in Figure 13-1 hyperlinks to a CDF that builds the subscription shown.

Note that user subscriptions require no processes on the Web server. The server builds no database of subscribed users, for example, nor does it construct a list of computers to thrust content on. The server's only role is delivering the CDF just as it would any other plain text file.

FIGURE 13-1.
This is the Front-Page Script Wizard window.

Explorer bar displays known channels.

Displays and hides channel list

Scrolls list up

Logo image toggles display of pages.

Loads pages as clicked

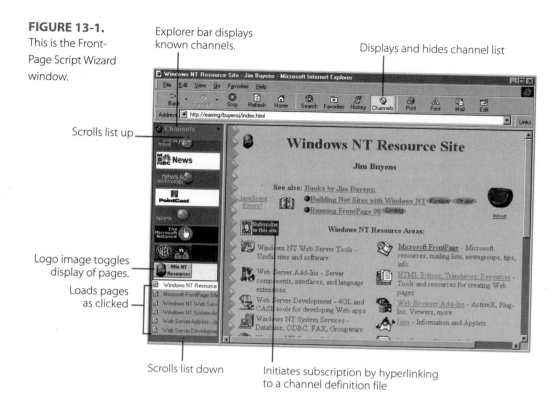

Scrolls list down

Initiates subscription by hyperlinking to a channel definition file

Adding channel capability to a new or existing Web site requires only that you create a CDF and some hyperlinks that point to it. To make creating CDFs easy, FrontPage provides a Wizard. Here are the step-by-step instructions.

1 To prepare for making the CDF

- Identify the Web pages you want included in the channel listing. Unless the channel will include all the files in your Web, it's usually best to put all files for a given channel in a corresponding folder.

- Make sure these pages are titled with the text you want remote users to see when they click the channel's logo image. These are the same page titles you see in FrontPage Explorer's Folders view.

- Select or prepare the channel's logo image. This image should be 80 pixels wide by 32 pixels high.

- Select or prepare the channel's icon image. This image should be 16×16 pixels.

2 Choose Define Channel from the Tools menu in FrontPage Explorer. The dialog box shown in Figure 13-2 will appear. Assume for this procedure that we're creating a new CDF and choose Create A New Channel Definition Format File For The Current FrontPage Web. Click Next.

FIGURE 13-2.
This is the opening dialog box for the Channel Definition Wizard. Create a new file or specify an existing one.

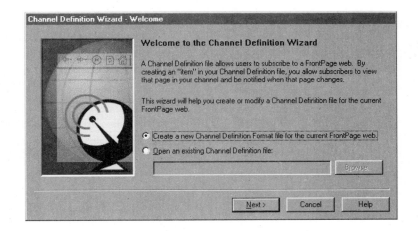

3 Figure 13-3, on the following page, shows the Channel Scheduling dialog box, the first step in building a new CDF. The input fields are described below.

- **Title** is the name of the channel in words, as remote users will see it. When defining a new channel this defaults to the name of the FrontPage Web.

- **Abstract** provides a slightly longer description than the title and is optional. Internet Explorer 4 displays this text when the mouse pointer rests over the channel's logo or title.

- **Introduction Page** identifies the first Web page received by a user who subscribes to the channel. By default, the Introduction Page is your Web's home page.

- **Logo Image** names an image that identifies your channel in the Explorer bar of the remote user's browser. This entry must be the URL of a GIF file 32 pixels high by 80 pixels wide. If you specify nothing, the browser displays a default image.

- **Icon Image** names a smaller image that identifies your channel in the remote user's browser. This entry must the be the URL of a 16×16 pixel GIF file. If you specify nothing, the browser displays a default image.

- **Last Modified** displays the date and time you started the Channel Definition Wizard or last modified the existing CDF.

FIGURE 13-3.
This wizard prompt controls your channel's home page and browser appearance.

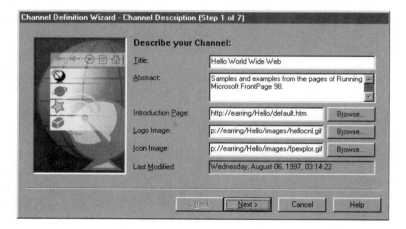

4 The second dialog box for creating a channel appears in Figure 13-4. In the Source Folder text box you can specify the starting folder for pages in the channel. The default is your FrontPage Web's starting folder, but you can specify any other. Turn on the Include Subfolders box if you want to include an entire folder tree. Click Next.

★ TIP

Specifying your Web's starting folder as a channel's starting folder makes sense only if the channel includes your entire Web. If the channel includes just *part* of your Web, you'll find that locating all channel files in a subfolder makes the channel easier to manage.

FIGURE 13-4.

This dialog box requests the folder containing your channel pages.

5 The Edit Page List dialog box shown in Figure 13-5 shows the Web pages residing in your channel's starting folder or tree. Exclude files you don't want to Webcast; those remaining will be periodically checked for updates by browers that have subscribed to your channel, and updated pages will be automatically downloaded.

FIGURE 13-5.

Here you select and exclude any listed files that shouldn't be part of the channel.

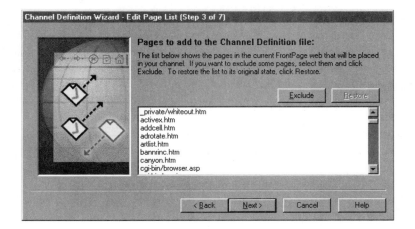

The more files you find yourself excluding, the more work you'll save by segregating channel files in their own folder. Pages within the channel can still hyperlink to pages outside it—that is, to pages elsewhere in your Web or anywhere on the Internet. To minimize the communications overhead of checking for channel updates and downloading them, move seldom-accessed pages outside the channel and let users access them as normal Web pages.

6 Figure 13-6 shows the Channel Item Properties dialog box. To set properties for a particular page, first select it and then specify its Abstract, Page Cache, and Usage options.

FIGURE 13-6.
This window sets properties for each file in the Channel Items list.

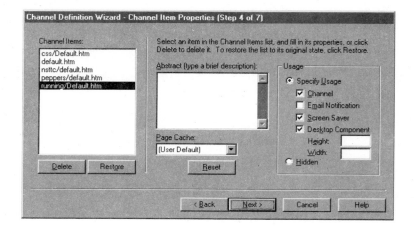

- **Channel Items** lists the pages you've selected for Webcasting.

- **Delete** removes the currently selected item from the list.

- **Restore** reinstates all items you've deleted from the list. This button is enabled only if there are deleted items to restore.

- **Abstract** provides a brief, optional description of the selected page. Internet Explorer 4 displays this text when the mouse hovers over the page icon or title.

- **Page Cache** specifies how the browser should download and cache the selected page.

    User Default caches the page based on browser settings.

    Don't Use Cache prevents the browser from caching the page. Instead, the browser must connect to your Web site every time the user wants to view the page. This precludes offline browsing.

Use Cache allows the browser to cache the page. This option permits offline browsing.

- **Reset** restores the Abstract, Page Cache, and Usage selections for the selected page to their original settings.

- **Specify Usage** controls how the selected page should function in a user's Web browser. Specify one or more of the following choices.

  Channel uses the selected page as an item in your channel. When a user's browser opens your channel, the page will appear in the list of channel items.

  Email Notification sends a message to the subscriber whenever the page is modified. Each browser, on detecting a change, sends mail to its own user.

  Screen Saver adds this page to the list of pages displayed by the channel screen saver on the remote user's computer. Although, as a channel author, you can add pages to the remote user's list, no pages will be displayed unless the remote user chooses to run the channel screen saver itself.

  Desktop Component displays summary or update information about your Web channel directly on a portion of the subscriber's desktop. It's useful for displaying such items as a stock ticker, a list of news stories, or a pop-up broadcast message.

⭐ **TIP**

Some Web browsers, on receiving a single desktop component, ignore the specified usage of all other items in your channel.

- **Hidden** offers an alternative to the usage options by downloading the page for offline browsing rather than displaying it as a channel item, screen saver, or desktop component.

7 The next window, the Channel Scheduling dialog box shown in Figure 13-7, controls the frequency and timing of downloads done in the background. These options are available:

- **From Start Date** specifies when remote users should begin downloading content from the channel. The default is (Now), which initiates downloading the same day a user subscribes to the channel. To make users wait until some future date, enter that date.

- **Until End Date** specifies that remote users should stop connecting to the channel as of the given date. The default is (Forever).

- **Check Every** controls how often remote users connect to the channel and check for updates. Type a number in the left field and choose a unit of measure—Days, Hours, or Minutes—in the right field.

- **Delay Checks Between** randomizes the timing of background connections from remote users. By default, all subscribed browers will connect at midnight as determined by the remote user's computer clock, and this might create an undesirable peak demand on your Web server. To avoid this problem, turn on the check box for this option, and then specify a range and a unit of measure—Days, Hours, or Minutes. Each remote browser will then choose a random start time within that interval.

FIGURE 13-7.
The Channel Scheduling window controls the timing and frequency of background downloads.

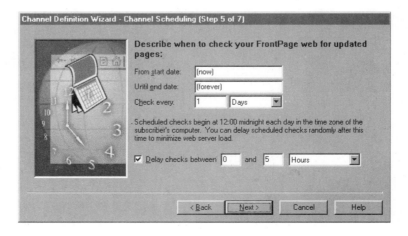

8 The next step in defining a new channel involves the Log Target dialog box shown in Figure 13-8.

FIGURE 13-8.
This dialog box prompts you for a form handler that can receive channel hit counts from a browser. FrontPage provides no such handler, so, unless you've obtained one elsewhere, leave this field blank.

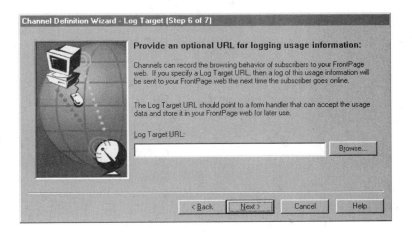

If you have a program that can receive channel activity (hit) counts from browsers, enter its URL in the Log Target URL field. If not, leave the field blank. FrontPage doesn't include such a program, so in all probability you'll leave this field blank. For more information about use of this field, see the sidebar "Counting Channel Hits," page 507.

9 The final dialog box required for defining a channel appears in Figure 13-9. It specifies the CDF's filename and subscription options.

FIGURE 13-9.
The filename and subscription options for your channel are specified here.

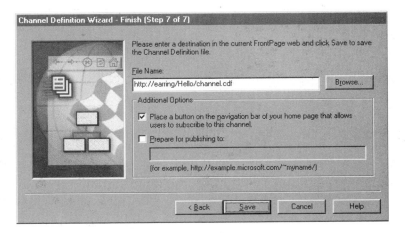

- **File Name** specifies the name and location of the CDF. You can have as many different CDFs as you want, but for maximum compatibility you should keep them all in your Web's top-level folder.

- **Browse** selects a different folder or file in your Web.

- **Place A Button On The Navigation Bar . . .** adds a node labeled Subscribe to FrontPage Explorer's Navigation View. This node will appear on your home page if it uses navigation bars.

   Repeated use of this option will create multiple channel subscription buttons, all captioned Subscribe. To give each button a unique name, edit the corresponding nodes in Navigation view.

- **Prepare For Publishing To** names the Web server that remote users will access to start subscriptions. If, for example, your development and production Web servers are different, enter the production Web server's name.

   Once you've named this server, the CDF will allow users to subscribe only on the specified server.

Unless you're using navigation bars to provide subscription choices, the last step in establishing a channel definition is adding subscription hyperlinks to one or more normal Web pages. These hyperlinks function as usual except that they point to a CDF instead of an HTM file.

To revise an existing CDF, double-click it in FrontPage Explorer. A second method is choosing Define Channel from the Tools menu in FrontPage Explorer, and then clicking Open An Existing Channel Definition File when the window shown in Figure 13-2, page 499, appears. Either method restarts the Channel Definition Wizard with your existing settings preloaded. Modify any settings you wish to change, and then save the file as described previously.

Counting Channel Hits

Hit counts are the most generally accepted measure of Web page activity. The Web server creates a log file record for each page request it receives, and subsequent analysis summarizes the number of times each page was accessed. This provides feedback to the Web designer, the site sponsor, the system administrator, and others.

Channel subscribers might "hit" every page in your site once a day, once an hour, or at any other frequency, but it's clear these hits aren't comparable to counts on conventional Web pages. Automatic downloads simply don't have the same usage significance as page requests that result in immediate display. In addition, the Web server can't possibly count how often pages are displayed offline or as part of screen saver rotations.

To provide something resembling normal hit counts, the channel specification provides a way for browsers to tabulate user access counts, and for browsers to upload these counts when they contact the Web server for channel updates. However, this is an advanced feature that FrontPage doesn't directly support. Contact the vendor of your log analysis program to ask about this feature.

Presenting Video

FrontPage can insert video clips into your Web pages as easily as it inserts still images. Doing so requires no special software in FrontPage or your Web server, though it does require a player on the remote user's browser. The most common video formats on the Web are AVI (Audio Visual Interleaved) from Microsoft and MOV (Active Movie) from Apple. Users can obtain player software from these company's Web sites, or through their browser supplier.

The section "Adding Multimedia Formats," page 284, describes the mechanics of adding video files to pages in your Web.

Animating Page Content

At two different levels, FrontPage can animate the way your Web pages come into view. At the page level, you can have FrontPage animate the way one Web page replaces another. Or, at the level of individual objects, it can animate the way objects appear on the page.

Both these capabilities require the Active HTML features of Internet Explorer 4. For browsers that lack these features, the Web pages simply appear without animation.

Animating Page Transitions

Figure 13-10 shows, in frozen form, an animation effect in progress as one Web page replaces another. Instead of just erasing the screen and painting the new page normally—from top to bottom—the browser displays it in an ever-widening circle. In this way the Black On White page gradually replaces the White On Black page.

FIGURE 13-10.
The page with the white background is gradually replacing the page with the black. You control such effects using the Page Transition command on the Format menu.

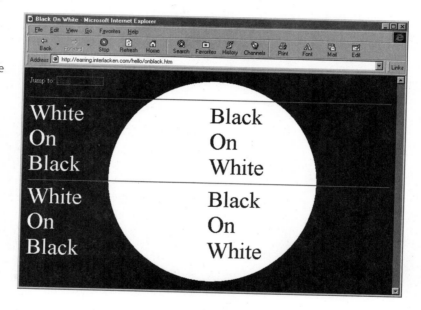

These transitions use special features of Active HTML present in Internet Explorer 4. Browsers that don't support these features display the pages normally, without animation.

To set page transitions, open the dialog box shown in Figure 13-11 by choosing Page Transition from the Format menu.

- **Event** specifies when the page transition will occur.
  - **Page Enter** displays a transition effect as the currently edited page appears on the user's browser.

FIGURE 13-11.
This FrontPage Editor window defines page transitions for Web pages.

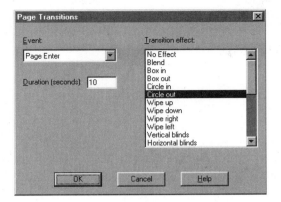

- **Page Exit** displays a transition effect as the currently edited page disappears from the user's browser.

- **Site Enter** displays a transition effect as the currently edited page appears on the user's browser, provided the previous page was from a different Web site.

- **Site Exit** displays a transition effect as the currently edited page disappears from the user's browser, provided the next page is from a different Web site.

- **Duration (Seconds)** specifies how long the transition effect will last.

- **Transition Effect** controls the animation pattern with over 20 effects. You can guess from each transition's name the type of effect it will produce. But the best way to become familiar with these effects is to simply try them on your own system.

Animating Page Objects

In addition to animating the appearance and disappearance of entire Web pages, FrontPage can animate the way individual elements arrive on-screen. Headings, images, and other objects can fly in from various borders, drop in one word at a time, spiral in, zoom in, and so forth. Figure 13-12, on the following page, shows such an animation in progress. The items on the menu bar in the Web page are flying in one word at a time from the upper-right corner of the window. *Backup, Diskettes,* and *Drink* have already arrived and *Holder* is en route.

FIGURE 13-12.

The menu bar on this Web page is flying in word by word from the upper right.

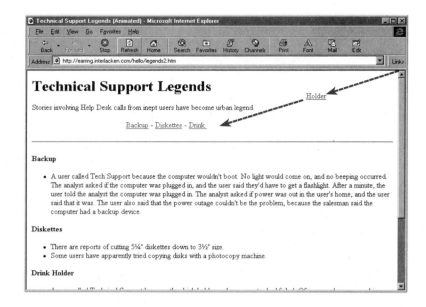

FrontPage creates these effects by adding browser scripts to your Web page. These scripts are written in JavaScript and use the positioning and overlap features provided by Active HTML. Internet Explorer 4 was the first browser to support these features; others may follow. Applying animation effects in FrontPage 98 is quite simple.

1 Set the insertion point anywhere within the object you wish to animate. This will usually be a paragraph.

2 Choose Animation from the Format menu.

3 Select the effect you want.

Among the animation effects are flying text onto the page as a block or by the word from any corner or side of the screen, dropping it in by the word, spiraling it, or zooming it in or out. Once again, seeing these effects is far better than reading about them. Get a compliant browser and try them on your system.

Incorporating Custom Script Code

The use of "under construction" phrases and icons on the World Wide Web has become an almost comical cliché; in reality, everything on the Web changes *constantly* or quickly becomes obsolete. Inevitably, making all these changes becomes tiresome, so savvy page creators, wearing their construction hard hats, search for ways to automate the work. Script languages meet this need.

Script languages can also provide a customized display for each user. Scripts can respond to database results or to a variety of environmental factors, effectively working as self-modifying HTML. They can also provide a measure of interactivity for the remote user without the delay of sending data back to the server and waiting for a response.

In the most general sense, a script is a set of instructions that describes how certain entities are to interact. The script for a stage play, for example, describes in some detail what the actors say, how they should interact, and when they enter and exit the scenes. In a computer sense, scripts are lines of high-level programming code that control the communication interaction, loading, and termination of software components.

Scripts in Web pages are a relatively new but extremely useful addition to the Web. Special HTML tags mark blocks of text as script code, specify the script language used in that block, and control whether the script runs on the server or within the browser. The server looks for server-side script code while transmitting Web pages; correspondingly, the browser watches for browser-side scripts as it receives pages. In either case, the server or browser examines and compiles the code immediately.

Various computer languages have come into use for scripting: awk, sed, Perl, REXX, VBScript, and JavaScript are a few examples. These languages are more general than macro languages tied to a specific program, yet less formal than large-scale development languages such as C and Pascal. Because most scripts are short bits of code connecting other objects and methods, programmers generally view great rigor in a script language as excess baggage. Instead, "quick" and "dirty" are the watchwords.

Code that runs during Web page transmission can insert HTML at the location that triggers the script. This makes any aspect of the page programmable; indeed, you could create a Web page that consisted of a script only. Such a script would need to write all the HTML required to display what you wanted the user to see. More common, however, is

> ### Scripts, Scripts, and CGI Scripts...
>
> Script languages have been used for server-side programming since the earliest days of the Web. A URL specified the name of the script and the server launched it. The script retrieved any user input from the tail of the URL or from form elements, performed any required processing, and wrote a complete HTML stream for transmission to the remote user. This is how CGI (common gateway interface) and ISAPI (Internet Server Application Programming Interface) work. CGI programs in particular are so often written in script languages such as Perl that many programmers and administrators use the term *scripts* for all CGI and ISAPI programs, even if they're written in C, C++, or some other formal programming language.
>
> CGI and ISAPI scripts aren't the subject of this section. The scripts discussed here are HTML scripts—scripts whose source code is stored line-by-line within a Web Page's HTML and executed directly from that location.

to author the static (unchanging) parts of the page in an HTML editor such as FrontPage and to code only the variable portions as scripts.

There are two script languages in common use on Web pages.

- **JavaScript** is the invention of Netscape Communications and first appeared in Netscape Navigator. Originally called LiveScript, this language has little in common with the Java programming language except that both bear a general resemblance to C++.

  JavaScript runs under both Netscape Navigator and Microsoft Internet Explorer, subject to slight implementation differences.

- **VBScript** is the invention of Microsoft and first appeared in Internet Explorer. VBScript is a subset of Microsoft Visual Basic for Applications, which is a subset of the Visual Basic retail product. Curiously, neither Visual Basic for Applications nor VBScript has a visual aspect of its own; instead, both run within the visual interface of the application that invokes them.

  VBScript runs under the Internet Explorer browser and, on the server side, under Microsoft Internet Information Server and Microsoft Peer Web Server. Because of differences in their environments, objects, methods, and events on the server differ from those on the browser.

> **Browser Support for Scripts—or Not**
>
> Support for browser scripts varies widely. Some browsers support no scripting at all, some support only JavaScript, and some support both JavaScript and VBScript. In addition, the level of support varies with the browser version. Even among browsers that *do* support scripting, most provide a way for users to turn it off.
>
> If you decide to use scripting on a Web page, be sure to
>
> - Test the script with all common browsers.
>
> - Note (perhaps at the bottom of the page) the minimum browser version the user should have.
>
> - Provide a way for users to navigate your site even if they lack script support.

Like most computer languages, scripts can define subroutines. When a browser receives code not within the bounds of a subroutine, it compiles and executes the code immediately. Code declared as a subroutine is compiled immediately but stored for later execution. There are three ways to invoke stored script routines.

- A block of immediate code residing elsewhere in the Web page can call the routine.

- Code in one stored routine can call another.

- Stored routines can respond to events such as the window loading, a particular form element gaining or losing the input focus, or the user clicking a push button.

Interesting (or not) as the above introduction may be, this book is about creating Web pages with FrontPage and not about the details and nuances of writing scripts. To gain true proficiency in writing scripts, you should obtain one or more books dedicated to that subject alone. FrontPage does have the capability to create certain kinds of scripts without programming, however, and to store script code within Script components in FrontPage Editor. The remainder of this section will discuss these facilities.

Generating Browser Scripts

The section "Validating Form Input," page 409, has already described one method of generating browser scripts. Establishing validation rules for form elements generates script routines the browser runs when the user clicks the form's Submit button. If the script detects no form element fields having values outside the prescribed range, it submits the form normally. If the script detects an incorrect value, it displays an error message to the user and submits nothing.

FrontPage also provides a Script Wizard that can generate code for many common applications. The Script Wizard is a specification-oriented tool that lets you specify what you want done rather than how to do it—that is, rather than requiring you to write lines of code.

Like most specification-oriented tools, Script Wizard works better for some problems than others. If your requirements are a simple list of "If this happens, do that" statements, the Script Wizard can be an excellent tool. But if your problem involves complex logic, looping, and procedure branching, be prepared to lay code.

To use the Script Wizard

1 Use FrontPage Editor to open or create a Web page containing form elements.

2 Right-click any form element.

3 Choose Script Wizard from the pop-up menu.

When the Script Wizard appears, it will look like Figure 13-13. This window contains three main areas.

■ **1. Select An Event** displays all events to which a script can respond. The top level is an expandable tree containing an entry for each form on the page, plus an entry for the browser window.

 TIP

You'll find it easier to use the Script Wizard if you give not only each HTML form element but also each HTML form on your page a descriptive name. To do so, right-click anywhere on the form and choose Form Properties from the pop-up menu.

IV

Activating Your Site

FIGURE 13-13.

The FrontPage
Script Wizard win-
dow lets you link
events with actions
and objects.

Object or
collection icon

Action
icon

Property
icon

Hollow event icon
indicates no actions
defined for the event.

Solid event icon
indicates event has
defined actions.

List indicates specific
actions to be taken
when event occurs.

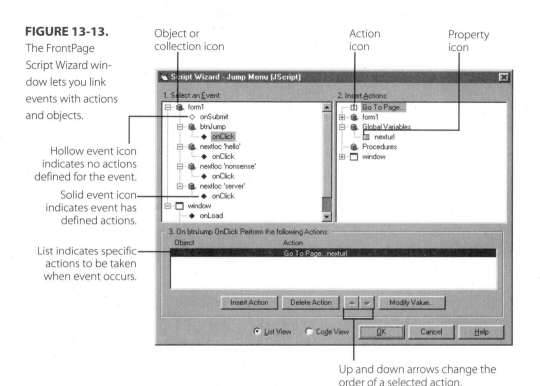

Up and down arrows change the
order of a selected action.

■ **2. Insert Actions** lists all the objects and properties your script
can affect. As before, there's an entry for each form and one for
the window, but in addition there are entries for Go To Page,
Global Variables, and Procedures. You can expand these trees to
view objects and properties beneath them.

FrontPage identifies objects with a cube icon. These icons
appear, for example, in pane 2 alongside the objects form1,
Global Variables, and Procedures in Figure 13-13.

The same view flags actions—also called methods—with an
exclamation icon. The Go To Page item in pane 2 of Figure 13-13
illustrates this.

A document icon flags object properties the script can modify.
The nexturl property under Global Variables in pane 2 of Figure
13-13 provides an example.

■ **3. . . . Perform The Following Actions** lists all actions the script will take when the event highlighted in Select An Event occurs. The actual prompt you see will vary according to the event selected.

The Script Wizard supports an event-oriented programming model, similar to the stimulus-response model psychologists study in lab animals. The Web page is considered at rest until one of many possible events occurs. If a script programmer has provided code for a particular event, the browser will run the code whenever that event occurs. The code can change the properties of various Web page objects or trigger additional events.

You can think of the Script Wizard dialog box as being divided into stimulus and response sections. The list of possible events (stimuli) is in the upper-left pane, the list of possible responses in the upper-right. The bottom pane specifies actual responses to a given event.

A single Script Wizard dialog box lists all events, actions, and variables on a Web page. It makes no difference which form element you right-click to display the Script Wizard; they all produce the same result. Similarly, there's no reason to quit the Script Wizard, right-click a different form element, and invoke the Script Wizard again. The Select An Event pane lists every element on the page, though you might have to click a plus (+) icon or two to find the one you're looking for.

To have the Script Wizard add code that responds to a given event

1 In the Select An Event pane, select the event that will trigger the action.

2 In the Insert Actions pane:

- Select the action you want to invoke or the property you want to modify.

- Either click the Insert Action button or double-click the desired action or property.

3 If you selected a property to modify, FrontPage will prompt for the new value you want the property to have. Enter a value or variable name, and then click OK.

The Script Wizard prompts for property values with two very similar dialog boxes, shown in Figure 13-14 and Figure 13-15.

- The prompt in Figure 13-14 is *Enter a text string*. The Wizard surrounds anything you enter, whether one word or several, with quotation marks and makes it a fixed value. You can't enter the name of a variable.

FIGURE 13-14.
The Script Wizard treats all entries in this dialog box as text strings.

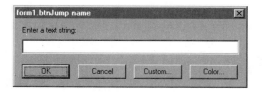

- Figure 13-15 prompts *Enter a single value or variable name*. If you enter a value, you must surround it in quotation marks yourself. If you enter the name of a variable, don't use quotation marks.

FIGURE 13-15.
In this dialog box, you use quotation marks to indicate values but not for variable names.

If FrontPage gives you the prompt of Figure 13-14 but you want to enter a variable name, click the Custom button.

4 After completing steps 2 and 3, you should find the corresponding action listed in the Event Actions pane.

- To view actions for any event, click that event in the Select An Event list.

- To delete an action, select it in the bottom pane, and then click the Delete Action button.

- If you've defined several actions for the same event and wish to change their order, first select an action and then use the up and down buttons (Figure 13-13, page 515) to move it.

IV

Activating Your Site

- To modify the value assigned to a property, select the corresponding action and then click the Modify Value button.

- To see the program code the Wizard generated, click the Code View radio button. To return to the event list, click the List View radio button.

Figure 13-16 shows a simple Web page that uses the Script Wizard. The user selects one of the radio buttons and then clicks the Jump button to display the corresponding location.

FIGURE 13-16.

The FrontPage Script Wizard generated the JavaScript that jumps selectively from this Web page.

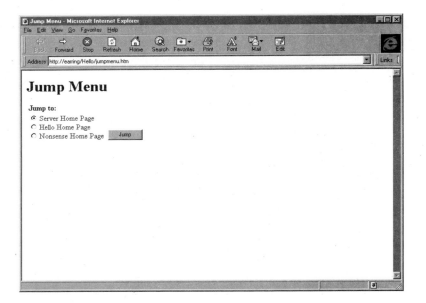

The creator of this page chose to use JavaScript for browser-side scripting because, at the time, support for JavaScript was more prevalent than support for VBScript. JavaScript, however, is a relatively quirky language. Features appear sporadically in various browser releases, and bugs similarly appear and disappear. Code that works in one context might fail in another, no matter how similar the situations may appear. *Testing is critical for both VBScript and JavaScript.*

An odd JavaScript problem arises with radio buttons and drop-down lists: Their values aren't available to browser-side scripts. You can access the value of a text box with the expression

```
text1.value
```

where `text1` is the name of a text box. But you can't access the value of a radio button or drop-down list the same way; the expressions are valid, though the values are always blank.

For this reason, the script in the Web page shown in Figure 13-13 (page 515) can't read the value of the radio buttons directly. Instead the script initializes a variable called nexturl to "/" when the page loads, and then updates nexturl whenever the user clicks a radio button. When the user clicks the Jump button, code tied to the button's click event jumps to the location currently in nexturl.

In Figure 13-17 you can see the definition of the nexturl variable; it's in the Insert Actions pane under Global Variables. To create a global variable, right-click Global Variable in the Insert Actions pane, choose New Global Variable, and give the variable a name.

FIGURE 13-17.
Here the Script Wizard generates code telling the browser to set the value of global variable nexturl to "/" when the web page loads.

Clicking this button jumps to location in nexturl variable.

Clicking these buttons updates value of nexturl.

The nexturl variable is defined here.

When the form loads, nexturl is set to "/".

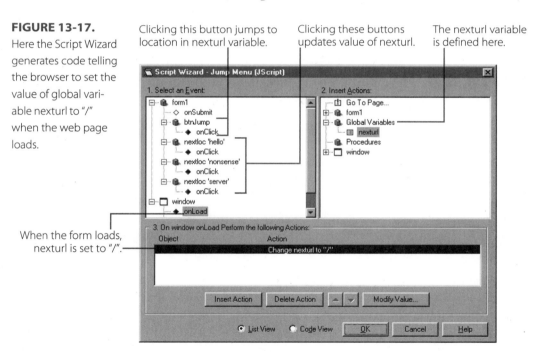

Note in Figure 13-17 that the window object's onLoad event is selected. The bottom pane lists scripted actions that will occur in response to this event—that is, whenever a browser loads the current Web page. In this case the action sets the value of nexturl to "/".

Figure 13-18 shows the Web page of Figure 13-16 open in FrontPage Editor. The two J icons contain JavaScript code to declare the variable nexturl and to initialize its value. We'll discuss these again later.

FIGURE 13-18.
Front Page Editor displays the Web page shown in Figure 13-16 (page 518).

The nexturl variable is defined here.

When the form loads, nexturl is set to "/".

Clicking these buttons updates value of nexturl.

Clicking this button jumps to location in nexturl variable.

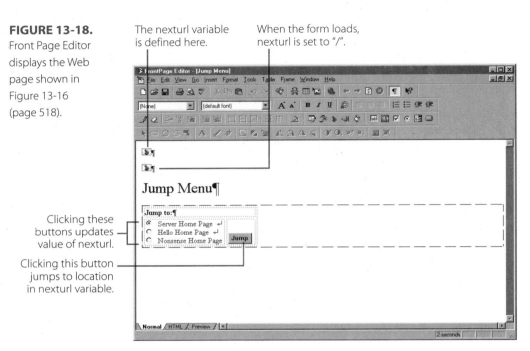

The HTML form in Figure 13-18 has the name form1. The radio buttons all have the name nextloc. You can distinguish one radio button from another by the value assigned on its property sheet: hello, nonsense, or server. The push button's name is btnJump. Notice how concise, intuitive naming of forms and form elements makes use of the Script Wizard more intuitive as well.

As you can see from the solid diamonds in Figure 13-17, each radio button has code associated with its onClick event. The user created this code by

1 Selecting the appropriate onClick event in pane 1

2 Double-clicking the nexturl variable in pane 2

3 Entering a value in the resulting dialog box, which resembles Figure 13-14, page 517.

The value for the server radio button is "/"—the same as the initial value assigned in Figure 13-17. For the hello radio button the value is "/hello/" and for nonsense it's "/nonsense/".

To create event code for the button, the Web page author selected the onClick event under btnJump and then double-clicked Go To Page in the Insert Actions pane. When a dialog box similar to Figure 13-14 (page 517) appeared, the Web page author clicked the Custom button and then entered the variable name nexturl. The Action listed in pane 3 would be

```
Go To Page . nexturl
```

Clicking the Code View radio button at the bottom of the window changes the Perform Actions pane to display the JavaScript or VBScript source code that will handle the event. In Code View mode you can also enter script statements yourself—if-then-else combinations, procedures calls, looping structures, and so forth. It's your responsibility to create these statements accurately; FrontPage won't check them in any way. If you create an incorrect statement, the browser will display an error message when loading or running the Web page, or the page will malfunction.

If you create statements by hand in Code View and then switch back to List View, FrontPage will interpret your statements in English if possible. If your code contains complex statements such as if-then-else combinations and loops, however, FrontPage will display a message in List View suggesting you switch to Code View.

Scripting associated with form elements has no visible appearance in FrontPage Editor—you must invoke the Script Wizard to see it. Other script code *does* appear in FrontPage Editor however, as Script components. In the case of JavaScript, these components are the J icons visible in Figure 13-18. Opening the upper Script component in Figure 13-18 by right-clicking it and selecting Script Properties produces the dialog box shown in Figure 13-19 (page 523). The significant controls in this display are the following:

- **Language** specifies the language being used for the script.
  - **VBScript** indicates that the script consists of VBScript statements.

Run Script On Server indicates that the script should run on the server. Make sure your Web server supports server-side scripts written in VBScript before using this option. Initially, only Microsoft Internet Information Server for Windows NT Server and Microsoft Peer Web Server for Windows NT Workstation supported server-side VBScript.

- **JavaScript** indicates that the script consists of JavaScript statements.

- **Other** indicates that the script is other than VBScript or JavaScript. Specify the name of that language.

■ **Script** displays the script's source code.

■ **Script Wizard** displays the Script Wizard window shown in Figure 13-17 (page 519).

The script in Figure 13-19 is extremely simple, consisting of the single line

```
var nexturl
```

This line of code creates a variable named nexturl. It resulted from using the Script Wizard to create a global variable.

Viewing the properties of the second script component in Figure 13-18 also reveals one line of code, namely

```
nexturl = "/"
```

which sets the value of the nexturl variable to "/". This resulted from using the Script Wizard to initialize the value of nexturl in response to the Windows onLoad event.

Assembling all these pieces, the script works as follows:

1 Defining a global variable created the variable named nexturl.

2 The onLoad form event triggers a line of code that sets the default value for nexturl to "/".

3 The onClick event for each radio button updates the value of nexturl accordingly.

4 The onClick event for the push button jumps to the URL contained in nexturl.

⊗ CAUTION

Before clicking the Script Wizard button, verify that the settings in the Language section are correct. If the Script Wizard saves any changes, it will write them in the language you specified in the Language section even if you originally created the code in another language.

FIGURE 13-19.
The Script dialog box provides a hidden container for script code.

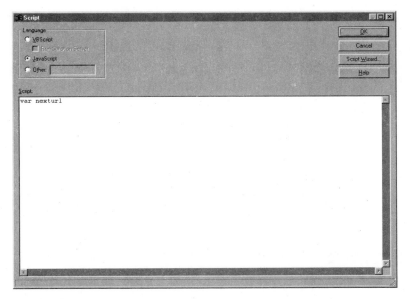

Procedures serve to organize complex routines and avoid redundant code needed in several locations. You can think of them as subroutines, functions, or methods. The next section in this chapter will include an example using a procedure. This is an outline of the steps you'll take:

1   Choose Advanced from the Insert menu, and then select Script. The dialog box of Figure 13-19 will appear.

2   Choose the Script language.

3   Click the Script Wizard button.

4   Turn on the Code View button at the bottom of the window.

5   Right-click the Insert Actions pane and choose New Procedure from the pop-up menu.

6   Change the default name (that is, Procedure1) to a meaningful name and specify any arguments the procedure will receive. *Don't* press enter with the cursor on this line.

7   Use the mouse to move the cursor to the second line of the procedure, and then enter the code for the procedure.

8   Click OK to see the procedure.

To modify the procedure later, repeat steps 1-4, then expand the Procedures object in the Insert Actions pane. Right-click the procedure you want to edit, then choose Edit from the pop-up menu. You can also create, edit, and view procedures after clicking the HTML tab at the bottom of the FrontPage Editor window.

> **NOTE**
>
> The numbered instructions on the previous page create procedures in the header of the Web page. This guarantees the procedure is available before any part of the Web page starts to display. You can also enter procedures after following step 1 to display the dialog box of Figure 13-20, but this will position the procedure in the body of the Web page.

The Script Wizard, like form field validation, can generate useful script code for a variety of applications. Choosing events, properties, and actions from hierarchical lists is certainly easier and more intuitive than locating the necessary documentation, identifying required keywords, and writing code by hand. In addition, the Script Wizard organizes your work around the built-in scheme of browser and Web page objects.

As with any high-level tool, the Script Wizard requires some understanding of underlying concepts. You should have some familiarity with event-driven programming, with the scripting language you decide to use (JavaScript or VBScript), and with the properties and methods of the various browser and form element objects.

Incorporating Browser Scripts

This section and the next will illustrate two scripts that accomplish the same purpose in different ways. The task is to mark items in a list of hyperlinks

- With a New! or Upd! (updated) icon if they're less than 14 days old.

- With a graphic bullet if they're more than 14 days old.

This section implements the function in JavaScript and runs it on the browser. The next section does the same job with VBScript on the server. Figure 13-20 shows the JavaScript version as displayed by a browser, while Figure 13-21 shows it open in FrontPage Editor.

FIGURE 13-20.
JavaScript programming in this page's HTML displays a New! or Upd! (updated) icon for items less than 14 days old, but automatically displays a graphical bullet for items that are older.

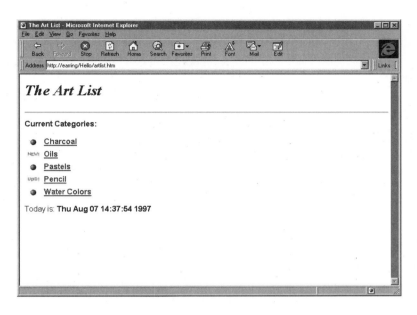

FIGURE 13-21.
Here's the Web page shown in Figure 13-20 as it appears in FrontPage Editor.

JavaScript containing
newicon function

Javascript components containing code that (a) calls the newicon function, (b) passes it a date and an action code argument, and (c) displays the appropriate icon

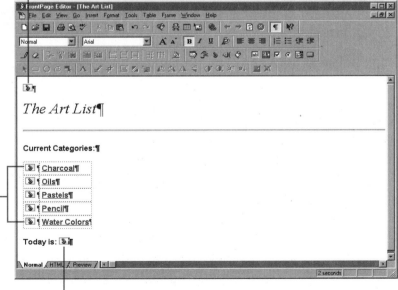

JavaScript containing code
to display current date

The Script component at the top of Figure 13-21 contains the code shown in Figure 13-22. This code was entered in the Script Wizard as a new procedure, though choosing Script from the Insert menu would have been just as easy.

FIGURE 13-22.

This is a JavaScript procedure that displays a graphic bullet, a New! icon, or a Upd! (updated) icon.

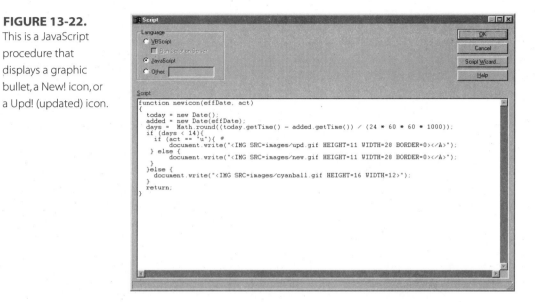

The function is named newicon and accepts two arguments, *effDate* and *act*. The *effDate* argument accepts the effective date of the listed item. The act argument accepts an action code—"a" for added items and "u" for updated ones. The function then creates two date objects and computes their difference. The date object named *today* contains the current date and the one named *added* contains the date received in *effDate*.

JavaScript dates are actually very large integers that count time in milliseconds. Subtracting two dates therefore produces a result in milliseconds. To convert this result to days, the script divides it by 24 * 60 * 60 * 1000 (24 hours times 60 minutes per hour times 60 seconds per minute times 1,000 milliseconds per second). The script saves the result in days to the variable named days.

- If *days* is less than 14 and *act* is "u", the script writes the characters `<IMG SRC=images/upd.gif HEIGHT=11 WIDTH=28 BORDER=0>` into the HTML stream as if they had come from the server. This is the function of the document.write statement. The characters shown constitute an HTML image tag.

- If *days* is less than 14 and *act* isn't "u", the script writes an image tag for the new.gif icon.

- If *days* isn't less than 14, the script writes an image tag for cyanball.gif.

The table cell preceding each menu choice contains another Script component. These scripts are one line each, as in

```
newicon("Aug 1, 1997", "a")
```

This statement runs the *newicon* routine with Aug 1, 1997, as *effDate* and "a" as *act*. The appropriate icon will appear in place of each such JavaScript statement when the browser displays the Web page.

The last Script component on the page displays the current date. It consists of the following two statements, which use concepts already explained in this section.

```
today = new Date();
document.write (today);
```

The advantage of a browser-side script is that it requires no special services or features on the Web server; the server delivers the script statements as part of the HTML with no special handling. The primary disadvantages are the uneven level of support among various browsers and the fact that no server-side resources are available. Also note that in this section's example, the date used to determine the proper icon is the date on the remote user's computer. For some applications, lack of control over that date (or other environmental factors) may be a limiting issue. In addition, users can turn off browser-side scripting and render the routines useless.

Incorporating Server-Side Scripts

This section will illustrate a server-side solution to the same problem posed in the previous example. This solution uses VBScript and the Active Server Pages feature of Internet Information Server 3. The results appear in Figure 13-23, on the following page.

FIGURE 13-23.

This Web page is very similar to that of Figure 13-20 (page 525) but uses server-side scripting. The filename extension is ASP rather than HTM, and it resides in an executable directory.

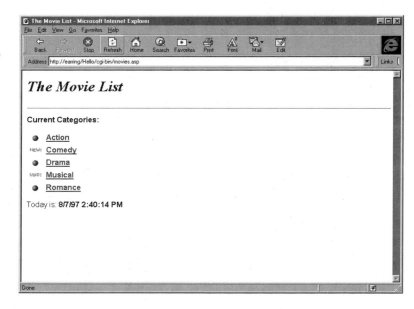

Microsoft uses the term Active Server Pages to denote Web files that contain server-side scripts. Such files must have an ASP filename extension and must reside in an executable directory. When the server gets a request for an ASP Web page, it processes the page, executes the server-side script, and sends only the results to the remote user. The results consist of plain HTML and not the original script statements.

 TIP

> There's no restriction against using server-side and browser-side scripts on the same page. The two script types are identified differently in the HTML, allowing the server-side script processor to pass browser-side script statements to the browser unmodified. Server-side scripts can even generate browser-side scripts by writing the necessary statements to the outbound HTML stream.

Within the HTML, server-side VBScript statements can be marked either with the tags

```
<SCRIPT LANG=VBSCRIPT RUNON=SERVER> statements </SCRIPT>
```

or with percent sign tags

```
<% statements %>
```

Using the latter form, the code to set the first item's graphic is

```
1 <%maxdays = 14%>
2 <%if (now - #8/1/97# < maxdays) then%>
3   <img src="../images/new.gif">
4 <%else%>
5   <img src="../images/cyanball.gif">
6 <%end if%>
```

Four features of VBScript make reading this code somewhat simpler than the Java Script version:

- The *now* function in VBScript returns the current date and time.

- Dates and times in VBScript are stored as whole numbers for days and fractions of a day for time—6:00 AM is 0.25, 12:00 noon is 0.5, 6:00 PM is 0.75, for example. Subtracting two dates immediately provides the difference in days.

- VBScript directly supports date values. Anything enclosed in pound signs (#) is considered a date.

- VBScript supports a document.write command as JavaScript does, but it also supports HTML code interspersed within if-then-else statements.

Given all this, line 1 in the listing above defines a variable that gives the cutoff period in days: 14. Line 2 subtracts the date 8/1/97 from the current date, giving the difference in days, and then compares the difference to the cutoff period. Line 3 is ordinary HTML that the server transmits to the browser only if the *if* condition is true—that is, only if 8/1/97 is within 14 days of the current date.

Line 4 is an *else* statement that negates the *if* statement on line 2. Line 5 is ordinary HTML that the server transmits to the browser only if the *if* condition on line 2 is false. Line 6 terminates the *if* condition.

The code on lines 2 through 6 can be repeated to generate the bullet for each item in the jump list. Since there's less code to repeat than in the JavaScript example, it isn't so tempting to create a procedure. Not creating a procedure also avoids the complexity of passing the item date and the add-or-update indicator as arguments. The date and icon (New! or Upd!) can simply be hard-coded.

Figure 13-24 shows the Web page of Figure 13-23 (page 528) open in FrontPage Editor. The VBScript component after the text Current Categories contains line 1 from the listing above, and each category row begins with three VBScript components containing the *if, else,* and *end if* statements from lines 2, 4, and 6, respectively. Lines 3 and 5 of the listing appear as ordinary HTML, which accounts for the appearance of the graphic bullets.

FIGURE 13-24.
The Web page of Figure 13-23 (page 528) is open in Front-Page Editor, showing the three VBScript components preceding each category item. These contain *if, else,* and *end if* statements so that only one icon appears on display.

Column of VBScript components containing "if" scripts with different date values
Column of identical VBScript components containing only "else" statements
Column of identical VBScript components containing only "endif" statements
VBScript component setting maxdays variable to 14

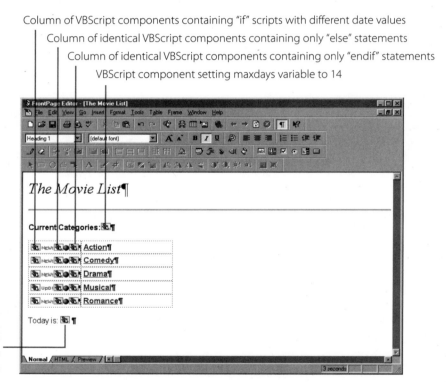

VBScript component consisting of "=now" statement to display current date and time

Figure 13-25 shows the result of double-clicking the left-most VBScript component for the first item. The Language section specifies VBScript as the script's language and indicates Run Script On Server. The <% %> delimiters don't appear for reasons of clarity but the dialog box will insert them when it saves the script. Double-clicking the middle VBScript component would display a similar screen containing only the word *else.* Double-clicking the third component would reveal the words *end if.*

FIGURE 13-25.
Here are the contents of the first VBScript component in row 1, column 1 of the category table in Figure 13-24.

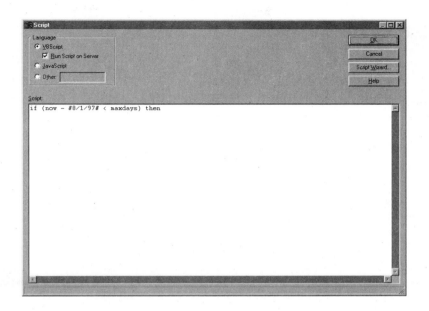

To create each of these components, set the insertion point in Front-Page Editor, choose Advanced from the Insert menu, choose Script, and specify VBScript and Run Script On Server.

To add additional categories, the Web page author would copy a set of three VBScript components and two icons from an existing row, double-click the first icon to set the date, and change the icon filename to new.gif if necessary. To flag a category as updated, the author would change the icon filename to upd.gif if necessary and then double-click the first component to reset the date.

The last Script component on the page displays the current date. Double-clicking this component produces a dialog box much like that of Figure 13-25 but containing this single line of code:

```
= now
```

Within an Active Server Page—a page that contains a server-side script—an equal (=) sign at the beginning of a script line is equivalent to `document.write`. That is, it evaluates the rest of the line and inserts it into the HTML stream. Type conversion is automatic in VBScript, so `<% = now %>` converts the current date and time to text and inserts the text into the outgoing Web page.

There are three primary advantages to server-side scripting.

- Browser compatibility issues are eliminated. There's no worry about whether your script will run on all browsers; you need to verify only that it runs on your server.

- Server-side resources are available. Although these features are not demonstrated here, server-side scripts can read and write files, query and manipulate databases, and make use of other resources on the Web server.

- Control is greater. All users receive information on the same basis—the server's date, for example—and remote users never see script code. Remote users can't turn off the script in their browsers either.

The chief disadvantages of server-side scripting are that your server must support it and your Webmaster must let you use it. Initially, only Microsoft Internet Information Server for Windows NT Server and Microsoft Peer Web Services for Windows NT Workstation supported Active Server Pages. Furthermore, Active Server Pages must reside in an executable directory and, for security reasons, many server administrators tightly control access to such directories.

Incorporating ActiveX Controls

Microsoft's vision of uniting Windows and the World Wide Web naturally involves a merger of Windows programming objects and active Web pages. This section explains how to incorporate such objects, called ActiveX controls, into your Web page.

ActiveX—A Brief Introduction

ActiveX controls are reusable software modules you can place on a Web page to extend the capabilities of HTML. The modules are actually Windows DLLs—dynamic link libraries—but usually have an OCX filename extension. They're closely related to OLE objects, widely used in Windows programming. ActiveX controls were initially available only for Windows platforms but their applicability is growing over time.

ActiveX controls have properties, methods, and events.

- **Properties** are data values accessible by the control and externally. Depending on how a control is written, a given property might be updatable or made read-only to external processes.

- **Methods** are software routines, programmed into the control, that external processes can trigger.

- **Events** are external incidents that trigger code to execute. Event routines run in response to external stimuli such as mouse clicks, keystrokes, and incoming data.

On Web pages, scripts modify ActiveX properties, invoke their methods, and respond to their events. In most cases, therefore, using ActiveX controls requires the ability to create scripts with JavaScript or VBScript. (You don't need to write scripts, however, if your sole objective is to display preset data.)

ActiveX controls run like any other OLE object on your computer. Not only can they manipulate the browser display and interact with scripts; they also can make any changes to the local system that the current local user could make. A Digital Signature scheme ensures that whoever downloads an ActiveX control knows who created it and thus whom to prosecute if the control is mischievous or destructive!

The difficulty of adding an ActiveX control to a Web page depends on two factors:

- Whether the control is installed on your computer

- Whether the control supports local editing of properties

SEE ALSO
For more information about using ActiveX controls, refer to "ActiveX Controls," page 81.

ActiveX controls, like other OLE objects, are normally installed in a computer's Windows folder and cataloged in the system registry. The setup program for any piece of software might install various ActiveX controls. In addition, accessing a Web page containing an ActiveX control can download and install the control automatically (subject to policies and responses set by the remote user).

Inserting a control that's installed on your computer is easier than installing one that's not, because FrontPage can display a list of controls known to the registry and obtain various property values there. If the control isn't installed on your computer, you'll have considerably more typing to do.

Support for local editing of properties means that FrontPage can query the control, display a property sheet, and preview the control's appearance. Not all controls support these functions, however. Some were written before these requirements were completed. Others are simply bare-bones, browser-only controls, minimized in size for maximal download performance.

Inserting ActiveX Controls

There are two ways to begin the process of adding an ActiveX control to a Web page.

- Choose Advanced from FrontPage Editor's Insert menu, and then select ActiveX Control.

- Click the Insert ActiveX icon on FrontPage Editor's Advanced toolbar. Table 13-1 describes that toolbar.

TABLE 13-1. The FrontPage Editor Advanced Toolbar

Icon	Description	Function	Menu Command
	Insert HTML	Inserts HTML code directly	Insert FrontPage Component Insert HTML
	Insert ActiveX	Adds an ActiveX control to the current page	Insert Advanced ActiveX Control
	Insert Java Applet	Adds a Java applet to the current page	Insert Advanced Java Applet
	Insert Plug-In	Adds a plug-in module to the current page	Insert Advanced Plug-In
	Insert Script	Adds JavaScript or VBScript code to the current page	Insert Advanced Script

Both methods open the same dialog box, namely that shown in Figure 13-26, on the following page. Supply values as follows.

- **Pick A Control** specifies the control to insert. For controls installed on your computer, click the drop-down button and select the control from the resulting list. To insert an ActiveX control *not* installed on your machine, type its class ID number directly into this field.

> **NOTE**
>
> A class ID is an identifier such as 99B42120-6EC7-11CF-A6C7-00AA00A47DD2 assigned to an ActiveX control. A formula that ensures uniqueness generates these identifiers when the control is created.

SEE ALSO
For guidance in performing local property editing, refer to "Using Local Property Editing," page 539.

SEE ALSO
For guidance in using the Object Parameters dialog box, see "Using the Object Parameters Dialog Box," page 540.

- **Properties** specifies parameters for the ActiveX control.

    If the control is installed on your computer and supports local property editing, a property sheet listing the control's properties and current values will open.

    If the control isn't installed or doesn't support local property editing, a simple Object Parameters dialog box will appear. This box requires you to know the names and data types of each valid parameter.

- **Name** gives the control a name. Scripts on the same Web page can use this name to reference the control.

- **Layout** specifies the control's page placement and appearance.

    - **Alignment** specifies the control's position relative to surrounding text. Table 8-1, on page 290, describes the possible values.

    - **Border Thickness,** if nonzero, surrounds the control with a border. The specified integer controls the border's thickness in pixels.

    - **Horizontal Spacing** controls the separation, in pixels, between the control and neighboring elements on the same line.

FIGURE 13-26.
This dialog box governs how to specify and display ActiveX controls on a Web page.

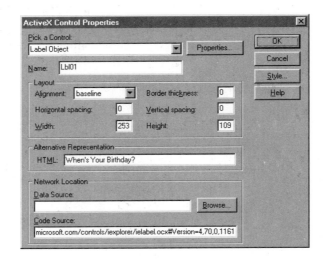

- **Vertical Spacing** controls the separation between the control and any text or images present in lines above or below it.

- **Width** specifies, in pixels, the horizontal space available to the control.

- **Height** specifies, in pixels, the vertical space available to the control.

TIP

You can also resize the area available to an ActiveX control by selecting the control in FrontPage Editor and then dragging its handles.

- **Alternative Representation** specifies what a browser should display if it doesn't support ActiveX controls.

  - **HTML** supplies HTML to display if a browser doesn't support ActiveX controls. This can be plain text, HTML tags, or both.

- **Network Location** optionally specifies a network location for the control and its data. This feature allows capable browsers such as Internet Explorer to fetch and install the control on demand.

  - **Data Source** specifies the URL of a file containing run-time parameters for a control. This file is necessary only for certain controls.

IV

Activating Your Site

- **Browse** searches the current Web, the World Wide Web, or the local file system for the Data Source file.

- **Code Source** provides the URL of the file containing the ActiveX control. If a control isn't installed on a Web visitor's computer, browsers such as Internet Explorer can download and install it using this URL.

> You may wish to specify a Code Source location at a provider's Web site rather than your own, to ensure that Web visitors will get the most current version.

Locating ActiveX Controls

Specifying a Code Source location for an ActiveX control can be a problem if you don't know the control's filename. Here's one procedure for finding the filename on a Windows 95 system that has the control installed. A similar approach should work on Windows NT.

1 Start Registry Editor by clicking the Start button, choosing Run, entering *regedit*, and clicking OK.

2 With My Computer (the top item) highlighted in the left pane, choose Find from the Edit menu.

3 In the field titled Find What, enter the name of the control as it appears in the ActiveX Control Properties drop-down list, and then click OK.

Registry Editor should find the control as shown below.

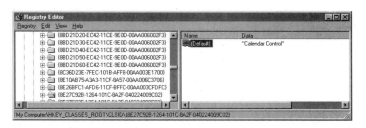

Locating ActiveX Controls *continued*

4 Press Shift+Tab and the object's Class ID will be highlighted in the left pane. Expand this entry by clicking its plus (+) icon, and then select its subentries one by one until you see a filename like the one shown below.

5 In this case, C:\WINDOWS\SYSTEM\MSACAL70.OCX is the control's filename. To provide copies of this control to your Web visitors, import MSACAL70.OCX into your Web, and then specify its URL in the Code Source field shown in Figure 13-26 (page 536).

> **NOTE**

Be sure to observe copyright restrictions when distributing ActiveX controls.

You can revisit the ActiveX Control Properties dialog box in any of four ways.

- Double-click the control in FrontPage Editor.

- Right-click the control, and then choose ActiveX Control Properties from the pop-up menu.

- Select the control and press Alt+Enter.

- Select the control, and then choose ActiveX Control Properties from the Edit menu.

Figure 13-27 shows FrontPage Editor displaying two ActiveX controls, while Figure 13-28 shows Internet Explorer displaying the same page. Neither control executes in the FrontPage environment—objects in FrontPage need to "hold still" for editing. This means ActiveX controls don't respond interactively, as they would in a browser situation. Some controls don't even display in WYSIWYG mode.

IV

Activating Your Site

FIGURE 13-27.
Here FrontPage displays two ActiveX controls on a page—a Label Object and a Calendar Control. Neither object executes in FrontPage.

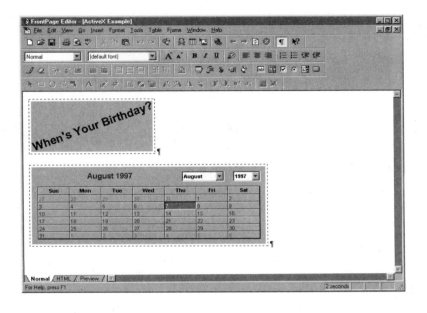

FIGURE 13-28.
The page edited in Figure 13-27 displays correctly in Internet Explorer.

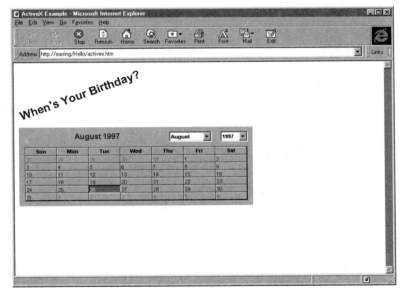

Using Local Property Editing

If an ActiveX control is installed on your computer and supports local property editing, clicking the Properties button in Figure 13-26 (page 536) will display a dialog box like that shown in Figure 13-29, on the following page.

FIGURE 13-29.
This is the local property editing dialog box for the Microsoft ActiveX Calendar Control.

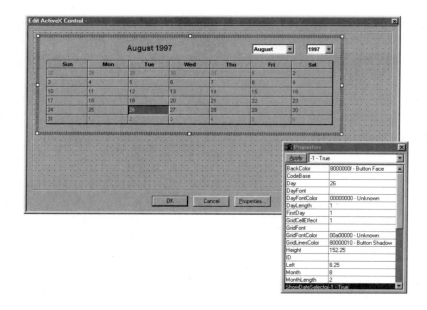

Note that two windows result: a preview window and a Properties window. The preview window shows the results of any parameter changes you make, and might allow direct manipulation such as resizing.

The Properties window automatically lists all available properties for the control and their current values. To change a parameter, select it, modify the existing value in the text box at the top of the dialog box, and then click the Apply button. When finished, click the OK button in the preview window.

Using the Object Parameters Dialog Box

Most ActiveX controls now support local property editing. However, for those that don't (or aren't locally installed), FrontPage displays the Object Parameters dialog box shown in Figure 13-30. Initially, the parameter table will be blank and you'll have to add all required parameters manually, one by one. The procedure for adding a parameter is given below.

1 Obtain a list of the control's required and optional parameters. This information usually comes as documentation from the control's provider.

2 Click the Add button in Figure 13-30. The dialog box shown in Figure 13-31 will appear.

IV

Activating Your Site

FIGURE 13-30.
The Object Parameters dialog box manages parameters of ActiveX controls that don't support local property editing.

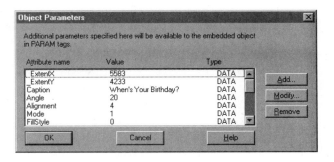

FIGURE 13-31.
The Edit Object Parameters dialog box specifies parameters of ActiveX controls that don't support local editing.

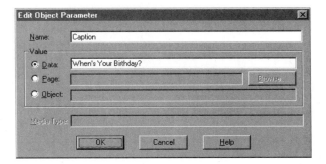

3 Specify parameters using the following fields.

- **Name** identifies the parameter. This name must be spelled exactly as shown in the control's documentation.

- **Data** is one of three ways to specify the chosen parameter's type and value. Select the type setting specified in the control's documentation. Choosing Data indicates that the parameter's value consists of data. Type the data into the associated text box.

- **Page** indicates that the parameter's value is the URL of a file. Enter the URL in the associated text box or use the Browse button to locate the URL.

- **Object** indicates that the parameter's value is the name of another ActiveX control on the same page. Type the name of the control in the associated text box.

- **Media Type** specifies the MIME (Multipurpose Internet Mail Extensions) type of the specified value. Media type can only be specified for the Page parameter type.

4 Click OK to close each dialog box.

To modify an existing parameter

1 Select it from the list shown in Figure 13-30, and then click the Modify button. (Alternatively, double-click the parameter's line in the list.)

2 Change whatever settings require correction.

3 Click OK to close each dialog box.

To remove a parameter setting, select it and click the Remove button.

Incorporating Java Applets

Java is a hugely popular programming language closely resembling C++ but with restrictions that help the innocent avoid hanging themselves. A team at Sun Microsystems invented Java, and Sun remains its guiding authority.

Java programs don't compile to a processor's native instruction set; instead, they compile to the instruction set of an imaginary computer called the *Java virtual machine*. Java programs are portable to any type of computer and any operating system that has a virtual machine emulator. The emulator is a piece of software that carries out Java virtual machine instructions using local native instructions so that the compiled Java program can run.

Java applets are small programs that run as part of a Web page. Applets are considerably less capable than ordinary programs—even ordinary Java programs. Applets can take up space on the screen, play sounds, modify the browser window, interact with scripts, and open various connections to the machine they were downloaded from. Applets can't, however, make changes to the local machine's files or hardware settings. The collective name for these restrictions is *the Java sandbox*. The idea is that an applet, playing within its sandbox, can't do anything at all to your computer, therefore it can't do anything bad. Neither can it do anything desirable, in the opinion of some…but that's another discussion.

About GraphicsButton

The examples in this section use a freeware Java applet called GraphicsButton. It works like a Submit push button but displays an image instead of text on the face of the button. In addition, the edges of the button depress when the user clicks the button.

To obtain GraphicsButton, its documentation, and other information about Java, visit PineappleSoft at *www.pineapplesoft.com/goodies/index.html*

Applets reside on a Web server. Browsers download applets just as they do images or other files used on a Web page, but of course the browser runs the applet rather than displaying it as an image.

Applets, like ActiveX controls, have properties and methods. The ActiveX distinction between methods and events is discarded in Java; both are simply considered methods.

To add a Java applet to one of your Web pages

1 Obtain a copy of the applet and its documentation.

2 Import the applet file, which normally has a filename extension of CLASS, into your Web. You'll probably find it convenient, as many Web developers do, to place all Java applets in a folder called *classes*.

3 Use FrontPage Editor to open the Web page that will contain the applet.

4 Perform *either* of the following actions:

  • Choose Advanced from the Insert menu, and then choose Java Applet.

  • Click the Insert Java Applet icon on FrontPage Editor's Advanced toolbar. Table 13-1, page 534, describes that toolbar.

Using either of these methods will produce the dialog box shown in Figure 13-32, on the next page.

FIGURE 13-32.
You use this dialog box to add a Java applet to a Web page.

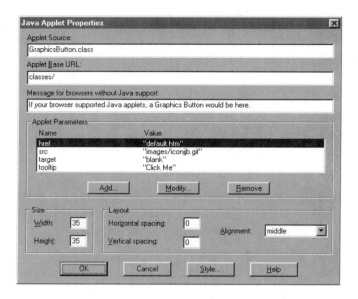

5 Fill out the fields in the dialog box as follows.

- **Applet Source** specifies the name of the Java applet file. Don't specify a complete URL or a path of any kind.

- **Applet Base URL** specifies the URL path to the applet file. Don't include *http://*, the computer name, the port number, or the name of the applet file itself.

- **Message For Browsers Without Java Support** controls what a browser should display if it doesn't support Java applets.

- **Applet Parameters** lists settings used by the applet. Use the Add button in this group box to specify a name and value for each required applet parameter. The next step describes this process in detail. Consult the applet's documentation for a list of mandatory and optional parameter names and data values.

- **Size** allocates screen space for the applet.

  Width specifies, in pixels, the horizontal space available to the applet.

Height specifies, in pixels, the vertical space available to the applet.

- **Layout** controls the applet's positioning.

Horizontal Spacing controls the separation, in pixels, between the applet and neighboring elements on the same line.

Vertical Spacing controls separation between the applet and any text or images present in lines above or below it.

Alignment specifies the control's position relative to surrounding text. Table 8-1, page 290, describes the possible values.

6 Clicking the Add button in the Java Applet Parameters dialog box shown in Figure 13-32 produces the Set Attribute Value dialog box of Figure 13-33. Enter data using the fields below.

- **Name** specifies the name of the parameter, spelled exactly as described in the applet's documentation.

- **Specify Value** indicates whether the parameter takes a value. Turn the box on for a parameter that takes a value, and turn it off for keyword parameters.

- **Value** supplies the parameter's desired value.

FIGURE 13-33.
This dialog box sets parameter values for Java applets.

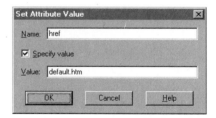

To modify a parameter setting

1 Select its entry in the Applet Parameters table (Figure 13-32) and click the Modify button. (Alternatively, double-click the table line for the desired parameter.)

2 Change whatever settings require correction.

3 Click OK.

To remove a parameter, select it and click the Remove button.

Figure 13-34 shows the GraphicsButton applet open in both FrontPage Editor and Internet Explorer. Like ActiveX controls, Java applets don't execute within FrontPage; this accounts for the difference in their appearance.

FIGURE 13-34.
Because Java applets don't execute in Front-Page, only by browsing them can you display their true appearance.

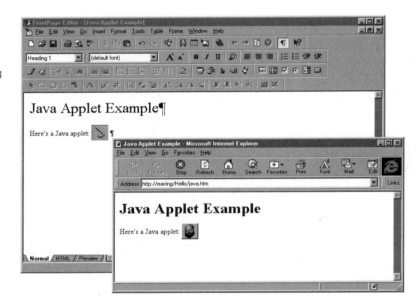

PART V

Maintenance and Utility Functions

Keeping Your Site Up-to-Date

A s time passes, your site will likely grow in size and complexity. Pages will evolve, gaining and losing both hyperlinks and images along the way. As this process continues, the difficulty of maintaining technical and visual continuity will grow as well. FrontPage provides a number of features to assist in ongoing maintenance. These include

- A way to update hyperlinks automatically when you move or rename a page

- A way to find or replace text anywhere in your Web

- Ways to globally check spelling and hyperlink accuracy throughout your Web

- A command for updating all cross-references and indexes for your site

- A means for integrating non-FrontPage editors into FrontPage Explorer, and for ordering FrontPage Explorer to automatically update indexes when such editors save changes

Moving, Renaming, and Reorganizing Pages

As the number of files in your site grows, organizing them into folders and establishing naming conventions will become increasingly important. The need to reorganize or rename pages isn't necessarily a sign of poor planning; more often it's simply a sign that your site has grown. A topic that began as a single Web page may, over time, become a dozen pages and warrant its own folder. And a small collection of image files will likely become difficult to search after growing to a hundred or so images.

? SEE ALSO

For details on the mechanics of moving, copying, and deleting files in FrontPage Explorer, refer to "Viewing and Organizing a FrontPage Web," page 173.

If you have local or file-sharing access to your Web's file area, you can move, copy, rename, or delete files with Windows Explorer, the command prompt, or any number of utility programs. Even if you don't have such access, you can make such changes with an FTP program. Unfortunately, these approaches do nothing to adjust hyperlinks from other pages to the moved or renamed files. Unless you locate and correct these links manually, your Web won't function properly.

Changing filenames and locations in FrontPage Explorer avoids the problem of broken hyperlinks because FrontPage corrects links automatically. FrontPage maintains indexes of all links within a Web, enabling it to find and update the necessary Web pages. To keep these indexes accurate, it's always best to use FrontPage Explorer for organizing Web pages.

Here are several cautions:

- FrontPage only corrects hyperlink and image references within the current Web. When you reorganize pages or images, the maintainers of other Webs will need to correct their references manually.

- If you have reason to suspect FrontPage's indexes are out of date, re-create the indexes before reorganizing files. The procedure is described later in this chapter. FrontPage can't update your Web correctly if its indexes are incorrect.

- Changing a FrontPage Web by any means other than FrontPage is the number one cause of incorrect indexes.

- FrontPage can't reliably identify image tags and hyperlinks coded as values within script code. Thus, FrontPage won't update hyperlinks and image references located within scripts.

- Close any Web Pages open in FrontPage Editor before reorganizing files. FrontPage doesn't update hyperlinks located within open pages.

- If you suspect that your site already has broken hyperlinks or image locations, refer to "Link Checking," page 559.

Finding and Replacing Text

From time to time you'll no doubt find it valuable to search your FrontPage Web for all occurrences of a certain word or phrase. You may need to locate all occurrences of a person's name, a product name, an address, or some other text expression and check those pages for accuracy. The Cross File Find command in FrontPage Explorer provides an excellent facility for such searches.

Cross File Find differs from the FrontPage Search component in that

- Cross File Find operates in the FrontPage Explorer environment. Once you find a matching page, a single mouse click will open it with FrontPage Editor. Cross File Find is always available.

- The FrontPage Search component operates at run time, using a browser, and has no direct links to authoring tools. Also, it must be activated in advance as part of your Web.

Cross File Find differs from file system search utilities as well.

- Cross File Find offers one-click access to FrontPage Editor.

- A file system search will locate word or phrase occurrences in both FrontPage index and cross-reference files, as well as in Web pages.

- A file system search will *miss* phrase occurrences that contain carriage returns, line feeds, tabs, or extra spaces.

? SEE ALSO
For more information about the FrontPage Search component, review "Search Form," page 388.

▶ NOTE

Cross File Find searches only the text portion of HTML pages. It doesn't search hyperlinks or other HTML objects, nor does it search other file extensions such as TXT.

V

Maintenance and
Utility Functions

To run Cross File Find on your Web

1 Open the Web in FrontPage Explorer.

2 To ensure accurate results, save any pages that are open for edit.

3 Choose Find from the Tools menu, press Ctrl+F, or click the Cross File Find icon.

4 The dialog box shown in Figure 14-1 will next appear. Configure the following settings.

- **Find What** specifies the word or phrase you want to find.

NOTE

> Cross File Replace finds and replaces only ordinary text in Web pages. It can't, for example, replace all occurrences of one URL with another.

- **Match Whole Word Only**, if turned on, specifies that Front-Page will match only complete words. The search term *basket*, for example, would not find the word *basketball*. Clearing the box searches for words of any length that contain the search term.

- **Match Case**, if turned on, indicates that matching terms must have exactly the same capitalization. If turned off, capitalization doesn't matter.

- **All Pages** searches all HTML pages in the current Web.

- **Selected Pages** searches only selected pages in the current Web. Highlight the desired pages in Folders view before beginning the search.

FIGURE 14-1.
This dialog box begins a Cross File Find operation in FrontPage Explorer.

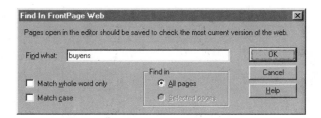

5 Click OK after completing the entries in Figure 14-1. FrontPage will then display the dialog box pictured in Figure 14-2. The button in the upper-right corner will be captioned Stop and the Close button at the lower right will be unavailable. A progress bar will appear across the bottom. Click Stop to pause or abandon the search.

FIGURE 14-2.
This window displays Cross File Find progress and, eventually, search results.

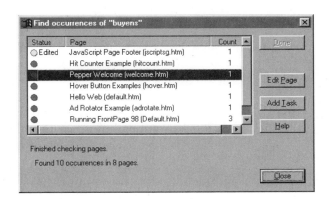

6 When the search finishes, the caption on the Stop button changes to Done and the button becomes unavailable. The Close button, by contrast, becomes available. The list box contains the following column entries for each page containing a match.

- **Status** initially displays a red circle, indicating that no action has yet been taken.

- **Page** displays the title and name of each page that contains the text you specified in the Find What field in step 4.

- **Count** reports the number of matches on each page.

7 To view or edit a found page, select its entry in the list box and then click the Edit Page button. As shown in Figure 14-3, on the next page, FrontPage Explorer will start FrontPage Editor and automatically find the first occurrence of the Find What text.

Opening a found page in FrontPage Editor changes the Status entry from a red circle to a yellow circle and changes the word Status to Edited.

FIGURE 14-3.

Clicking the Edit Page button in Figure 14-2 (page 553) opens the selected page in FrontPage Editor.

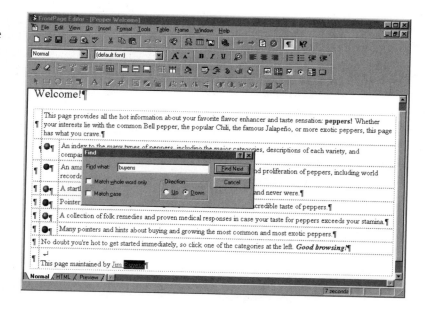

8 To create a Task list entry for a found page, select the page in the Find Occurrences dialog box (Figure 14-2, on the previous page) and then click the Add Task button.

- The Status entry will change from a Red circle to a yellow circle and to the words Added Task.

- To view the task, in FrontPage Explorer choose Tasks from the View menu or click the Tasks icon. The list in Figure 14-4 shows the new task.

As you might expect, the process of running a Cross File Replace greatly resembles that for Cross File Find. There are two major differences, however.

■ When specifying the text to find, you must also specify the text to substitute.

■ When you open a Web page from the Find Occurrences list, FrontPage Editor displays its Find/Replace dialog box instead of its Find dialog box.

Cross File Replace has no unattended Replace All option. First it displays a list of pages, and then you must select and edit each found page. You can click the Replace All button when FrontPage Editor opens a page

FIGURE 14-4.
The Add Task button in Figure 14-2 (page 553) created the task high-lighted (with dotted lines) in Tasks view.

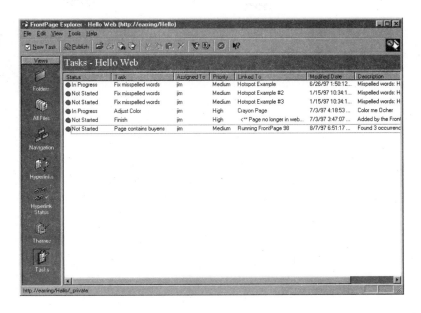

and displays its Edit Replace dialog box, but this replaces all occurrences in the current page and not all occurrences in the current Web.

Here's the full procedure for performing a Cross File Replace.

1 Open the FrontPage Web in FrontPage Explorer.

2 Close any editing sessions.

3 Choose Replace from the Tools menu or press Ctrl+H.

4 When the dialog box shown in Figure 14-5 appears, configure the settings as described in step 4 of the Cross File Find procedure. There is one additional field, namely

   • **Replace With** specifies the word or phrase that should replace the found text.

FIGURE 14-5.
Begin a Cross File Replace operation with this dialog box.

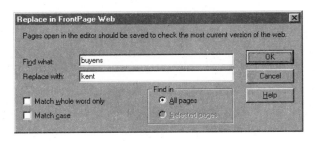

V

Maintenance and Utility Functions

5 After you Click OK, FrontPage will run the Cross File Find process and display, as before, the dialog box shown in Figure 14-2 (page 553).

6 At this point in the Cross File Replace process, no actual replacements will have occurred. To replace text on a listed page, select it, and then click the Edit Page button. As shown in Figure 14-6, FrontPage will start FrontPage Editor, automatically find the first occurrence of the Find What text, and offer to Replace it.

To replace all occurrences on a page, click the Replace All button.

7 If you click Replace All or click either Find Next or Replace past the end of the page, FrontPage will offer to save the current page and open the next page containing found text.

8 You can add found pages to Tasks view using the same procedure as for Cross File Find—that is, by clicking the Add Task button.

Each page you examine will be marked Edited when you return to the list of matches, even if you don't make any changes.

FIGURE 14-6.

To replace text on a given page, use the Edit Page button in Figure 14-2 (page 553). FrontPage Editor will display an Edit Replace dialog box automatically.

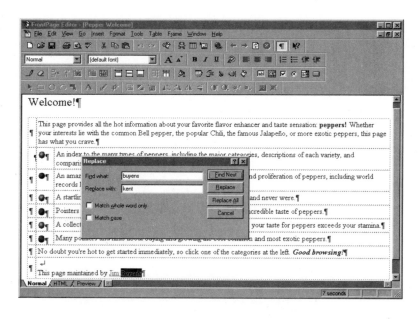

Spell Checking

The procedure to check spelling throughout an entire site or group of pages strongly resembles using Cross File Replace. Instead of replacing one word or phrase with another, however, Cross File Spelling replaces misspelled words with correct ones. Like other Cross File functions, Spelling first builds a list of pages containing misspelled words, and then provides choices for editing pages or adding them to Tasks view. If you choose to edit a listed page, FrontPage Editor steps through the misspelled words.

To spell check an entire Web or group of files

1   Close any pages that are open for editing.

2   To check only part of a Web, select the desired pages from Folders view in FrontPage Explorer.

3   Choose Spelling from the Tools menu, press the F7 key, or click the Cross File Spelling icon.

4   The dialog box shown in Figure 14-7 will next appear. Configure the following settings.

   • **Check Spelling Of** specifies the range of pages to check.

     All Pages checks all pages in the current Web for correct spelling.

     Selected Pages checks only pages you highlighted in step 2.

   • **Add A Task For Each Page With Misspellings** indicates that you want to bypass the list of pages containing misspelled words and instead add each page to Tasks view.

V

Maintenance and Utility Functions

FIGURE 14-7.
This dialog box initiates Cross File Spelling.

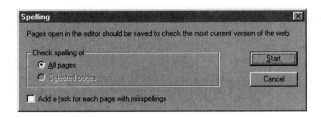

5 After you click Start, FrontPage will check the specified pages for spelling.

- If you chose Add A Task For Each Page With Misspellings, FrontPage will display a simple progress bar during the spell check, and then will exit. This was the origin of the tasks titled Fix Misspelled Words in Figure 14-4 (page 555).

- If you didn't choose Add A Task For Each Page With Misspellings, FrontPage will display a dialog box similar to Figure 14-2 (page 553) listing any pages with misspelled words. You can edit these pages in FrontPage Editor or add them individually to Tasks view. Figure 14-8 shows FrontPage Editor opening a page with the first misspelled word ready for correction.

You can also invoke the dialog box of Figure 14-8 yourself to check an individual page you've opened in FrontPage Editor. Choose Spelling from the Tools menu, and then use the elements in this window as follows.

- **Not In Dictionary** displays the word identified as misspelled.

- **Change To** supplies a corrected word. You can accept the word FrontPage suggests, type a word on the keyboard, or pick a word from the drop-down list of suggestions.

FIGURE 14-8.
FrontPage Editor uses this dialog box to correct spelling of questionable words.

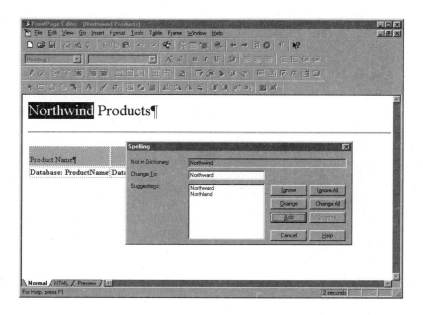

- **Suggestions** provides a list of possible corrections to the misspelling.

- **Ignore** bypasses the current word.

- **Ignore All** ignores the current word if it appears again in the same Web page.

- **Change** replaces the misspelled word with the contents of the Change To field.

- **Change All** replaces the current misspelled word with the contents of the Change To field everywhere on the current Web page.

- **Add** places the current word in the custom dictionary. Future spelling checks will no longer report this word as an error.

 NOTE

FrontPage uses the custom dictionary at c:\windows\msapps\proof\custom.dic (where c:\windows is the folder in which Windows was installed). Because this file is on the FrontPage user's local machine, dictionary additions made by one user won't be available to other users of the same Web.

V

Maintenance and
Utility Functions

Link Checking

A widely accepted principle of physics is that, left to itself, order inevitably reverts to chaos. Hyperlinks provide a perfect example of such entropy at work. While FrontPage can greatly reduce instances of broken hyperlinks within your Web, still, typing errors and changes at remote sites inevitably break even the most carefully created hyperlinks. FrontPage provides the Hyperlink Status view to detect and correct such errors.

All Web authors should check hyperlinks occasionally, because there's no reliable means to catch changes as they occur throughout the entire World Wide Web. The frequency of checking will vary, depending on the number of links, their volatility, and the level of service you wish to provide.

For more information about Hyperlink Status view, refer to "Working with Hyperlink Status View," page 187.

Reindexing Your Site

FrontPage maintains a number of databases and index files that cross-reference hyperlinks and other elements in your Web pages. If these files and your Web pages get out of sync, FrontPage may produce incorrect search results, incorrectly size images, or incompletely update hyperlinks.

CAUTION

It's best to close any open files in your Web before recalculating hyperlinks.

Fortunately, both FrontPage Explorer and FrontPage Editor always update the necessary indexes whenever they make changes to a Web, but other programs and utilities don't. You should reindex your site every time you make changes with external tools, anytime you suspect indexes of being corrupted, or in general anytime your Web seems to be acting strangely.

To reindex a Web, open it in FrontPage Explorer and choose Recalculate Hyperlinks from the Tools menu. This accomplishes three things.

- It updates the display for all current views of the FrontPage Web.

- It instructs the server to regenerate all dependencies. If, for example, you use an external editor to modify an included page, any pages that include it will continue to display the old version. Recalculating hyperlinks refreshes the affected Include Page components.

- It rebuilds the text index used by the FrontPage Search feature. This can get out of date if you externally add, change, or delete files in your Web.

Recalculating hyperlinks can take several minutes for a large FrontPage Web. FrontPage warns you of this before starting the recalculation. Once recalculation starts, FrontPage Explorer will flash its logo at the right of the toolbar area until recalculation finishes, and only then can you do further work in FrontPage.

Invoking Other Editors from FrontPage

You can configure FrontPage Explorer to invoke the editor of your choice for any given file type. Doing so minimizes the need to recalculate hyperlinks and, at the same time, builds a more integrated environment. The procedure is as follows:

1 Start FrontPage Explorer.

2 Choose Options from the Tools menu.

3 Choose the Configure Editors tab to display the dialog box shown in Figure 14-9. The list box shows each currently defined file type and its associated editor.

- **Add** displays a dialog box for adding a file type and its associated editor.

- **Modify** displays a similar dialog box that alters the editor associated with the currently selected file type.

- **Remove** deletes the editor association for the currently selected file type.

FIGURE 14-9.
FrontPage Explorer can associate a different editor with each filename extension.

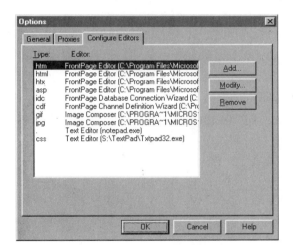

4 Figure 14-10, on the next page, shows the dialog box for modifying an editor association. Use the controls in this window as follows:

- **File Type** specifies the filename extension associated with the editor. There can only be one editor associated with a given file type. You can't, for example, define two GIF entries to give yourself a choice of image editors. However, see the sidebar "A Bug in the Alphabet Soup?" page 563.

- **Editor Name** gives the editor's name in words.

- **Command** specifies the name and, if required, the path to the editor's application file, which would normally be an EXE file.

- **Browse** locates the editor's application file.

FIGURE 14-10.
This dialog box associates an editor with a file type.

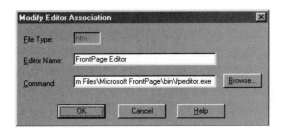

When you double-click a file in FrontPage Explorer or use the Edit button in a dialog box, FrontPage honors the normal file association. To choose a secondary editor (one defined on a wildcard entry), right-click the file in FrontPage Explorer and choose Open With from the pop-up menu. FrontPage will present the dialog box shown in Figure 14-11, so you can open the file with the editor of your choice.

FIGURE 14-11.
Right-clicking a file in FrontPage Explorer and choosing Open With produces a list of program choices such as this.

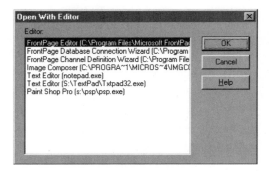

When FrontPage opens a file with any editor other than FrontPage Editor, it follows this six-step process.

1 Copies the file to a temporary area

2 Notes the temporary file's size and date stamp

3 Launches the editor, passing it the name and location of the temporary copy

4 Watches for the editor to terminate

5 Compares the size and date stamp of the temporary file to that of step 2

6 If the comparison in step 5 is unequal, imports the updated file from the temporary area to the FrontPage Web

There are two reasons for this process. First, it's unlikely that the external editor can read and save files via HTTP as FrontPage does. Second, importing the updated temporary file triggers a limited hyperlink recalculation and keeps all FrontPage indexes, cross-references, and FrontPage components up to date.

Be aware, however, that until FrontPage imports the modified page, no changes will be visible in FrontPage or in your browser. The File Save command in the external editor only updates the temporary copy; FrontPage doesn't import the copy until the editor terminates.

A Bug in the Alphabet Soup?

FrontPage exhibits a curious behavior when displaying the Open With Editor dialog box shown in Figure 14-11. Any editor associated with a wildcard file extension, such as *gi?*, is always listed, regardless of the currently selected file type. This may be a bug but, even so, it's a convenient one; it means you can add as many editors as you like regardless of file type, by specifying extensions containing an asterisk or question mark wildcard character: *gi*, g?f, ht*, do?, tx?*, and so forth.

The only downside to making very many wildcard entries is that you'll have a long and confusing list to sort through every time you use the Open With command.

Testing Your Web

Utilities such as Hyperlink Status view and Cross File Spelling provide excellent ways to check the content of your site, and using FrontPage Editor produces error-free HTML. Nevertheless, there's no substitute for browsing your own Web and testing its functions online.

Two fundamental things to check are the correct operation of all hyperlinks and reasonable page transmission times under typical conditions. However, you should also do a test drive to confirm proper appearance and operation under the following conditions.

- **Different Browsers.** Test your pages with at least the current production versions of Internet Explorer, Netscape Navigator, and any other browser used by your audience, plus perhaps the previous production version and current pre-release version of each.

- **Different Browser Settings.** Remember that users can turn some browser features on and off, such as the ability to run scripts, run Java applets, and load ActiveX controls. If you use these facilities, make sure your pages degrade gracefully, rather than crash and burn, if users turn them off.

- **Different Color Depths.** View your pages in 256 color mode as well as 24-bit true color. Depending on your user base, you might also wish to test at 16 colors and in 64K high-color mode.

- **Different Screen Sizes.** Make sure your pages are viewable on systems with 640×480 pixel displays.

- **Different Servers.** Don't assume that everything on multiple servers will work the same way (presuming your environment uses more than one, such as a Microsoft Personal Web Server for authoring and an ISP's Unix server for production). The more different the servers, the more that can go wrong. Test and debug each server environment thoroughly.

Scripts are probably the most sensitive components in your Web. JavaScript, in particular, hasn't benefited from a formal language specification, nor does it have a comprehensive test suite. Bugs and features seem to come and go with each browser version, so testing is an absolute necessity. Remember that browser-side VBScript isn't supported by Netscape browsers.

Test after each change to your Web—each set of page changes, each Copy Web, each server upgrade, each new version of FrontPage, each new browser version that appears. Even if nothing else changes, hyperlinks will; verify them periodically.

The FrontPage Security Model

S ecurity is a constant concern on the Internet. Most Web sites allow any and all to visit, but restrict editing and administration to a few authorized individuals.

FrontPage supports these requirements with an intuitive, built-in security model involving usernames, passwords, and three levels of access.

- **Browse** allows users to view the Web with browsers such as Internet Explorer, but not to open it with FrontPage or make changes.

- **Author and Browse** allows FrontPage users to open the Web and change its content, but not to modify Web settings or permissions.

- **Administer, Author, and Browse** permits users to change content, settings, and permissions.

FrontPage depends largely on your Web server's security functions for control. Security commands issued within FrontPage communicate with FrontPage software on the server and instruct it to implement the required settings, thereby insulating users from many of the differences in security approaches among Web servers.

Initializing FrontPage Security

During setup, FrontPage installs a program called FrontPage Server Administrator but doesn't add it to the Windows Start menu. This program modifies the configuration of a Web server by installing the FrontPage Server Extensions and initializing various settings, including security.

If FrontPage Setup installs or detects a Web server on the local machine, it automatically runs Server Administrator as part of the setup process. Later, if required, you can also run Server Administrator manually. You might need to do that if

- You've changed your Web server software

- You need to change settings

- You want to install, upgrade, remove, or check the FrontPage Server Extensions

SEE ALSO
For more information on the FrontPage Server Extensions, see Chapter 16, "Choosing and Configuring Your Web Server."

Figure 15-1 shows FrontPage Server Administrator's opening screen. FrontPage Setup doesn't create a Start menu option for Server Administrator, but it does create a shortcut in the FrontPage software folder. If you run Server Administrator often, consider copying this shortcut to your desktop or Start menu. If you can't find the shortcut, you can always run the program directly by double-clicking its name in Explorer. Look for the file FPSRVWIN.EXE, probably located in your FrontPage \bin folder.

SEE ALSO
For an explanation of Port Numbers, see the sidebar "Port Numbers," page 568.

The list box titled Select Server Or Port displays an entry for each TCP/IP port where a Web server on the local machine is responding. The figure shows the simplest case: one server responding on port 80.

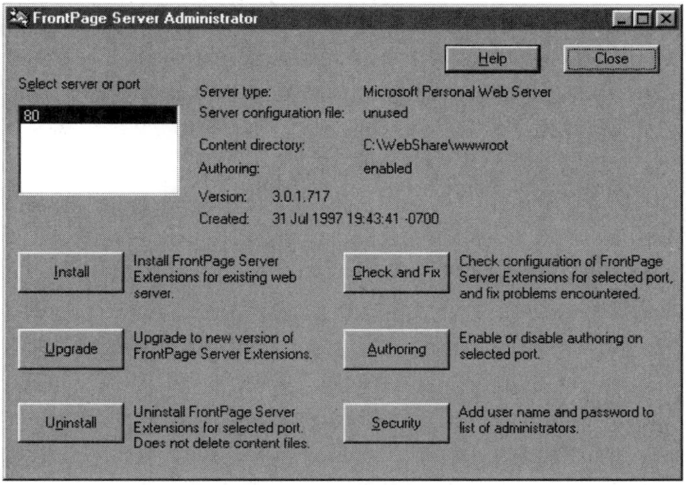

FIGURE 15-1. To start FrontPage Server Administrator, look for a shortcut in the folder where you installed FrontPage.

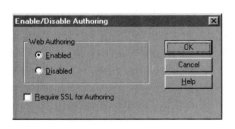

The Server Type, Server Configuration File, Content Directory, Authoring, Version, and Created fields display information about the server on the selected port.

The Install, Upgrade, Uninstall, and Check And Fix buttons pertain to the server and port you select. The next chapter will discuss these options, but it's worth noting here that the Check And Fix option can apply a comprehensive set of valuable security rules.

SEE ALSO

To read about authoring control for individual FrontPage Webs, see "Administering Security for an Existing FrontPage Web," page 571.

Figure 15-2 shows the result of clicking the Authoring button in Figure 15-1. By default, Web authoring is enabled, but the administrator can freeze the site's content by changing this setting to Disabled. The Web Authoring setting controls all FrontPage Webs on the selected server—it can't enable authoring on some FrontPage Webs and disable it on others.

FIGURE 15-2. This dialog box appears when you click the Authoring button in Figure 15-1. Settings affect all FrontPage Webs on the selected server.

V Maintenance and Utility Functions

Port Numbers

 SEE ALSO

For an explanation of TCP/IP, see "Server Connectivity and TCP/IP," page 585.

When a single machine provides several TCP/IP services, clients need a way to identify which of these services they wish to use. Port numbers provide such a method.

When a TCP/IP service starts up, it registers with the local machine's network software and indicates which ports it wishes to respond to. The network software then forwards all incoming traffic on those ports to that service.

If a service requests a port that's already in use, it receives an error code. Allowing two services to register the same port would be ambiguous; the network software would again be unable to identify which service should receive traffic arriving on that port.

By default, HTTP servers listen on port 80. This is also the default port number in an *http://* URL. If a system administrator wants to run several kinds of Web server software at the same time on the same machine, the administrator must configure each piece of software to listen on a different port number, and users must specify the same port numbers in their URLs. For instance,

http://www.pfew.com

will access an HTTP server on port 80, and

http://www.pfew.com:8080

will access an HTTP server on port 8080. Port 8080 is a common choice for Web servers running on computers where port 80 is already in use. If you ask Front-Page Setup to install FrontPage Personal Web Server and Setup finds that port 80 is already in use, setup will install FrontPage Personal Web Server on port 8080.

The check box Require SSL For Authoring specifies whether FrontPage authors need to turn on the Connect Using SSL box in FrontPage Explorer when accessing Webs on this server. SSL, or Secure Sockets Layer, is a way of securing Web traffic so that it can't be mimicked, tampered with, or deciphered by others with access to the network.

 WARNING

Don't activate the Connect Using SSL option if your Web server doesn't support SSL. Doing so will block all authoring to the server (including yours).

Clicking the Security button in Figure 15-1 (page 567) invokes the Administrator Name And Password dialog box. It allows the system administrator to change a FrontPage Web's administrator name and password. Figure 15-3 shows a full version of the Administrator Name And Password dialog box. The Password, Confirm Password, and Advanced options may not appear, depending on your Web server and its operating system.

- **Web Name** names the FrontPage Web to be updated. Root Web is the default.

- **Name** specifies the administrator's user name.

- **Password** supplies a password for the administrator. If the name is already an administrator, its password will be changed. If the name was not an administrator, it will become one.

- **Confirm Password** prompts a second time for the administrator password. The Password and Confirm Password entries must agree.

- **Advanced** limits administrator access based on IP (Internet Protocol) address.

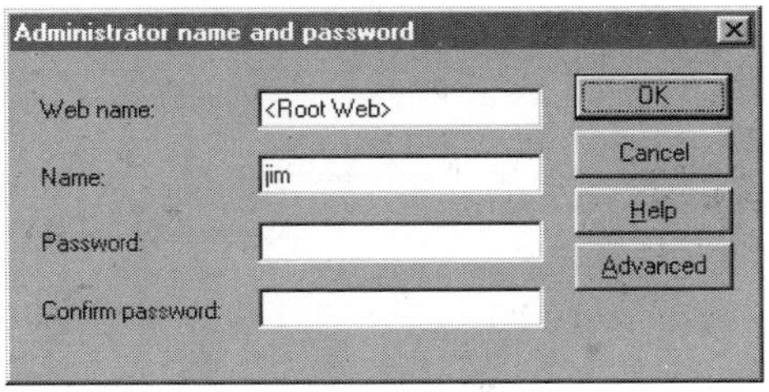

FIGURE 15-3.
The appearance of this dialog box will vary, according to the selected server.

Port 443 and Secure HTTP

Port 80 is the default port for normal HTTP, while port 443 is the default for secure HTTP. Servers that respond to both types of HTTP show up twice in FrontPage Server Administrator, but you only need to maintain one port—port 80.

For an example of a more complex environment, consider Figure 15-4. In this case the server type is Microsoft Internet Information Server running on Windows NT Server. There are two virtual Web servers, one at the system's default IP address and one at 192.168.180.100. Both servers respond to ports 80 and 443.

FIGURE 15-4.

This is the same dialog box shown in Figure 15-1 (page 567), but in a more complex environment. Note the virtual Web server on 192.168.180.100 and the multiple ports per server.

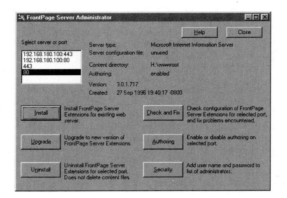

Even if FrontPage Extensions were already installed on the default virtual server and on 192.168.180.100, an additional virtual server created on, say, 192.168.180.101 wouldn't automatically appear with the FrontPage Extensions and FrontPage security in place. To install these features on a new virtual server, the system administrator would select its IP address in Server Administrator and then click Install.

Virtual Servers

Many Web servers support a concept called *virtual servers*. Virtual servers allow Web sites to have names like *www.apples.com* and *www.oranges.com* without requiring a separate physical machine for each site. A virtual server works this way:

- A single machine responds to several IP addresses.

- Each of these IP addresses has a different DNS name, such as *www.apples.com* and *www.oranges.com*.

- The Web server uses a different document folder, depending on the IP address an HTTP request arrived on.

Administering Security for an Existing FrontPage Web

Installing FrontPage Server Extensions, initializing security, and creating new FrontPage Webs are usually tasks done by a system administrator—someone responsible for the overall stability and performance of the server. If you're running a personal Web server, this is probably as far as you'll go by way of security. It's like being the president, chief engineer, and janitor of a one-person company.

In a multiuser environment, however, the system administrator usually turns ongoing maintenance over to the new Web's owner. The owner then designates any additional administrators and authors.

Administering Web-Level Security

FrontPage Explorer provides an administrative front end to your Web server's security system. Not only may your security rights change as you connect to various Webs, but FrontPage may display different security options for different kinds of Web server software. This section will examine the most common variations.

To change permissions via FrontPage on a particular Web server, you must open the applicable FrontPage Web *on that server*. This requires the presence of the FrontPage Server Extensions. If the extensions aren't installed, you or an administrator will have to control permissions using the server's native security system.

Updating a Web's permissions on your authoring machine and then publishing your Web to a production server doesn't affect security on the production server. This is because, in most scenarios, security on the two servers *ought* to be different. You may be an administrator of your Personal Web server, for example, but only an author (allowed to change content but not permissions) on the production server. In a shared development environment, many Web authors could have permission to update the group's authoring server, though only the project leader or librarian might have rights to publish content on the production server.

To change permissions for an existing Web, the Web's administrator opens the Web in FrontPage Explorer and then chooses Permissions from the Tools menu. This displays the dialog box shown in Figure 15-5. The Tabs available will vary, depending on the capabilities of the Web server and the installed FrontPage Server Extensions.

> The Permissions choice on the Tools menu will be disabled for servers having no security in effect, or for those whose security isn't configurable through the FrontPage Server Extensions.

FIGURE 15-5.
The Permissions dialog box in FrontPage Explorer lets administrators establish permissions for the current Web that differ from those of the Root Web.

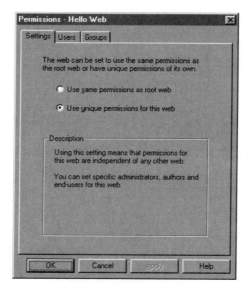

The Settings tab controls whether the current Web will use the same permissions as the Root Web or unique permissions of its own. While new Webs always inherit permissions from the Root Web, this is seldom appropriate for ongoing use. In all but the simplest environments, different people will maintain the Root Web and subordinate Webs. Therefore, after creating a new Web, the Root Web administrator will generally activate unique permissions so that the appropriate users or groups can begin setting their own permissions and creating content.

Choosing the option Use Unique Permissions For This Web unlocks the remaining tabs on the dialog box. These might include Users, Groups, and Computers, depending on the Web server.

Controlling User-Level Web Access

There are two major variations for the Users Tab: one for Web servers that use a Windows NT User Account Database and another for servers that maintain Web-specific user lists. The dialog box shown in Figure 15-6 depicts the Users tab for a server that takes the Windows NT approach.

FIGURE 15-6.
This Users tab dialog box is typical for Webs running on servers that support Windows NT security.

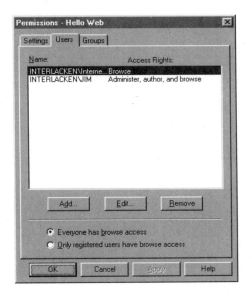

Most Microsoft Web servers employ a Windows NT user account database to control Web access. These include

- Internet Information Server for Windows NT Server

- Microsoft Peer Web Server for Windows NT Workstation

- Microsoft Personal Web Server for Windows 95, provided that the following two conditions are true:

  - The User Level Access Control is turned on.

  - The Obtain List Of Users And Groups From text box specifies a Windows NT computer or domain.

  Open the Access Control tab of the Control Panel's Network applet to set or modify these items.

NOTE

If User Level Access Control based on a Windows NT User Account Database isn't available, Microsoft Personal Web Server provides no security at all. If you're working in a nonnetworked environment, such as your home, this may not be a concern. In a multiuser environment, consider running at least one Windows NT workstation or server.

The list box at the top of the Users dialog box shows which users have permission to access the current FrontPage Web and tells what activities are permitted. To begin adding a user to the list, bring up the dialog box of Figure 15-7 by clicking the Add button.

FIGURE 15-7.
This dialog box allows users with Windows NT accounts to be granted access to a FrontPage Web.

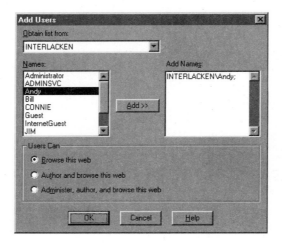

If the server supports multiple User Account Databases, the drop-down list titled Obtain List From can retrieve usernames from the database you want. In Figure 15-7, for example, INTERLACKEN is the name of the Windows NT Domain, and the Names box lists user accounts in that domain. If you log into a Windows NT Domain, operate a Microsoft Web server in the same domain, and open a FrontPage Web on that server, FrontPage will automatically use the current login account to log into the FrontPage Web. To grant any of the listed users access to the current Web, follow these steps:

1 Select the username in the Names list and then click the Add button. You can also add users by double-clicking their entries in the Names list.

2 Select the most appropriate privilege in the Users Can section.

3 Click OK.

You can add as many names as you like before clicking OK, but all the names will receive the same permissions. To give various users different permissions, close and reopen the dialog box. FrontPage can't create, modify, or delete Windows NT accounts, nor can it change passwords. These are functions provided in Windows NT User Manager.

Clicking Edit in the Permissions dialog box (Figure 15-6, page 573) displays the Edit Users dialog box shown in Figure 15-8, where you can change a user's level of access. Clicking Remove in the Permissions dialog box deletes the selected user from the authorized list.

FIGURE 15-8.
This dialog box changes the permissions of the currently selected user.

V

Maintenance and
Utility Functions

Note the following options at the bottom of the Permissions dialog box:

- **Everyone Has Browse Access** means that anyone with network access to your Web server can browse it, using programs such as Internet Explorer or Netscape Navigator.

- **Only Registered Users Have Browse Access** means that Web browsing is available only to authorized users and to members of authorized groups. To verify authorization, the Web server will prompt visitors for a qualifying username and password.

Most Web servers other than the three listed on page 573 have Web-specific user lists that are quite distinct from the operating system's list of login accounts. This avoids the security concerns of granting Web users system-wide login accounts, but it also means that people needing both type of access will have to remember an additional username and password.

ⓧ CAUTION
Password-protected Web pages are accessible only if the browser and Web server use the same authentication scheme. If the server and browser come from different providers, they might not reveal their security algorithms to each other for security reasons. If you have trouble getting valid passwords accepted, change or add authentication schemes until you find a compatible set.

In many of these cases, you can maintain Web-specific user lists directly from within FrontPage. FrontPage Personal Web Server provides this capability. The Users Tab and the Add Users dialog box take on the appearance shown in Figure 15-9.

FIGURE 15-9.
These dialog boxes appear for Web servers that maintain their own user databases.

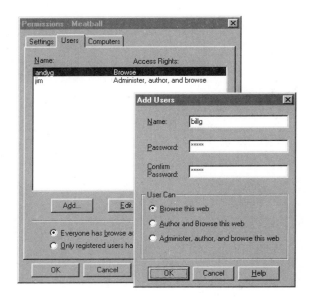

Clicking the Add button in Figure 15-9 brings up the Add Users dialog box shown. Enter the new username, enter the new password twice, specify the level of access, and then press OK.

Controlling Web Access by Group

Groups are simply collections of users granted identical security privileges. Grouping all users in a certain department, in a certain job classification, on a client site, or from another category makes it easy to grant or revoke privileges for the whole group. Granting privileges by group also eases maintenance as individuals enter and leave the group; rather than updating security in many different locations, you need only update the group's membership.

Support for groups varies from one Web server to another, as does the ability to create, delete, and modify groups from within FrontPage. In

Figure 15-10 the Web server is Microsoft Internet Information Server and the groups listed are those in the Windows NT Server's domain. The Windows NT User Manager tool creates, modifies, and deletes these groups. Other Web servers maintain groups in their own way, and might permit maintenance via FrontPage. The Add, Edit, and Remove buttons in Figure 15-10 work very much as they do in the Permissions dialog box shown in Figure 15-6 (page 573).

FIGURE 15-10.
This dialog box sets the access level for groups of users.

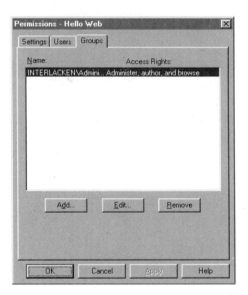

Controlling Web Access by Network Address

Some Web servers can control access based on a remote user's IP address. Because IP addresses are typically assigned to organizations in blocks, granting or denying access based on IP address can provide a form of security broadly grounded in organizational membership.

The Computers tab shown in Figure 15-11, on the following page, controls access to a FrontPage Web based on the IP Address. This tab is available only for Web servers that support this feature, such as FrontPage Personal Web Server. It's not available for Internet Information Server 3 and earlier, for Microsoft Peer Web Server 3 and earlier, or for Microsoft Personal Web Server.

V

Maintenance and
Utility Functions

FIGURE 15-11.

The Computers tab grants or limits Web access based on IP address.

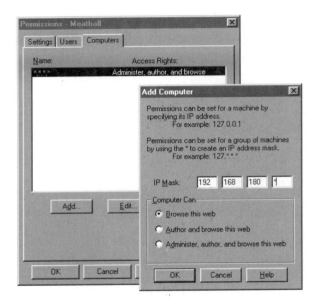

To provide Web access for a given computer, click the Add button, enter the computer's IP address in the IP Mask field, choose the level of access, and then click OK. The access levels work the same as those for users and groups, except, of course, that you can exercise no direct control over who might be sitting at the computer that you're granting Web access.

To control access for a range of IP addresses, enter asterisks (*) in one or more boxes in the IP Mask field. In Figure 15-11, the Web server will allow browsing by all users having IP addresses 192.168.180.0 through 192.168.180.255.

The Edit button in the Permissions dialog box shown in Figure 15-11 modifies the permissions of an existing IP address entry. The Remove button just to its right deletes the selected entry from the list.

Administering Folder-Level Security

Using a new feature of FrontPage 98, the administrator of a FrontPage Web can now control access to individual folders within a Web. To do this, locate the folder in FrontPage Explorer, and then either select the folder and choose Properties from the Edit menu or right-click the folder and choose Properties from the pop-up menu. The dialog box shown in Figure 15-12 will appear.

FIGURE 15-12.
The folder Properties window in FrontPage Explorer controls execute and browse access for the selected folder.

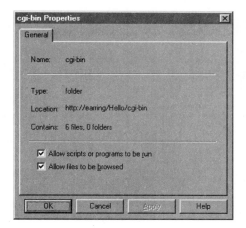

■ **Allow Scripts Or Programs To Be Run**, if turned on, allows the Web server to run executable programs in the selected folder. Valid program types include CGI, ISAPI, NSAPI, ASP, and any other script languages (such as Perl) that your server is configured to recognize.

■ **Allow Files To Be Browsed**, if turned on, permits file access from Web browsers. Turn this option off to prevent ordinary remote users from accessing the folder. This option will be absent from Web servers that don't support it, such as FrontPage Personal Web Server.

Setting these options modifies the security settings on your Web server. If your server's system administrator hasn't granted you permissions to do this, the commands will fail. Contact the system administrator for assistance.

Security administration is a complex, critical, and judgmental task. It always involves tradeoffs among the degree of protection, ease of administration, and ease of access for authorized users. There are no universal answers or pat solutions—but FrontPage at least provides a start.

For more information about choosing, configuring, and administering a FrontPage Web server, proceed to the next chapter.

V

Maintenance and
Utility Functions

PART VI

Integrating FrontPage and Your Web Server

CHAPTER 16

Choosing and Configuring Your Web Server

C hoosing Web servers for your development and production environments is a major site-planning decision. Microsoft provides two Web servers for Windows 95, one for Windows NT Workstation, and another for Windows NT Server. This chapter reviews those servers and discusses the environments for which each is best suited. It also explores alternatives in case your Web server isn't a Microsoft product.

This chapter will primarily interest those who install and maintain Web servers—Webmasters, network administrators, and system administrators—as well as FrontPage authors running personal Web servers on their own machines. If your responsibilities mainly involve content development and someone else administers your Web server, you may decide to skim or skip this chapter.

Understanding Web Servers

To become proficient in publishing to the Web requires at least a basic understanding of how the Web itself works. While making no claims of comprehensive coverage, the material below provides an overview of the Web's core technologies; later sections will use this information to discuss managing specific Web servers.

HyperText Transfer Protocol—A Simple Concept

Using Web browsers like Internet Explorer to retrieve and view Web pages is generally a pleasant and easy experience. The data you see, however, is obviously stored somewhere else on the network, and your browser retrieves it using a relatively hidden transfer mechanism. In the case of the World Wide Web, the data comes from a Web server and the transfer mechanism is hypertext transfer protocol—HTTP.

As originally conceived, both HTTP and Web servers are very simple. The browser sends the server a command such as

```
GET /sports/hockey/standings.html
```

and the server responds by locating a folder named /sports/hockey/, looking for a file named standings.html, and transmitting that file to the browser.

Notice that the GET command in the previous paragraph contains less information than a normal URL. The corresponding URL might have been

http://www.nws.com:80/sports/hockey/standings.html

SEE ALSO

For an explanation of port numbers, refer to the sidebar "Port Numbers," page 568.

where *http* specifies the protocol, *www.nws.com* is the name of the Web server, and *80* is a port number on that server. The browser uses the information in *http://www.nws.com:80* for connecting to the Web server, and it transmits the rest as a command to locate and deliver the file—that is, as the GET request shown above.

The file standings.html probably contains hypertext markup language—HTML—and might call for additional files. If so, the browser retrieves each additional file by issuing another GET request. The server handles all ordinary GET requests identically, regardless of file type. The job of assembling multiple files and formatting the finished page falls entirely to the browser.

Proxy Servers and GET Requests

There's one instance where a browser sends out GET requests containing the remote hostname and port number: that is, when it uses a proxy server.

For security reasons, many sites require their users to access the Internet through a proxy server. A proxy server is simply a relay agent that retrieves Internet Web pages for local users but prevents Internet users from accessing the site's internal resources. To use a proxy server, a browser must be configured to

- Send all GET requests to the proxy server and not to the host specified in the URL, and

- Include the full URL, including the server name and port, in all GET requests.

Essentially, the browser sends the proxy server GET requests containing host names. The proxy server then connects to the named host and sends a GET request with the host name removed. With or without a proxy server, the remote Web server receives GET requests not containing its host name.

To have Internet Explorer 3 use a proxy server

1   Choose Options from the View menu.

2   Click the Connection tab.

3   Turn on the check box titled Connect Through A Proxy Server.

4   Click the Settings button.

5   Specify the proxy server's location.

6   List the names of any servers that shouldn't be accessed through the proxy server. (These would typically be internal machines.)

Server Connectivity and TCP/IP

? **SEE ALSO**
If your working environment doesn't include a TCP/IP network, you may decide to use a disk-based Web for development rather than a Web server. See "Creating Disk-Based Webs," page 633.

All communication on the Internet uses a group of protocols collectively called Transmission Control Protocol/Internet Protocol—TCP/IP. For any sort of Internet client and server to communicate, both must be running TCP/IP and have an active network link between them.

Browsers, Web servers, and PCs running FrontPage are no exception; all need TCP/IP connectivity to operate. This applies even within your own PC. If you want FrontPage or a browser to connect to a Web server on the same machine, that machine will need working TCP/IP

VI

Integrating FrontPage
and Your Web Server

software complete with an *IP address*. An IP address consists of four numbers in the range 0–255, separated by periods; 192.168.180.2 is a typical IP address (the periods are pronounced "dot").

If your PC is on a campus or enterprise LAN (local area network), your network administrator has probably assigned it an IP address. For this discusson it makes little difference whether the administrator assigned your address manually or via an automated network service, or whether the administrator configured your network software personally or simply provided instructions. If your PC has an IP address, Front-Page can communicate with Web servers also running on your PC or elsewhere on the network.

WARNING

> It's absolutely critical that no two computers on the same network have the same IP address. Duplicate IP addresses prevent both computers from working and lead to other network problems as well. Never use an IP address you guessed at, chose randomly, or copied from someone else's computer.

If you connect to the Internet by a dial-up link, your PC probably has no assigned IP address. Instead, software at your service provider assigns a temporary address every time you dial in. FrontPage can use this temporary address to connect to Web servers on the Internet or on your local machine, but once you disconnect, the IP address disappears and even a Web server on your own PC becomes inaccessible. Some Internet service providers will provide a permanent, or *static,* IP address for an additional fee.

A LAN IP address is clearly preferable to a fleeting dial-in address, though getting one presents a problem if you don't actually have a LAN. One solution is to build your own LAN. Ethernet adapters are available for less than $100, and hubs to connect them are just as cheap. If you have more than one computer in your home or office, connect them together! This makes it easy to share printers and data among your computers, and you can even set up your own Web.

The complete details of setting up a small LAN are beyond the scope of this book, but generally it involves adding an expansion card to each computer, connecting the expansion cards with the proper cabling, and installing the proper network software. Windows 95 and Windows NT include all the software you need for a wide variety of network cards.

TIP

> Unless you've installed network cards, cabling, and software before, get help from someone with experience or from another book. The material presented here is only an overview.

Windows 95's Plug and Play operating system will usually detect the new network card, prompt you for the necessary disks and CDs, and walk you through the installation automatically. If not, open the Control Panel's Network applet, click Add, and choose Adapter.

If your PC is on a LAN managed by a network administrator, the administrator will give you an IP address. For private networks, choose addresses from Table 16-1. In all but the most unusual cases, this means choosing 192.168.*xxx.yyy* where *xxx* is a fixed number between 1 and 255 and *yyy* is a different number between 1 and 255 for each computer.

TIP

> If you don't know your IP address, try using 127.0.0.1 or the name *localhost*. These are special values that mean *myself* on every computer running TCP/IP.

TABLE 16-1. IP Addresses for Private Networks

Class	From IP Address	To IP Address	Subnet Mask
A	10.0.0.1	10.255.255.255	255.0.0.0
B	172.16.0.1	172.31.255.255	255.255.0.0
C	192.168.0.1	192.168.255.255	255.255.255.0

NOTE

> These IP addresses are assigned by an Internet standard called RFC 1597. However, they can't be used on the Internet, which makes them safe to use for a private network.

When the network setup program prompts you for protocols, be sure to choose TCP/IP. When prompted for an IP address, enter the IP address you chose in the preceding paragraph and the corresponding subnet mask from Table 16-1 (page 587)—probably 255.255.255.0. Leave the Default Gateway, DNS, and WINS dialog boxes blank.

Server Names and the Domain Name System

Because IP addresses are difficult to remember and subject to change, Internet authorities (such as they are) invented the Domain Name System—DNS. Essentially, DNS is an online, distributed database that translates easily remembered names such as *www.intel.com* and *ftp.microsoft.com* to IP addresses. When your browser, for example, tries to open the URL

> *http://www.microsoft.com/frontpage*

it actually begins by using DNS to translate *www.microsoft.com* to an IP address. The browser then connects to the IP (numerical) address and not to the DNS name.

Like most Internet applications, DNS is a client-server system. The client software is called a *resolver* and, in the case of Windows, it's part of the TCP/IP software that comes with the operating system. *Name resolution* is the process of translating computer names to IP addresses, and vice versa.

A DNS server usually resides centrally on a network and contains the databases that allow DNS to work. When a user requests a connection to a named host, the user's computer sends the name to the local DNS server, and with any luck the DNS server responds with the corresponding IP address. If the local DNS server can't resolve the request, it might contact additional DNS servers until it *can*.

Each dot (period) in a DNS name normally indicates a different database and possibly a different machine. If your network software asks your local DNS server for the IP address of *www.microsoft.com*

1 The local server first contacts a *root* DNS server that knows all the COM entries in the world.

2 The root server provides the names and IP addresses of all DNS servers in the *microsoft.com* domain.

3 Your local server would contact one of the *microsoft.com* DNS servers to get the IP address for *www.microsoft.com*.

The inner workings of DNS really aren't important for Web authoring. However, if someone asks you for your DNS name, you should know what they're talking about. You'll also need to understand a little about DNS so that you can ask your service provider or network administrator to establish a name for your server, as well as understand the error messages you'll get if DNS isn't working.

If your environment lacks a DNS server—or if you have computers not included in your DNS server's database—you can provide name-to-IP-address translation using a hosts file. This is a simple text file named *hosts* (with no extension) and is located in the following folder.

- **Windows 95:** the Windows folder (that is, c:\windows)

- **Windows NT:** <systemroot>\system32\drivers\etc. (where <systemroot> is typically c:\winnt)

You can create this file using any simple ASCII editor, such as Notepad. Each line in the file contains an IP address, one or more spaces, and a computer name. After saving the file in the correct location, you should find that your computer translates the entered names to corresponding computer names as if they were in DNS.

 TIP

> If you use Save As to save the hosts file with Notepad, be sure to enclose the filename—hosts—in double quotes. Otherwise, Notepad will add a TXT extension and the file won't work.

The primary disadvantage of hosts files is that each computer needs its own copy of the file. Keeping all these files up to date becomes unwieldy in large environments.

Server Home Folders

It's hard to imagine a case where any server administrator would want to make a Web server's entire file system available to everyone on the World Wide Web. Web servers therefore assign a *home folder* as the starting point for all GET requests. The term *home folder* is used interchangeably with any of the following: *home directory, root folder, root directory, document root,* and *home root.* If the server's home folder was

```
H:\wwwroot
```

and the server received

```
GET /sports/hockey/standings.html
```

it would actually look for and deliver the file

```
H:\wwwroot\sports\hockey\standings.html
```

Virtual Folders

For one reason or another, it's frequently convenient to view data as though it resided within a server's home folder even though it doesn't. The data might reside on a different drive letter for space management or historical reasons, for example, or it might reside on another machine. *Virtual folders* solve this dilemma by making folder locations outside the server's home folder appear to be within it.

Suppose, for example, a site kept its local announcements in a folder at

```
I:\sitenews
```

but its server home folder was

```
H:\wwwroot
```

The server administrator could define a virtual folder called /news that represented I:\sitenews. If the server then received

```
GET /news/default.html
```

it would look for and deliver

```
I:\sitenews\default.html
```

rather than

```
H:\wwwroot\news\default.html
```

A frequent reason for setting up virtual folders is security. An administrator may feel more confident of a system's security by physically locating important files outside the server's home folder. In addition, many Web servers use virtual folders to implement folder-level security provisions. Any folder-level settings used by the Web server but not by the local file system usually reside in virtual folder definitions.

Virtual Servers

Contrary to popular belief, no law of nature dictates that all Web sites have DNS names beginning with *www* and ending in *com*. Nevertheless, this is what most Web surfers now expect, and it creates problems for large and small sites alike.

For large sites, problems arise building servers powerful enough to handle hundreds (or thousands) of incoming requests per second. The solution is normally to keep upgrading hardware and software, or to set up additional servers for menu choices one or two levels removed from the home page.

For small sites, the problem is the cost of building a separate server for each client, even if the number of hits per day is small or moderate. The obvious solution is locating several small clients on one server, but clients want direct, custom names like *www.cats.com* and *www.dogs.com*, not *www.provider.com/~cats* and *www.provider.com/~dogs*.

Virtual servers provide an elegant solution to this common dilemma. An administrator sets up a different DNS name and IP address for each client, and then configures the server's network software to respond to each such address. Finally, the administrator configures the Web server to access a different home folder, depending on which IP address the remote user specified. This allows different DNS names like *www.cats.com* and *www.dogs.com* to access different home folders on the same server.

 TIP

To display the dialog box that makes a Windows NT computer respond to more than one IP address, open the Windows NT Control Panel, double-click Network, and click the Protocols tab, then select TCP/IP Protocol, click the Properties button, click the IP Address tab, and then click the Advanced button.

VI

Integrating FrontPage
and Your Web Server

Server-Side Programming

Delivering prewritten Web pages is quite a useful function, but generating pages on the fly offers considerably more flexibility. This is possible using a variety of techniques.

- **CGI—common gateway interface.** The remote user submits a URL that identifies not a file the server should transmit, but a program the server should run. Such programs typically receive input from HTML forms or from data appended to the URL, and as output they generate HTML for delivery to the remote user. They can also update files or databases on the server, send mail, and perform other useful functions.

- **ISAPI—Internet Server Application Programming Interface.** This approach is similar to CGI in function but implemented differently. ISAPI programs are dynamic link libraries (DLLs) that the operating system needs to load only once for any number of executions. By contrast, CGI programs are EXE files that must be loaded, initialized, run, and unloaded for each incoming request. The user submits a URL containing the name of the DLL.

- **ASP—Active Server Pages.** Unlike CGI and ISAPI, Active Server Pages consist of ordinary HTML intermixed with program code. The Web server interprets and executes the program code as it delivers the Web page. Web pages containing server-side scripts have the filename extension ASP.

  Programmers usually create code for Active Server Pages using simple script languages such as JavaScript and VBScript. These languages can then invoke services from built-in server functions, ActiveX controls, Java applets, and other objects.

Because of the damage an errant or mischievous program can inflict, server-side programming raises significant security concerns. No Webmaster or system administrator wants users interfering with normal operation or tampering with content. For this reason, most Web servers are configured to execute only programs in specially designated folders. Administrators then allow just a few trusted individuals to place programs there.

Understanding the FrontPage Server Extensions

FrontPage lives intimately on the Web. Not only does it create and manage Web content; FrontPage itself is a distributed, Web-based, client-server system. FrontPage has processing components on both Web clients and Web servers, and these components communicate via Web protocols.

Server Extension Functions

FrontPage Explorer and FrontPage Editor provide client-side processing for Web development. Your Web server plus the FrontPage Server Extensions provide the complementary server processes. The FrontPage Server Extensions provide four kinds of services.

- **File and Folder Access.** When you open a page in FrontPage Editor, FrontPage normally retrieves the page over the network by HTTP and not by reading a local file system. The data files for the Task list, Navigation view, and Text indexes reside in hidden FrontPage folders on the server, and clients retrieve these by HTTP as well.

  At some point, however, the needs of FrontPage exceed the capabilities of standard Web servers. FrontPage needs to create, replace, rename, move, copy, and delete files on the server based on commands received from the client—that is, from FrontPage Explorer and FrontPage Editor. The FrontPage Server Extensions provide the server-side software for these client-server functions.

  Compared to local file access or traditional file sharing, using Web protocols for file handling may initially seem awkward. Consider, however, that many Web developers lack facilities for local file-sharing but do have Web connectivity. In this environment, using Web protocols and Server Extensions indeed makes sense.

- **Background Services.** The FrontPage Server Extensions also provide a number of content services that run in the background on the server. Choosing Recalculate Hyperlinks from FrontPage

VI

Integrating FrontPage
and Your Web Server

Explorer's Tools menu, for example, brings up the dialog box shown in Figure 16-1, informing the user that FrontPage is about to launch a server-side process.

FIGURE 16-1.
FrontPage clients can initiate server-side processes installed by FrontPage Server Extensions.

- **Browse-Time Services.** Features like text search and server-side form field validation obviously require programs that run on the server not when the developer creates or uploads the page, but every time a Web visitor submits a request. The FrontPage Server Extensions provide this programming in a standard way.

- **Security Services.** The ability of remote users to add, update, delete, and reorganize files and folders carries with it the necessity to differentiate authorized and unauthorized users. For more information, see Chapter 15, "The FrontPage Security Model."

Despite running with different Web servers and on different operating systems, each implementation of the FrontPage Server Extensions provides the same services and application protocols. This allows FrontPage Explorer, FrontPage Editor, and other clients to utilize the FrontPage Server Extensions in a platform-independent way.

Server Extensions Documentation

The FrontPage 98 CD contains detailed Server Extensions documentation in HTML format. If you chose during FrontPage setup to install the Server Extensions Resource Kit, these files will reside at <<FrontPage>>\version3.0\serk, where <<FrontPage>> is the location of your FrontPage program files. You can also find these directly on the CD, in the \serk\enu\ folder. Substitute another language code for *enu* if necessary.

You can view the Server Extensions Resource Kit documentation directly, as shown in Figure 16-2, or by defining a virtual folder that points to the serk folder on your disk. Copy the \serk\enu\ folder to a folder on your Web server disk if FrontPage Setup hasn't already done so.

FIGURE 16-2.
The FrontPage Server Extensions Resource Kit provides detailed information about installing and configuring a FrontPage Web server.

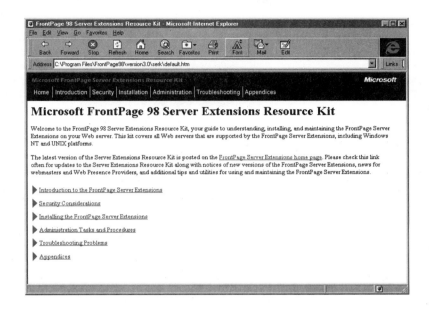

Software Platforms and Availability

The FrontPage Server Extensions are available for all popular Web server software on all popular platforms. Table 16-2 lists the servers supported as this is being written, while Table 16-3, on the next page, lists the operating systems.

TABLE 16-2.   Web Server Availability for FrontPage Server Extensions

Provider	Web Server	Operating System
Apache Project	Apache	Unix
CERN	CERN	Unix
Microsoft	FrontPage Personal Web Server	Windows
Microsoft	Internet Information Server	Windows NT Server
Microsoft	Microsoft Peer Web Services	Windows NT Workstation
Microsoft	Microsoft Personal Web Server	Windows 95

VI

Integrating FrontPage
and Your Web Server

(continued)

TABLE 16-2. *continued*

Provider	Web Server	Operating System
NCSA	NCSA	Unix
Netscape	Netscape Commerce Server	Unix, Windows
Netscape	Netscape Communications Server	Unix, Windows
Netscape	Netscape Enterprise Server	Unix, Windows
Netscape	Netscape FastTrack	Unix, Windows
O'Reilly	WebSite	Windows

TABLE 16-3. Operating System Availability for FrontPage Server Extensions

Operating System	Hardware Platform
BSD/OS 2.1	Intel x86
BSD/OS 3.0	Intel x86
Digital Unix 3.2c, 4.0	DEC Alpha
HP/UX 9.03, 10.01	HP PA-RISC
IRIX 5.3, 6.2, 6.4	Silicon Graphics MIPS
Linux 3.03 (Red Hat Software)	Intel x86
Solaris 2.4, 2.5	Sun SPARC
SunOS 4.1.3, 4.1.4	Sun SPARC
Windows 95	Intel x86
Windows NT	Intel x86, DEC Alpha, Silicon Graphics MIPS, Motorola PowerPC

As you might expect, versions of the server extensions for various servers and operating systems tend to appear at intervals rather than all at once. To check the current availability of FrontPage Server Extensions for your environment, browse Microsoft's Web site at

http://www.microsoft.com/frontpage/wpp

Obtaining FrontPage Server Extensions

There are three ways to obtain and install the FrontPage Server Extensions. The method you use depends on your Web server's operating system and software.

- **Delivered with FrontPage.** The FrontPage CD provides Server Extensions for most Windows-based Web servers. Running Setup from the CD will normally detect any Web servers on the same machine and install the appropriate extensions.

- **Delivered with Web Server Software.** Some Web servers include FrontPage Server Extensions on their distribution disks. Check your product documentation for availability and instructions.

- **Downloaded from Microsoft.** Many FrontPage Server Extensions are available from Microsoft's Web site at *http://www.microsoft.com/frontpage/wpp*. Even if you obtain FrontPage Server Extensions from another source, it's usually worthwhile to check the Microsoft site for a newer version.

Installing the FrontPage Server Extensions Under Windows

The procedure for installing the FrontPage Server Extensions varies somewhat, depending on the Web server, the operating system, and the server extensions version. In general, though, you should

1 First install the Web server software.

2 Test the server by displaying a few default pages over the network.

3 Install any other extensions or add-ons.

4 Test by exercising the provided functions.

5 Install the FrontPage Server Extensions.

6 Test by opening the Root Web with FrontPage Explorer and creating a new FrontPage Web.

7 Start adding content.

? SEE ALSO
For more information on installing FrontPage Server Extensions on Microsoft products, see "Choosing a Microsoft Web Server," page 602.

VI

Integrating FrontPage and Your Web Server

"Initializing FrontPage Security," page 566, provided a brief introduction to the Windows version of FrontPage Server Administrator. This program installs and initializes the FrontPage Server Extensions on most Windows-based Web servers. FrontPage Setup runs Server Administrator automatically as part of the setup process, but you can also run it later by double-clicking the shortcut in your FrontPage software folder. Figure 16-3 shows FrontPage Server Administrator running manually.

FIGURE 16-3.
To start FrontPage Server Administrator, look for a shortcut in the folder where you installed FrontPage.

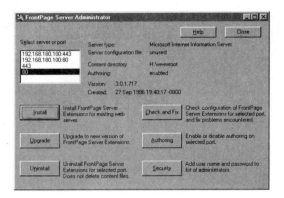

The following buttons control installation, update, removal, and verification of the FrontPage Server Extensions.

- **Install** adds the FrontPage Server Extensions to an existing Web server on the selected port. Table 16-4 lists the available options.

  After clicking the Install button, you'll be asked to confirm the type of Web server. Server Administrator will then prompt you for any necessary parameters and finally display a confirmation summary of actions it will take. Clicking OK at that point allows installation to proceed.

- **Upgrade** updates the FrontPage Server Extensions on an existing Web server to agree with a newer version of Microsoft FrontPage.

- **Uninstall** removes the FrontPage Server Extensions from an existing server.

- **Check And Fix** verifies the configuration of the server extensions installed on the selected port.

- **Authoring** displays a dialog box that enables or disables FrontPage authoring for the entire Web server.

- **Security** displays a dialog box that designates users as Web administrators and controls their passwords.

TABLE 16-4. Server Options in FrontPage Server Administrator

Server	Windows 95	Windows NT Workstation	Windows NT Server
FrontPage Personal Web Server	Yes	Yes	Yes
Internet Information Server	No	No	Yes
Microsoft Peer Web Server	No	Yes	No
Microsoft Personal Web Server	Yes	No	No
Netscape Commerce Server	Yes	Yes	Yes
Netscape Communications Server	Yes	Yes	Yes
Netscape Enterprise Server	Yes	Yes	Yes
Netscape FastTrack Server	Yes	Yes	Yes
O'Reilly WebSite Server	Yes	Yes	Yes

Installing the FrontPage Server Extensions from the Command Line

In addition to the Windows-based FrontPage Server Administrator described in the previous section, Microsoft also provides a command line version of the program, called fpsrvadm.exe. This can be useful for performing operations in batch files or on a timed basis. It's also the only method for installing the FrontPage Server Extensions on Unix-based systems.

Table 16-5, on the following page, summarizes the command line switches for fpsrvadm.exe. For more information about the fpsrvadm.exe program and its options, consult the admin.htm page in the Server Extensions Resource Kit.

VI

Integrating FrontPage and Your Web Server

TABLE 16-5. **Command Line FrontPage Server Administrator Switches**

Switch	Abbrev.	Argument	Function
-help	-h	N/A	Displays a help screen summarizing command line syntax.
-operation	-o	install	Installs the FrontPage extensions.
		upgrade	Upgrades existing FrontPage extensions to match the current version of FrontPage.
		uninstall	Removes the FrontPage extensions.
		check	Verifies proper installation of the FrontPage extensions.
		security	Adds to or removes administrators, authors, or end users from a Web. Sets IP address restrictions.
		chmod	On Unix only, chowns and chmods the FrontPage folders, Server Extension files, and Web content to a Unix username and groupname.
		enable	Enables authoring.
		disable	Disables authoring.
		recalc	Recalculates links for the specified Web.
		putfile	Adds a file to the specified Web. -web specifies the Web. -destination specifies the relative URL. -filename specifies the file.
		recalcfile	Recalculates links as if the specified file had changed. -destination or -filename specifies the file.
-port	-p	nnnn	The port on which the server is running. If virtual servers exist, specify them as hostname:port or ipaddress:port. For some operations, such as recalc, this switch can be specified as a11.
-web	-w	web name	The name of the FrontPage Web. Specify "" for the Root Web.

(continued)

TABLE 16-5. *continued*

Switch	Abbrev.	Argument	Function
-type	-t	apache apache-fp apache-manual-restart cern cern-manual-restart ncsa ncsa-manual-restart netscape netscape-manual-restart	The server type.
-servconf	-s	server config file	The name of the server's configuration file. The default location is the folder where the server is installed plus conf/httpd.conf (for NCSA or Apache) config/httpd.conf (for CERN) config/magnus.conf (for Netscape)
-multihost	-m	hostname	The name of a virtual server configuration. This can be either a fully qualified DNS or an IP address.
-username	-u	username	The administrator username. This is required if -operation is install or security.
-password	-pw	password	The administrator password. This is required if -operation is install or security.
-ipaddress	-i	IP address	Specifies IP addresses administrators may use. FrontPage will accept administrator functions only from matching addresses. The asterisk wildcard can be used in any of the IP address's four parts; for example, 143.45.*.*.
-access	-a	remove administrators authors users	The type of FrontPage Web access being granted.
-destination	-d	destination url	The destination URL for a document in a FrontPage Web on the server. This address is relative to the FrontPage Web specified with -web.

VI

Integrating FrontPage and Your Web Server

(continued)

TABLE 16-5. *continued*

Switch	Abbrev.	Argument	Function
-filename	-f	filename	The full pathname of a file on the server machine.
-xUser	-xu	Unix username	A Unix account name.
-xGroup	-xg	Unix group	A Unix group name.
-noChown Content	-n	yes	Chowns only FrontPage _vti folders and no user content.

The program fpsrvadm.exe also has a prompted mode. Simply enter *fpsrvadm* with no switches at the command line.

For examples of typical commands, search FrontPage Help for the string *command line version* or type *fpsrvadm -h* at the command line.

Choosing a Microsoft Web Server

This section will briefly review several Web servers that support Front-Page and its Server Extensions.

Internet Information Server for Windows NT Server

The flagship of Microsoft's Web server line is Internet Information Server (IIS). This is an extremely powerful, commercial-grade Web server suitable for a wide range of production environments. IIS runs on Windows NT Server, and thus on a variety of processors, as listed in Table 16-3, page 596.

If you want your FrontPage environment or your server environment to be 100 percent Microsoft, Internet Information Server should be your production Web server. The various Web servers tend to leapfrog one another in terms of features and performance, but IIS is perennially near the top. IIS's large installed base ensures a wide variety of third-party add-ons, and Microsoft is a leader in bringing new technologies to its server. Finally, IIS ships at no extra charge with every copy of Windows NT Server.

You can install IIS when you first install Windows NT Server, or you can add it later. Figure 16-4 shows the dialog box sequence for adding it later. The sequence is

1 Open Control Panel.

2 Double-click the Network icon.

3 Choose the Services tab.

4 Click the Add button.

5 Select Microsoft Internet Information Server.

6 Click OK.

FIGURE 16-4.

You can add Internet Information Server to Windows NT Server through the Control Panel Network.

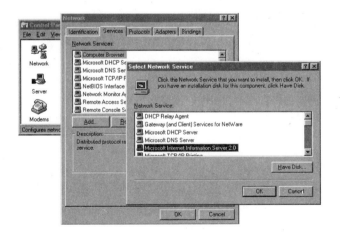

The remainder of the setup process will prompt you for various installation options, including locations for the IIS software itself and for Web, FTP, and Gopher home folders. A full discussion of IIS configuration and management is clearly beyond the scope of this book, but it's usually best not to locate service home folders on the Windows NT boot drive.

VI

Integrating FrontPage and Your Web Server

To manage IIS after installation, Microsoft provides an application called Internet Service Manager. On Windows NT Server the icon to start this program resides within the Start menu's Microsoft Internet Server program group. On Windows NT Workstation, the program group is Peer Web Services. Starting Internet Service Manager brings up the dialog box shown in Figure 16-5, which displays all Microsoft Internet Services installed on your machine. You must be logged onto the server as an administrator to use Internet Service Manager.

FIGURE 16-5.
Internet Service Manager lists Internet services installed on your machine or others on the network. To manage a service, double-click its entry.

There's no requirement to run Internet Service Manager on the same machine as the service being administered; you can even run Internet Service Manager on Windows NT Workstation and administer a Windows NT Server. Wherever you run Internet Service Manager, though, your login account must have administrator privileges for the target Windows NT Server.

> You can locate Internet Services running on other Windows NT machines at your site by choosing Find All Servers from the Properties menu. The magnifying glass icon provides an equivalent toolbar function.

Administering IIS Service Properties

Double-clicking any entry in Internet Service Manager brings up a tabbed dialog box for managing that service. The first tab for the WWW service appears in Figure 16-6.

The input fields control these properties:

- **TCP Port** specifies the port number on which the server will operate.

FIGURE 16-6.
This dialog box manages WWW Service Properties for Internet Information Server.

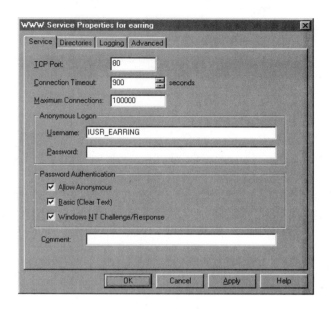

- **Connection Timeout** is the number of seconds the server will wait for network responses.

- **Maximum Connections** limits the number of simultaneous connections the server will allow. In extremely busy environments, it may be better to turn away some connections than to provide substandard service to everyone who connects. Browsers will usually retry refused connections.

- **Anonymous Logon**

  - **Username** provides the name of a Windows NT account the server will use if a Web visitor supplies no other username. IIS Setup creates an account named IUSR_<computername> for this purpose.

  - **Password** provides the password required to use the above account.

- **Password Authentication** controls the method for prompting and verifying usernames and passwords.

  - **Allow Anonymous**, if turned on, instructs IIS to determine whether the Anonymous Logon Username has access to a

VI

Integrating FrontPage
and Your Web Server

file before prompting the remote user for a username and password. If the Anonymous Logon Username has access to the requested file, no username/password prompting will occur. If the Anonymous Logon Username doesn't have access, IIS will prompt the remote user for a username/password combination that does.

- **Basic (Clear Text)**, if turned on, instructs IIS to accept unencrypted passwords from remote users. Unencrypted passwords are a security risk because others on the network can capture, decipher, and use them without proper authority. Unfortunately, this is the only authentication scheme many Web browsers support.

NOTE

> After receiving a password prompt and a successful response from a Web server, browsers continue sending the same password to the same server until they receive another prompt.

- **Windows NT Challenge/Response**, if turned on, indicates that IIS should verify passwords using a very secure process also used for network logins to a Windows NT server. As of this writing, Internet Explorer was the only browser that supported this option.

NOTE

> If Basic authentication and Windows NT Challenge/Response are both enabled, IIS will use Windows NT Challenge/Response if possible and Basic authentication otherwise.

- **Comment** provides a line of text that will appear in the Internet Service Manager listing.

As illustrated in Figure 16-7, you can also administer IIS services remotely, using a Web browser. This is an option when you install or reinstall IIS.

FIGURE 16-7.
This HTML form
manages WWW
Service properties for
Internet Information
Server. Note the similar-
ity to Figure 16-6.

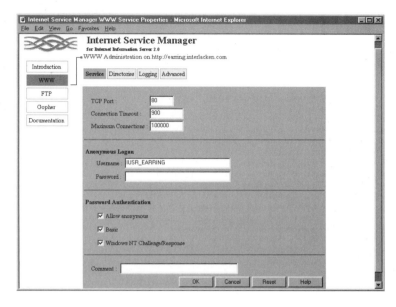

Administering IIS Content Directories

The second tab in the WWW Service Properties dialog box pertains to
directories. An example appears in Figure 16-8. *Folders* and *directories*
are synonymous.

FIGURE 16-8.
The Directories tab
manages folders for
the IIS WWW Service.

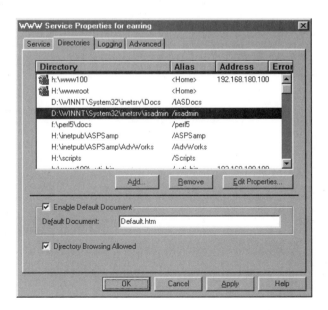

VI

Integrating FrontPage
and Your Web Server

Securing Web Page Delivery with IIS

In addition to storing file and folder information, the Windows NT File System (NTFS) stores *access control lists* (ACLs) that specify which users can access a given file or folder, as well as what permissions they have. If a file's ACL doesn't authorize a user to perform an operation, NTFS blocks the attempt and returns an error message.

When retrieving pages for Web delivery, IIS normally accesses the file first with an Anonymous Logon Username. If that access succeeds, IIS delivers the page. If it fails, IIS prompts the Web visitor for another username and password. If the user responds with a username and a password that have access, IIS delivers the requested page. If not, IIS repeats the prompt.

FrontPage establishes the following NTFS permissions for the various Front-Page access levels.

- **Browse.** Users and groups at this access level have Read permissions in the Windows NT file system.

- **Author and Browse.** Users and groups in this category have Change permissions in NTFS.

- **Administer, Author, and Browse.** Web administrators have Full Control permissions over their Web files; they can update both files and permissions.

It's best to use FrontPage, rather than native Windows NT dialog boxes, to set permissions for FrontPage Webs. This avoids problems caused by FrontPage's finding permissions in an unexpected state.

The multicolumn listing at the top of the window gives all special directory assignments currently in effect for both the default server and any virtual servers. This includes both home directories and virtual directories.

The check box Enable Default Document controls whether IIS will look for a document with the given filename when someone submits a URL without one. This situation occurs when, for example, a user submits a URL such as *http://www.microsoft.com/*. If Enable Default Document is turned on, the server will switch to the directory specified in the URL and then search for the given default document.

The check box Directory Browsing Allowed controls what happens if no default document is available. If the box is turned on, the server will supply a directory listing of files and allow the user to choose. If the box is turned off, the server returns an error message.

Figure 16-9 illustrates the procedure for setting up virtual directories and virtual server home directories. Click the Add button in Figure 16-8 (page 607) to obtain it.

FIGURE 16-9.
The Directory Properties dialog box maps the physical directory at the top of the window to the virtual directory entered in the Alias field.

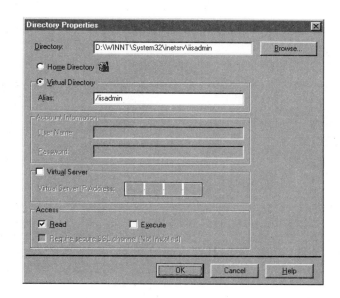

The entry requirements for the fields in Figure 16-9 are the following:

- **Directory** contains the physical location of the directory that contains the files you wish to publish. Specify locations on the local machine with drive letters. Specify network locations using universal naming convention (UNC). UNC names begin \\<servername>\<sharename>\.

- **Home Directory**, if turned on, indicates that the specified directory is the server's home directory.

- **Virtual Directory**, if turned on, indicates that the specified directory should be accessible as if it were located within an existing home directory tree.

  - **Alias** specifies an artificial name for the virtual directory.

VI

Integrating FrontPage and Your Web Server

- **Account Information** is applicable only if Directory specifies a UNC name. Enter a username and password capable of accessing the network resource.

- **Virtual Server**, if turned on, indicates that the home or virtual directory is for a virtual server.

  - **Virtual Server IP Address** specifies the virtual server's IP address.

- **Access** controls availability of documents to Web visitors.

  - **Read** indicates that Web visitors can retrieve files from the specified directory.

  - **Execute** indicates that Web visitors can cause files from the specified directory to be executed on the server.

  - **Require Secure SSL Channel** indicates that files in this directory can only be accessed securely; that is, using Secure Sockets Layer. To use this feature, your server must be configured with a valid public/private key pair.

In Figure 16-9 (on the previous page), physical directory D:\WINNT\ System32\inetsrv\iisadmin is being mapped to virtual directory /iisadmin on the default server. D:\WINNT\System32\inetsrv is the location where IIS setup installed the IIS software. The iisadmin directory within that location contains the HTML files for Web-based administration. You could physically copy these files into a physical directory within the Web server home directory, but setting up a virtual directory is a better solution. If a future update to the IIS software updates the Web-based administration pages, the virtual directory will reflect the changes automatically.

Many Internet-style services now provide documentation in HTML format and Web-based administration tools. It's usually worthwhile to look for these files in the service's software directory and set up virtual directories to make them accessible.

Administering Logging

The third tab of the WWW Service Properties dialog box controls logging and appears in Figure 16-10. With logging turned on, IIS extends

FIGURE 16-10.

This dialog box in Internet Service Manager controls activity logging for the WWW service.

a log file by one record for every HTTP request. You can subsequently analyze these logs to determine usage patterns.

The Enable Logging check box turns logging on and off. Turning logging on activates the Log To File and Log To SQL/ODBC Database option buttons.

Choosing Log To File enables the left section of the dialog box and activates the following input fields.

- **Log Format** provides two choices: Standard Format and NCSA. Choose the format your log analyzer expects.

- **Automatically Open New Log**, if turned on, instructs IIS to periodically stop appending records to its existing log file and create a new one. This can occur daily, weekly, monthly, or whenever the log file reaches a certain size. IIS names the log files in accordance with the Log File Name message near the bottom of the dialog box.

- **Log File Directory** specifies the folder where IIS will write log files.

Choosing Log To SQL/ODBC Database activates the four input fields beneath the button.

- **ODBC Data Source Name (DSN)** specifies the name of an Open Database Connectivity (ODBC) System Data Source Name. To define an ODBC System DSN, use the ODBC 32 applet in Windows NT Control Panel.

> If no ODBC 32 applet appears in Control Panel, or if the applet doesn't list drivers for your database type, you probably need to install the database software or additional features on your server.

- **Table** supplies the name of the database table that will receive the log records. Every HTTP request arriving at the server will create a record in this table. It's your responsibility to define the table with the field names and types that IIS will use.

> For more information about setting up SQL tables for IIS logging, consult /iisadmin/htmldocs/07_iis.htm (assuming you've set up an iisadmin virtual folder as described in the previous section).

- **User Name** provides a username capable of opening and updating the specified SQL table.

- **Password** supplies the password for the username above.

Administering Network Access

The last tab in the Internet Service Manager WWW dialog box is simply titled Advanced. It appears in Figure 16-11.

The upper part of this dialog box controls which IP addresses can access the service. By default, there are no IP address restrictions. If you wish to block access from certain computers or groups of computers, you can exclude them by clicking the Add button and specifying their IP addresses. To exclude an entire block of IP addresses, enter a network number and a subnet mask. Figure 16-11, shows all IP addresses except 192.168.180.241 and 192.168.190.* having access.

FIGURE 16-11.
The Advanced tab controls network access by IP address and traffic volume.

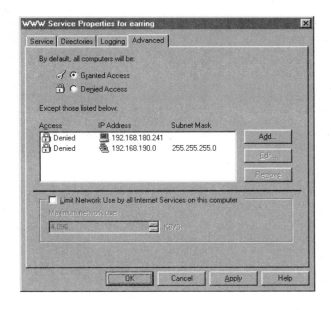

A subnet mask looks like an IP address but only indicates which parts of a real IP address are significant. After converting both the IP address and subnet mask to binary form, 1-bits in the subnet mask indicate address bits that are significant and 0-bits indicate those that aren't.

? SEE ALSO
For more information on installing, configuring, and managing Windows NT in general or IIS in particular, consult the product documentation, Microsoft's Web site at *http://www.microsoft.com*, or books dedicated to these topics.

If, under the heading By Default All Computers Will Be, you choose Denied Access, the meaning of the exception list reverses. The exception list then indicates which computers *have* access.

The check box captioned Limit Network Use By All Internet Services On This Computer is off by default. If you turn it on, you can use the text box just below it to specify the maximum bandwidth your server will consume for Internet services. Administrators may need to limit bandwidth at the server if, for example, the server frequently overwhelms an Internet connection with outgoing traffic.

Microsoft Peer Web Server for Windows NT Workstation

Realistically, only a small percentage of FrontPage authors are likely to administer a Windows NT Server or a full-blown version of Internet

VI

Integrating FrontPage
and Your Web Server

Information Server. But many Web authors and programmers need access to the Windows NT and IIS environments for testing and development. Microsoft Peer Web Server for Windows NT Workstation satisfies these requirements. Microsoft bundles a copy of Peer Web Server at no additional charge with each copy of Windows NT Workstation.

Peer Web Server is a version of IIS that runs, with a few restrictions, on Windows NT Workstation. The restrictions are

- There's no support for virtual servers.

- The Advanced tab for the WWW service in Internet Service Manager is omitted. That is, the dialog box of Figure 16-11, on the previous page, doesn't appear.

- Licensing prohibits more than 10 different IP addresses from connecting to a Windows NT Workstation in any 10-minute period.

These restrictions conform to Windows NT Workstation's pricing and positioning as a single-user desktop operating system. Windows NT Workstation's machine-to-machine connectivity is intended for small workgroups, not for large enterprises or the world.

Peer Web Server provides an excellent platform for running FrontPage, for group or individual authoring, and for testing a site prior to production. Developing and testing Webs on Peer Web Server provides a high degree of confidence that the same Webs will operate as intended when moved to full-blown IIS.

The procedure for installing Peer Web Server is the same as that for Internet Information Server; look for it under the Network command of the Control Panel's Network applet. If Peer Web Server isn't installed on a Windows NT Workstation when you install FrontPage, FrontPage will display a dialog box similar to Figure 16-12, and will offer to install Peer Web Server for you.

The easiest way to integrate FrontPage with Peer Web Server is to install Peer Web Server first, test it, and then install FrontPage. FrontPage Setup will detect the installed copy of Peer Web Server and automatically install the FrontPage Server Extensions. If you install FrontPage before installing Peer Web Server, you'll need to run FrontPage Server Administrator to add the Server Extensions after Peer Web Server has been installed. Administering Peer Web Server is almost exactly like administering Internet Information Server, described in the previous section.

> Not all FrontPage authors running Windows NT Workstation need their own copy of Peer Web Server. It's perfectly acceptable—and frequently desirable—to set up one Peer Web Server per workgroup, especially in collaborative environments.

Microsoft Personal Web Server

If you need a personal or workgroup Web server that runs under Windows 95, Microsoft Personal Web Server (MS-PWS) is an excellent choice. MS-PWS is supplied with FrontPage.

Installation

One of the first tasks FrontPage 98 Setup performs on a Windows 95 system is checking for the presence of Microsoft Personal Web Server. If MS-PWS isn't already installed, Setup displays the dialog box shown in Figure 16-12. Click OK to accept installation of MS-PWS. When the installation completes, it reboots your system and restarts installation of FrontPage. For a quick check that MS-PWS installed correctly, look for a Control Panel icon captioned Personal Web Server.

FIGURE 16-12.
Setup recommends
Microsoft Personal
Web Server.

> Remove any other Web servers from your Windows 95 system before installing MS-PWS. You can usually find and remove these using Control Panel, with the Add/Remove Programs or Install/Uninstall command.

VI

Integrating FrontPage
and Your Web Server

 **TIP**

MS-PWS Setup may require files from your Windows 95 CD or disks during installation.

If you choose the custom FrontPage 98 Setup option, the prompt shown in Figure 16-13 will offer to install FrontPage Personal Web Server as well. FrontPage PWS is covered in a later section in this chapter, but for now take note that you probably don't need two Web servers on the same computer.

FIGURE 16-13.
This dialog box is displayed if you choose a custom installation of FrontPage. You can install the FrontPage Personal Web Server, even if the Microsoft Personal Web Server is installed.

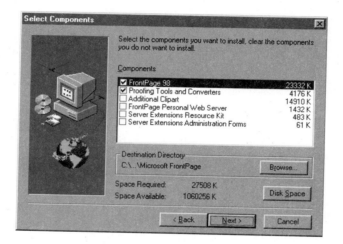

In total, there are four scenarios for installing Personal Web Servers on Windows 95.

- **Install No Personal Web Server.** Decline installation of Microsoft Personal Web server when the dialog box shown in Figure 16-12 (page 615) appears, and then choose custom installation during FrontPage setup and decline installation of FrontPage Personal Web Server as well. This presumes you'll be using an existing FrontPage Web server on your LAN or a disk-based Web. Disk-based Webs have reduced functionality, as discussed, in "Creating Disk-Based Webs," page 633.

- **Install Microsoft Personal Web Server.** Accept installation of Microsoft Personal Web server, and then choose Typical installation during FrontPage Setup. If you choose Custom installation, decline installation of FrontPage Personal Web Server. This is the normal and *recommended* configuration.

- **Install FrontPage Personal Web Server.** Decline installation of Microsoft Personal Web server, choose Custom setup for FrontPage, and specify installation of FrontPage Personal Web Server. Choose this approach only if you need features of FrontPage PWS (such as self-registration) that Microsoft PWS doesn't provide.

- **Install Both Personal Web Servers.** Accept installation of Microsoft Personal Web server, and then choose Custom setup for FrontPage and specify installation of FrontPage Personal Web Server as well. This is an extremely unusual setup, but useful if you need to test results or compare features of both servers. Microsoft PWS, which installs first, will run on port 80 and FrontPage PWS will run on port 8080.

To construct URLs that access FrontPage PWS when Microsoft PWS is also present, append *:8080* to the computer name.

Security Modes

Windows 95 lacks the robust user database, file system security, and other security features of Windows NT. These deficiencies lead to some compromises when using Microsoft Personal Web Server to provide Web service. Depending on the level of file-sharing Windows 95 is configured to provide, there are three MS-PWS security scenarios. These are summarized in Table 16-6, on the next page.

- If the Windows 95 system isn't sharing local files or printers, FrontPage MS-PWS uses a local user database. For information on creating and maintaining this database, refer to the discussion of Figure 16-26, on page 628.

- If Windows 95 is sharing local files or printers with share-level security, the FrontPage Server Extensions operate with no security restrictions on anyone.

- If Windows 95 is sharing local files or printers with user-level security, the FrontPage Server Extensions will control security using the same user database as file and print sharing, typically a Windows NT User Account Database elsewhere on the network.

TABLE 16-6. Effect of Windows 95 File Sharing on MS-PWS Security

	Control Panel Network Settings		
File Sharing	**Configuration: File and Print Sharing**	**Access Control**	**MS-PWS Security**
Off	Both options off	N/A	Local User Database
Share-Level	Either option on	Share-Level	None
User-Level	Either option on	User-Level + Domain	Domain User Database

When FrontPage Server Administrator installs the MS-PWS Extensions on a machine with share-level file sharing enabled, it uses the dialog box of Figure 16-14 to recommend a change to user-level file sharing. To implement this change

1 Run FrontPage Server Administrator and remove the FrontPage Server Extensions from MS-PWS.

2 Quit FrontPage Server Administrator.

3 Open Windows 95 Control Panel.

4 Double-click the Network Icon.

5 Choose the Access Control tab. This is the dialog box shown in Figure 16-15.

6 Choose the User-Level Access Control option.

FIGURE 16-14.
FrontPage Server Administrator suggests configuring your network software to obtain a user list from another source.

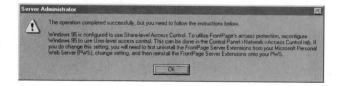

FIGURE 16-15.

The Network dialog box from the Windows 95 Control Panel governs the system's access control approach.

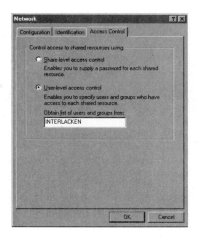

7   In the text box titled Obtain Users And Groups From, enter the name of a Windows NT Domain or computer. If possible, this should be the Windows NT Domain or computer Web that authors log onto when they start their computers.

8   Click OK. At this point, Windows 95 may require files from your Windows 95 CD or disks.

9   Restart the computer.

10   Run FrontPage Server Administrator and reinstall the FrontPage Server Extensions.

With user-level security in place, Web administrators can grant FrontPage author and administer privileges to any person or group in the specified domain. If a user's computer is already logged onto the domain with a valid account, FrontPage uses that account automatically. In any other case, FrontPage prompts for a valid username and password.

User-level security probably isn't a concern if you work at home, remotely, or independent of any LAN. If your computer is on a network with other users, however, you should take great care to protect your work from deliberate or accidental tampering.

Administering MS-PWS from Control Panel

Installing Microsoft Personal Web Server adds this icon to the Windows 95 Control Panel.

Personal Web
Server

VI

Integrating FrontPage
and Your Web Server

A similar (but smaller) icon may also appear in the tray area of the Windows 95 taskbar. Double-clicking either icon brings up the dialog box shown in Figure 16-16. This dialog box, like many in MS-PWS, is merely a front-end to certain browser displays. The buttons work as follows.

- **Display Home Page** starts the computer's default HTML browser and displays the local server's home page.

The dialog box's General tab displays the Default Home Page filename, but to make changes you must choose the Services tab and click the Properties button.

- **More Details** displays the Web page shown later in Figure 16-21, page 623. This is the main entry point to online documentation about MS-PWS.

You may find it easier to save important MS-PWS Web pages as Favorites in your browser than to access them from the Personal Web Server button on the Control Panel.

FIGURE 16-16.
This is the opening dialog box of the Microsoft Personal Web Server applet of the Control Panel.

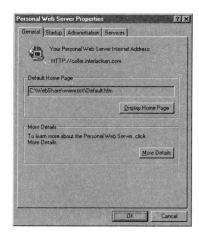

MS-PWS's Startup tab appears in Figure 16-17. The section titled Web Server State displays the Web server's current condition and provides buttons for starting and stopping it. Two check boxes control

- Whether the Web server will start automatically when the system boots

- Whether a Personal Web Server icon should appear in the taskbar tray

> You can also start and stop the Web server from the Services tab.

FIGURE 16-17.
Personal Web Server's Startup tab controls service startup and shutdown.

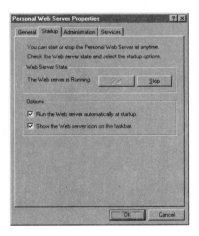

The Administration tab, pictured in Figure 16-18, on the following page, contains a single button titled Administration. Clicking that button starts the default Web browser and displays the page shown later in Figure 16-22, page 624.

The Services tab provides ways to start, stop, and reconfigure both PWS's Web server and its FTP server. This is the dialog box shown in Figure 16-19. To start or stop a service, first select it and then click the Start or Stop button as appropriate. To change properties, select the desired service and then click the Properties button.

VI

Integrating FrontPage and Your Web Server

FIGURE 16-18.
Clicking the Administration button under the Administration tab displays the dialog box shown in Figure 16-22 (page 624).

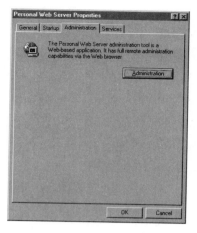

FIGURE 16-19.
This is the Personal Web Server's Services tab.

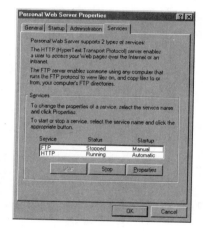

Figure 16-20 shows the Properties dialog box for MS-PWS's HTTP service. It results from selecting HTTP in Figure 16-19 and clicking Properties. From here you can control whether the Web server starts automatically when the system boots, just as in Figure 16-16 (page 620). The following buttons allow changing the Web server home folder and default home page, respectively.

- Change Home Root

- Change Home Page

The property sheet for the FTP services is very similar to that of Figure 16-20, but there's no default home page setting.

FIGURE 16-20.
This property sheet allows setting startup mode, the Web server's document home root, and the Web server's home page.

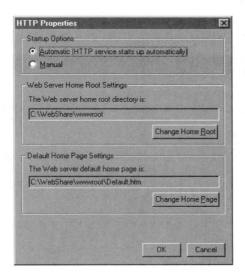

Administering MS-PWS with Web Pages

As was likely apparent in the preceding section, most Personal Web Server administration occurs through Web pages. Microsoft has documented these pages in HTML, as shown in Figure 16-21. The URL, except for the host name, should be the same on any computer.

FIGURE 16-21.
This is the starting point for the online documentation on MS-PWS. The host name will vary from system to system.

VI

Integrating FrontPage and Your Web Server

Figure 16-22 shows the main menu for PWS administrative functions. Clicking WWW Administration, FTP Administration, and Local User Administration jumps to HTML forms for the corresponding functions. The hyperlinks under Other PWS Resources jump to outside sites.

FIGURE 16-22.
This is the main menu for Personal Web Server administration. The host name will vary from system to system.

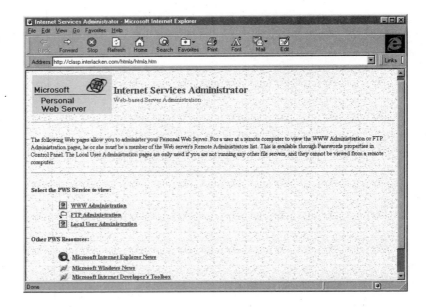

Clicking the WWW Administration hyperlink in Figure 16-22 jumps to the Web page in Figure 16-23. Note the family resemblance to Figure 16-6 (page 605) and Figure 16-7 (page 607). As before, you can modify the following:

- **Connection Timeout** specifies the number of seconds a Web connection can remain inactive without being canceled.

- **Maximum Connections** limits the number of Web server connections that can be open at once. Additional connections are rejected, forcing the browser to retry or give up.

- **Password Authentication** selects the methods available for validating user access to Web pages.

  - **Allow Anonymous** specifies that remote users can display Web pages without entering a username and password.

- **Basic** supports a simple username/password scheme that all browsers support but that doesn't safeguard passwords in transit.

- **Windows NT Challenge/Response** implements an advanced username/password scheme that safeguards passwords in transit but that, as of this writing, only Internet Explorer supports.

■ **Comment** supplies an optional remark that appears in various informational displays.

FIGURE 16-23.
This is the Services configuration tab for Microsoft Personal Web Server.

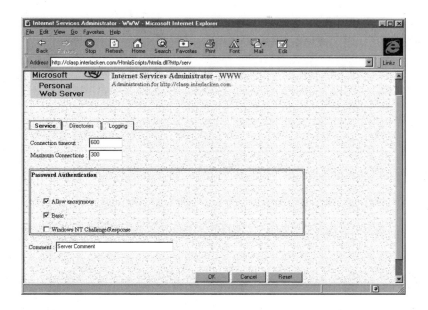

The PWS Directories page appears in Figure 16-24, on the next page. This is typically a long page, so only the lower portion is shown. The top of the page contains headings and more virtual folder definitions.

■ To modify a virtual folder definition, click its Edit hyperlink, type over the data, and click OK.

■ To delete a definition, click its Delete hyperlink.

■ To add a virtual folder, click the Add hyperlink in the lower-right corner of the listing.

FIGURE 16-24.
This is the Microsoft Personal Web Server's Directories administration page.

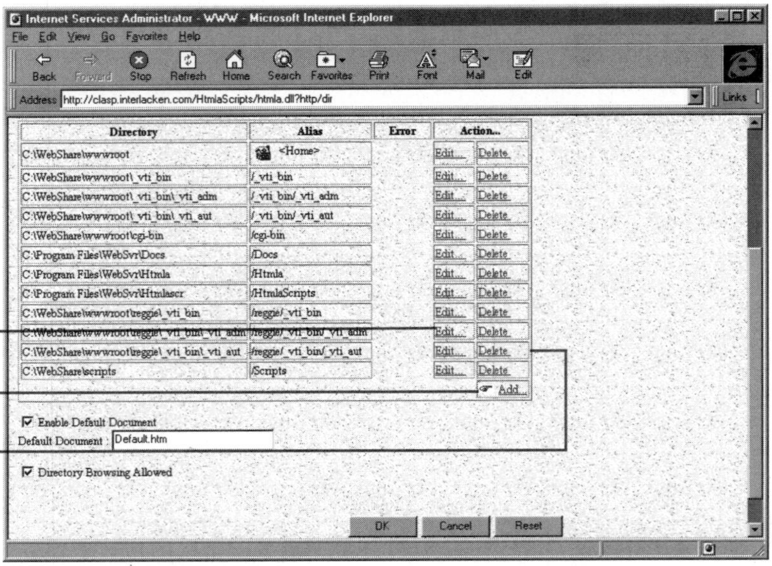

Click to modify a virtual folder.

Click to add a new virtual folder.

Click to delete a virtual folder.

If Enable Default Document is turned on, MS-PWS will search for the given Default Document filename whenever it receives a URL whose document filename is blank.

If Directory Browsing Allowed is turned on, MS-PWS will transmit a clickable file listing whenever it receives a URL with a blank document filename and no default document is available. If it is turned off, failure to locate a default document results in an error message to the user.

The MS-PWS Logging page appears in Figure 16-25.

- **Enable Logging** controls whether logging occurs.

- **Automatically Open New Log** controls whether MS-PWS will periodically start logging to a new file.

- **Log File Directory** specifies where the log files will reside.

Clicking FTP Administration in Figure 16-22 (page 624) displays a similar set of HTML forms; you should have no trouble with these if you understand how the Web server's configuration pages work.

FIGURE 16-25.
This Web page controls logging in Microsoft Personal Web Server.

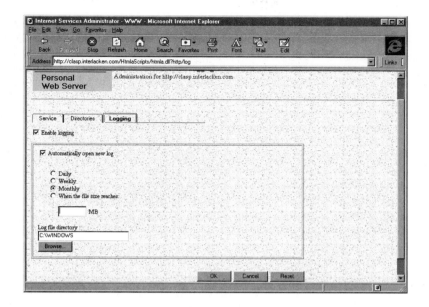

Clicking the Local User Administration hyperlink in Figure 16-22 (page 624) jumps to the Web page in Figure 16-26, on the following page.

 NOTE

> MS-PWS uses its own user and group list only if User Level Access Control, pictured in Figure 16-15 (page 619), isn't in effect.

- The list box titled User List displays usernames currently in the database.

- Selecting a user and clicking the Properties button brings up a form for changing the user's password.

- Clicking the New User button displays a page where you can add new users to the database and assign passwords.

- Clicking the Remove button deletes the selected username from the database.

Clicking the Groups tab in Figure 16-26 (on the next page) displays the Web page in Figure 16-27 (page 629). Selecting a group and clicking the Properties button shows the group's members, but allows no changes

VI

Integrating FrontPage
and Your Web Server

from that display. The New Group and Remove buttons add and delete entire groups, respectively.

Clicking the User/Group tab in Figure 16-26 or Figure 16-27 calls up the Web page shown in Figure 16-28. To add a user to a group

1 Select the user.

2 Select the group.

3 Click the Add User To Group button

To remove a user from a group

1 Select the user.

2 Click the Remove User From Group button

Microsoft Personal Web Server can't match the performance, stability, and security of Microsoft's Windows NT-based Web servers, though it provides a close match fully suitable for use by individuals, students, and small workgroups. Compared to FrontPage Personal Web Server, described next, Microsoft Personal Web Server is faster and provides a better test bed for developing and testing Webs that will run on Windows NT in production. In most cases, MS-PWS will be the preferred Microsoft Web server for Windows 95.

FIGURE 16-26.

This HTML form provides a way to add, maintain, or delete local usernames for Microsoft Personal Web Server. Clicking the Groups and User/Group tabs jumps to associated pages.

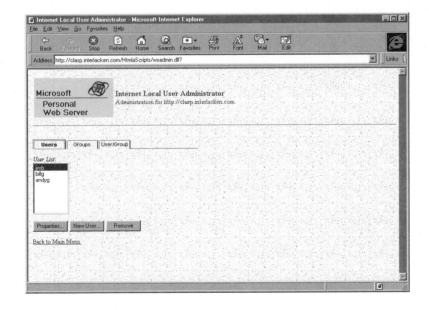

FIGURE 16-27.
This Web page displays, adds, and deletes MS-PWS groups. It doesn't control group membership.

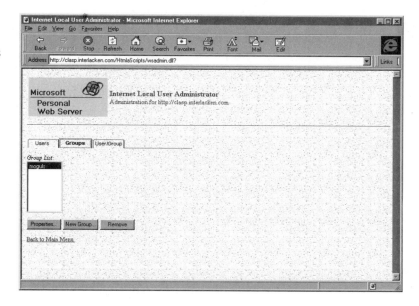

FIGURE 16-28.
The User/Group page adds existing users to existing groups, or removes them from existing groups.

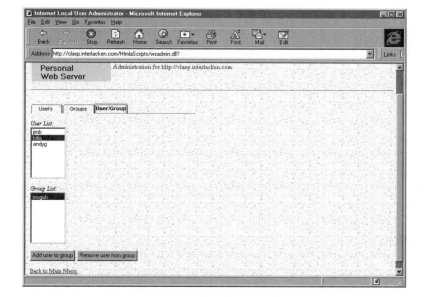

FrontPage Personal Web Server

This section describes the oldest and least capable of Microsoft's Web servers: the FrontPage Personal Web Server (FrontPage PWS). This server was part of FrontPage before FrontPage was part of Microsoft, and may eventually be phased out.

VI

Integrating FrontPage and Your Web Server

(X) CAUTION

FrontPage PWS names and passwords are case-sensitive. Check the Caps Lock state, particularly before entering passwords.

The previous section in this chapter discussed installing FrontPage Personal Web Server during FrontPage setup. In addition to the dialog box of Figure 16-13, page 616, FrontPage Setup displays one additional dialog box when installing FrontPage PWS: the dialog box shown in Figure 16-29. This prompts for the new server's Root Web administrator name and password. Enter the password twice for confirmation.

FIGURE 16-29.

When installing Front-Page Personal Web Server, Setup prompts for the initial Root Web administrator name and password.

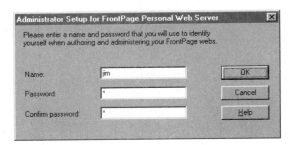

FrontPage PWS runs as a minimized foreground application, not as a background service. If you want the server to start whenever you boot, you'll need to add it to the Startup folder in your Start menu. The default program location is

```
c:\frontpage webs\server\vhttpd32.exe
```

The normal way of using FrontPage PWS is not to start it on bootup, but to let FrontPage itself start the server. FrontPage will start the server automatically when you try to access a Web on your own machine.

FrontPage PWS has no integration with Windows security, so on opening a Web you'll always be prompted for a name and password having author or administrator privileges. This involves the simple dialog box pictured in Figure 16-30.

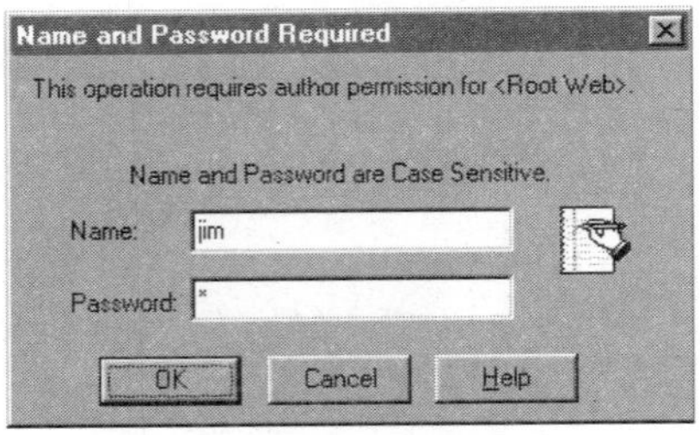

FIGURE 16-30.

When opening a Web, FrontPage uses this dialog box to prompt for an author or administrator name and password.

When a Web resides on a FrontPage PWS, choosing Change Password from the Tools menu in FrontPage Explorer displays the dialog box shown in Figure 16-31. This allows a FrontPage user or administrator to change his or her own password. Enter the old password, enter the new password twice, and then click OK.

FIGURE 16-31.
This is the FrontPage Explorer Change Password dialog box for a Web residing on Front-Page Personal Web Server.

? SEE ALSO
For a discussion of inheriting Root Web permissions, see "Administering Web-Level Security," page 571.

As is the case for other Web servers, the first tab of the Permissions dialog box, selected from the Tools menu, controls whether Webs other than the Root Web will inherit Root Web permissions. For Root Webs, this tab has no meaning and is thus absent.

The Users tab displays, adds, edits, and removes users. Figure 16-32 illustrates adding a new user. Specify the new user's name, password (twice), and privilege level, and then click OK.

FIGURE 16-32.
This dialog box adds, edits, and removes users of a FrontPage Personal Web Server database. The Edit and Remove buttons are behind the Add Users window.

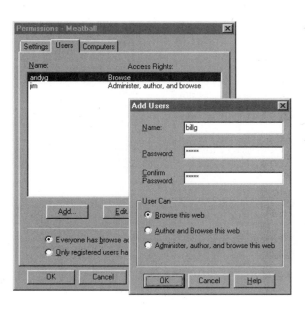

Selecting a user and clicking the Edit button brings up the Edit Users dialog box, very similar to the Add Users dialog box shown in Figure 16-32 (on the previous page), where an administrator can change that user's password or privileges.

Clicking the Remove button deletes the user from the database.

The Computers tab for a FrontPage PWS controls access by IP address as illustrated in Figure 16-33. By default, computers having any IP address (that is, *.*.*.*, with the asterisk standing for wildcard numerals) can administer, author, and browse the current Web. In the figure, all computers have Browse access, but only computers with IP addresses beginning 192.168.180 will have authoring and administrative capability. Prohibiting authoring and administration from computers outside your site provides additional security, compared to using passwords only.

FIGURE 16-33.
FrontPage PWS can control which computers can browse, author, and administer its FrontPage Webs.

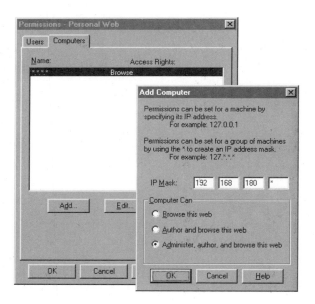

Installing FrontPage Personal Web Server creates the default home page shown in Figure 16-34. Unfortunately, there's no HTML documentation or Web-based administration for FrontPage PWS.

FIGURE 16-34.
This is the default home page for Front-Page PWS. No Web-based administration is available.

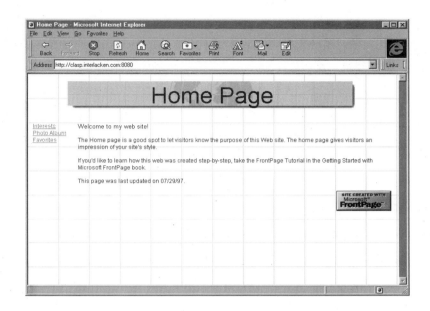

Creating Disk-Based Webs

Itself an object of the Web, FrontPage requires the presence of a Web server to deliver its full complement of features. There may be cases, however, when it isn't possible to have access to a Web server—not even a personal Web server operating on your own computer. Some possible reasons include the following:

- Your computer isn't on a TCP/IP network and has no IP address.

- You find configuring your own Web server impractical.

- You have access to a Web server, but for some reason FrontPage Server Extensions can't be installed. The extensions might not be available for the particular server and platform, for example.

- You notice that performance is inadequate when you're running a personal Web server.

Fortunately, FrontPage can provide most of its features in a completely serverless environment called a disk-based Web. Instead of having a

Web server read and write files on the server's local disk, FrontPage simply reads and writes the files directly, using either your computer's local hard disk or space on a network file server.

Unfortunately, a disk-based Web has no way to run CGI or ISAPI programs. Such programs provide dynamic services, at either authoring time or browse time. They're designed to run in a Web server environment, and can't run without one, so the following FrontPage features won't work on a disk-based Web.

- Confirmation Field component

- Discussion Group component

- Form Results component

- Registration component

- Search component

- Server-side scripts (Active Server Pages)

- Any other user-written, shareware, or commercial server-side programs

In addition to these restrictions, disk-based Webs have no security features at all; anyone with at least read permission to the disk-based Web's file area has access. Because of the many restrictions inherent in disk-based Webs, Microsoft is deemphasizing them and not guaranteeing future support.

Using a disk-based Web doesn't prevent you from creating Web pages using these features; it only prevents you from running or testing them. Still, this is a significant list of features to lose.

Creating a disk-based Web is relatively simple.

1 When FrontPage starts, choose Create A New FrontPage Web and then click OK. Alternatively, if FrontPage Explorer is already running, choose New from the File menu, and then select FrontPage Web.

2 Choose the kind of FrontPage Web you want (that is, choose the type of initial content), give the Web a name, and then click the Change button to override the suggested Web location.

3 When prompted to specify the location of the new Web—as in Figure 16-35—enter the name of a folder in your file system rather than the name of a Web server on your network. The name can be either a drive:folder combination or a universal naming convention (UNC) name. UNC names have the format \\<computer>\<sharename>\<path>\<file>.

4 Click OK once to enter the disk-based Web's location, and then again to create the Web. If you specify a location that was never a disk-based Web before, FrontPage will create a Root Web in that location. If you specify a location that contains the path of an existing disk-based Root Web plus one folder name, FrontPage will create a user Web.

FIGURE 16-35.
To create a disk-based Web, enter a local or network file location rather than a Web server address.

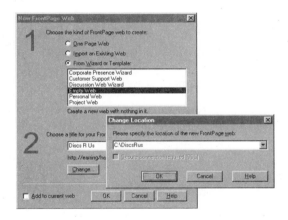

Figure 16-36, on the next page, shows the result of creating the disk-based Web started in Figure 16-35. Note that the top folder in the left pane reports a file location rather than a Web server address. All the other FrontPage Explorer screen shots in this book show a Web server address.

Note the file system location at the top of the left pane of this window, which indicates a disk-based Web. Note also that FrontPage has created several—but not all—of its usual folders. The _private and images folders are present, but the cgi_bin, _vti_bin, and _vti_txt folders are not.

You can create a disk-based Web in a location where HTML files already exist, but FrontPage will *webify* that location by adding its own

FIGURE 16-36.
FrontPage displays the location of a disk-based Web as a file location rather than a Web server name.

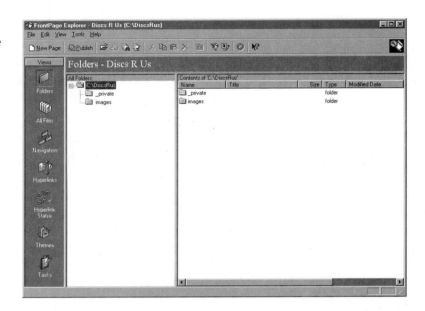

folders and files. To keep your original location clean, first create a new disk-based Web in a different location and later import the existing content.

You can publish a disk-based Web to another disk-based Web or to a real Web server. Likewise, you can publish a real FrontPage Web to a disk-based Web. Simply specify the correct location, whether Web server or disk, when you open the source Web and also when you specify the target Web.

Using a Non-Microsoft Web Server

The FrontPage Server Extensions are designed to minimize differences among Web servers. Assuming FrontPage Extensions are available for the target server and the server administrator has installed them, Web page authors shouldn't have to concern themselves greatly about which Web server is in use. For programmers and administrators, however, the differences aren't nearly as transparent.

Regardless of the type of Web server in use, authors will need to learn the default document name. This name is default.htm on most Microsoft servers and index.html on most others, though local configurations can vary in either case.

Security is another area where no two servers tend to be alike. Web authors, Web administrators, and system administrators will need to learn how security works on each server—target and development—and must control access on each machine appropriately.

SEE ALSO
To learn about the availability of Front-Page extensions for non-Microsoft Web servers, review "Software Platforms and Availability," page 595, and "Obtaining Front-Page Server Extensions," page 597, earlier in this chapter.

Each Web server tends to provide a slightly different environment for running programmed elements such as CGI programs, ISAPI programs, server-side includes, and server-side scripts. Different versions of such tools are usually required for each different Web server, and few are available for all. This variance also affects programs you or others at your site may write; in general, without modification they won't be portable from one type of server to another.

If FrontPage extensions aren't available for the target Web server or aren't installed, authors will have to publish Webs manually or using the Web Publishing Wizard. In addition, browse-time services provided by the extensions obviously won't be available—services such as search and server-side form field validation.

If the FrontPage extensions on a server aren't up-to-date, you'll get various errors when authoring and publishing. The best solution is to upgrade the extensions. If that isn't possible, do as much work as possible on a server that has up-to-date extensions, and then publish the results to the out-of-date server later. Before using any browse-time features, test them on the outdated server to determine whether they work as expected.

The more active services you expect from your Web server, the more difficult mixed server environments will be. If at all possible, use the same server or at least the same family of servers for development, testing, and production.

Other Windows Web Servers

All Web servers must, by definition, implement the hypertext transfer protocol similarly. This means that virtually all Web servers deliver simple Web pages the same way, transparently to Web authors.

As just stated, differences are more pronounced with respect to executables, such as CGI, ISAPI, and server-side scripts. Before using any of these facilities, verify that your target Web server supports them.

Web Servers on Non-Microsoft Operating Systems

? SEE ALSO

For information about installing the Server Extensions on non-Windows operating systems, see "Installing the FrontPage Server Extensions from the Command Line," page 599.

All the cautions mentioned in the previous section apply as well to Web servers operating in a non-Windows environment. In addition, such servers raise issues involving non-Windows file systems.

Unix file systems are usually case-sensitive, limited to 32 characters per filename or folder name, and subject to different restrictions on filename characters. This means, among other things, that a URL for Index.html will not retrieve a file named index.html; instead, the server will return a Not Found message. The best policy, therefore, is to limit filenames and folder names, both in the file system and in URLs, to lowercase letters and numbers only.

Some executables will run on more than one Windows Web server, but virtually none will run on both Windows and non-Windows systems. Most executables are completely nonportable between Windows and Unix, even on the same hardware. If Windows-based authors need to invoke Unix-based server-side programs, they'll have to work carefully from the documentation and, in the best of circumstances, test their results in an environment closely resembling production.

Afterword

Concepts, Ink, and Bits

The previous chapter concludes our travels through FrontPage, at least for this edition of the book and this version of the software. There are always more questions to be asked, and there is always more material to write about…but only so much time and paper and ink. I hope the book has answered at least most of your questions and given you some ideas and techniques you might not have encountered otherwise. In short, I hope the book was worth what you paid for it.

But even more, I hope that the combination of this book and the Front-Page software will expedite the flow of your thoughts and ideas from concept to expression. I hope you've learned to express yourself more completely, more powerfully, more effectively, and more eloquently than would otherwise have been possible—and thus more honestly as well.

The World Wide Web is the most democratic publishing medium yet created. No other medium allows so many people to present their ideas so rapidly, so cheaply, and so broadly to such an audience both large and diverse. The result is the tumultuous chorus of ideas flowing today across the Web, educating the curious, opening vistas for the isolated, rousing the apathetic, and multiplying appreciation of the human condition. There's no more powerful force for peace, prosperity, and progress than diverse people discovering each other, communicating, and building understanding.

With this thought I repeat my hope that this book and FrontPage itself provide the means for you to express yourself, convey your message, and attract the attention of others in ways unparalleled. May it lead to relationships and experiences you never dreamed possible. Let's go to press…

Index

Register Today!

Return this
Running Microsoft® FrontPage® 98
registration card for
a Microsoft Press® catalog

U.S. and Canada addresses only. Fill in information below and mail postage-free. Please mail only the bottom half of this page.

1-57231-645-4A   *RUNNING MICROSOFT® FRONTPAGE® 98*   *Owner Registration Card*

_____
NAME

_____
INSTITUTION OR COMPANY NAME

_____
ADDRESS

_____

_____
CITY   STATE   ZIP

Microsoft*®*Press
Quality Computer Books

**For a free catalog of
Microsoft Press® products, call
1-800-MSPRESS**